M000100257

The Other Modernism

The Other Modernism

F. T. Marinetti's Futurist Fiction of Power

Cinzia Sartini Blum

UNIVERSITY OF CALIFORNIA PRESS

Berkeley   Los Angeles   London

University of California Press
Berkeley and Los Angeles, California

University of California Press
London, England

Library of Congress Cataloging-in-Publication Data

Blum, Cinzia Sartini.
    The other modernism : F.T. Marinetti's futurist fiction of power /
Cinzia Sartini Blum.
        p.   cm.
    Includes bibliographical references and index.
    ISBN 0-520-20048-9 (alk. paper). — ISBN 0-520-20049-7 (pbk. :
alk. paper)
    1. Marinetti, Filippo Tommaso, 1876–1944—Criticism and
interpretation. 2. Futurism (Literary movement)—Italy. I. Title.
PQ4829.A76Z57   1996
858'.91209—dc20   96-3604
                                                                  CIP

Printed in the United States of America
9 8 7 6 5 4 3 2 1

CONTENTS

PREFACE / *vii*

1. The Other Modernism: Futurism and Its Contradictions / *1*

    Historical Roots / 3
    Literary Origins / 7
    The Futurist Fiction of Power / 16
    Methodological Questions / 20

2. The Rhetoric of Gender in the Manifestos / *29*

    Barricades / 31
    The Text as a Locus of Violence / 36
    The Futurist Mythopoeia / 41

3. The Superman and the Abject: Mafarka le futuriste / *55*

    The Rhetoric of Abjection / 56
    Failing Dikes / 59
    Total Art / 73

4. The Heart with Watertight Compartments and the Travel-size Woman:
Futurist Strategies in Love and War / *79*

    Grim Pictures of the Home Front / 81
    Sour Grapes / 85
    Cooking with Women / 89
    Bellicose Sex and Sexy War / 99

5. The Hero's War and the Heroine's Wounds: *Un ventre di donna*   /   *105*

A Prescription of Courage and Truth   /   *112*
The Surgical Novel   /   *114*
The Wombs of Other Women   /   *116*
Echoes in the Master's House   /   *117*
The Scarred Womb   /   *122*

6. Transformations in the Futurist Mythopoeia   /   *125*

Resorbing the Rejected   /   *126*
From Political Activism to Aesthetic Escapism   /   *130*
Tactilism and Transformism   /   *133*
Art as Salutary Distraction and Cosmetic Compensation   /   *135*
Recycling the Past   /   *137*
Pathetic Fallacy in the Technological Mythopoeia   /   *140*
Fashioning a Fascist Discourse   /   *143*
Realignments in the Mythopoeia of War   /   *145*
The Ultimate Transformation: Art as Transubstantiation   /   *155*

Afterword: The Rhetoric of Violence and the Violence of Rhetoric   /   *163*

NOTES   /   *165*

INDEX   /   *205*

PREFACE

F. T. Marinetti's provocative propaganda was a catalyst in the emergence of futurism as the first, most vociferous, and ultimately most influential movement of the modernist avant-garde. Its very exuberance, however, has in many ways hindered a critical understanding of futurist textual practices. His strident slogans glorifying war, demeaning woman, celebrating technology, and advocating the destruction of the past have generated reductionist interpretations of the movement's political and aesthetic ambitions. The ideological affinities between fascism and futurism have provoked facile condemnations of the movement, leading to an all too hasty dismissal of its historical and cultural significance. Analyses focusing on the politics of futurism have failed to address the complexities the movement's aesthetic production presents. Conversely, the rediscovery of futurism that began in the late 1960s (spurred on by a new wave of "neo-avant-garde" experimentation) has generally dissociated assessments of the movement's artistic achievements from ideological and political concerns.

The methodological dichotomizing of the political and the aesthetic circumvents a problem that is crucial to any understanding of futurism: the relationship between apparently divergent or unrelated goals of the movement, particularly its technical "revolution," its call to violence, its avowed contempt for woman, and its rejection of literary tradition. My study attempts to explore these issues by identifying an overarching ideological construct in Marinetti's writings: a mythopoeia of individual and national regeneration that I call the "futurist fiction of power." From this vantage point, it is possible to chart isomorphic patterns and synergistic effects in futurist strategies, ranging from the experimentation with "words in freedom" to the belligerent rhetoric of the manifestos.

At its inception, futurism was a reaction against the fin de siècle malaise that took the form of a pervasive sense of a dislocation in the logical, causal relationship between past, present, and future. Marinetti's antidote to the ills of modern decadence is the formulation of a mythical new subjectivity that rejects the limits of history and empowers itself by appropriating the marvels of technology to create a utopian futurist wonderland infused with primal life forces. This regenerative program incorporates irrationalist ideologemes like the Nietzschean notion of the *Übermensch* and the Sorelian idea of the revolutionary force of myth, combined with scientific theories of evolutionary perfectibility, notably Herbert Spencer's "survival of the fittest" and Jean Baptiste de Lamarck's "transformism." Its founding myth is the (re)birth of a futurist *superuomo*, predicated on the liquidation of the old rational, introspective, and sentimental "I" and on a hyperbolic expansion of the New Man's energy, intuition, imagination, and will to power.

The destructive and constructive dynamics of the fiction of power is driven by the transforming force of figurative language. The Marinettian self is configured metaphorically in the most grandiose terms (miracle worker, space conqueror, or armored fighting machine). Natural or societal obstacles to his limitless expansion are either eradicated (through a rhetoric of abjection) or mastered by way of assimilation, that is, transformed into objects of desire and conquest. This destruction/construction is (re)produced by the discursive strategies of Marinetti's poetic revolution: the ellipsis of syntactic (hence logical) links; the accumulation of sensorial effects and bold imaginary associations. Conventional and experimental strategies converge to restore the writer's power to represent and act upon reality. On the one hand, the esoterism of words in freedom revolutionizes the experience of lyric expression, reasserting control over the epistemological and referential realm: the fragmented, chaotic text conforms to and claims mastery over the fragmented, chaotic world in which rational and historical links have failed to order meaning and stabilize identity. On the other hand, through their characteristic oratorical impetus and exalted epic tone, the manifestos display power of action in the sociopolitical realm, reclaiming the public function that art has lost in modern society. The futurist affirms his role as armed prophet and guide of a new, powerful Italy, finding in patriotic war and modernity a cause for his rebellion and an inspiration for his art.

The global effect of these strategies is a totalizing affirmation of the self through annihilation or assimilation of the other. Viewed from this perspective, Marinetti's misogynist aphorisms can be seen as one incarnation of a pervasive discursive practice and the most blatant manifestation of the centrality of sexual relations and gendered rhetoric in the fiction of power. Sexual difference shapes virtually all aspects of the imaginary relationship between the futurist (male) subject and the (feminine) world of objects. The polarized, asymmetrical configuration of masculine totality and feminine lack provides a bedrock and a blueprint for the futurist destruction and reconstruction of the universe. Thus an examination of the fiction of power through the methodological lens of gender illuminates the ideological foundation of Marinetti's writing. Furthermore, a gender analysis reveals its unarticulated emotional underside, the "other" within the self: a radical sense of crisis, producing a need for unlimited control and a desire for absolute domination, to which the rhetorical strategies of the futurist fiction of power provide a violent, artificially optimistic, compensatory response. In this respect, Marinetti's works speak compellingly to issues that are central to contemporary scholarship. His rhetorical annihilation and assimilation of the feminine other—a code for woman, nature, and reality, as well as for the inner dissolution produced by the flow of desire—can be traced both to changes in the social configuration of gender relations and to a destabilization of the Western ideal of the separate, bound, and autonomous subject. The fiction of power illustrates how that ideal, when frustrated, may degenerate into violent aggression and repression of the other, both within and without the self.

To establish a theoretical and methodological framework for this investigation, I rely on models derived from gender studies and psychoanalysis—more specifically, from discourses that foreground the figural dimension of the text, highlighting interrelations between rhetorical strategies, ideological constructs, psychic processes, and social practices. I draw upon a notion of gender as a fundamental parameter of (self-)representation and as the complex product of social and cultural practices. Because of my concern with the origins and the temporal developments of the fiction of power, I also adopt a historical perspective. Through this shifting methodological focus, I pursue my analysis on two different levels: that of diachronic changes in the configuration of the futurist mythopoeia and that of synchronic, psychological, and rhetorical processes that convert "deep structures" of unconfessed anxieties into the "surface structures" of the futurist vision of the modern age.

My ordering of the chapters is in part chronological and in part determined by criteria of thematics and genre. Chapter 1 explores the origins of the futurist movement as a reaction to the cultural crisis of the modernist era in which it was originally embedded. It considers the ideological and aesthetic background of futurism's antipasséist revolution in relation to the decadent sensibility at the turn of the century, with particular emphasis on Marinetti's prefuturist production. Here, the naked body of woman stands for the impossibility of the ideal and the imperfection of the real, and thus for the perpetual frustration of desire. Such frustration, often enacted in sadomasochistic erotic fantasies, results in destructive and self-destructive rebellion against both the unattainable ideal and a reality perceived to be intolerable: a violent version of decadent "neurosis," characterized by hyperbolic expenditure, rather than deliquescence, of vital forces.

The difference between the decadents' contemplative aestheticism and Marinetti's agitated activism is radically accentuated in the futurist manifestos, where he programmatically reacts against the fin de siècle's overwhelmingly pessimistic and disempowering view of civilization's vulnerability to the destructive forces of nature and society. To counter such negativity, the futurist leader advanced the formula of *arte-azione* (art-in-action or art-as-action), heralding it as a new principle of "mental hygiene," ostentatiously assuming a stance of creative, "healthy" expansion and appropriating the new technological sources of power to drive at full speed, with optimistic determination, toward the future. Chapter 2 examines the workings of this fiction of power in the futurist manifestos. My analysis centers on Marinetti's use of language as a reality-structuring principle, focusing, in particular, on his "massive" deployment of the femininity seme to demarcate an "other" against which the self (individual, group, nation) can be negatively defined. My chief contention is that the symbolic configuration of femininity unwittingly projects ambivalent value markings: attention to these valorizations permits one to identify lacunae in ideological constructs whereby that which is rejected, negated, unacknowledged—the sense of crisis that is the source and undercurrent of Marinetti's writing—is rendered evident.

Mafarka le futuriste (Mafarka the Futurist) illustrates paradigmatically how woman haunts Marinetti's imaginary world as a catalyst of fear and fascination— a locus of ambivalences in which the modernist crisis resonates. Chapter 3 explores the primacy of feminine identity in a novel about an all-male generation of the futurist superuomo. Mafarka is the protagonist of a fatal struggle against an abject feminine other that, however, turns out to be a fundamental part of his own self. In the end, the divided protagonist is killed in order to give life to an armored, hypervirile, omnipotent hero, who rises to the sky while an explosion of apocalyptic forces destroys Mother Earth. By highlighting the pervasive imagery of feminine abjection, one can discern an obsessive phantasmatic economy, a subtextual drama about the dissolution of identity, that overrides the novel's utopian conclusion.

Further exploration of the psychological roots and historical grounds of the fiction of power requires moving beyond the mythopoeia of the futurist superuomo and examining the connection between Woman in her mythical form (as Magna Mater, eternal feminine) and woman in her social, historical reality (as partner in modern family and sexual relations). Chapter 4 charts Marinetti's shifting positions on matters of sexual politics throughout his vast output of polemical writings and erotic literature. His discourse on love, marriage, and the family is marked, on the one hand, by blatant chauvinism and, on the other, by radical polemics on behalf of feminist concerns such as divorce, suffrage, and the right to equal salaries. These inconsistencies pose an obstacle to the labeling of Marinetti's stance as purely revolutionary or reactionary. They suggest that, at heart, his writing is fueled by a complex reaction to changes in gender roles and power relations. The utopia of "metallized man," predominant in Marinetti's earlier work, represents the threatened male's ultimate goal: total rejection of woman. This goal can be achieved only when man completes his evolutionary metamorphosis into a superhuman type impervious to affect. A more pragmatic discourse, characteristic of Marinetti's wartime and postwar output, realizes that contemporary man still needs a healthy, ego-boosting "diet" of seduced women to sustain his threatened masculine identity. This "presentist" strategy is bodied forth by a rhetoric of metaphorical depersonalization and synecdochic reduction that molds and parcels woman into a "manageable," "assimilable," and "appetizing" object

of desire. The recurrent association of sex and violence, both in erotic and in battlefield scenarios, points to an intimate connection between the discourse on love
and the discourse on war. Warfare, like sexual violence, allows for a "legitimate"
eruption of emotions: an explosion of boundaries that, paradoxically, is predicated on affirmation of difference.

Chapter 5 explores two different experiences of war in *Un ventre di donna* (The
Womb of a Woman). This "surgical novel" combines Marinetti's letters from the
front—brief sketches of his exhilarating exploits—and an autobiographical narrative of the futurist woman writer Enif Robert, a story of intimate (physical and
psychological) struggle against a mysterious disease. Although futurism is generally considered a misogynist movement, it encouraged the active presence of
women artists in its ranks. Futurist rhetoric's abjection of the "feminine other"
does not conform to the actual standing of women in the movement. It does, however, account for the two different kinds of self represented in *Un ventre di donna*:
the surgically separate identities constructed by the hero's war against a foreign
enemy and by the heroine's struggle against her own body. Because of its duplex
authorship, this two-tiered narrative offers interesting and symptomatic interpretive problems concerning the uneasy position of futurist women writers vis-à-vis
the Marinettian fiction of power.

Finally, chapter 6 considers Marinetti's output in the period usually referred to
as "second futurism," which coincides with the exhaustion of the avant-gardist
impetus and with a general *rappel à l'ordre* in the European cultural scene after
World War I. The texts examined in this section are the least known and the least
studied of Marinetti's works, though they present interesting developments in the
futurist mythopoeia and significantly complicate the issue of Marinetti's *modernolatria* (worship of modernity). The vision of modernity for which Marinetti is famous is the celebratory one loudly proclaimed in the manifestos. The tensions underlying this enthusiastic outlook have for the most part been ignored by his
critics. In Marinetti's later works, similarly neglected by critics, those tensions
come to the surface in the wake of a thematic *riflusso, a* "reflux" or "resorption" of
the rejected themes of sentiment, nostalgic memory, nature, and Christian love.
Seen through the prism of gender, and from the vantage point of the overarching
fiction of power, the developments in Marinetti's later output no longer appear to
be merely a tired and tiresome return to tradition after the wearing out of the
original revolutionary impetus, but a return to the origins, or an eruption of the
primal psychological forces driving his textual production.

Parts of this book have been previously published, in somewhat different form.
Portions of chapter 2 appeared as "Rhetorical Strategies and Gender in
Marinetti's Futurist Manifesto" in *Italica* 62.2 (1990): 196–211, and a shorter ver-
sion of chapter 5 appeared as "The Scarred Womb of the Futurist Woman" in
Carte Italiane 8 (1986–1987): 14–30. Illustrations are reprinted with permission from
Giovanni Lista, the National Library of Florence, the University of Iowa Li-

braries (Iowa City), and the Beinecke Rare Book and Manuscript Library, Yale University.

Quotes are given in translation with key words and phrases interpolated when necessary. I have enclosed ellipses marking omissions in square brackets to distinguish them from suspension points in the quoted material. Unless otherwise noted, all translations are mine. In developing my translations of Marinetti's works, I consulted Marinetti, *Selected Writings,* ed. R. W. Flint, trans. R. W. Flint and Arthur A. Coppotelli (New York: Farrar, Straus and Giroux, 1971). My thanks to Sean Caulfield, Monique Manopoulos, Suzanne Morrison, Rosemarie Scullion, Scott Sheridan, Lara Trubowitz, and Russell Valentino for helping me with the translations and to Robert Herschbach for his skillful editorial assistance.

The work for this book has been sustained by the generosity of many other people, and I wish to acknowledge it here. In the early stages of this project, a Cornell University Fellowship supported my research in Italy, and my mentors at Cornell provided encouragement, advice, and critical insight. I am particularly grateful to Jonathan Culler, Anita Grossvogel, Mary Jacobus, Marilyn Migiel, and Jeffrey Schnapp for creating a tremendously stimulating intellectual environment (special thanks to Marilyn for her inspiring example and continuing friendship). My gratitude also goes to Leonardo Clerici, Claudia Salaris, Primo Conti, Antonio Pantano, and the *aeropittrice* Barbara for allowing me access to their private collections as well as for sharing their scholarly and personal experiences with me.

The University of Iowa enabled me to develop and bring the project to completion with an Old Gold Summer Fellowship and a semester's leave. I have greatly appreciated the supportive atmosphere offered by the University of Iowa and especially by the Department of French and Italian. All of my colleagues have been generous with their encouragement and assistance. In particular, I owe very warm thanks to Deborah Contrada for her invaluable friendship. I also want to acknowledge the colleagues who have generously read sections of this book: Geoffrey Hope, Michel Laronde, Rosemarie Scullion, and Steven Ungar. A very special thanks goes to Alan Nagel who has read the entire manuscript and offered incisive suggestions. For their assistance in finding and reproducing illustrations, *grazie* to Kathy Wachel and Thomas Sulentic.

Finally, I am grateful, beyond words, to my family and especially to my husband, Tom. They have been a source of unfailing support. This book is, appropriately, dedicated to them.

ONE

The Other Modernism

Futurism and Its Contradictions

Futurism is characterized by striking ambivalences and contradictions. These, in turn, are epitomized by its dual historical legacy. On one hand, this earliest incarnation of the modernist avant-garde was instrumental in foreseeing, instigating, and initiating revolutionary developments in the arts. The futurists are credited not simply with specific technical innovations like synthetic theater, visual poetry, and tactile poetry (*tattilismo*) but especially with affirming and divining ideas that have come to make up our modern conception of art: in particular, the conflation of traditionally separate genres and media, the breakdown of boundaries between world and text, and the conviction that art should match a rapidly changing reality and inhabit the regions colonized by technology. At the same time, futurism was instrumental in the development of Italian politics toward fascism. The movement supported Benito Mussolini's political enterprise from start to finish. Furthermore, the futurists responded actively to the contemporary sociopolitical climate by helping produce an ideology for the fascist era: futurist aesthetics are, indeed, bound up with the construction of a vision that provided a powerful impetus to belligerent patriotism and, later, to fascism.

The question of futurism's contradictions cannot be reduced to an incongruity between innovative aesthetics and reactionary politics, or bypassed by drawing a clear-cut boundary between the two domains. Even granting that any such line can be drawn (as it has been) for critical purposes, each domain is bound to include antithetical, apparently unreconcilable concepts to define each domain. Futurist politics has been characterized as both anarchist and nationalist, while futurist aesthetics has been seen as compounding romantic, elitist notions of heroic creative genius with twentieth-century strategies of mass culture. One may perceive further incongruities in the futurist stance toward the sweeping changes affecting the modern world: while celebrating the new forces of flux and exchange that transgressed national boundaries, the futurists fanatically embraced a militant nationalism and defended, with great enthusiasm, their homeland's borders in both world wars. Their positionings with respect to the question of the New Woman also appear to vary. Marinetti, in particular, blatantly displayed his misogyny and antifeminism. Yet he also sponsored the careers of several women artists (including his wife) and clamored for such feminist issues as divorce, equal pay, and political emancipation. Though he frequently relied on phallic metaphors of domination and penetration to figure the creative individual's mastery of reality, he also advocated an aesthetic of "polymorphous" sensuality that, according to today's literary theory, undermines phallocentrism. These and other complexities seem to warrant Luciano De Maria's 1968 prescription for futurist scholarship: in order to examine futurism, one must examine its contradictions.[1]

De Maria's critical edition of Marinetti's writings catalyzed the interest of scholars in the futurist movement. Since that time, a growing body of research has explored the phenomenon of futurism, calling attention to its complexity. (Not accidentally, this rediscovery of futurism—the so-called historical avant-garde—coincides with the revival of interest in formal experimentation and in the political implications of art that, in Italy, were most conspicuously manifested in the neo-avant-garde.) As previously suggested, however, critics have tended to spotlight one or the other of this movement's most visible faces. The tendency to split along political lines is particularly evident in the case of Marinetti. Founder, leader, and chief propagandist of futurism, his life and career (from 1909 to 1944, the year of his death) span the life of the movement. Studies of Marinetti's work seem to have had great difficulty in reconciling his "radical" experimentation and his political choices. Critics who are outraged by the latter tend to discount the former. Jo Anna Isaak, for instance, stigmatizes the futurist "new mimeticism" by relating it to the modern phenomenon of reification and by portraying Marinetti as "the greatest adman" of commodity capitalism and of fascism.[2] In similarly summary fashion, Alice Yaeger Kaplan qualifies Marinetti's stylistic innovations as an aesthetic "bribe" that has secured futurism's place in the avant-garde, anarchic tradition, thus obfuscating its fascist affinities.[3] Conversely, those who accentuate the importance of futurism as an avant-garde movement tend to disregard or play down its political affiliations. Marianne W. Martin exemplifies this tendency: she masses together problematic aspects of the futurist program—glorification of conflict, violence, misogyny, and anarchism—and explains them away as "expressions of universal dynamism."[4] Marjorie Perloff, who offers a valid analysis of futurist experimental techniques, also discounts the belligerent nationalistic ideology by viewing it as a product of the "avant-guerre" climate in which prowar sentiments fermented.[5]

Apologetic and condemnatory approaches tend to gloss over problematic aspects of the futurist experience, thus hindering the investigation of its historical significance and contemporary relevance. Ignoring what is puzzling and disturbing in this experience, or demonizing it as a mere premise to fascism—or, worse, discounting it as a "miracle in stupidity"[6]—results in oversimplification, dismissal, and misunderstanding. To avoid these pitfalls, I believe that futurism should be considered in all its contradictions and ambivalences against the background of, and as a response to, the cultural crisis of the modernist era in which it was originally embedded.

HISTORICAL ROOTS

Although the term "modernism" is controversial in many respects, it has acquired wide currency in reference to the radical developments in Western art, literature, and thought that had their most conspicuous early manifestation in the innovations of French symbolism, reached a peak of intensity in the first quarter of the twentieth century, and continued until about World War II or shortly thereafter.[7] At the core of those developments is a sense of crisis in the human existence that can be seen as an early stage of the "modern neurosis" still affecting us: a reaction to traumatic historical change, to the breakdown of secure communal ideologies, to the destruction of beliefs and illusions that function as shields against existential anxieties, as barriers against exposure to meaninglessness and absurdity.[8] The causes of this sense of crisis can be predicated in a variety of conditioning factors that have transformed the essential parameters of experience and knowledge: changes in modes of production and marketing, in class structures and class conflict, in social institutions and gender roles, in means of communication and means of waging war, and, finally, in the scientific, religious, philosophical, and political systems of beliefs for ordering and making sense of the world. New applications of technology to industry, agriculture, war, and everyday life radically altered the foundations of experience and the material basis of value in European society. These developments resulted in an unprecedented expansion of human possibilities, but also in the dissolution of old support structures and in the empowerment of conditioning apparatuses and agencies. Corporatism, bureaucracy, mass communication, advertising, and state propaganda contributed to the creation of an alienating environment for the individual. The evolution of new classes and communications, in addition, led to the pluralization of perspectives and the destabilization of traditional worldviews, while class conflict threatened to undermine the establishment. Furthermore, the erosion of gender divisions and of the authoritarian patriarchal family—related to women's increasing economic, political, and sexual freedom—produced a masculinity crisis and whipped up an antifeminist backlash. Finally, scientific discoveries, along with new philosophical, psychological, and socioeconomic theories, fostered a more materialistic and relativistic view of human nature and of its role in the universe. The cultural crisis of modernism thus can be essentially described as one of metaphysics and language: a collapse of transcendental values and old systems of belief (meanings and hierarchies); a failure of social institutions—foremost, for the writer, language—in their function of providing meaningful structures for human experiences; and, ultimately, a breakdown in the framing assumptions of Western civilization so far as they rest on the

traditional conception of individuality, on the anthropocentric notion of the rational control and supremacy of man over reality.[9]

Artists responded to the modern age with a variety of attitudes that ranged
from total refusal to enthusiastic acceptance. However, within the proliferation of
movements and individual styles commonly associated under the label "modernism," we can isolate an essential core of common tenets and attitudes: a tendency toward experimentation and technical display; an aesthetics of abstraction,
discontinuity, and subversion; and, finally, the problematization of the role of the
artist. Although the modernist consciousness defines itself in opposition to the
past, romanticism and naturalism constitute the breeding ground of the new sensibility, which can be detected in a flourish of aesthetic theories influenced by
Schopenhauerian pessimism and by Nietzschean irrationalism. As realism and
naturalism decline in influence, the positivistic (scientizing, rationalizing, democ-
ratizing) view of historical progress gradually gives way to a fascination with irrational and unconscious forces, and the notion of modernity becomes increasingly
associated with a sense of hopelessness, alienation, and impotence, with a pessimistic view of man's relationship to society.[10] As George Mosse notes, the growing influence of Arthur Schopenhauer's *Die Welt als Wille und Vorstellung* (The
World as Will and Representation; 1819) testifies to the reorientation of European
thought. According to Schopenhauer, man is driven by his blind and aimless will
against a chaotic, alien reality; hence, his only escape from a world of misery re-
sides in denial of the will. Some artists and intellectuals resorted to a Schopenhauerian escapist solution against the materialistic chaos of modernity—a retreat
from the world into the realm of aesthetics: " 'Art for Art's Sake' was a slogan
which appealed to many, and scholarship for the sake of scholarship became
quite popular."[11] Other new theories were inspired by an active, utopian sense of
change: avant-garde movements, characterized by a blend of nihilism, activism,
antagonism, and agonism,[12] saw in art the only way of meeting the challenge of the
modern world and advocated programs of aesthetic and even social revolution.

The fin de siècle crisis assumed in Italy a somewhat different configuration,
due in part to the underdevelopment of the Italian economy, politics, and national identity relative to other European powers. The climate out of which futurism grew was characterized by a widespread sense of frustration: the consensus
was that the ruling class had betrayed the "spirit" of the Risorgimento and failed
to give the new nation a solid internal organization, as well as international power
and prestige.[13] Italy's unification had ended the multiplicity of governments but
had not filled the gap between local and national systems of power. In the 1890s
Italian national politics was brought into a state of crisis by a combination of factors, most notably, government corruption, expensive but ineffective colonial adventures, and pressure from an increasingly organized labor militancy, which
produced waves of strikes, demonstrations, and riots. The prewar era saw an ag-
gravation of labor-management conflict, important new political alignments
under Giovanni Giolitti's reformist leadership, and increasing polarization on the

question of Italy's foreign policy between the liberal and socialist opposition to war and the nationalists' propaganda for military intervention. While class and geographic frictions produced a sense of sociopolitical instability, changes in the social structuring of gender relations (such as the entry of women into the workforce) threatened established roles, stirring up concerns about "the future of the family and of the race" and sparking animated debates on the so-called *questione femminile*, or woman question.[14] At the same time, the belated Italian industrial revolution had set the ground for economic expansion, engendering, in addition to social problems and labor trouble, new hopes of progress and an impulse to be part of the international competition for industrial expansion. These hopes and impulses were concomitant with a trend of positivism, which pervaded large sectors of Italian culture at the beginning of the twentieth century.[15] Many intellectuals, however, denounced positivist rationalism and materialism as leading to the demise of individual and spiritual values. Among artists, there was a sense of frustration about Italian provincialism and backwardness vis-à-vis the modern artistic movement: irrationalism and aestheticism played a role in Italian culture, particularly through the popular Gabriele D'Annunzio; on the whole, however, Italy remained in a marginal position with respect to the ferment of change in the European cultural scene.[16]

The journals of militant culture that flourished in Italy, particularly in Florence, during the first two decades of this century offer compelling evidence of the political, institutional, philosophical, and psychological aspects that compounded the pervasive sense of crisis. Writers of different ideological orientations expressed similar concerns and anxieties, voicing the disappointments and hopes of a generation of intellectuals affected by "premature senescence," by the burden of "a life which was not theirs," because they had not experienced the fire of passions, ideals, and beliefs that was smoldering in the "crepuscular" dawn of the new century.[17] Giuseppe Antonio Borgese defines the crisis in existential terms, as a loss of roots, goals, and certainties. He invokes the image of the Flying Dutchman (Il vascello fantasma) to describe the curse of his generation: prematurely old in spirit, modern youth drifts aimlessly toward an abyss of nihilism and a vortex of Dionysiac activism, driven by "hate for what is rotting and not by desire for the new."[18] Similarly, Giovanni Amendola speaks of a ghastly intellectual void haunting contemporary writers. As the romantic critique of classical ideals gives place to a postromantic skepticism that discards individual beliefs like old clothes, the modern man who wanted to be "naked will" realizes that nothing is left but a "nebulous ghost."[19] He thus faces a crucial ideological dilemma: to pursue current theories of relativism and voluntarism to their nihilistic extremes or to revisit the classical shores of absolute value. Should he choose a return to belief, he can take the rational road of abandoning voluntaristic theories, or he can surrender himself to the irrational impulse that will drive him back down the path of individual ideals until he reaches the "romantic bridge" between postromanticism and the shores of classicism.

Many writers chose the voluntaristic path to belief. In journals such as *Hermes*, *Il Regno*, *Leonardo*, *La Voce*, and *Lacerba*, they waged war against Italy's political, social, and cultural ills. Although they often pursued different strategies, their objective was ultimately the same: an intellectual revolution that would embrace modernity and counter the disintegrating effects of modernization through a new, unifying "religion" of the nation, a secular mythology of national palingenesis that reconciled spiritualism and industrialization. Announcing the goals of *Il Regno*, Enrico Corradini (leader of the Italian nationalist movement) lamented "the cowardice of the present national hour" and set out to incite the glorious resurgence of the fatherland.[20] In less heroic terms, this nationalistic program was a reaction to the "social question" (class antagonism, organized labor, the growth of the Socialist party) and to the government's strategy of compromise with the Left. The prime target of Corradini's campaign was socialism, which "destroyed values" to appease the "base instincts" of the masses; however, he also attacked the bourgeoisie for having grown soft to liberal doctrines of freedom and internationalism and for having been contaminated by the "syphilis" of sentimental socialism. Giuseppe Prezzolini and Giovanni Papini (founders of *Leonardo*) also diagnosed the disease affecting the ruling class and prescribed a cure of antiproletarian reaction and "spiritual revival." Advocating a voluntaristic pragmatism, they rejected the new "metaphysics" of positivist materialism, which they viewed as an instrument of socialist reformism and a means to the democratic leveling of all minds.[21] To bourgeois "decay" (i.e., liberalism and internationalism), they opposed individualistic and nationalistic ideals influenced by Spencer, William James, Max Stirner, and D'Annunzio.[22]

In his campaign to form a new intellectual elite of heroes, Papini expresses disgust for the disease of mediocrity and idleness that affects his generation of "Hamlets," enfeebled by hesitation and self-reflection. With a rhetorical turn recurrent in much literature of his time, he figures the effects of this disease as de*gender*ation: today's spirits, he claims, are "effeminate" because they prefer words, which are "female," rather than acts, which are "male."[23] A few years later, this rhetorical move gives place to an outrageous "philosophical" disquisition on the need to "massacre" women.[24] Drawing on the authority of Friedrich Nietzsche and Otto Weininger (who had unveiled the "truth" about woman, the "animal/hag"), Papini announces the imminent and inevitable liquidation of the female sex, cause of man's degradation and powerlessness. Anticipating the objection that woman is necessary for procreation, he retorts that the human race is doomed in any case, since the number of women who refuse to make babies keeps growing every day. This conclusive argument suggests that the topos of degeneration can be traced to another source of modern malaise: a concern with the social changes that undermined gendered identity.[25]

Fertile territory of cultural production and consumption in Italy, the militant journals constituted the primary breeding ground (and, in the case of *Lacerba*, a forum) for many of the ideas developed by futurists. However, futurism's origins cannot be traced solely to developments in Italy. International trends in literature also play a key role—not only because the cultural environment in which it rose was characterized by an unprecedented fluidity and circulation of ideas but also because its creator, Marinetti, embodied the cosmopolitan spirit of modernism (the crossing of cultural boundaries and national frontiers) in his life experience.[26] He was born of Italian parents in Alexandria, Egypt, where he lived until he was seventeen (1876–1894). His earlier multicultural exposure included being nursed by a black Sudanese woman and being taught French by the Jesuits of Saint François Xavier College. His mother, meanwhile, introduced him to Italian literature. In Alexandria, he founded a small literary review, Le Papyrus (1894), where he published poems and articles in defense of naturalism and modern literature. He received his baccalauréat ès lettres in Paris, then studied law in Pavia and Genoa (his father was a successful lawyer and entrepreneur). Marinetti's earliest work, inspired by the French literary milieu of the fin de siècle, gave him the reputation of a "Franco-Italian" poet. His career took a radical turn in 1909 with the launching of the first futurist manifesto on the first page of an internationally prominent mass circulation newspaper, the Parisian daily Le Figaro. From the beginning, Marinetti collaborated in a variety of international reviews and then founded his own, Poesia (Milan, 1905–1909), an eclectic poetic forum with which he intended to expose the provincial Italian scene to the latest cultural trends and particularly to French symbolism. In his successive roles as promoter and propagandist of futurism, he traveled indefatigably (in Europe, Russia, and even Brazil), gaining the nickname "the caffeine of Europe." Cosmopolitanism was also a distinguishing trait of Marinetti's activities as founder, financial backer, and editor of the publishing house Edizioni di «Poesia» (1905), later renamed Edizioni futuriste di «Poesia» (1910–1943). Volumes such as Enquête internationale sur le Vers libre (International Inquest on Free Verse; 1909), Zang Tumb Tumb (1914), and Les mots en liberté futuristes (Futurist Words in Freedom; 1919) were addressed to foreign as well as Italian audiences, and perhaps had a greater resonance abroad.[27]

LITERARY ORIGINS

The futurist experience is rooted in the late symbolist mode of Marinetti's prefuturist output: a paroxysmal development, both sclerotic and hypertrophic, of the symbolist style and of the decadent pursuit of extreme experiences and sensations. The destructive impetus and hyperbolic excess characteristic of the manifestos already inform Marinetti's first major literary effort, La Conquête des Étoiles (The Conquest of the Stars). The poetic persona engaged in this epic, the symbolist "I" in search of the Absolute, is a frustrated idealist who launches an offensive against the bastions of the "impure" ideal. Much like a disillusioned lover who directs outbursts of verbal violence against all women, the poet vents his frustration by attacking the personified symbols of the "lost" ideal: the stars—traditional icons of pure spirituality—are metaphorically transfigured into wicked, lascivious courtesans who torment man with "their putrid / staring, through the damp slit / of their eyelids, half-closed and like vulvas" (115).[28] Such representations of feminine sexuality are typical of Marinetti's imagery. They point to an essential continuity of vision between the prefuturist and the futurist production: the "putrid" female genitals are the sign of the material limitations that doom organic life to imperfection, decomposition, and death, limitations that also contaminate the spiritual realm, the old symbolic order represented by the stars. These fallen but still desirable beauties are held responsible for the suicide of innumerable disillusioned lovers, shipwrecked in their search for the ideal and now piled up in the depths of the sea: "They died / from having fanned the fire of the Ideal in their blood, / the great shrouding flame of the Absolute! / They died because they believed in the promises of the Stars!" (62).

According to Marinetti, the means to the conquest of the stars are not to be found in the rationalizations of science. Syllogizing scholars, like lecherous old men, are incapable of laying their rude hands on "fragile" young truths. At most, their "impotent" logic can lust after the mere traces of such elusive beauties: "the impotent Syllogisms, / grey haired and broken, lick the traces / of fascinating Truths which pass by, elusive!" (58). The poet, instead, turns to the illuminating power of his "dream," a delirious vision, in order to break through the citadel of the Infinite and gorge on "sidereal flesh." This vision takes the form of an epic prosopopoeia that dramatizes an explosion of irrational forces: the sovereign sea and his cohort of unbridled natural elements, turning the petrified cadavers of suicidal lovers into ammunition, mount a destructive and self-destructive attack, which results in a slaughter of apocalyptic dimensions. The scene is presented in gory colors, with a bombastic tone and a plethora of hyperbolic, hallucinatory imagery. Through rhetorical surfeit or "apoplexy," symptomatic of a sort of linguistic bulimia, the poet attempts to satisfy his insatiable desire, to fill the unbreachable distance that separates him from the ideal, and to impose his creative (redeeming) mark on the engulfing abjection of nature evoked by recurrent images of decay. In other words, the rhetorical excess is a fetishistic artifice designed to compensate for, denaturalize, or "kill" the limited/limiting nature. When the stars are finally conquered, however, and the old poetic ideal of loving harmony between man and nature (symbolized by a fallen star that has been washed ashore) succumbs to the attack, the poet kisses the dying beauty and is left with nothing but deadly nostalgia: "I gently kissed her curving lips, / which were barely opening before pearly gleams of moonlight. / For a long time, I savored this funereal embrace / so as to die from it, to die from it!" (128).

The same themes and imagery return with obsessive repetitiveness in the other texts of this period. *Destruction* explores further the inner drama that leads to the apocalyptic explosion of destructive forces: in fact, this work can be seen as a premise to *La Conquête* even though it is, chronologically, its sequel.[29] The poem is framed by two desperate appeals to the "omnipotent" "avenging" sea: an initial invocation "to be freed from the Ideal" and a final invocation "to be freed from the

Infamous Reality." The poetic "I," a "beggar of love hungry for the Ideal," is caught and torn between his unappeasable desire for the Absolute (love, knowledge, power, happiness) and his disgust for (terror of) abject reality—the limited and limiting material world that is his lot. In this phantasmatic scenario, woman—the desired and abhorred other—embodies both poles of the conflict. The ideal is symbolized by the beautiful, beloved woman whom the stars promised the poet in the past days of his youth. But since that celestial woman is never to be found, the frustrated lover seeks oblivion in the "brothel" of the flesh, symbolized by the feminine sexual (as opposed to ideal) body, which "strangles" the "pure Dream" with the ecstasy of the senses. Such a split representation of woman is doubly emblematic: it is the projection of an inner break within the self between spirit and matter, dramatized by a dialogue between the sensual, pragmatic "I" and his idealist "Soul"; and it is also a figure for the maiming rupture between self and other—the painful gap between infinite desire and infamous reality, which is represented in terms of alienation, wounding, devouring, and annihilation.

In her degraded role, woman stands both for nature and for society; more specifically, she stands for the unruliness of nature and the ruling vulgarity of a materialistic, utilitarian society in a world without transcendent values. These two functions are best exemplified by Loulou, the Soul's lover: in her seductive sensuousness, she represents the surrender of the Soul's dream to the "reality" of the flesh. In her obtuse insensitivity to the Soul's genius, she epitomizes the imbecility of the crowd that does not understand the value of poetic creation. The realistic, pragmatic half of the poet—the "I"—betrays the idealistic half—the Soul—by accepting Loulou's degraded love as a necessary surrogate for glory in a world where all values, including the poetic, have lost their aura. This degeneration is rhetorically underscored by the shift from verse to prose, a shift that is heralded in the section's title, "Dans les Cafés de Nuit (chant qui finit en prose grossière)" (In the Night Cafés [melody that ends in coarse prose]). The fall of desire into the compromise of sexual intercourse with woman evokes the vision of a red, flaming-hot, bleeding island, floating in the sea like a "wound" and like a "velvet rose" (227)—a thinly disguised figuration of the threat of castration associated with the female genitals. Like Loulou, all the "obscene" women whom the poet meets at "the crossroads / of [his] defunct will" (163) are phantasmatically associated with loss of identity by organic lesions that open gaping mouths of voracious desire in their bodies and that resonate with other recurrent images of dismembering, bleeding, and decomposition.

Such imagery, especially the bleeding, flowerlike island, recalls the monstrously obscene Nidularium in Joris-Karl Huysmans's *À Rebours*—perhaps the most notorious example of the abhorrence of female sexuality, expressed in terrifying visions of organic decomposition, which pervades the male literary imagination at the end of the nineteenth century. As Rita Felski notes, the feminine body, particularly the "deviant" body of the prostitute, is recurrently identified both with the baseness of nature, "as a primary symbolic site for confronting and controlling the threat [of its unruliness]," and with the vulgarity of contemporary

society, "as a blatant embodiment of the commercialization of sexuality"—
which, in turn, symbolizes the commodification of the artist in the marketplace.[30]
In Felski's view, the fin de siècle aesthete attempts to exorcise this double threat
through an imaginary identification with the feminine. By colonizing the feminine body as the locus of artistic creation, the aesthete sublimates the boundaries
it signifies. Having appropriated its subversive power, he can then deploy it
against the dominant cultural discourse.[31]

Des Esseintes, the protagonist of *À Rebours,* and the archetypal literary incarnation of the effeminate aesthete, exemplifies this strategy: he withdraws from society into total isolation, displaying jaded detachment from the vulgar reality embodied by women and crowds; he cultivates his hyperrefined taste, creating his
own life as an aesthetic artifact through artificial pleasures and techniques of illusion; and he indulges in sexual perversions, challenging the hypocritical codes of
bourgeois society and exposing the artificiality of its cultural constructs. Ultimately, however, he illustrates the failure of the decadent strategy. A paralyzing
neurosis destroys his vital forces, rendering him totally unable to function in the
world. Feminization, rather than a sign of creative transgression, becomes the
mark of self-division and impotence. Such failure is particularly evident in the
novel's conclusion, where Des Esseintes's "attempted indifference" is swept away
by rage when he recognizes that there can be no refuge against the flood of "pesti-
lential filth," "the waves of human mediocrity" that engulf the world.[32]

A comparison between the decadent Des Esseintes and Marinetti's prefuturist
hero can help situate the origin of the futurist revolution in relation to the milieu
of the turn of the century. These two companions in misfortune share obvious
links and suffer the same crisis of values. Marinetti's poetic persona hyperbolically
intensifies Des Esseintes's "feverish desire for the unknown, the unsatisfied longing for an ideal, the craving to escape from the horrible realities of life, to cross the
frontiers of thought, to grope after a certainty, albeit without finding one, in the
misty upper regions of art" (115). Both heroes are haunted by anxieties about the
dissolution of the boundaries of identity. However, Marinetti's prefuturist poetic
persona is unlike the effeminate, passive, impotent dandy in that he experiences a
violent expenditure, rather than deliquescence, of vital forces. The poetic "I" displays sadistic aggressiveness toward woman, turning the sexual relationship into
an act of warlike aggression.

> I want the supreme communion
> of our two agonies, so that her body
> might thank me after all, in ecstasy,
> for the slowness of my daggers! . . .
> . . . so that at last the countless lips
> of all of her wounds might earnestly embrace
> these glaives for which they weep and die
> pierced through and happy!"

(171)

This kind of erotic scenario is clearly a symptomatic attempt to bridge the paralyzing gap, to exorcise the (decadent) phantasm of impotence through violent gestures of self-assertion that apotropaically counter gaping wounds with phallic swords. The prosaic sermon of the pragmatic "I" to the Soul pinpoints the "utilitarian" logic of such a rhetorical strategy: "Art is elusive and distant like a Star; and it is indeed sad to love a Star! Besides, one must satisfy one's pride through domination; so you must have immediate Glory . . . women offering up their lips" (231).

Marinetti represents his hero's evasion from abominable reality as a violently active liberation of irrational forces, an empowering symbiotic union with the vital elements of nature (the sea) and technology (the train), resulting in ultimate destruction. Leaving behind all charted territories, the poet accepts the challenge of the stars—which, having abandoned their traditional role as meaningful guides, rush toward a mysterious goal. He does so by identifying himself with a train launched at frenzied speed toward the unknown. In a famous passage of *À Rebours*, Huysmans also incorporates the locomotive into the aesthetic domain, celebrating the beauty of the machine over woman's beauty. The attitudes of the two protagonists, however, differ significantly: Des Esseintes's is one of passive contemplation, whereas that of Marinetti's protagonist is one of active identification. The latter's delirious race dramatizes the experience of liberation in terms that clearly anticipate the futurist motifs of pride, courage, speed, and violence. But here Marinetti has not yet reached the determination to join in the technological race to the future with total optimism: the black, voracious, abysslike mouth of the unknown looms at the end of the tracks, and the vertiginous race is haunted by terrifying visions of aggression and death. The poet is possessed by the "demon of speed" in an infernal, agonizing, suffocating urban scenario, where "frantic," "rabid" trams "bite each other like ogres biting children's bodies" and threaten the poet with hateful blood-injected eyes (186–187), sweeping him away into a dizzying "torrent" of speed. During his journey he confronts Death in another infernal city, where he must face the dissolution of his own identity in an amorphous, engulfing crowd, embodiment of the soulless quality of modern life.

> Tottering plumes of thick greasy smoke
> cover with an awful slime the crowding mob
> extending around me its colossal
> octopus tentacles with their wreaking suckers . . .
> Male and female . . . they all look like me!
> It is still you, Demon of Frenzies,
> who devoured their faces . . . Oh, the eternal leprosy! . . .
> . . . Like me? Just like me! . . .
>
> Did no one feel the anguish
> and the deep remorse of having thus lost
> their features . . . their mask . . . their face,

at the hands of an unknown,
for the love of Heaven or Hell?
for the love of Clouds! . . .

Ah, here is a woman! . . . My fingers have recognized you! . . .
I grab hold of your breasts. So yell at me, can't you sense
the horror of my pared face?

(217–218)

The poet is "the condemned man" and the hateful tentacled mass drags him toward "nothingness" ("le néant de [ses] vengeances," 218), an annihilating "revenge" that echoes the class antagonism that threatened to overturn social order.
The vengeful urban crowd and the sexual woman converge to mirror a dual anxiety about loss of identity: the poet's horror of the mechanizing, depersonalizing
effects of modern life and his terrifying realization that the explosion of the irrational "demon" has "corroded" his old self, alienating him from his own image
and dissolving the "difference" of sexed identity. Just as Papini's rhetoric of degenderation, this image of self-dissolution reflects contemporary concerns about
shifting gender roles.

Speed, trains, and the industrial city—celebrated emblems of progress in the
futurist manifestos—are charged with ambivalent, even negative connotations in
this early imaginary encounter between self and the modern world. So is the sea,
inspiring muse of the poem, and symbol of irrational forces. From these forces,
such as the fluid energy of the universe and the chaotic flux of the inner drives, the
poet draws the power to flee the prison of old ideals and infamous reality. The sea
is presented as an immense, comforting "lap" (147) and as a divine, omnipotent
"sword" (148)—that is, as a sort of phallic mother who combines masculine and
feminine features in a reassuring phantasmatic image of potent wholeness. At the
same time, however, the sea shares the attributes and destructive power associated with the prostitute and the crowd: its sensual, lascivious curves and mouths
are fatally seductive (159–162); and its sweeping, crushing, dismembering waters
blend with the torrent of the "automatic, bituminous" (219) crowd, engulfing the
poet in an overwhelming (con)fusion. Significantly, in describing these oceanic[33]
experiences, Marinetti casts his poetic persona in a role of feminine, masochistic
passivity not unlike that of Des Esseintes, thus pointing to irrationality's self-
destructive potential. This sinister implication is brought home in the conclusion.
Death presides over the ultimate (re)union between the self and the sea, which engenders only hate and devastation, leaving no hope for a new beginning. The
poem ends on a note of total pessimism, underscored by a refrained call to destruction ("Détruisons! . . . Détruisons!") and by an ominous sound of approaching war ("fanfares guerrières," 269).

In the play *Le Roi Bombance* (King Revelry), the theme of existential pessimism is
interlaced with a grotesque satire of political power and social ideologies, seen as
mere superindividual projections of the law of hunger (or desire) that governs
human nature.[34] The poet's hunger for the Absolute—a metaphor central to

Marinetti's early poems—is developed into a dystopic allegory of global appetite: "the social stomach" (10), an unjust digestive system in which bulimic structures of power (led by King Revelry) overeat, starving the famished masses of the Hungry. Social revolution, in turn, is presented as a periodic upsetting of the system, and progress as the evolution of the "jaws" with which men, from epoch to epoch, continue to perfect "the art of devouring one another with increasing agility" (267). When the king can no longer control the hungry populace, power is taken over by the scullions Tart, Siphon, and Bechamel—demagogues who wear the uniforms of "Cooks of Universal Happiness" (2). They mystify the masses with promises of a universal banquet; their only real aim is seizing control of the kitchens of power. Their bad faith is exposed by the true advocate of the stomachs' revolution, Emptystomach (Estomacreux). He leads the Hungry into a truculent, but ultimately ineffectual, revenge: a great feast that degenerates into a cannibalistic orgy, followed by indigestion, regurgitation of the victims, and a final reestablishment of the previous order, with the Hungry (who had died of indigestion) resuscitated and returning to haunt the undigestible Strong or Powerful.

On one level, the play is clearly a satirical caricature of socialist ideologies of materialistic progress: such polemical intention is particularly obvious in the Italian translation of 1910, which is dedicated to the socialist and syndicalist leaders Filippo Turati, Enrico Ferri, and Arturo Labriola—labeled, like the scullions of the play, "great cooks of universal happiness."[35] But the sociopolitical satire is ultimately assimilated by a visceral existential pessimism, embodied in the dystopic *dea ex machina* of the play: Saint-Putrefaction, who presents herself as "Goddess of Fertility and Destruction" (259), "incessant life teeming in death" (258), and "life of crowds that is renewed through the death of individuals" (258). In the play's economy, there is no transcending the cycle of life, decay, and death symbolized by this voracious, morbidly productive, all-embracing mother.

While femininity, embodied by Saint-Putrefaction, is given a primary role at the existential level, women, in their social role as wives and companions, are absent. They abandon the Kingdom of the Blunders (les Bourdes) at the beginning of the play, accusing their husbands of impotence. Men, for their part, do not ostensibly mourn the loss: women, they argue, cannot be easily served "in a plate" and cannot be easily "digested" (166–167), since their lust is insatiable and uncontrollable.

In this materialistic scenario, the poet, significantly named the Idiot, stands for "the Dream," or "the impossible that cries" (200): he is an alienated outcast, suffering for the degradation of all ideals and conscious of his inability to act. His impotence is symbolized by his broken heroic gear (dagger and helmet), thus already intimating the bellicose nature of his futurist rebirth. In other words, the Idiot is a rebel without a cause, unable to find the right "food" (or inspiration) within society or in the spiritual realm of the stars. He vainly attempts to console humanity with beautiful images but cannot satiate the obtuse appetites of the crowd or overcome his aristocratic disgust for life. Therefore, he finally chooses the "freedom" of death.

Another authorial persona, named Eel, stands for "Irony," or "the possible that laughs" (200). His cynically realistic perspective, elastic and resilient attitude, and capacity for transforming pain into play are later inherited by the futurist New Poet. He is the mouthpiece for Marinetti's pessimistic view of man as "a hilarious tragedy that . . . will never be performed" (184). This image, which anticipates Luigi Pirandello's theatrical metaphors, is extended into a definition of history as "so many dress rehearsals for this absurd tragedy" (185), in which the triumph of the worm crowns the apocalyptic conclusion. It then develops into another aphoristic figuration of the human condition: "Humanity? it is a small, low-born child, hanging from the earth's breast, stripping the skin from it with small clawing fingers, already clenched in agony" (185). The representation of mankind as an ill-fated, agonized infant recalls the characterization of the poet's perpetually hungry and disgusted soul as "puerile" in *Destruction* (150). Such formulations are symptomatic of a semantics of desire restricted to the body's perspective, to "the viewpoint of the pleasure-ego, for whom to say 'yes' means that it wants to introject into itself what is good, i.e., to 'devour' it, and to say 'no' means that it wants to eject from itself what is bad, i.e., to 'spit it out.' "[36] In psychoanalytic terms, this perspective is an archaic stage in the psychic constitution of the self, antecedent with respect to the consciousness of the "reality-ego"—the ability to recognize and accept the limitations imposed on the subject's desire by reality (or by another subject's desire). Philosophically, Marinetti's stance is a regressive one, marked by inability or unwillingness to accept the limitations of life and avoid the resurgence of narcissistic illusions. As I will argue, this stance is at the core of the futurist tendency to primitivism, violent antagonism, and juvenile rebelliousness.

While *Le Roi Bombance* offers the most articulated expression of Marinetti's bleak outlook in the prefuturist years, *La Ville charnelle* (The Carnal City) points to the way out of the pessimistic impasse. It was published in 1908, just one year before the birth of futurism. The first section of the poem, "Le Voyageur mordu,"[37] presents the poetic persona as a compulsive, bewitched traveler, who maintains an uneasy balance in his effort to keep ahead of the earth in its "laborious march [. . .] / like a juggler balancing upon a wobbly / rolling ball" (273)—Marinetti's globe-trotter version of a modernist topos, the poet as acrobat and tightrope walker. He is a beggar—hungry and thirsty for love, driven by a desire for absolute fulfillment, and haunted by fear of an all-consuming void ("the burst mouth / of devouring horizons," 279), the realization of being nothing but a mouse destined to be caught in the "black trap / of death" (311).

In his pilgrimage, the poet attains the goal of all those who crave boundless pleasure: an exotic "carnal" city with rosy flesh and feminine curves; a personified icon of lust, which provides shelter from the biting rays of solar ambition; and a harbor where he may rest from his journey. He attempts to quench his yearnings and drown his existential anxieties ("the unbridled / horrors of traveling," 279) by drinking at the spring of lust in the "cave" of the vulva, a grave and a cradle where he no longer fears "the mouth of the voracious horizon" (282). But his own cravings cannot be satisfied, and momentary oceanic ecstasy gives way to insatiable desire, ushered in by sadistic pleasure.

> The happiness of drowning in your vastness
> illusive and burning,
> like a tropical ocean, overflowing Vulva,
> dainty and so fragile, and yet
> larger than my soul right now! . . .
> The world is done away with! Desire is killed!
> The infinite is full, since you are the goal!
> And yet, hurting you feels so good,
> biting into you like a luscious fruit,
> to devour you,
> to drink up the sobs and fierce heavings
> of your liquid sensuality!
>
> You see, I am writhing in delight and ecstasy
> in your hollow, gushing and soft like a spring [*source*]!
> I want to dig into your sand with my teeth, my fingers,
> ever deeper, further, as far as unfathomable
> depths, so as to know
> and find the lode of joy,
> the wonderful lode of metallic happiness!
>
> (282–283)

Sexual "heroics" ("Héroïsme du sang," 282) turn into sadistic aggression—the impulse of biting, devouring, inflicting pain, dominating—as the carnal, feminine city (or "source"), with her soft, moist, corrupt(ible) nature, is rejected for the sake of a hard and shiny ideal, a vein of "metallic," untainted happiness. The clash between such a pursuit and the realization that the human creature is just another fruit of the earth, and equally destined to rot, results in a state of frustration and rage, expressed through the metaphor of a rabid dog infected by unrealizable ambitions:

> And the Sun cried out: «You will never enter
> the holy city with her happy terraces,
> which the dawn and the sea have made fragrant with honey!
> Cursed rabid dog, bitten by the snake
> festering and fetid with millenary arrogance,
> with my teeth I have crushed your powdery ankles,
> and, since then, my ambition's poison
> flows in your veins and clouds your eyes! . . .
> You roll forever in my resounding rays,
> weightier than chains, for you are a mere slave
> condemned to offer up your ripe heart,
> each day, like a fruit.
> I snatch it while biting your fingers, savoring them
> as they slowly and methodically turn gamy!»
>
> (277)

Anticipating a central theme of the novel *Mafarka le futuriste,* Marinetti chains his protagonist with a double bind: a despotic, castrating, degenerate power (embodied by the sun) condemns him to the "disease" of an impossible desire (the pride that flows in his veins like a poison) and to the awareness of his mortal, degraded, enslaved condition. Marinetti combines modernist encodings with images of biblical resonance—the bitten fruit and the serpent of pride that induced man's fall from grace—to play out the theme of universal degeneration that contaminates the very symbol of divine authority: the sun, initially figured as the violent idol of a primitive culture, is then disparagingly addressed as "panting juggler on the sky's stage," as "yapping mountebank" (278–279), and thereby demoted to the condition of a modernist fallen god.

The recurrent metaphors of carnality and decay echo the breakdown of spiritual beliefs and values brought about by modern consumer culture, which sets up barriers between inner being and outer world. The poet's pervasive use of material and corporeal imagery suggests that he is biting, or being bitten by, the materialistic spirit of the new age: "To sing of you again [Carnal City] I must remember / the past joys and beautiful days of my youth, / or unclench the teeth of the famished hyena / called Future, so as to have a scrap / of the purulent flesh she endlessly chews" (292). The poet is no longer a romantic martyr, but a self-conscious victim; the ideals that have ruined him are neither lofty nor pure. Rather, they are corrupted, contaminated, and fallen. The muses of the past, the stars, are no longer divine guides: they are, instead, satanic "golden Courtesans" (333), who prey on his fears and desires.

Since the past offers no escape, no astral signs to direct his course toward the "Infinite," the poet turns to the future. In the dithyramb "A mon Pégase" (To My Pegasus), he rhapsodizes over the automobile, the new "demon" and inspiring muse, "vehement God of a race of steel" (346), with which he will achieve the conquest of infinite, untainted, "metallic" freedom and happiness. In the epilogue ("La Mort tient le volant . . ." [Death at the Wheel]), death "bites the dust" in a symbolic race that marks the triumph of will and desire over time and space. Lust for the Carnal City, displaced onto the new mechanical idol, becomes desire for and intoxication with speed. *Lussuria Velocità* (Lust Speed), as the poem's Italian translation is titled, synthesizes this displacement, summarizing the trajectory of the text—from decadent, anguished desire to optimistic, energetic futurism.

THE FUTURIST FICTION OF POWER

As we have seen, futurism originated as a violent reaction to the turn-of-the-century crisis. It was programmatically attuned to modernity and sought to bridge the gap between currents of irrational thought—in particular, Nietzschean anarchist irrationalism and Sorelian theories on the function of myth and violence in modern society—and what appears to be a positivistic faith in progress. While rejecting the notion of a historical evolution informed by logic, along with the optimistic scientism and belief in political emancipation characteristic of positivism, futurism forcefully conveyed a bright vision of man's future, based on technological advances.[38] Calling for the radical liquidation of tradition and celebrating visionary intuition, vitality, dynamism, violence, and virility, the movement responded to the challenge of the modern age by constructing a fiction of the individual's power vis-à-vis the world—a modern myth for reimposing symbolic control on a world without absolutes, in which power seemed to have become the only measure of the self and the subjective imagination the only measure of reality. As T. S. Eliot was to say of James Joyce, and as could be said of other modernist myths, this creation of the imagination was "a way of controlling, of ordering, of giving a shape and a significance to the immense paradox of futility and anarchy which is contemporary history."[39] But while other modernist myths were typically divorced, or ironically distanced, from the material forces and pragmatic workings of the industrial world, the futurist "formula for renewal" (*TIF*, 329) was aimed at enthusiastically integrating the poetic experience into modern life and reconquering the public role that artists of the postromantic generation felt they had lost. The futurist claimed for himself the role of armed prophet and guide of a new powerful, bellicose Italy, finding in patriotic war and modernity—in the cultural utopia of an Italian revolution—a cause for his rebellion and an inspiration for his art. The alienated poet of *Le Roi Bombance,* the Idiot, abandons his broken helmet and sword (his anachronistic role as disenfranchised court jester) in favor of new, state-of-the-art weaponry.

Old ideals (*Amore*) and modern pessimism (the Schopenhauerian "disease" of the will brought on by disillusionment with the ideal) were equally subject to barrages of futurist rhetoric: "Our frank optimism is thus sharply opposed to the pessimism of Schopenhauer, that embittered philosopher who so often handed us philosophy's seductive revolver in order to kill our deep nausea of Love with a capital L" (*TIF*, 301). To borrow his own metaphor, Marinetti sought to turn the Schopenhauerian revolver away from himself, directing a violent attack against whatever threatened his optimistic, aggressive image of individuality. Hence his rejection of psychologism—the introverted exploration of inner conflict—and his emphasis on extroverted action.

The futurist fiction of power is rooted in a number of philosophical sources, prominent among which is pragmatism. General definitions of pragmatism are hard to come by; many divergent, even conflicting, points of view have been termed "pragmatic." Nevertheless, cultural historians have identified a substantial core of ideas shared by many variants of pragmatic philosophy. In the words of Philip P. Wiener, "Common to this substantial core [. . .] is an opposition to the absolute separation of thought from action, of pure from applied science, of intuition or revelation from experience or experimental verification, of private interests from public concerns."[40] Within this framework of shared values, however, a considerable ideological distance separates the subjective individualism of William James from the scientific experimentalism of mathematical logicians and philosophical experimenters such as Charles S. Pierce and Giovanni Vailati.

Marinetti's position is more akin to the psychological and nominalistic views of James than to the philosophy of science of Pierce and Vailati. An even more immediate precursor is the "magical" pragmatism enthusiastically advocated by Papini in the Florentine journal *Leonardo* during the years 1903–1907. Papini locates the lowest common denominator of all pragmatist views in the plasticity or flexibility of theories and beliefs, that is, in the recognition of their purely instrumental value.[41] Ignoring the criticism of James's nominalism by Pierce, he lumps James and Pierce together as proponents of a theory of meaning that emphasizes the particular consequences of ideas in future practical experiences. He himself relies heavily on the Jamesian version of pragmatism, particularly its doctrine of Will to Believe. His own "magical" version, however, carries the romantic elements of James's philosophy to an extreme, shifting the emphasis from internal psychological reality to the outside world and affirming that in certain men the will has the magical power of transforming external things.

Papini, in fact, views pragmatism as a collection of methods for expanding man's power to change the world. In this utilitarian perspective, power is the ultimate measure of the difference between pragmatism and the movement from which it derives and departs, positivism: the one fosters antiagnosticism and stands for empowerment, whereas the other leads to agnosticism and is synonymous with impotence. The pragmatist, according to Papini, scorns metaphysical questions not because they are too high, beyond the reach of human intelligence, as the positivist believes, but because they are senseless and stupid. In Papini's words, "Refusing to deal with them is not evidence of the *impotence* but of the *power* of our minds" (339; emphasis in original).

The connection between magical pragmatism and Marinetti's futurist fiction of power is suggested by Papini himself. Notions such as the influence of will on belief and belief on reality are, he argues, likely to attract practical minds as well as poets and utopian thinkers. The former will find in pragmatism the theory of their contempt for senseless and impractical questions and their sympathy for everything that is clear, effective, and quick. The latter will be attracted by suggestive views that encourage imagination and hope of extraordinary things. In this fashion, concludes Papini, pragmatism is capable of reconciling opposites (342).

In a similar manner, futurism combines a penchant for outrageous utopian visions with a persistent interest in the practical, efficient aspects of modern life. Like Papini's pragmatism, the futurist fiction of power can be defined as a collection of strategies of empowerment. Power is the ultimate, shared goal of seemingly contradictory drives of destruction and creation, deterritorialization and reterritorialization, internationalism and nationalism, anarchic dispersion and totalizing condensation, projection toward the technological future and recuperation of primitive forces. This double movement reproduces, exposes, and even celebrates the intrinsically contradictory dynamics of progress, which Norbert

Elias describes as a dialectic of expansion and contraction of bodies and the world.[42]

The genealogy of several aspects of futurism (including the prominent themes of modernity, antipasséism, violence, and emotional nationalism) can be traced back to other end-of-the-century authors and schools.[43] The shocking iconoclastic program announced in the first manifestos—destroying museums, monuments, libraries, and academies in order to foster a dynamic, ephemeral art capable of keeping pace with the modern world—was the most extreme expression of the negative view of the past and its effects that many authors shared. Nietzsche, Joyce, and Henrik Ibsen variously address the suffocating, paralyzing, guilt-sustaining weight of the past.[44] Many European intellectuals hailed war as a force of rejuvenation—a remedy against decadence, corruption, and sclerotization in society and art. Marinetti himself recognized a small number of authors—Émile Zola, Walt Whitman, Rosny Aîné, Gustave Kahn, Émile Verhaeren—as precursors of futurism's poetics; other "intellectual fathers"—Edgar Allan Poe, Charles Baudelaire, Stéphane Mallarmé, Paul Verlaine, D'Annunzio—he acknowledged by negation, as he repudiated them for their cult of the past, or *passatismo*.[45]

Futurism's anti-intellectualism, antitraditionalism, and aesthetic experimentation link it with several other avant-garde movements. For instance, futurism and expressionism both valorize the vital and instinctive, react violently against bourgeois culture, and advocate outrageous, shocking positions. Unlike expressionism, however, the futurist revolt against the establishment produced no radical social criticism and discouraged pessimism and alienation. Emphasis was placed instead on the necessity for the artist to embrace the phenomena of modern life (such as industrial production and mass communication) and on his ability to dominate the new reality. Dadaists and surrealists also chose to accept the chaos of the modern age, to dive into the abyss of change, rather than withdraw into the ivory tower of solipsism and nostalgia. But they surrendered the old, collapsed fiction of man's mastery of the universe and of language, while the futurists sought to reclaim it.

In their efforts to formulate and affirm a new myth of "Italianism," nationalist/modernist intellectuals such as Prezzolini, Papini, Corradini, Giovanni Boine, Scipio Slataper, and Mario Morasso anticipated some of the motifs, principles, and strategies of the futurists' program of national rebirth: the cult of youth, heroism, and regenerative violence; the irrationalist valorization of mythic thought against the Enlightenment values of liberal reason; and the celebration of the machine as a new aesthetic paradigm—"emblem of modern life," model of "disciplined energy" and of "inflexible power."[46] What set the futurists off from the other circles of militant ideologues and artists was their total rejection of tradition, their cohesive organization and collective identity as a movement driven by an all-encompassing project, and their concerted efforts to master the multifarious challenges of modernization. Marinetti indeed created the novel idea of a globally

active avant-garde that would embody the revolutionary spirit of the age and assimilate the resources of mass commodity culture to promote its artistic and political program.

METHODOLOGICAL QUESTIONS

Later chapters will address the various fields embraced by futurism, as well as
some of the many authors who became associated with the movement. However,
the contours of this study are, by necessity, limited to the work of Marinetti, in
which the origins, workings, and transformations of the fiction of power can be
best investigated. While other artists unquestionably contributed to the creation
of a futurist aesthetic, the overall vision bears Marinetti's signature. So do the
rhetorical strategies that shaped it into a movement, as well as the galvanizing impetus, organizing effort, and style of behavior that translated it into action. While
Marinetti's fundamental role in the creation of the movement and in the formulation of its program has been universally recognized, the significance of his production has not yet been explored in all its complexity. Marinetti's allegiance to
fascism has focused the attention and alienated the sympathy of literary critics to
a greater extent than the fascist leanings of other major modernists. This is almost
certainly a consequence of his brash, violent rhetoric and of the clamorous, belligerent style of action he advocated and displayed. Outrageous formulations
such as love of war and contempt of woman have been major stumbling blocks in
the study of Marinetti's work: they have become ready-made formulas used to
simplify and often dismiss it, leading to the reductive, derogatory portrayal of
Marinetti as the "charlatan" of modernism. Such labels, applicable to his most
extreme and most obvious pronouncements and posturings, paper over numerous cracks and gaps in critical understanding.

   Marinetti's political stance and futurism's contribution to the success of fascism have been explored extensively.[47] However, critical considerations of gender
issues have tended to address only the most conspicuous aspects of Marinetti's
rhetoric, as employed in his most well-known texts: the sexual violence and hy-
pervirility of the futurist superuomo in *Mafarka le futuriste* and the attack on woman
and feminine values in some manifestos.[48] Shortcomings in this field of inquiry
may be, at least in part, imputed to the fact that Italian criticism has been tendentially refractory to issues of gender; in addition, they may be seen as a consequence of the aforementioned split between apologetic and condemnatory tendencies in futurist scholarship. On the question of the meaning and role of
woman in Marinetti's writing, interpretations tend to take two opposite but
equally dismissive directions. On one hand, Marinetti's apologists redeem his unsettling misogynist aphorisms (such as the infamous slogan "We will glorify [. . .]
scorn for woman" launched in the first manifesto) by reading them as an indict-
ment of the sentimental idealization of woman in passéist literature. This is actually a long-lived critical commonplace, which can be traced back to Marinetti's

own defensive reply to the critique of his contemporaries[49] and which is still recycled in today's commentaries. The two introductory essays in the recent edition of Marinetti's *Taccuini* are representative of this tendency. Renzo De Felice interprets Marinetti's "antifeminism" as an antisentimental stance: the refusal of a "horrible and heavy" kind of love, which hinders the progress of men and women alike.[50] In similar fashion, Ezio Raimondi's discussion of Marinetti's "anti-D'Annunzian" eroticism reproposes Marinetti's own justification of the futurist antisentimental campaign: it pits Marinetti's "erotic bravado" against D'Annunzio's aestheticizing "mystical sublimation"; moreover, it reduces the pervasive thematic and rhetoric of sex to the surface of elementary, uninhibited, demystified physical desire—a "modernization" of sexual relations warranted by modern life and by war.[51]

From a different (more explicitly political) perspective, Maria-Antonietta Macciocchi offers another sympathetic reading of the futurist discourse on issues of sexual policy. She denounces D'Annunzio's elitist "morale de la débauche" and attributes revolutionary value to Marinetti's anticonventional stance: "Before it was put in step and denatured by fascism, Marinetti's futurism jostled bourgeois ethics and its familism which in D'Annunzio went along with a morality of debauchery for the privileged elite. It preached divorce, free love, the abolition of female bondage, and women's suffrage."[52] These remarks exemplify another common tendency in apologetic commentaries: parlaying an ideological ambivalence into a chronological dualism—between a first, "true" futurism and a second futurism "denatured," "perverted" by fascism—in order to reckon with the incontrovertible alliance between futurism and fascism.

On the other hand, studies that focus on Marinetti's misogynist formulations tend to view the issue of woman in futurism as evidence of the antidemocratic, procapitalist, or proto-fascist nature of the movement.[53] Kaplan's reading of Marinetti as the paradigmatic fascist modernist may be cited as an example of this critical tendency, though she succeeds in underscoring the fundamental role played by the feminine as that against which the futurist man must define himself: "The earth is played by woman—so is war, the machine, the sea, and, in fact, nearly every possible thing except woman herself, who, having given over her essence to everything around her, is completely void of intrinsic meaning."[54] Kaplan does not pursue this line of inquiry far enough to explore the complex implications of her insights. She does not, for instance, investigate the problematic association of woman with both the abhorred earth and the celebrated technological war, the shifting rhetorical (and psychological) function played by the ubiquitous feminine throughout Marinetti's production, or the "intrinsic," historically grounded meaning of woman in his discourse on sexual politics. Instead, she proceeds to identify the links between Marinetti's writing and "generalized European fascist topoi" (88). Her analysis is, in fact, subordinated to a more general agenda: defining "fascist desire" through an ideological inquiry into the complicity of intellectual culture in fascism—where ideology is understood, following

Ernesto Laclau, "as a reproduction of desires and *discourse*, that is, in terms of the persuasive language used by fascists" (20; emphasis in original).

While desire-oriented political theories, starting with Wilhelm Reich's 1933 *Die Massenpsychologie des Faschismus* (The Mass Psychology of Fascism), have tradition- ally predicated susceptibility to fascism in father-bound feelings (fundamentally, the desire to identify with the leader-as-father, with the authoritative protector of the nation-as-family), Kaplan identifies other, in her opinion more crucial, emo- tional components in fascism's power to seduce or "fascinate": "mother-bound" impulses, "oceanic" feelings of symbiotic unity, the desire for an all-encompassing, reassuring authority.[55] Fascism's ability to "fascinate," she argues, was produced by a technologically empowered propaganda machine. Using images (posters and cinema) and, especially, sound (microphones and radio), it established a sense of immediacy between the subject and object world and a feeling of unity with the maternal leader and the nation-as-mother. Fascism's gathering power, she points out, also derived from its ubiquitous ideological positioning: its "splitting" and "binding" strategies for scapegoating and idealization, its "crosspollination" and "displacement" of traditional ideological polarities and conceptual categories, such as modern/antimodern, construction/destruction, revolutionary/conservative, and populism/elitism.

This theoretical framework, once applied to textual analysis, should make it possible to identify the "symptoms" of a fascist sensibility at work in a modernist text. Indeed, Kaplan offers an insightful reading of certain crucial aspects of Marinetti's writing; in particular, his binding of the construction/destruction po- larities and his predilection for an aerial, totalizing perspective through which the futurist self is both disseminated and synthesized. The concepts of splitting and binding, projective identification, and oceanic unity, which Kaplan uses as "diag- nostic" tools in her analysis of fascist desire, are of crucial importance in the study of many mechanisms and strategies at work in Marinetti's writing. One can, how- ever, raise some objections to Kaplan's analysis on theoretical and methodologi- cal grounds. From a theoretical standpoint, it can be argued that Kaplan's "shift to the maternal"—her emphasis on mother-bound desire as that which put fas- cism in power—upstages the regressive, utopian role of father-bound narcissism in fascist desire, that is, the role played by identification with the idealized father figure in sustaining an infantile fantasy of omnipotence against a sense of help- lessness and vulnerability. Indeed, the definition of fascism's early appeal as es- sentially mother-bound and the characterization of the hypnotic, seductive leader as "maternal" seem to underwrite the age-old dualism between the mother's utopian (irrational) seduction and the father's pragmatic (rational) authority, along with the related psychoanalytical assumption that the maternal is to the preoedipal as the paternal is to the oedipal.

This equation (and split) of stages and agencies has been placed under critical scrutiny by feminist psychoanalysts such as Jessica Benjamin, in an effort to ex- plore the interplay between the work of culture and psychic processes. In what follows, I shall take Kaplan's approach to task and define my own, drawing from Benjamin's work on desire and domination, which will later provide theoretical support to my discussion of the emotional underpinnings of the futurist fiction of power. Benjamin offers a lucid critique of the "mother-bound" approach to the problem of domination and submission as exemplified by the work of the French psychoanalyst Janine Chasseguet-Smirgel. Questioning the assumption that the roles played by mother and father in psychic development are part of an essential, universal structure of the unconscious, she takes issue with the inevitability of the gender polarity whereby "the mother exercises the magnetic pull of regression and the father guards against it," as "he alone is associated with the progression toward adulthood, separation, and self-control."[56] For Benjamin, what is missing from this polarized scheme is the provision that the oedipal mother may play a role in differentiation, just as the archaic father may be "the magnet for the (pre-oedipal and oedipal) strivings of narcissism: reunion and omnipotence" (*BL*, 153). Accordingly, she argues against equating fascism's power of seduction with the seductive maternal ideal: "The notion that return to the omnipotent mother was the predominant motive in Nazism is an exemplary demonstration of the theoretical attempt to attribute all irrationalism to the maternal side and deny the destructive potential of the phallic ideal. Chasseguet-Smirgel's alignment of the ego ideal with the mother in general, and her example of Nazism in particular, are whitewashes of the vital part played by narcissistic identification with the father in the mass psychology of fascism—a part anticipated full well by Freud" (*BL*, 154).

Benjamin's critique of Chasseguet-Smirgel is part of a broader discussion of desire-oriented political theories, which leads to the formulation of a new and compelling view of the intricate intertwining of familial, gender, and social domination. The mother-bound approach, says Benjamin, reformulates, or displaces, the split between good and bad father on which earlier psychoanalytic theories of fascist desire are predicated. Such theories, most prominently advanced by the Frankfurt school, recuperate the ideal of rational (democratic) paternal authority by splitting off the notion of the preoedipal father (as prototype of the hypnotic leader), whose authority appeals to dread and to narcissistic currents of identification. From this perspective, mass participation in fascism is explained as the fascination (narcissistic tie) of a "fatherless society" (a society in which the "rational," "democratic" authority of the oedipal father is in crisis) with a powerful figure of identification.[57] Against this interpretation, Benjamin maintains, "one could plausibly argue that the surrender to the fascist leader is not caused by the absence of paternal authority, but by the frustration of identificatory love: the unfulfilled longing for recognition from an early, idealized, *but less authoritarian father*" (*BL*, 146; emphasis in original).[58] If this is the case, the problem is to be identified, not with the absence of authority (or the presence of a "maternal" seducer), but rather with the absence of a nurturing authority that engenders submission: "It is the combination of narcissistic disappointment and fear of authority that produces the kind of admiration mingled with dread noted by observers of fascism in the mass love of the leader. The fascist leader satisfies the desire for ideal love, but this version of ideal love includes the oedipal components of hostility and authority" (*BL,* 146).

From the vantage point of Benjamin's extensive inquiries into the dynamics of power and desire, the notion of a subjugating, idealized leader, who combines features of the authoritarian oedipal figure and the omnipotent archaic father of narcissistic identification, seems more convincing than the idea of a maternal *Duce* or *Führer,* who seduces through the "rhythms" and "tone" of a "feminine authority" or "voice."[59] Kaplan's reflections on the "maternal voice" of fascism are based on the assumption that the privileging of vocal presence and immediate communication are inherently symptomatic of "dangerous desires for the acultural, the anti-intellectual, the seductive, the *fascist*" (8; emphasis in original). Such an assumption is simplistic, in that it fails to take into account the actual rhythm and tone of the voice in question. It is difficult to relate the dictatorial voice of the fascist leader addressing the rallied crowd with the nurturant voice of a mother talking to her infant.

Psychological states and mechanisms such as splitting, binding, projective identification, and the narcissistic desire for oceanic oneness—the desire for an all-encompassing authority—are not unique to fascist desire. Rather, they are generally at play in the dynamics of identity formation and group psychology. Other mass movements, such as the collectivist mystiques of twentieth-century socialism, were attuned to the "oceanic" and relied on "seductive" propaganda techniques—techniques that, it should be emphasized, are a product and a characteristic of modern mass society, not a distinguishing trait of fascism.[60] Likewise, the early twentieth-century obsession with antifeminism crossed political boundaries in the literature of the prefascist and fascist periods.[61] Without the anchorage of historical and textual specificity, fascism risks becoming what Michel Foucault calls a "floating," "oceanic" signifier, and the critic, as the Italian saying goes, "rischia di fare di tutta l'erba un fascio" (risks binding too many different weeds in the same bundle). Foucault argues that the "non-analysis of fascism" has enabled "fascism to be used as a floating signifier, whose function is essentially that of denunciation."[62] One can hardly accuse Kaplan of "non-analysis"; however, the methodological framework of her study, which lumps together authors of divergent backgrounds and nationalities under the aegis of a boundaryless fascist desire, is conducive to sweeping generalizations.

De Felice, by contrast, argues for a distinction between periods and cultural sectors. Scholars should consider "patterns of historical continuity" between the fascist period and the one that preceded it and should avoid being "conditioned by other models, by other realities such as that of Nazism."[63] Though De Felice's approach is historical, rather than psychological, his warning about the importance of cultural variables is applicable to the study of desire. There are, for instance, discrepancies between the fantasies and configurations that, according to Klaus Theweleit, characterize the writings of the *Freikorpsmen* and those that recur in futurist texts. The futurist's penchant for erotic scenarios (as displayed, for example, in Marinetti's 1917 handbook *Come si seducono le donne* [How to Seduce Women]) contrasts sharply with the German writers' tendency to portray relationships between desexualized women and sexless officers who manifest attraction solely for their leaders, comrades, or horses (1:52–63). It is more than plausible that culturally specific notions of masculine identity—in this case, the Prussian and the Italian conceptions of maleness—are at least partially responsible for such differences.[64]

When considering the fantasies of a particular author, it is essential not to blur differences between individual and collective imagination—and, even more important, between individual and hegemonic discourse. Kaplan herself warns about the ambivalences and complications the critic must reckon with when approaching the texts of fascist modernism. But she seems to disregard this caveat in her discussion of Marinetti as "the 'clean' fascist modernis[t]" (109) and in her classification of the futurist movement as "a fascist lobby" (75). This self-certain stance, and her tendency to see Marinetti and Italian futurism as the "ridiculous," "blatant" version of fascist modernism, may account for the fact that she does not quite square her theoretical premises with the complexities of Marinetti's texts and does not seem to entertain the possibility that the traces of splitting and binding one finds in his writing may not neatly coincide with those one detects in the "fascinating" discourse of fascism, or in the work of other "fascinated" writers. I agree with Kaplan's summary remarks about the existence of connections between futurism and fascism, connections that she describes as both "accidental—as culturally unconscious—and as perfectly obvious." Her specific examples, however, do not always support her claims. "Mussolini," Kaplan asserts, "owed the futurist avant-garde for their revolutionary methods of disseminating propaganda and for their use of aesthetic and sexual criteria in analyzing social issues. One of his often-quoted lines is pure Mafarka: 'War is to man what maternity is to woman' " (88). The quote is problematic: taken in context, the maternity = woman equation actually applies to Mafarka, who rejects woman's procreative role and trains the "ovary" of man's genius to give birth to an all-male immortal creation.

Barbara Spackman, focusing more specifically on questions of gender, locates Marinetti's stance toward women within the context of fascism's rhetoric of virility. Although her reading of Marinetti, like Kaplan's, is part of a broader project, it is more nuanced in its conclusions. On one hand, Spackman argues against Macciocchi's positive valorization of Marinetti's sexual politics, identifying reactionary (proto-fascist) underpinnings in the "ambiguously progressive" elements of Marinetti's discourse: " 'all the beautiful freedoms' (as Marinetti himself puts it in *Come si seducono le donne*) that futurism has to offer women are designed not only to liberate women from slavery to men and to the bourgeois family, but also to safeguard virility and insure the future of the nation and of the race."[65] Stripped of its "ambiguously progressive" elements, futurism's reactionary core is evident:

a concern with the interplay of boundaries, both individual and national, is Marinetti's contribution to the rhetorical "currency" of the regime. On the other hand, Spackman indirectly admits that Marinetti's notion of *uomo italiano* does not coincide with the fascist notion by stating that the virility D'Annunzio praised "was far closer to Roman *virtù* than to that of Marinetti's Italian male" (99). The distance between futurist virility and Roman virtù is a significant one because it separates Marinetti's rhetoric from the fascist celebration of the (Roman, imperial) past as repository of the values of authority, obedience, and classical order. As Spackman notes in her conclusive argument, "what Mussolini will absorb from his 'precursors' must be weighed against what he will discard; the *Duce* will mint his own version of virility, welding new materials to the old" (101).

Spackman makes a compelling case for her approach to the study of the fascist rhetoric of virility. She argues against the two predominant critical tendencies, which "represent the Scylla and Charybdis of approaches to fascism": the tendency to trivialize the fascist rhetorical obsession with virility as a "linguistic tic" or to demonize it as a symptom of "pathological aberration." She then charts a third course. Acknowledging that all political rhetoric, especially nationalist rhetoric, is a rhetoric of virility, she emphasizes the necessity of analyzing this rhetorical and ideological commonplace in order to avoid a partial and ideological understanding of fascist culture: "An investigation of the rhetoric of virility would thus seem doubly banal; not only do we 'know' that fascist rhetoric is a rhetoric of virility, we also 'know' that all political rhetoric is a rhetoric of virility. But such 'knowledge' is based upon an ideological sedimentation so thick that it seems as natural as the ground we walk on, and easily leads to an acceptance of those gender politics as equally natural. Though layer upon layer of culture have made it appear 'natural,' that common ground is a commonplace—rhetorical and ideological—that is neither trivial (simply to be expected) nor demonic (completely unprecedented)" (87–88).

An analogous argument can be made for the study of Marinetti's gender-inflected rhetoric: it should not be disregarded as a trivial "futurist tic," nor should it be considered a demonic "fascist aberration"; rather, it should be analyzed in its idiosyncrasies, as well as in its genealogies and filiations. It is my aim to address these questions by examining, through the lens of gender, the futurist fiction of power as it appears in Marinetti's writings. Such an approach, in my view, is a most fruitful one, as it contributes to contemporary inquiries into the problematics of modern subjectivity. In order to *understand*, rather than just postulate, the crucial nexus between aesthetics, politics, and desire in the futurist fiction of power, I rely on psychoanalytically informed theories of gender and on close readings of a large variety of texts, some of which have been virtually ignored by critics. Any ideological investigation of the futurist aestheticopolitical project requires continued reference to the textual manifestations of Marinetti's rhetoric, politics, and psychology of gender.[66]

My methodological choice is predicated on considerations of the crucial role played by gender in Marinetti's work, in modernist literature in general, and, on a broader theoretical plane, in the discourse of identity and power. With regard to those aspects of Marinetti's prefuturist production that constitute a premise to, or an anticipation of, the futurist "revolution," I have already pointed to the centrality of Marinetti's figuration of woman and erotic scenarios as metaphors for the poet's relationship to reality and art. Recent scholarship has offered ample evidence that modernism is a gender-marked territory, in which the relations between the sexes function as a fundamental layer of identification (permeating the other layers of class, nation, and race) and in which the crisis in gender identification is figurative of an overall sense of crisis.[67] Finally, various critical and theoretical studies have highlighted and explored an intrinsic link between issues of gender/sexuality and the discourse on identity/power.

In his inquiry into the fascist mystique of war and violence, Theweleit has discussed, extensively, the central role that male-female relations of inequality play in the maintenance of a system of domination within the changing power structures of patriarchal capitalist society. From this perspective, even fascist terror appears to be the extension of "a particular conception of culture [that] had emerged during the course of European history, one framed in terms of a centralistic subjection of nature, of femininity, and, finally, of the individual unconscious, all of which have been banished from the male ego" (2:49).

Building on the materialistic analysis of the ideal subject in philosophical idealism, psychoanalytic feminism has, by exposing its gender roots, advanced a critique of the Western notion of individuality as separate, bounded, and autonomous. As Benjamin notes, "The salient feature of male individuality is that it grows out of the repudiation of the primary identification with and dependency on the mother," which "leads to an individuality that stresses [. . .] difference as denial of commonality, separation as denial of connection," rather than "a balance of separation and connection."[68] The psychological mechanisms through which this one-sided autonomy results in a power structure of gender domination are elucidated as follows: "Since the child continues to need the mother, since man continues to need woman, the absolute assertion of independence requires possessing and controlling the needed object. The intention is not to do without her but to make sure that her alien otherness is either assimilated or controlled, that her own subjectivity nowhere asserts itself in a way that could make his dependency upon her a conscious insult to his sense of freedom."[69]

Other feminist theorists have explored the ramifications of the ideal of autonomous individuality in relation to scientific thought, which relies on metaphors of male control over a feminized nature. Evelyn Fox Keller, in particular, points to the dual constitutive motives that underwrite the scientific, rationalist ambition to "objectivity": power and integrity of the subject. She illustrates the workings of this emotional substructure by referring to Francis Bacon's metaphor of knowledge as "chaste and lawful marriage" between mind and nature, "a metaphor for power and domination, designed to safeguard the integrity of the knower."[70]

Beginning with different theoretical premises, Julia Kristeva offers insights into the exacerbated manifestations of these mechanisms of individuation in situations of ideological and psychological crisis, both through her readings of modernist texts, which dramatize the breakdown of rationalist notions of the autonomous, bounded self, and through her case studies of "borderline" subjects.[71] In her psychoanalytic investigations, which span early infancy, primitive ritual, literary language, and religious discourse, she underscores the universality of the dynamics of victimization and abjection (abhorrence, abomination) of women, which she relates to the maternal matrix of individuation: the anxiety-laden separation, fear of the engulfing power of the maternal, and the threat to survival and identity that characterize the earliest phase of psychic development, when the first precarious boundaries of human subjectivity are drawn. Through ritual, religion, and culture, she asserts, maternal abjection can be symbolically sublimated but never entirely transcended; its mechanisms are exacerbated and exposed by the crisis of the symbolic order.

The essential interrelatedness among gender, identity, and power, particularly as it emerges in the extreme circumstances of crisis explored by Kristeva, marks the rhetorical function of gender as a site of crucial interest for the analysis of the fiction of power. Moving beyond the infamous, attention-getting aphorisms, we find that the representation of woman, the scenario of sexual relations, and genderization as a rhetorical strategy are intricately bound up with Marinetti's construction of reality. The rejected feminine, in particular, plays a paramount role in his entire production as a major locus of ambivalence: a catalyst of conflicting or complicitous repugnance and fascination, disgust and desire. By tracking the feminine/feminized other through the various domains of Marinetti's imaginary, its workings can be explored in depth.

Drawing largely from Kristeva's and Benjamin's work on ideological fantasies, this project seeks to investigate the futurist fiction of power within a broad theoretical and historical framework, in order to understand its genealogy and its relevance to the still very topical problematic of the relationship among rhetoric, gender, and violence. Kristeva casts light on the constitutive force of violent exclusion and abomination of the feminine in a variety of cultural and textual productions, from the rituals of ancient religions to the modernist rhetoric of abjection. Benjamin shifts the focus on the power structure of gender domination, mapping the "bonds of love" between "normal" mechanisms of abjection and fascist terror. Most important, she goes further in opening a theoretical space for change, where the goal of relatedness to others replaces the ideal of, or need for, autonomous individuality and the specter of self-dissolution.[72] This perspective has made my work on the disquieting rhetoric of gender and violence a less disheartening experience and, I hope, a more useful effort.

TWO

The Rhetoric of Gender in the Manifestos

The importance of Marinetti's contributions to the avant-garde aesthetic revolution has been a subject of controversy since the beginnings of the futurist movement. Nevertheless, critics generally acknowledge Marinetti's innovativeness in establishing "the art of making manifestos." Most recently, in her remarkable study on the "language of rupture" of the avant-garde movements prior to World War I, Perloff locates the originality of the futurist manifesto in its hybrid, multifaceted nature. Its genealogy can be traced back to the agonistic mode of discourse of the nineteenth-century political manifesto and to the programmatic statements of aesthetic renovation, modernity, nationalism, and heroism articulated in the manifestos of other turn-of-the-century movements. But the Italian futurist manifestos differ from their precursors because of "their brash refusal to remain in the expository or critical corner, their understanding that the group pronouncement, sufficiently aestheticized, can, in the eyes of the mass audience, all but take the place of the promised art work."[1] Marinetti's first manifesto, "Fondazione e Manifesto del Futurismo" (The Founding and Manifesto of Futurism), not only inaugurated the futurist movement but also created a new genre straddling poetic and theoretical discourse—a collective statement directed at a mass audience, in which the articulation of an aesthetic and political program is transformed into a literary construct.[2]

The futurist manifesto qualifies as a genre of rupture in two ways. As the theoretical and propagandistic arena of the futurist "global" revolution, the manifesto was the principal instrument in a campaign aimed at fomenting change in art and society. Launching fiery attacks against the establishment and the conventional tastes of the public, manifestos such as "Uccidiamo il Chiaro di Luna!" (Let's Murder the Moonlight!), "Contro Venezia passatista" (Against Passéist Venice), and "Abbasso il tango e Parsifal" (Down with the Tango and Parsifal) promised the rejuvenation of the Italian spirit through violent action in the theaters, on the streets, and on the battlefields. Furthermore, a series of technical manifestos are the springboard of revolutionary aesthetic principles such as the breakdown of barriers between the individual arts, the destruction of syntax, and the elimination of the psychologizing literary subject.

As an artwork, the manifesto subverts traditional codes, obliterating boundaries between different genres and expressive registers. It assembles a collage of disparate verbal strategies: passionate, often fervid lyric prose, wrought with metaphors, symbols, and allegorical narratives; trenchant satire, with comic hyperboles and outrageous metaphors; didactic, normative proclamations of the futurist credo, with numerical lists of formulaic statements; the sensational, telegraphic quality, and typographic novelty of advertising; and dialogic strategies, including exhortations, aggressive apostrophes, and moments of pretended conversation with the public.[3] Marinetti's use of oratory and theater accentuates the oral dimension of the futurist manifesto. It is a text intended to be declaimed—as opposed to conventional literature, which privileges the book. Occasionally, as in the 1912 "Risposte alle obiezioni" (Responses to the Critics) and the 1913 "Il Teatro di Varietà" (The Variety Theater), the manifesto is not only a springboard but also a testing ground of the new antigrammatical and antisyntactical model.[4]

An aesthetic of rupture that subverts literary conventions and linguistic constraints is capable of undermining hierarchical, centralizing ordering systems predicated on a unitary, authoritative speaking and thinking subject. Traditionally, those studies of Italian futurism that emphasize the novelty and importance of its formal experimentation have tended to avoid ideological inquiry. Some apologetic studies pay a cursory visit to this territory, abstracting formal categories from content to posit an unproblematic congruence between the formal and the ideological realms. Such an approach may lead the reader to unwarranted conclusions concerning the ideological stakes of the futurist aesthetic revolution.[5]

Futurist experimentation is psychologically rooted in anxieties about the fragmentation of identity and the confusion of codes. In the manifesto "Il teatro futurista sintetico" (The Futurist Synthetic Theater), for example, Marinetti posits "reality" as a condition of threatening chaos and overwhelming impact: "reality vibrates around us assaulting us with *squalls of fragments of interconnected events, wedged into each other, confused, tangled, chaotic*" (*TIF*, 117; emphasis in original). The barrage of external forces conjures up a hostile reality at war against a besieged subject. The ideological framework of futurist experimentation redirects doubts about subjectivity and representation into an acritical, boisterous affirmation of the epistemological and artistic powers of the "multiplied" futurist man. The iconoclastic attack on linguistic conventions is governed by an effort to control the life of matter—a fantasy of omniscience and omnipotence.

> There is no more beauty, except in struggle. Without an aggressive character, no work can be a masterpiece. Poetry must be conceived of as a violent assault against unknown forces, so that they will be reduced to prostrating themselves before man. (*TIF*, 10)

Today, more than ever, one does not make art if he does not make war. No one appears worthy of glory except he who stands erect to violate Mystery, to challenge the tempting monstrosities of the Impossible. (*TIF*, 28)

Only the asyntactical poet who unleashes words will be able to penetrate the essence of matter and destroy the deep hostility that separates it from us. (*TIF*, 52)

The object of the poet's quest is expressed in terms of negativity and impossibility ("unknown," "monstrosities," "Impossible," "deep hostility," "separates"). In the first two passages, the marked choice of negative periphrases to affirm his power reinforces the effect of the lexical choice. But the semantics of negativity and impossibility is countered by a semantics of sexual aggression: the futurist poet—a violent successor to the romantic notion of the artist as explorer in the perilous realm of knowledge—is imagined as a warrior, his head raised to violate, or rape, the mystery of reality. The sexual overtones of these passages cast the futurist epistemological and aesthetic model into a gendered situation, which sets up an aggressive, virile subject against a feminized reality that must be conquered or destroyed. The mapping out of femininity in Marinetti's manifestos provides a sort of blueprint for the futurist project. Such a project involves three logically successive steps: (1) identifying targets to be destroyed; (2) producing the text as a site for violent action; (3) creating new myths.

BARRICADES

The first step—the definition or demarcation of the enemy—associates the feminine principle with everything futurism is supposed to fight against: all past traditions in art (particularly sentimental poetry), the parliamentary system, pacifism, as well as constrictive mores and institutions that lead to the country's decadence while stifling virile energy and courage. For instance, in "Uccidiamo il Chiaro di Luna!" Marinetti writes, "Yes, our nerves demand war and despise woman, because we fear that the supplicating arms will wrap around our knees on the morning of our departure! . . . What do women, the sedentary, the invalid, the sick and all the prudent counselors expect? To their vacillating lives, broken by dismal agonies, by fearful sleep and heavy nightmares, we prefer violent death and we glorify it as the only one worthy of man, beast of prey" (*TIF*, 15). The manifesto hinges on a rhetorical strategy that brings gender into relation with political and aesthetic issues, and in which femininity works as a mark of impotence, disease, and fragmentation. These, in turn, are attached to mental attitudes that futurist hubris seeks to contradict. The glorification of futurist artistic potency is shored up by a polemical discourse in which the terminology of sexual dysfunction is frequently used to dismiss nonfuturist artistic and political tendencies. For example, Proustian introspective writing is stigmatized as "fragmentary, effeminate, ambiguous" (*TIF*, 173); pacifist sentiments are contemptuously attacked as a form of "castration" of the race (*TIF*, 290); academic culture is deplored as "castration" of genius (*TIF*, 308).

Marinetti programmatically refused the symbolist and decadent response to the fin de siècle crisis; namely, a poetic discourse in which the female body represents unstructured truth, to be grasped through momentary revelations, or a pervading loss, lack, and impossibility—the abyss in which the self is engulfed. While his prefuturist output was fundamentally influenced by French symbolism and decadent culture in general, the futurist Marinetti took a strong stance against the "sickly" drift of this literature and scourged his "symbolist masters" for their enfeebling influence. In particular, he targeted Gabriele D'Annunzio, "lesser brother of the great French symbolists, like them nostalgic and hovering over the naked female body" (*TIF,* 304). D'Annunzio was to be fought "at all costs" because he had "distilled" four dangerous "intellectual poisons" that the futurists wanted to destroy forever: "1° the morbid and nostalgic poetry of distance and memory; 2° the romantic sentimentalism dripping with moonlight, which rises toward the ideal and fatal Woman-Beauty; 3° obsession with lust, with the adulterous triangle, the pepper of incest and the seasoning of Christian sin; 4° the professorial passion for the past and the mania for antiquities and collections" (*TIF,* 304). Those intellectual poisons contain obvious elements of symbolic femininity: the ideal, fatal body of woman, which Marinetti rejects as a morbid obsession of the fin de siècle imaginary, is traditionally the object of unfulfilled desire and the idol of a solipsistic, self-reflexive kind of poetry. By colonizing the feminine body as the locus of artistic creation, the decadent aesthete attempts to sublimate the limits it symbolizes, but in so doing he withdraws from the "virile" world of ideas and action into the "feminine" world of sensuality and introverted passivity. Thus femininity and feminization become "symptomatic" of a pathological, renunciatory attitude toward reality. As an antidote, Marinetti proposes arte-azione—a new principle of "mental hygiene," ostentatiously assuming a "healthy" stance of creative expansion and appropriating new, technological sources of power.

As will become apparent in the following chapters, an undercurrent of decadent "poison" (eroticism, sentimentalism, and nostalgia) occasionally resurfaces in Marinetti's writing and becomes particularly conspicuous in his later works. Nevertheless, the antisentimentalist, antipasséist rhetoric of the manifestos is the "loudest" aspect of futurist propaganda, and the trademark with which critics identify Marinetti's movement.

Following World War I, Marinetti directed his aggressively "therapeutic" language and "hygienic" creativity toward what he diagnosed as the "deep and mysterious" disease that affected artists and thinkers in the aftermath of the war. Again, the symptoms of the disease have an obvious feminine component: Marinetti describes them as "a sad indolence, an excessively feminine neurasthenia, a hopeless pessimism, a feverish indecision of bewildered instincts and an absolute lack of will" (*TIF,* 160). The rhetoric of healthy masculinity and pathological femininity often recurs in the writings of Marinetti's followers. Mario Carli's "Arte vile e arte virile" (Vile Art and Virile Art; 1919), in particular, is entirely constructed around the topos of sexual degeneration.[6] Encamped in a sound fortress of bois-

terous virility ("healthy and noisy futurist vitality"), the futurist artist launches a virulent attack against the sickly, effeminate other: "the artist immersed in the wom-
anish aristocracy of his mind, disdainful of rolling up his sleeves for a boxing
match, and worried solely about the delicate subtlety of his images, fragile like
embroideries of clouds." According to Carli, almost all nonfuturist artists are
wretched or sexually degenerate: "If they are not lymphatic, they are acidic; if they
are not acidic, they are neurotic; if they are not neurotic, they are pederasts."

The obsessive preoccupation with gender distinction underlying the futurist
fiction of virile power is most explicitly expressed in Francesco Cangiullo's "La
scoperta del sostantivo anatomico o del sesso in esso" (The Discovery of the
Anatomical Noun or of the Sex within It; 1926), a text that foregrounds the relation of language to sexuality. Cangiullo's declared concern is "*to feminize the Woman
and masculinize the Male*" (emphasis in original). Sexual perversion, he argues, results from linguistic perversion—specifically, from the practice of naming female
anatomical parts with masculine nouns, and vice versa.

> Well, can anybody tell me what kind of a funny game is it when feminine *things* [*cose*]
> must have masculine nouns and, let's say, when masculine *things* [*cosi*] must have
> feminine nouns? [. . . .] Men with abnormal sensibility—and there will be more and
> more of them—can be influenced to the point of *not feeling woman anymore* by naming
> those parts of the female body as masculine. And vice versa, women of similarly ab-
> normal sensibility, by continuing to name those parts of the male body as masculine,
> *will one day no longer sense man.*[7]

Cangiullo's solution is to straighten out such ambiguities, to close the "arbitrary
gap" between signifier and signified and thus exorcise sexual deviance. Although
futurism generally subverts linguistic rules in the name of artistic freedom, in this
case Cangiullo invokes one of the most archaic conceptions of language—that of
the intrinsic, organic relationship between signifier and signified. However, this
seemingly reactionary position is premised on thoroughly modern concerns—
anxiety about the instability of gender's "natural" foundations and an understanding of the performative force of symbolic systems (forerunning postmodern
theories on the discursive construction of the subject).

Cangiullo's is one of a number of strategies aimed at a sharply dichotomized,
proscriptive definition of gender distinction. In particular, Marinetti advocated
the masculinization of social ethos through war—a catalyst of virilizing male
bonds—and through an educational system structured to protect boys from feminine influence. The boundary between such homosocial bonding practices and
homoerotic desire is a slippery one.[8] Manifestations of displaced homoeroticism
can be seen in futurism's fetishization of the machine—an other that reassuringly
mirrors the subject's desire for power. Furthermore, the violent misogyny advocated by futurism contains homoerotic undercurrents. Hidden in the manifestos,
they rise to the surface in *Mafarka le futuriste*, a text that dramatizes the permeabil-
ity and uncertainty of the subject's borders and affective valences.

Homophobia, gynophobia, and the homoeroticism inherent in both can ultimately be traced to the disruption of the parameters, codes, and material conditions in which the individual's sense of identity and power is grounded. The manifesto's hybrid nature enacts the disruption of codes by transgressing literary
boundaries. The rhetoric and thematics of gender, however, strive to rebuild a
foundation for the integrity of the subject by postulating a rigid system of authority and subordination. In short, barriers between genres can be broken; gender
barriers cannot.

The polarization of gender functions as the bedrock on which other barricades
are erected. Marinetti's writing (especially in manifestos and polemical texts)
seems to be controlled by the necessity of producing a rigidly binary construction
of reality. This tendency was apparent from the very beginning of the futurist
movement, particularly in "Fondazione e Manifesto del Futurismo," Marinetti's
first declaration of a war on the past and worship of aggressive action. The following are examples of the peremptory divisions drawn by the manifesto.

> 9. We want to glorify war—the world's only hygiene—militarism, patriotism, the
>   destructive gesture of freedom fighters, beautiful ideas one dies for and scorn
>   for woman.
> 10. We want to destroy museums, libraries, academies of every kind, and fight
>   against moralism, feminism and any opportunistic or utilitarian cowardice.
>   (*TIF*, 11)

At play in this strategy is the creation of a new binding ideology for revolutionary
artists and, concomitantly, a destructive radicalization of the relationship with the
other as enemy ("us" versus "them")—a typical feature of the "bellicose-destructive"
mode of conflict.[9]

The binary structuring of reality is tied to the founding of a new religion. In
"La nuova religione-morale della velocità" (The New Religion-Morality of
Speed; 1916), Marinetti argues that speed, whose essence is "the intuitive synthesis of all forces in movement," is, by nature, "*pure.*" Slowness is "naturally *foul*" because its essence is "the rational analysis of every weariness at rest." Futurism thus
replaces the old notions of good and evil with "a new good: speed, and a new evil:
slowness" (*TIF*, 132; emphasis in original). The cult of speed is proposed as an alternative to a no longer effective Christian morality, which has lost "divinity"—
that is, power to control man's instincts and to instigate his progress. Whereas the
Christian morality had defended "the physiological structure of man from the excesses of sensuality," the futurist one would protect it from "the decay brought
about by slowness, memory, analysis, repose and habit" (*TIF*, 130). According to
this pragmatic creed, speed realizes the Absolute in life (as opposed to the Christian afterlife) by affording man victory over time and space. Like other modern
writers, Marinetti confers on art a religious function, in the sense that he attributes to the artist's imagination the power of reinventing regulatory ideals in a

world where old values are ineffective and corrupted. While the poetic persona in prefuturist writings is an alienated, frustrated rebel without a cause, "hungry" for absolute ideals, the poet of the manifestos is the creator of a new religion in a world without God, and the spokesman for a collective "we" bound by the cause of galvanizing the nation into regenerative action. Modernization and patriotism are the two main articles of faith embraced by futurism as an antidote against the decay of secure communal ideologies of redemption, a decay that leads to self-destructive nihilistic despair.[10]

Kristeva's psychoanalytical and anthropological studies on abjection offer a theoretical framework for examining futurism's religious aspects as well as, more generally, the pervasive imagery of defilement, corruption, and decay in Marinetti's texts.[11] In *Powers of Horror*, she locates the origin of phenomena such as anti-Semitism, rituals of defilement, phobias, and the repudiation of femininity in the fundamental psychic processes of the subject's accession to meaning and identity.[12] According to Kristeva, the primal process of separation from and rejection of the maternal entity results in repugnance, or abjection—a corporeal symptom or sign that serves to defend the subject's power of identification. The abjection of corporeal waste and, in general, that which traverses the boundary of the self, accompanies that power as its other.[13] Citing primitive societies where defilement is synonymous with supreme danger or great evil, Kristeva notes that the ritualization of defilement is accompanied by a strong concern for separating the sexes: "[Women], apparently put in the position of passive objects, are none the less felt to be wily powers, 'baleful schemers' from whom rightful beneficiaries must protect themselves" (*PH*, 70). Defilement rituals and behavior prohibitions are meant to ward off the danger; by establishing separations, they lay the foundations for social order. Such rituals and the concomitant abjection of the feminine are traced to the absence of "a central authoritarian power" (*PH*, 70).

These observations offer some insight into the note of sacrality that is often sounded in Marinetti's texts. They illuminate the possible links between his misogynist strategies and the early twentieth-century crisis of cultural order. The concept of abjection plays a fundamental role in Kristeva's analysis of modern literature, which, in her view, has assumed "the role formerly played by the sacred, at the limits of social and subjective identity" (*PH*, 26). A fundamental question informs her literary criticism: "If language, like culture, sets up a separation and, starting with discrete elements, concatenates an order, it does so precisely by repressing maternal authority and the corporeal mapping that abuts against them. It is then appropriate to ask what happens to such a repressed item when the legal, phallic, linguistic symbolic establishment does not carry out the separation in radical fashion—or else, more basically, when the speaking being attempts to think through its advent in order better to establish its effectiveness" (*PH*, 72). We have already seen how Marinetti's response to the inadequacies of the symbolic system involves marking off boundaries along gender lines between a virile self and a feminine or feminized other—a structuring of reality that sets up an enemy to be ostracized and fought. We thus arrive at the second step of the futurist project: the construction of the text as a site for violence, where woman often figures as a target.

THE TEXT AS A LOCUS OF VIOLENCE

Violence, along with its derivatives—strife, war, destruction—is a crucial thematic focus and a fertile semantic field in Marinetti's writing. War, in particular, is celebrated as a natural phenomenon—élan vital, "world's hygiene," a necessary regenerating, purifying process. It is aestheticized as spectacle, an exhilarating expenditure of energies. Human suffering is upstaged by the beautiful performance of the machine. "I noticed," recalls Marinetti, "how the shining and aggressive muzzle of a cannon, red-hot with sun and rapid fire, makes the spectacle of torn, dying human flesh almost negligible" (*TIF,* 101).[14] Pain is replaced by orgasmic pleasure; war is repeatedly fantasized as violent defloration or forceful and fecund copulation. The following, one of Marinetti's most disturbing battle-inspired erotic scenarios, appears at the end of "Uccidiamo il Chiaro di Luna!": "Here is the furious coitus of battle, gigantic vulva inflamed by the heat of courage, *shapeless vulva* [*vulva informe*] that rips apart to offer itself better to the terrific spasm of imminent victory! Ours is the victory" (*TIF,* 26; emphasis added).

If war, as we have seen, entails man's liberation from woman's enfeebling, enthralling influence and from the obsession with lust, how is it that the feminine body also personifies war in scenes of sexual violence? One possible answer is that such imagery, by pairing violence and sex, death and pleasure, constructs a picture of war as desirable, thus performing a propagandistic function.[15] But Marinetti's formulation conveys more than a pleasurable scenario of exciting adventures. A more interesting line of inquiry is that which aims at identifying the common ground on which the equation woman = war is posited. In the above passage, Marinetti's use of the word *informe* points to a less obvious link between the vehicle and the tenor of the metaphor, suggesting an unarticulated vision of war as chaos: lack of form is the negative property shared by woman and battle.

Three journal entries in Marinetti's *Taccuini* lend support to this interpretation. One passage defines battle as a "bordello," a term that means not only "brothel" but also "mess," "chaos": "Brothel sensations. Packed full and confused. Noise. Comings and goings. All the unforeseeable. All the disorder and all the rush. Victory goes to the most energetic mess that contains a stronger aggression."[16] This passage may be read as a gloss to the accumulation of fragmentary perceptions in Marinetti's representations of battle.[17] The products of the brothel-like chaos of war—rubble, refuse, excrement, decomposition—are explicitly linked with femininity in another entry, in which Marinetti juxtaposes the spectacle of his (female) dog, Gaby, with that of a young girl searching among piles of refuse and carrion: "Gaby is happy to lead the assault on those mountains of stench. Up there she

meets a little girl from Gorizia who also spends her days rummaging in the ma-
nure dung mud and garbage. What is she looking for? That which women look
for in life: debris and rubble" (61). Marinetti's use of verbs that connote activity
("frugare," "cercare") and aggression ("dare l'assalto") suggests an association between femininity—typically identified with passivity, pacifism, and romantic
love—and the processes and products of war. Fragmented, decaying matter corresponds to Kristeva's abject matter, which traverses the boundary of the self, simultaneously defining its margins and undermining its integrity.

Woman figures as bearer of the sign of castration in another emblematic moment of the notebooks, in which Marinetti recounts the episode of a young girl exposing her genitals at the beach: her "small vulva" is described as a "half-open
perpendicular wound with scarred lips" (272). As the image of formlessness, or
"lack," woman triggers existential anxieties derived from a historical situation of
crisis; these anxieties reactivate, and are sustained by, primal anxieties linked to
the process of identity formation.[18] In other words, the feminine threat stands for
the disempowerment of modern man in a rapidly changing world that baffles ex-
isting ethical and epistemological codes. By repeatedly displaying the female body
in a condition of violent sexual/verbal subjugation, Marinetti exorcises the threat
of chaos and supplants it with his fiction of male power.

Succeeding chapters will investigate further the intimate connections between
love and war, pleasure and destruction. For now, we can assert that sexual violence provides a model for the wished-for relationship between the subject and his
world: the subjugation of a "shapeless" (feminine) object by a powerful (male) subject. The role of woman in the manifestos is comparable to that of the scapegoat
in ancient myths and rituals: the scapegoat becomes the repository of all the
effects of sacrificial crisis, which can thus be represented in a reassuring version
and exorcised.[19]

These considerations can be extended to the manifesto's aesthetic of violent
rupture. Marinetti's texts are a locus of aggression and violence, not merely on
the thematic but also on the syntactic level: his poetics of "destruction of syntax"
and "wireless imagination" attacks linguistic conventions to produce syntactic violence. The ultimate target is the old "I" of traditional literature, "subjected to
frightful logic and wisdom" (*TIF*, 50): "We systematically destroy the literary I so
that it may scatter into the universal vibration, and we reach the point of expressing the infinitely small and molecular agitations" (*TIF*, 100). The epistemological implications of this stance are less iconoclastic than they might, at first,
appear to be. The scattering (*sparpagliamento*) of the self in the universe (brought
about by the fast pace of modern life) is presented as a means to a more powerful unity freed from the limits of human nature: "Victory of our I over our
Weight, with its treacherous plots to murder our speed and drag it into immobility's ditch. Speed = *scattering* + *condensation* of the I. All the space covered by a
body *condenses* in this very body" (*TIF*, 136–137; emphasis added). Destroying the
"I" of passéist literature, the futurist subject disseminates himself to penetrate the

molecular life of matter. With the help of *aeropoesia* (aeropoetry or aviation poetry), he becomes a winged, mechanically propelled "super I," capable of wielding power in the immense spaces revealed to twentieth-century consciousness by the totalizing—both detached and dominating—perspective of the airplane.[20]

Just as the self is not actually dispersed in the futurist imaginary universe, the subject is not lost/fragmented in the chain and texture of signifiers. The beginning of *Zang Tumb Tumb* (1914) clearly illustrates the paradoxical, totalizing effect of the futurist destruction of syntax.

Correction of proofs + desires in speed

No   poetry   before   us
with   our   wireless   imagination   words
in   freedom   longggggGGG   live   FUTURISM   fi-
nally   finally   finally   finally
finally

FINALLY

ᴘᴏᴇᴛʀʏ BEING BORN

train   train   train   train   **tren   tron**
tron   tron   (iron   bridge: **tatatluuun-**
tlin)   sssssssiii   ssiissii   ssiissssiiii
                train   train   fever   of   my
train   express-express-expресssssss   press-press
press-press-press-press-press-press-press-press-
press-press-presssssss   tingled   by   the   sea
salt   aromatized   by   the   oranges   seeking   sea
sea   sea   jumping   jumping   rails   rail
lllls   jumping   rrrrrrailllls   rrrrrrrraills
(GLUTTONOUS   SALTY   PURPLE   DROLL   IN-
EVITABLE   INCLINED   IMPONDERABLE   FRA-
GILE   DANCING   MAGNETIC)   I   will   explain
these   words   I   mean   to   say   that   sky   sea
mountains   are   gluttonous   salty   purple   etc.
and   that   I   am   gluttonous   salty   purple   etc.
all   that   outside   of   me   but   **also   in**

me   absolute   totality   simultaneity   synthesis   =
superiority   of   my   poetry   over   all   others   stop

(*TIF*, 643–644; emphasis in original)

Ellipsis of syntactical and logical links produces fragmentation, chaos, obscurity. However, Marinetti always combines, and "overcompensates" for, strategies of *detractio* with those of *accumulatio* (accrual of details), so that an effect of fullness and totality is created. Even at its most experimental, his writing displays mechanisms of "suture,"[21] which beget the subject's unity and ability to produce meaning. These include "free, expressive orthography and typography" that reproduce "the facial mimicry and the gesticulation of the narrator" (*TIF*, 104); onomato-poeia, synesthesia, and numerical symbols that convey that poet's sensations with "intuitive precision" (*TIF*, 106); mathematical signs that arrange the elements of discourse according to a precise logical system;[22] parenthetical indications of tempo that direct the reading pace; and even glosses that clarify obscure aspects of the text, as exemplified by the *epiphrasis* in the above passage ("I will explain these words I mean to say that sky sea mountains are gluttonous salty purple etc. and that I am gluttonous salty purple etc. [. . .] superiority of my poetry over all others stop"). Like the subject of idealistic cognition theory, the futurist subject is hypostatized as a self-assured center of intuition and representation. This self-present, "condensed" subject regards poetic language as an extension or emana-tion of his own "field of force" (in Marinetti's words, "the lyric and transfigured prolongation of our animal magnetism" [*TIF*, 104]), which must be freed from the hindrance of syntax as an instrument of logic and mobilized to conquer reality: "We shall set in motion the words in freedom that burst the boundaries of litera-ture marching toward painting, music, the art of noises, and casting a marvelous bridge between the word and the real object" (*TIF*, 141).

The futurist attack on linguistic conventions, its destruction of the symbolic, is governed by a desire to master the life of matter, "to penetrate it and know its vi-brations" (*TIF*, 105). Marinetti's rejection of cerebral, psychologizing writing and his emphasis on intuitive and sensory experiences betray a romantic longing for the "organic" fusion of inner sensibility and external experience—for the return to a more primitive, immediate poetic experience. The notion of an organic rela-tionship between artist, art, and world seems, in fact, to inspire the famous metaphorical definition of art as **"prolongation of the forest of our veins, which spreads, outside the body, in the infinity of space and time"** (*TIF*, 54; em-phasis in original). In pursuit of immediacy, Marinetti produces a willed, sensory tour de force—a violent overcoming of the distance between subject and world—that foregrounds technique, inscribing the intellectual self-consciousness of the artist-as-critic in the text. The "intellectualized" aspect of futurist poetics is evi-denced by Marinetti's prescriptive definition of the new rules of poetic expression.[23] In the manifestos, which were often published or republished as introductions or appendixes to "creative" texts, an egotistical "I" (or an elitist "we") harangues, explains, prophesies, and rhapsodizes, playing the ambivalent role of prophet/ advertiser of a new religion/product. The conventional rhetoric of the manifestos establishes the ideological and mythical framework in which the fragmented, chaotic materiality of "free-word" texts serves a constructive end. Ultimately, futurism destroys in order to resymbolize and reaffirm mastery over that which threatens to exceed the control of language. In relationship to this project, one can understand the futurists' interest in occult science and the "magic" function of neologisms, or formulas, such as *paroliberismo* (paroliberism or words in freedom), *tattilismo* (tactilism), *poliespressività* (polyexpressivity), *tavole sinottiche e sintetiche* (synoptic and synthetic tables), and *simultaneità* (simultaneity).[24]

Even the typographic revolution is fundamentally a mimetic device, and a means of gaining absolute control over how the text is declaimed and read. It is a sort of corrective measure, compensating for the text's esoteric difficulty.[25] The apparent contradiction between futurism's liberating and controlling tendencies is particularly evident when paroliberist texts are compared with the conventional language of the manifestos. Both tendencies, however, serve the demands of Marinetti's fiction of power. On the one hand, the esoterism of words in freedom restores the poet's power in the epistemological and referential realm by erasing preconceptions and expectations concerning lyrical expression. The fragmented, chaotic text mirrors, and claims mastery over, the fragmented, chaotic world. On the other hand, the conventional syntax, oratorical impetus, and exalted, epic tone of the manifestos are a way of displaying power of action in the sociopolitical realm and affirming the artist's public role in mass society—hence Marinetti's introduction of mass communication techniques and commodity economy strategies into the new domain of artistic activism. In order to "sell" the futurist program of aesthetic renovation and national reawakening, he assimilated the persuasive systems of political propaganda and industrial advertisement: inflammatory and hyperbolic rhetoric, signposting, the distribution of leaflets, and a massive use of the media for promotional purposes. The "marketing" of futurist "products" was managed (and largely financed) by Marinetti himself through an extensive cultural entrepreneurship. Acting as a publisher, impresario, promoter, and publicist for his followers/friends, he founded his own publishing house, organized theatrical tournées, sponsored exhibitions, and conducted intensive propaganda campaigns both in Italy and abroad. The futurist manifestos were sent to Italian and foreign newspapers, with attached circular letters soliciting reviews and comments.[26] Gift copies of the new books published by Edizioni futuriste di «Poesia» were also accompanied by fliers that offered suggestions for glowing reviews and promised forthcoming volumes in exchange for free publicity. Indeed, only a small percentage of each new run was channeled onto the market. Most volumes were distributed gratis to intellectuals, journalists, political and industrial leaders, and socialites—including not only active and potential supporters of the futurist effort of national renewal but also notorious opponents of the movement.[27]

From the beginning, the futurist program transcended the literary realm in its efforts to orchestrate collective action, extend the agency of art beyond its traditional confines, and affirm the supremacy of Italian "genius." Celebrating the multimedia creation of futurist cinema in 1916, the futurists described themselves as "**disassembling and reassembling the universe according to [their] marvelous whims [*capricci*],** to centuplicate the power of Italian creative genius and its absolute predominance in the world."[28] This statement echoes Giacomo Balla and Fortunato Depero's 1915 manifesto, "Ricostruzione futurista dell'universo" (Futurist Reconstruction of the Universe), which offered blueprints for mixed-media art and for the marriage of artistic and industrial worlds—perhaps futurism's most significant innovation and most enduring legacy. However, the language of the 1916 manifesto also suggests a link between aesthetic revolution and virulent nationalism, bordering on imperialism. At the same time, it evokes infantile play and caprice, a child's all-or-nothing attitude (*capricci* means both "whims" and "tantrums").

"Ricostruzione futurista dell'universo" offers insight into the connections between these two overlapping aspects of the futurist "deconstruction and reconstruction" of the universe. One of the proposed examples of multimedia creation is the "futurist toy," aimed not only at stimulating the child's laughter, elasticity, imagination, and sensibility but also at inciting a pugnacious disposition by getting him accustomed *"to physical courage, to fighting and to* **WAR.**"[29] Outrageously comical and dangerously aggressive, the toy is a miniature model of the futurist style of action: a combination of ludicrous excess and violent fanaticism.[30] As an adult, of course, the futurist child will continue to play his power games by transforming war into an exciting aesthetic experience and, as we shall see, by perverting love into a relationship of domination and annihilation.

Ultimately, no true ideological conflict exists between the gender-inflected rhetoric of violence and the gestures of formal disruption: in both cases, the fundamental goal is not to subvert the phallogocentrism of the old symbolic order, but to produce a reassuring representation of self, founded on exclusive opposition and on the devaluation, domination, or negation of otherness. The declared destruction of the literary "I" does not involve the deconstruction of the unitary subject, but its expansion, its transformation into a new all-powerful "I." Accordingly, modern reality in the futurist manifesto is not, as in other modernist texts, a problematic world of contradictions to explore; rather, it is a world to be colonized and subjugated—fuel for a self-assertive, self-aggrandizing enterprise.

THE FUTURIST MYTHOPOEIA

As we have seen, Marinetti's disruption of syntax and other linguistic habits coexists with reconstructive efforts. Similarly, the theme of destructive violence that pervades his work is inextricably linked to notions of creative progress and the construction of new myths: the utopia of multiplied, metallized man, immunized against love and death; the celebration of technological advances—life in the industrial city, "electric war," mechanized agriculture; and the exaltation of the all-powerful but controllable machine, which replaces woman as the ideal of beauty and as the object of man's narcissistic love.

As Marshall Berman notes, creation (perpetual renewal, progress, infinite development, insatiable desire, inexhaustible drive) and destruction (nihilism, insatiable violence, war, horror, despair, death) are the polarities that "shape and animate" the culture of modernity. Art in the modernist era, Berman continues, is possessed and driven by both forces reproducing and expressing "the inward rhythms by which modern capitalism moves and lives."[31] Marinetti's texts openly exhibit this thematic and ideological interplay, celebrating the violent impetus that unites capitalist expansion and the sexual economy of phallic domination. In *8 Anime in una bomba: Romanzo esplosivo* (8 Souls within a Bomb: An Explosive Novel; 1919), the central idea of creative power is expressed in a series of formulas or multiplied analogies, which produce the effect of continuous, unlimited dynamism, projected ad infinitum by the indefinite quantifier "etcetera."

Formulas

VIRILE MEMBER = deflowering - vulva - fecundation - kisses blood, etc.

PISTON = going coming - boiler - industry - vapor, etc.

PROW = sailing - sea wind - trade - foam, etc.

PLOW = opening - soil - agriculture - sap, etc.

SHRAPNEL = splitting - enemy body - war - tears blood, etc.

VOICE PEN CHISEL = creating spirit - art - light, etc.

SCALPEL = anatomizing - friendly body - surgery - pus - health or death, etc.

(*TIF*, 838)

The phallic power evoked in the first analogical chain is projected onto, and multiplied by, succeeding chains (in themselves marked by patently sexual connotations), so that it becomes the paradigm and point of origin of all the other manifestations of power: agricultural and industrial forces of production, economic expansion and trade, artistic creativity, medical and military technology (the power of giving life and death). Conversely, the violent, masculine connotations of the multiplied analogy reverberate in the procreative act. Reproductive power is thus appropriated, made male, and identified with the power of destruction, while nature/reality is implicitly imaged as a subdued, fecundated feminine body—a tabula rasa inscribed by the omnipotent stylus of man's will.

In this vision of dynamism and creativity, the flow of images generates an undercurrent of suffering and destruction ("blood," "tears," "pus," "death"), thus reproducing the paradoxical dynamics of progress. The last equation of the series, in particular, introduces elements of uncertainty and unease, as anatomy and surgery expose the extreme vulnerability of the human body. But this darker side of technology, contiguous with pain and death, is ultimately contained within the celebratory picture of unconstrained phallic power, which "naturalizes" and domesticates technological progress by collapsing the distance between libidinal and mechanical forces. The formulas are a sort of ritual attempt to dominate/propitiate the forces of both nature and technology—or, as Marinetti himself suggests by placing the formulas after a brash definition of his optimistic "fifth soul," a prescription for "impetuous hard sure optimism that doesn't yield wants smashes through opens ploughs creates and fecundates" (*TIF*, 837).

In "La guerra elettrica" (Electrical War; 1915), sexual imagery offers further clues to the ideological and emotional currents that underlie the convergence of themes (and aesthetics) of war and technology. The "vision-hypothesis" begins by envisaging a futurist wonderland, where famine and the drudgery of labor have been conquered through mechanized agriculture. This technological utopia inspires sexually charged imagery, thus invoking a science fiction version of an age-old topos: the equation of earth with the female body, a "territory" that man is entitled to exploit. While old, lazy, and unproductive Italy is described as a "money squandering," "wicked" courtesan, the futurist homeland, regenerated and harnessed by the new electrical forces, becomes a hyperfertile body, under the thumb of the "vast electrical hand of man."

> The energy of distant winds and the rebellions of the sea, transformed by man's genius into many millions of Kilowatts, will spread everywhere without wires, through the muscles, arteries and nerves of the peninsula, with a fertilizing abundance regulated by keyboards that throb beneath the fingers of the engineers. (*TIF*, 319)

> Finally the earth gives its full yield. Tightly held in the vast electrical hand of man, it expresses all its juice of wealth, beautiful orange so long promised to our thirst and finally won! (*TIF*, 321)

Technological instruments are represented as organic extensions of the human body, multiplying its force and reach. In his metallic, mechanized environment, man is sublimely removed from the earth ("only merchandise still creeps on the earth. Man, having become airborne, sets his foot on it only once in a while!" *TIF*, 321). Free from natural and social limitations—hunger, poverty, class conflict, and the weakness of the flesh—he is finally able to nourish his immense willpower and ambition: "the pure idea of the ascensional *record*," "an anarchy of perfections," "a surplus of pleasure," the universal reign of "free human intelligence" (*TIF*, 322; emphasis in original). Unexpectedly, however, the result is not perpetual peace but a most inhuman kind of war in which monstrous machines suck up the air and storm the unbreathable vacuum with devastating electrical discharges.

Instead of transcending national boundaries, the futurist Eden turns into an imperialistic "hell" of twenty-five technocratic superpowers fighting over the markets for their surplus production. Retrospectively, the germs of war can be detected already in the agonistic and antagonistic notion of individual freedom as pursuit of "surplus pleasure": "Every intelligence having become lucid, every instinct having reached its greatest splendor—they clash with each other for a surplus of pleasure" (*TIF*, 322). The various transfigurations of the Italian peninsula (first represented as a wicked courtesan, then as a prolific body bent to the satisfaction of man's greed, and finally as a science fiction wasteland destroyed by unrestrained ambition) solicit the reader's attention to an intrinsic connection between oppressive masculinity, imperialistic aggression, and the technological violence with which nature is subjugated and reduced to a monstrous, hyperproductive but unlivable environment.[32]

How does this vision of destruction square with the utopia of the futurist superuomo? One might say that the idea of the metallized, mechanized man is both an antidote to the poisons of nature ("fragility," "debilitating softness," "tiredness," "sleep") and a safeguard against new technological threats: men at war will wear oxygen-producing armors, and radiotherapists will be protected against "the perforating and curative danger of radium" as they enlist it to wipe out sickness. There will be no room in this aggressive environment for the weak and the infirm, who will be the inevitable victims of progress: "crushed, crumbled, pulverized by the vehement wheels of intense civilization" (*TIF*, 324).

The characteristic features of the futurist superuomo are crystallized in "L'uomo moltiplicato e il Regno della macchina" (Multiplied Man and the Reign of the Machine; 1910–1915), in which questions of sexuality are foregrounded. A fundamental attribute of the "multiplied" man of the future is his immunity to love. Having jettisoned sentiments and lust for woman, he engages in casual sexual encounters with no aim other than mechanical relief and reproduction. Victory over "the disease of love" translates into the ultimate triumph over "the tragedy of death." To achieve this futurist goal, warns Marinetti, it is necessary that modern young men "methodically learn to destroy all the sorrows of their hearts, methodically lacerating their affections and infinitely distracting their sex with quick, casual female contacts" (*TIF*, 301). The utopia of the New Man presented in "L'uomo moltiplicato e il Regno della macchina" and the technological wonderland envisioned in "La guerra elettrica" bespeak the same desire: to subjugate, transform, or destroy the unruly forces of nature. Winds and waters must be bridled and all the juices hidden in the entrails of the Italian peninsula squeezed out, so that man can pursue his fantasy of detached control and transcendence. Affects and drives must be channeled or drained in the territory of the male body, so that its energies can be supernaturally multiplied.

The genesis of the futurist multiplied man involves surrender to the empowering qualities of the machine—energy, precision, discipline—and the expulsion (projection onto the other) of weakening human qualities—sensibility, sensualism, skepticism, pessimism. This logic of exclusion culminates in Marinetti's manifesto-preface to the novel *Mafarka il futurista,* which triumphantly announces man's victory over nature and predicates the birth of a futurist superuomo on the exclusion of woman from the (pro)creative act. Having incited his futurist brothers to free themselves from the condition of "sons and miserable slaves of the vulva," the poet makes the following prophecy: "In the name of the human Pride that we worship, I announce to you the coming hour in which men with wide temples and steel jaws will prodigiously give birth, only with their exorbitant willpower, to infallible giants . . . I announce to you that man's spirit is an untrained ovary . . . And we are the first to fecundate it!" (*TIF,* 255). Once man is freed from woman's power to trap him into the instrumental role of generation, he will conquer immortality through a process of parthenogenetic filiation. Thus the futurist myth of rebirth foregrounds gender only to elide woman as subject in the act of male (pro)creation: the expenditure of the female principle serves the purpose of masculinizing creative economy, and the erotic imagery conveys the excitement and pleasure invested in fantasies of mastery over nature.

Marinetti's metaphor of sexual violence is a radical version of a very old phallic fantasy: the exposure or unveiling and subsequent penetration of nature. Keller has shown how the genderization of knowledge (or science) as masculine and nature as feminine pervades Western thought through its history. In particular, she focuses on Bacon's description of knowledge as a "chaste and lawful marriage" between mind and nature. This metaphor, Keller suggests, is a prescient vision of rational, objective thought ("a metaphor for power and domination, designed to safeguard the integrity of the knower," 95). The vision of "a conjunction that remains forever disjunctive" exposes the dual constitutive motives underwriting the aspiration to "objectivity": the subject's desire for power and integrity (95).[33] Exploring the emotional substructure that gives birth to claims of objectivity, Keller links the conceptions of autonomy, masculinity, objectivity, and power that emerge from the child's developing sense of self, gender, and reality. She identifies "patterns of male and female socialization that reproduce a sexualization of aggression, power, and domination," patterns that enforce the association of love with female "impotence" and autonomy with male "power," aggression, and separation from the other—starting with maternal love, then expanding to human others and nature (114). In a footnote, the connection between these psychosocial premises and sexual violence is spelled out: "There is little question that the denial of interconnectedness between subject and object serves to nullify certain kinds of moral constraint; it *allows* for kinds of violation (even rape) of the other that would be precluded by a respect for the relation between subject and object. At the same time, however, it ought logically also serve as a protection against forms of violence provoked by a relation between subject and object that is experienced as threatening to the subject" (96n. 1; emphasis in original). This sociological explanation indirectly squares with Kristeva's psychoanalytical perspective. When promiscuity (chaos) explodes, destroying the "chaste and lawful marriage" between subject and object (and, consequently, the subject's integrity and control), violence erupts. Hence Marinetti's obsession with violation and rape can be seen as evidence of a problematic relationship with the other—a sense of crisis that exacerbates the desire for control and domination.

Similar questions inform the quality of rhetorical excess evident in much of Marinetti's writing. The multiplication of sensory notations eventually becomes mere repetition, mirroring the "possession" of reality. The baroque quality of Marinetti's analogical technique responds to the need to control and domesticate all possible relationships between subject and other. The theory of analogy is a central tenet of futurist poetics, as expounded in the "Manifesto tecnico della letteratura futurista" (Technical Manifesto of Futurist Literature; 1912).

> Analogy is nothing other than the *deep love* that connects distant, seemingly different and hostile things. An orchestral style, at once polychromous, polyphonic, and polymorphous, can *embrace the life of matter* only by means of the most vast analogies.
> [. . . .]
> Images are not flowers to be parsimoniously selected and picked, as Voltaire said. They are the very blood of poetry. Poetry must be an uninterrupted sequence of new images without which it is nothing but anemia and chlorosis.
> [. . . .] The analogical style is thus *absolute master* of all matter and its intense life.
> (*TIF*, 48; emphasis added)

A poetics of imaginative profusion and expressive force is also affirmed in "Distruzione della sintassi—Immaginazione senza fili—Parole in libertà" (Destruction of Syntax—Wireless Imagination—Words in Freedom; 1913), which offers a "combative" critique of the decadent sensibility epitomized by Mallarmé's desire for the unique word: "I combat Mallarmé's decorative, precious aesthetic and his search for the rare word, for the one irreplaceable, elegant, suggestive and exquisite adjective. I do not want to suggest an idea or a sensation with passéist grace or affectation: on the contrary, I want to grasp them brutally and hurl them right in the reader's face" (*TIF*, 77). The analogical style, for Marinetti, makes use of the vital, expansive, aggressive corporeality of language to enact the desire for absolute possession. The vigorous style he propounds, hypertrophically infused with "the blood" of images, contrasts sharply with the "anemic" poetics of classical measure and the "inert" poetics of decadent rarefaction. The poetic modes that Marinetti dismisses involve different attitudes toward language, subjectivity, and reality: classical economy entails an ideal of harmony and control in the relationship between the subject and his world (the "chaste and lawful marriage"); the suggestiveness and refined artifice of symbolist reverie implies introversion and linguistic sublimation of unfulfilled desire (the contemplative aestheticism of the "effeminate" dandy). Marinetti does not offer his reader a carefully picked selection of poetic "flowers"; nor does he "waste" his energy searching for a perfect, rare image to suggest, gracefully, an idea or sensation. Instead, he "brutally" grabs images by the handful and "hurls" them at his reader.

Peter Nicholls perceives gender-inflected implications in the difference between the linguistic opacity of symbolism and the futurist objective of sensory immediacy: "Futurism's preoccupation with speed and simultaneity derived not simply from an obsession with technology, but from a need to find aesthetic means by which to deny linguistic materiality as the province of 'feminine' inwardness."[34] Futurism, he notes, replaces the self-reflexive, static strategies of symbolism (echo-play, deferrals, the vertical relations presupposed by the symbol) with "a horizontal cross-weave of images which brings together different, initially unrelated zones of experience" (207). Nicholls's account, however, focuses solely on certain programmatic aspects of the futurist project and takes Marinetti's claims to the "destruction" of the literary "I" at face value. Through the futurist strategy of superficial, horizontal, depersonalizing externalization, Nicholls concludes, the self is dehumanized, "decentered," drained through the holes of the "strict net of images or analogies" (Marinetti's phrase), and transformed into a "purely functional conduit of external rhythms" in the expansive, fast-moving circuit of consumerist capitalism (208–209). On the basis of this conclusion, Nicholls draws a distinction between the Italian futurists and the Anglo-American modernists, arguing that they assume opposite attitudes in matters of sexual difference: "because their [the Anglo-Americans'] particular Modernism was a *rappel à l'ordre* which [. . .] depended on a forceful restatement of sexual difference, the feminine 'other' could not be effaced, as it was in the 'cosmic vibrations' of the futurist world" (212). Instead, he posits an analogy between futurism and postmodern nihilism à la Baudrillard, arguing that they both imply "delirious surrender to forces which must always lie beyond control and understanding;" hence the " 'end' of the speaking subject" and the "end of language as a social means" (217).

Closer investigation of Marinetti's rhetorical strategies shows that the strict nets of images are tight enough to contain a real drainage of subjectivity. Rather than surrender to forces of modernity, the futurist "I" claims control over them though the power of intuitive, imaginative divination and synthesis. Rather than anticipate postmodern "subjectlessness," futurism reclaims the heritage of the poet-demiurge as "chosen" hero, seer, and genial creator.[35] This poetic "I" is further contained (and expanded/empowered) by a homosocially bound "we" in the prescriptive, performative rhetoric of the manifestos. Marinetti does not conceive of the futurist response to modernity as surrender, but as a Spencerian struggle for the survival of the fittest—survival though adaptation to and assimilation of new empowering forces.[36] Furthermore, his fiction of power is predicated not only on the destruction of old boundaries but also on the reconstruction of stronger ones (particularly along national and gender lines); hence, the feminine other can be rejected, subjugated, or co-opted, but never entirely effaced in the futurist world. If, as in Jean Baudrillard's theory of commodity culture, any opposition or difference is flattened out by the total circulation of the signifier, no such vision of power is possible, only the dystopia of absolute indifference, passivity, resignation, and silence. If an analogy can be found between futurism and postmodern ni-

hilism, it lies in the totalizing attitude of both toward the "paradox" of literature—the gap, or difference, between subject and object, signifier and signified.
While futurism pursues a fantasy of total control (of forcefully bridging the gap),
however, nihilism dead-ends in total impotence.

Marinetti's imaginary world is less dehumanized and often more deeply psychological than it might at first appear. The futurist poetics of "the marvelous"
(*TIF,* 82) is characterized not only by the utopia of the dehumanized, metallized
man but also (and much more conspicuously) by the prosopopoeia of natural elements and inanimate objects. Despite Marinetti's avowals to the contrary, humanized matter recurs throughout futurist texts.[37] Even the machine, which
stands for a superhuman power uncontaminated by organic limitations, is often
personified and represented as man's faithful, responsive lover: "his great faithful
devoted friend with her quick and ardent heart," "his beautiful steel machine that
[shines] with pleasure beneath his lubricating caress" (*TIF,* 298). Through a reading of the technological mythopoeia in the first two manifestos, I will argue that
this futurist pathetic fallacy projects onto matter a fiction of willpower, absolute
strength, and fulfilled desire. By focusing on the role played by the feminine in this
fiction, I will also attempt to explore its underside: an unarticulated anxiety about
modern reality that futurist scholarship has generally failed to recognize.[38]

The first futurist manifesto, "Fondazione e Manifesto del Futurismo," recounts the birth of a new poet-hero who is symbiotically joined with his automobile. From this central symbol, an entire narrative unfolds: three "famished automobiles" lure the poet and his friends from a decadent, opulent setting, and from
old myths and ideals, into a frenzied race through the streets of the city.

> We had stayed up all night—my friends and I—under mosque lamps with domes of
> lacy brass, starred like our souls, like them shining with the caged radiance of elec-
> tric hearts. For a long time we had trampled our atavistic indolence into oriental
> rugs, arguing before the extreme confines of logic and blackening many reams of
> paper with frenzied writings.
>
> [. . . .] But as we listened to the exhausted prayers muttered by the old canal and
> to the creaking bones of palaces dying on their beards of damp greenery, under the
> windows we suddenly heard the roar of famished automobiles.[39]
>
> —Let's go, I said; let's go, my friends! Let's leave! Mythology and the mystic
> ideal are overcome at last. We are about to witness the birth of the Centaur, and
> soon we'll see the first Angels fly! . . . [. . . .]
>
> We approached the three snorting beasts, to amorously feel their torrid breasts.
> [. . . .]
>
> The raging broom of madness swept us away from ourselves and drove us
> through streets as rugged and deep as the beds of torrents. (*TIF,* 7–8)

In one breath, Marinetti proclaims the end of mythology and creates new myths.
Having abandoned the paraphernalia of a decadent, prisonlike setting, the poet
breaks out of his indolent confinement by asserting kinship with the automobile,
a tamed beast, which supplants woman as the ideal of beauty and object of man's

desire, affording new power to sustain the futurist drive toward revitalizing change and a more active connection with the modern world. The new mechanical idol functions as the common object of love and identification from which the collective "we" derives binding force. The race that plunges the futurist poets into the "torrents" of modern life is a foundational myth and an initiatory ritual for the futurist group.

The empowering union of man and machine allows man to challenge and tame death (the epitome of the devouring female figure that, as we shall see, is often encountered in Marinetti's texts), while the feminine idols of passéist poetry (the "ideal Mistress," the "cruel Queen") are repudiated.

> And, like young lions, we ran after Death, her dark coat blotched with pale crosses, as she ran down the vast violet living and throbbing sky.
>
> And yet we had no ideal Mistress raising her sublime form to the clouds, nor any cruel Queen to whom to offer our corpses, twisted like Byzantine rings! There was nothing to make us wish for death, but for the wish to be free at last from the excessive weight of our courage!
>
> [. . . .] Death, domesticated, passed me at every turn to hold out her paw gracefully, and once in a while laid down with a noise of strident jaws, making velvety caressing eyes at me from every puddle. (*TIF*, 8–9)

On a rhetorical level, the poet domesticates death (the ultimate symbol of material chaos and unintelligibility) by personifying it as a seductive and tamed lover. Death (or the fear of death) is mastered further by means of an "immunity bath," symbolized by an automobile accident, which marks the climax of the rebirth or initiation narrative.[40] Swerving to avoid the obstacles of reason (personified by two teetering cyclists), the poet-hero dives with his car into the invigorating waters of a technological "womb": "Oh! maternal ditch, almost full of muddy water! Fair factory drain! I relished voraciously your nourishing sludge, which reminded me of the blessed black breast of my Sudanese wet nurse" (*TIF*, 9). The event is a primal fantasy with a technological twist: the maternal "factory drain" is a hybrid image in which regressive feminine elements (the maternal womb, the breast of the black wet nurse) are linked with, and displaced by, a modern element (the drainage ditch filled with fortifying industrial waste)—thus signifying regeneration. Associating the unpalatable sludge of the industrial age with milk, Marinetti transforms it into prime nourishment for poetic inspiration. In so doing, he plays out the fantasy of an organic fusion between instinctual human nature, poetic imagination, and the forces of technology in a state of prenatal or preoedipal oneness. The feminine is simultaneously eschewed and retained, becoming a symbol of recovered primal forces that acquire supernatural power when channeled into technological structures through poetry.[41]

This line of inquiry can be extended to pursue the psychological underpinnings that inform the aesthetic and epistemological program advocated by the manifesto. The futurist revolution is predicated on the destruction of the old symbolic order by an explosion of rejuvenating irrational forces. The irrational, however, is perceived as hiding feminine-connoted threats to identity, which the futurist fiction of power tries to ward off. The clash between the fiction of power and the specter of femininity/feminization is dramatized in "Uccidiamo il Chiaro di Luna!"; taking the form of an allegorical tale, this second manifesto proclaims the unleashing of a pure, violent destructive/creative energy that will flout tradition and annihilate passéism. To accomplish the great futurist project (symbolized by the construction of a military railroad designed to reach the flanks of the world's summit), the poets ally themselves with the forces of the irrational: madmen ("those Pure ones, already cleansed of any filth of logic," *TIF*, 19), unchained wild beasts, and the unrestrained might of the ocean. Significantly, the climactic moments of the narrative are staged in Asia: the futurists, having launched a preliminary attack against the decrepit European world, enter the cradle of civilization as if returning to a mother's womb.[42] Here they will finally build the emblems of their new religion, means to the ultimate victory: the futurist railroad and the airplane. Before this can take place, an insidious, patently feminine threat hidden in the primitive scenario must be exorcised.

> Suddenly a piercing cry split the air; a noise spread out, everybody rushed . . . It was a very young madman, with the eyes of a virgin, struck dead on the Railroad track.
>
> His body was immediately hoisted up. In his hands he held a desirous white flower, whose pistil flickered like a woman's tongue. Some would touch it, and it was bad to do so, because a sobbing vegetation prodigiously rose from the earth rippled by unexpected waves, as rapidly and easily as dawn spreads over the sea.
>
> From the azure fluctuations of the prairies there emerged the vaporous hair of innumerable swimming women, who sighed as they opened the petals of their mouths and of their moist eyes. Then, in the inebriating flood of perfumes, we saw a fabulous forest spreading around us, its arching foliage seemingly exhausted by an idle breeze. (*TIF*, 21–22)

The futurists struggle to free themselves from the terrible embrace of this "forest of delights" seething with invisible phantoms. As they are wrestling the last, clinging lianas, the "carnal Moon, the Moon with lovely warm thighs," enters the fray, "abandoning herself languidly against [their] prostrate backs" (*TIF*, 22). To ward off the seductive moonlight and beat back the phantoms of irrationality, electric light must be created. Now the military railroad can be built and a decisive attack launched against the forces that obstruct progress. The narrative's resolution dramatizes the futurists' intent in mixing primitive and technological imagery. The collapse of the old order unleashes a force in individuals and in society; having erupted, this force must now be channeled into new structures of protection and empowerment (railroads, airplanes, electricity), which will exorcise the threats inherent to it. In the battle scene, Marinetti's word choice indicates a relationship between the fantasies aroused by the moonlit scenario and the passions driving the futurist aviators: the airplanes are described as "delicious lovers who swim, with open arms, on the undulating foliage" (*TIF*, 25), thus recalling the seductive swimmers emerging "from the azure fluctuations of the prairies." All potentially self-destructive drives are, however, channeled into the attack against the enemy, "the eternal enemy that we would have to invent if it didn't exist" (*TIF*, 16).

The aesthetic of "geometric and mechanical splendor" and "numerical sensibility" articulated in the 1914 manifesto thus provides the model for a new mode of being. Marinetti defines its essential features as "hygienic oblivion, hope, desire, harnessed force, speed, light, willpower, order, discipline, method; a feeling for the big city; the aggressive optimism that results from the cult of muscles and sports; wireless imagination, ubiquity, the laconism and simultaneity that derive from tourism, business and journalism; the passion for success, the newest instinct for record breaking, the enthusiastic imitation of electricity and the machine; essential concision and synthesis; the happy precision of gears and well-oiled thoughts; the concurrence of energies converging into a single victorious trajectory" (*TIF*, 98–99). Far from being reducible to a naive enthusiasm for the marvels of modern technology, this aesthetic of the machine betrays a deep need for new paradigms of order, power, and control: the search for a new all-male symbolic structure to "harness" the eruption of feminine-connoted irrationality. The technological wonderworks proposed as new aesthetic models embody tremendous energy and superhuman precision; the mechanized aesthetic denaturalizes man and subverts the boundaries of organic reality.

Given that the machine symbolizes freedom from the past and from nature and given that femininity is used to express the threat to the self in a form capable of being comprehended, dominated, and exorcised, what is to be made of the recurrent association between woman and machine? Complex defense mechanisms of projection and identification seem to be at play. The new, mechanical object of desire and identification enables the poet to imagine an empowering relationship with reality: it allows for the narcissistic rejection or domestication of female difference and mirrors man's ambition for supernatural power. Unlike real women, whose modern emancipation is the controversial topic of much futurist literature, the machine is a consistently "faithful, devoted friend with a quick and ardent heart" (*TIF*, 298) that fulfills male desire for total possession. Unlike psychologically symbolic "woman," benefactor of a limited, imperfect life tainted by mortality, the powerful machine with replaceable parts allows for the fantasy of a triumph over death. Unlike the literary feminine ideal—traditional symbol of the impossible, unreachable, and mysterious—the machine symbolizes the realization of ideals and the conquest of time and space.

The woman-machine association also performs the converse function of domesticating new technological realities—the technological "monster"—by embodying them in a familiar object of love and mastery. My use of the word *monster* is justified by Marinetti's diction in the first manifesto, which often evokes the metaphorical language and sinister representations of machinery found in the naturalistic novel. The first manifesto's depiction of automobiles as "snorting beasts" and the steering wheel as a "guillotine blade" acquires a literal resonance when the factual events underlying the tale are considered. The real-life car accident that brought Marinetti's driving career to a premature end was the result of his inability (or, according to his driving instructor, his ineptitude) to control the automobile (figs. 1, 2).[43]

Psychoanalytic theories of the defense against persecution anxieties offer an approach for understanding the notion of a beautiful and threatening machine. In Franco Fornari's terms, the child identifies with the internalized enemy object because this identification results in a sense of omnipotence.[44] This behavior foreshadows the war psychology of adults, in which the subject avoids depression by assuming a defiant, aggressive stance toward the world. The futurist mythicization of the machine is a phantasmatic transformation of an enemy into a friendly object. This process of identification or introjection results in a sense of belonging to the new modern reality. It affords an illusory amplification of power, a feeling of sadistic omnipotence. The futurist mythicization of war and Marinetti's rhetoric of violence and destruction are other examples of such a defense. War (more specifically, the nation at war) is an object of identification through which both self and group (the artistic movement, the Italian people) are unified. Unification results by means of paranoid projection of internal threat and incorporation of external threat, manifested by aggressive posturings and by denial of anxiety-causing dangers.

Other problematic implications of the futurist mythopoeia become evident when we shift from the psychological to the social perspective. Myths of individual and national empowerment through "unifying" mechanization and belligerence ignore or mystify the reality of the class tensions that threaten to tear apart the fabric of society—tensions that become more and more acute as Italy belatedly follows the more advanced European countries in the industrialization process. In "L'uomo moltiplicato e il Regno della macchina," eroticization of the machine transfigures the relationship between the worker and the technological means of production.

> Have you never observed an engineer as he lovingly washes the great powerful body of his locomotive? His is the minute, knowledgeable tenderness of a lover caressing his adored woman.
>
> It has been ascertained that during the great French railway strike, the organizers of the sabotage were unable to persuade even a single engineer to sabotage his locomotive. (*TIF*, 298)

The threat of class conflict is exorcised so long as the worker's desires and ambitions are displaced onto, and satisfied by, his new love—the machine. The ideal of mechanized man complements that of the humanized machine; both ideals evoke values of discipline, inexhaustible energy, and imperviousness to emotion.[45] In Marinetti's words, this futurist superuomo is "a nonhuman type in whom moral suffering, goodness of heart, affection and love, the sole corrosive poisons of inexhaustible vital energy, the sole interrupters of our powerful physiological

Fig. 1. Marinetti at the wheel. Published in Giovanni Lista, *Futurismo e fotografia* (Milan: Multhipla Edizioni, 1979). Reprinted courtesy of Giovanni Lista.

Fig. 2. Marinetti's car after the famous accident, 15 October 1908. Reprinted by permission of the Beinecke Rare Book and Manuscript Library, Yale University.

electricity, will be abolished" (*TIF*, 299). However, the mechanization of man also neutralizes another "poison" that Marinetti does not mention: the contradictions of industrial life and class antagonism that stand in the way of social cohesion and national unity.

In conclusion, Marinetti's manifestos on the futurist syntactic revolution proclaim his determination to clear the linguistic ground by destroying the barriers of traditional syntax and the old, introspective literary "I." The goal is to open an infinite space in which "multiplied" man—having surpassed the limits of nature—can meet the challenges of modern reality. Woman is consistently co-opted to construct this fiction of power, and just as consistently rejected as subject. Ultimately, however, the representation of the feminine produces meanings in excess of the fiction of power, exposing the anxieties that underwrite it. Virulent misogyny, homophobia, and the eroticization of violence add up to a paranoid, anxious self-definition, pointing to an unarticulated psychoanalytical tale.

THREE

The Superman and the Abject
Mafarka le futuriste

The clash between the fiction of virile power and the specter of femininity/ feminization resounds loudly in Marinetti's "African novel."[1] Critics have remained deaf to this most crucial aspect of the text, however. "Orthodox" Marinettian criticism reads *Mafarka* as an allegorical tale of initiation, death, and resurrection, which mythologizes the genesis of futurism: in De Maria's words, the birth of Mafarka's son is "the birth of a god, miraculous as in the myths of the most various of religions," the act of foundation of the futurist "religion of manifested Will and daily Heroism" (*TIF*, XXXVI). This kind of interpretation scarcely departs from the apologetic model provided by Marinetti's own defense at his trial for "offending public decency": "I have described the impressive ascension of an African hero, temerarious and cunning. After displaying, in manifold battles and adventures, the most vehement will to live and dominate, [. . .] still unsatiated by molding the world to his own liking, he abruptly rises from the heroism of war to that of philosophy and art. In a superhuman struggle against matter and mechanical law, he wants to and does create his ideal son, a masterpiece of vitality, a winged hero whom he transfuses with life by a supreme kiss, without the concurrence of woman who witnesses the tragic superhuman birth."[2]

At the opposite end of the interpretive spectrum, James Joll dismisses *Mafarka* as a "tedious, rhetorical tale of rape and battle in a mythical Africa."[3] Rinaldo Rinaldi calls it a feuilleton "dressed up" in the avant-garde clothes of a revolutionary experiment,[4] and Kaplan indicts Marinetti's prose for "its inevitable affinity with fascist politics."[5] Unlike Joll and Rinaldi, Kaplan provides an insightful analysis of the text, underscoring the role played by the female principle as the obstacle against which the new futurist perspective is affirmed. She culls the elements of a "fascist fantasy narrative" that binds the polarities of destruction and creation. In so doing, however, Kaplan focuses on Mafarka's display of supernatural powers, overlooking the more hidden complexities and ambivalences of the text. As a result, the various episodes of the novel (which, from her perspective, "appear foreign to each other") are seemingly unrelated to "the most surprising and most crucial moment of the novel: the place where Marinetti's authorial intentions, as stated in the preface, appear to break down through some involuntary return to the maternal."[6]

Giusi Baldissone's analysis, part of a monograph on Marinetti,[7] and Glauco Viazzi's stylistic study, "Ainsi parla Mafarka-el-Bar,"[8] are located between these two extremes of critical sentiment. Viazzi points to the semantic density of Marinetti's language but stops short of pursuing an interpretation of the whole text. Baldissone, meanwhile, assumes a psychoanalytical perspective in order to fathom the most opaque aspects of the text. She foregrounds the incestuous elements and oedipal conflict apparent in *Mafarka*. Her conclusions, however, are grounded in Marinetti's biography: his love for his mother, his rivalry with his brother, and traces of homosexual affect, which is also present throughout Marinetti's novel in the form of the "cult of male beauty's superiority over female beauty."[9] The problem with such an approach is that it limits itself to pursuing a hidden referential content in the author's life, drawing an equation between Marinetti's psychology and Mafarka's. Psychoanalytic insights can prove more useful to an understanding of the text and its workings when attention is focused on language and figurality.

Considered in its entirety, with sufficient attention to its figurative dimension and to the fundamental, complex role played by the feminine element, *Mafarka* resists being pigeonholed as a mythical foundation narrative of a new religion, the literal transcription of Marinetti's own family romance, or a fascist gesture that erases the difference between destruction and creation. While the conclusion presents a monolithic embodiment of the futurist fiction of power, the rest of the text reveals feminine-connoted crevices. These provide access to the inner lining of the fiction of power: the sense of crisis that constitutes the rejected premise of the futurist project.

THE RHETORIC OF ABJECTION

With the exception of the final cathartic apotheosis, the text exudes a rhetoric of putrescence, wetness, foulness, and death. Mafarka's actions take place in a murky "hyperorganic"[10] setting, seething with decomposing bodies and represented in terms that evoke fetid entrails. Images of corporeal excretions recur with obsessive frequency, accompanied by descriptions of Mafarka's terror and repulsion. Such a rhetoric of abjection, in Kristevan terms, constructs the sphere where the body's confines are established and overcome and where the drama of individual identity and power is played out. In Marinetti's novel, abject imagery is associated with loss of individuality and with the protagonist's hatred of the sociopolitical agencies that threaten his power. Such agencies are embodied by Kaïm-Friza, leader of the farmers—a "sordid," foul dwarf who tries to win over

Mafarka to a politics of peace for the masses' sake, somberly reminding him also of the existential condition that limits his ambitions. Metaphors of flooding, engulfment, and vortical motion represent the overwhelming forces that determine the destiny of individuals: Kaïm-Friza's sobering call to reality, for instance, is illustrated by a blindfolded ass, yoked to a waterwheel that turns around the axis of the ego's ambitions (28).

Sexual and affective drives are foregrounded as the main engines in the existential "press" that destroys individual identity. The following quote, from the episode of the rape of the slaves, exemplifies the liquefying, decomposing effects of lust on the "stinking human tide" (43) of Mafarka's sailors, drawn by orgiastic intoxication to be churned into a putrid pond of fetid human "oil."

> Mafarka-el-Bar tried three times to defeat the gyratory thrust of this shrieking, fuming mass, to discern the mysterious center around which it fatally revolved.
>
> Finally, pulling himself up on the stirrups, he saw that the strange human cyclone was swirling around a pond coated with green putrescent growths that were being perturbed by hundreds of delirious bathers, which exuded an acrid, pestilential smell of hemp, urine, fat and sweat.
>
> It was a fantastic compressor of jaundiced bodies stacked in pyramids, which collapsed secreting juice like monstrous olives, under the blazing teeth of the weighty solar wheel. It hurled its atrocious movement as it crushed all these human heads like enormous screeching and agonizing seeds; and the pond seemed to have been formed little by little with this frothing greenish paste. (37–38)

This passage, one of a number that establish a causal connection between sexuality and decomposition, also points to woman's intrinsic relation to the abject. The semantic field of abjection is linked to the feminine both literally and figuratively. In literal terms, "original sin"—the contamination of humanity with germs of decay—is blamed on woman. In a famous quote, Mafarka indicts the female genitalia as matrix of death: "Oh! what joy to have brought you into the world so beautiful and free of all the stains that come from the evil vulva and predispose one to decrepitude and death! . . . Yes! you are immortal, my son, the sleepless hero!" (214). Such is the rationale underlying the futurist program of generating a son (or regenerating the self) "without the concurrence and foul complicity of a woman's womb" (169). Figuratively, the association between woman and abjection is displaced in the prosopopoeia of feminine natural elements. The clouds, for instance, are feminized in the action of smothering the sun with their "smelly nursing breasts" (95). And death itself is imaged as a devouring femme fatale who feeds on the flesh and blood of her lovers: "Death grips you in her purplish lips and sucks your blood; her caresses turn your body into marble, and her voluptuous kisses rip the flesh off your bones" (173).

The fantasy of sexuality as oral aggression illustrates woman's threat throughout the text, most notably in the climactic episode wherein Coloubbi ("the keeper of hyenas," 218) attempts to seduce Mafarka on the eve of Gazourmah's birth. This episode, which signals the protagonist's most fascinating and horrifying confrontation with feminine sexuality, provides telling clues as to the significance of such a recurrent motif.

> In all truth, he felt small, no larger than a fruit in the mouth of the woman, clasped between her teeth, which she suddenly flashed, like one might draw a dagger out of its sheath. And it was as if she had shown one of her body's most intimate, tasty crannies . . .
>
> At the sight of the fresh, honeyed sweetness of lips that spread open on to white sensuality, a tortured, unbearable anguish gripped Mafarka by the throat. The juice of heavenly fruits! . . . As well as the inner folds of a wound she wistfully showed her mother so it could be treated. (189)

In Mafarka's anxiety-laden vision of Coloubbi, the main codes are those of "lack" and "power," "wounded" and "wounding." The gaping mouth, an image of aggressive desire that incorporates the other, also conjures up the female "other mouth"—a seductive, hidden recess, but also a terrifying wound.[11] Further images qualify this experience as one of a veiling/unveiling of truth. Coloubbi's smile is compared to an enlightening disclosure: "No! No! Remove your mouth! Remove your mouth! Smile, just smile, slowly, like that, as if to unveil a lamp!" (191). Her eyes are portrayed as vitreous screens over a ghastly, engulfing void: "Nothing, nothing . . . there is absolutely nothing behind the windows of your eyes, in the tower of your forehead! I know! . . . And yet you can unravel, one strand at a time, the tightly knit web I carry about in my mind!" (192). What is the light (truth) hidden by the veil of the lamp, the destructive nothingness behind the glass of the woman's eyes? The emphasis on emptiness, on absence, and on the horror of the beholder suggests that woman is fantasied as the passive and active repository of the emblematic icon of castration, which, as already suggested, may encode a more radical anxiety of symbolic impotence and self-dissolution. Mafarka's perceptions and words testify eloquently to an interplay between projection of lack and fear of recontamination. His initial sensations at the sight of woman's castrating mouth are of vulnerability ("he felt small, no larger than a fruit in the mouth of the woman, clasped between her teeth, which she suddenly flashed, like one might draw a dagger out of its sheath"). His sense of lack is immediately and pleasurably projected onto what is exclusive to the female other: her anatomic difference ("one of her body's most intimate, tasty crannies"). Projections, however, are reversible: the gaping void is reflected back and threatens to engulf the beholder who may recognize himself in it and must therefore protect his "wholeness" with fetishistic gestures of distancing and disavowal.

A later moment of confrontation supports this reading. As Coloubbi sneaks onto the scene of his all-male creation, Mafarka responds with words of phobic rejection: "Back off, sinister keeper of hyenas! . . . Get far away from here, with your pack of rotten genital eaters [*ton troupeau mangeur de sexes pourris*]! . . . [. . . .] Cover your face . . . And don't get undressed! Hide your throat! . . . Your skin is so transparent that I see two snakes furiously beating their heads within your breasts, as if they were two small silk pouches!" (209). Having unveiled the light of "truth" (an engulfing void), Mafarka reveils it in a more reassuring fashion: Coloubbi is endowed with symbolic figurations, or trophies, of the phallic power she is accused of devouring. Her furiously aggressive breasts, animated by snakes, call to mind the Medusa's head. Mafarka's effort to shield himself provides further links with the mythological subtext. The snakes suggest an apotropaic gesture meant to defend the beholder from the horror aroused by the gaping mouth, which evokes the loss of gender differentiation and, simultaneously, woman's castrating power.[12] Later, the plurality of reference is made more explicit: "Shut up, gluttonous beast! . . . What do you want to know? And you couldn't hear me, with your sleek ears— poor shells deafened by the frightful cry of lust! Your body has nothing but starving orifices! . . . If I offer you a heroic idea you are overcome with a desire to suck it like a sugar cane, admit it!" (216). The feminine "ravenous mouths" stand for a pervasive and radical danger: they intimate an unspoken anxiety about the boundaries of identity, a concern about the dissolution of borders sweeping away any possibility of distinction and symbolization.

The mechanism of misogynist scapegoating at work here closely resembles that which is deployed in the manifestos. Unlike the latter, in which the predominant rhetorical strategies shore up polarized definitions of self and other, the founding myth of the futurist "religion" defers the containment and exorcism of the "pollution" until the conclusion. An epidemic of abjection—a progressive, contagious loss of differentiation between masculine and feminine, sacred and abject, life and death—is played out with increasing virulence to be finally resolved in a universal, purging holocaust. My project in the following pages is to follow this thematic and rhetorical line, highlighting its central role in the novel. Such a focus offers leverage with which to uncover the emotional substratum of the fiction of power. More specifically, I will argue that the novel parlays the never-resolved tension between Marinetti's pessimistic view of reality and his futurist program into diachronic terms; namely, into a narrative of the miraculous origin of the futurist superuomo. The setting of this narrative is an indefinitely primitive world, vaguely located in the Arab region of Africa (conceivably, the Egypt of Marinetti's childhood). It is consistent with the futurist view of progress as mythical rebirth rather than historical development—a notion that is clearly connected with the radical pessimism that pervades prefuturist works. Given that the ideology of futurism originates in a tangle of pessimism, irrationalism, and vitalism of Schopenhauerian, Nietzschean, and Bergsonian extraction, its program for change can only be predicated on a drastic rupture with the historical past, and on the power of a willful imagination.[13]

FAILING DIKES

At first sight, the heroic Mafarka seems to fit the paradigm of aggressive virility: "He had the poise and stature of a young, invincible athlete, armed to bite, strangle, and crush" (22). He is endowed (if only in the "double fiction" of a tale within the tale) with an eleven-meter-long penis.[14] He is the successful defender of his country from the destructive assault of neighboring "black hordes" (Mafarka and his people, by contrast, are characterized as African Arabs). Indeed, we are told, his chest is "stronger than a dike" against a "flood" of abjection: "the ocean of tar that crested the wild hills" (25). In addition to the external menace of the black armies, who use packs of frothing rabid dogs ("the inundating tide of yellow beasts," 85) as their weapon, the hero successfully fends off an internal uprising (the "stinking human tide," 43) of tumultuous, intoxicated sailors, as well as the swelling tide of a turbulent, undifferentiated crowd that war has driven inside the city walls like "a devastating torrent" (24). Mafarka, in other words, seems to be armored against a rampant threat to individual identity and power, figured by the pervasive imagery of engulfing liquid masses. Symptomatic traces of "wetness" may, however, be detected in the introductory portrait of the strong African king: his "sensual" mouth, "meek" forehead, and "liquescent" eyes are melted links in the ironclad chain of qualities otherwise attributed to Mafarka (22).

Mafarka's virility and self-control contrast with his brother's ambiguous nature, which arouses the king's anxiety and horror.

> —Oh! I know how courageous you are, but I loathe this ridiculous feminine sappiness that, one minute, throws you into insane exaltations, and the next, subjects you to childish weaknesses . . . Listen to me: these unpredictable, inexplicable mood swings must be done away with today! . . . Oh my beloved brother, I sense so well that you don't have my catapulting muscles, to suffocate an enemy while pretending to kiss him. Despite your best efforts, your body has remained soft and fragile like the juicy body of a young maiden. Your eyes, made to be kissed, are not, like mine, scarecrows for birds of misfortune; but you have to harden them, your eyes, and arm them, like I have, with fangs! (30–31)

Mafarka's brother, Magamal, straddles the dangerous boundary between masculinity and femininity, bringing the threat of abjection closer to the hero. The novel's central drama of self-dissolution and self-regeneration is played out along this boundary, which becomes progressively more contorted and confused. Magamal turns out to be the object of ambiguous feelings on Mafarka's part, blurring the difference between fraternal affection, maternal love, and homoerotic attraction. Later, an unexpected feature of the protagonist's character is revealed by a gesture of "maternal tenderness" for his brother: "he turned toward his brother and looked deep into his eyes with the quenching tenderness of a mother, gently taking his head in the grasp of his large hands" (31).

Eventually, we learn that Mafarka is himself susceptible to swaying tides of emotions and oscillating moods, which he reads in Magamal's demeanor as a horrifying sign of psychological femininity. The rhetoric of liquidity and decomposition, most conspicuously associated with the amorphous crowd and enemy hordes, also signals Mafarka's loss of self-control, caused by surges of lust or sorrow and by the resurgence of mother-bound memories of the past. When, for instance, a "crop" of virgins is offered to Mafarka as the prize for his victory, he feels drowned by an inundation of sensuality.

> —Don't abandon me yet, fierce Sun, Sun of energy and cruel force! Here you are, pulling from my limbs one by one the fangs of will that have become encrusted in my flesh . . . It is your rays of red lava that flow in my veins . . . Oh sea of fire, do not run away from me! . . . I will be nothing more than a sandy port, I will be nothing, if you leave my chest, oh Sun! . . . Because, you can see, my soul is terribly frightened . . . It no longer knows how to receive this oppressive joy, and I feel suffocated by this tide of exquisite ecstasy! (97–98)

His reaction to sensual and emotional stimulations totters between ecstatic surrender (especially when the stimuli conjure up sensually and sentimentally charged memories of childhood)[15] and repulsion, which results in the unleashing of sadistic drives. This alternation of power and impotence, vulnerability and violence, is framed and underscored by alternating descriptions of day and night, with their opposing symbolic values of virile, aggressive energy and feminine, extenuating lunar seduction. In some instances, as in the passage quoted above, the text explicitly establishes a relation between the daily cycle of light and darkness and Mafarka's cyclothymia—the alternation of dynamism and aggressiveness on the one side, languidness and anguish on the other. It is usually when the feminine, maternal night takes over that Mafarka feels unable to resist the mounting tide of sensuality.

Underneath the framework of this naturalizing symbolism lie the workings and the failures of the cultural ideal of autonomous individuality. Mafarka's reaction to the physical contact with a seductive sacred dancer shows that his typical violence is triggered by intimacy perceived as a threat to the individual's boundaries.

> Suddenly Mafarka felt a woman's body, *at once burning and glacial,* glide into his arms. Wasn't it the scaly belly of one of the sharks that had disappeared at moonset?
> But the unknown mouth falling asleep on his own was smooth, and sinuous, *and his entrails stirred with ecstasy and terror.* He leapt up and, pushing the woman's body away, howled:
> —Enough! enough! Go away! go away! Back off! slaves, light your torches! Shackle these women, and throw them to the fish!
> [. . . .]
> —Yes! Yes! Throw them to the fish! You will love them more when they are dead! . . . But alive, no! no! . . . They cannot live among us! (121–122; emphasis added)

Like a Petrarchan lover, Mafarka simultaneously experiences sensations of heat and cold, delight and terror. To portray the divisive effects of desire, Marinetti relies on a characteristic topos of Western love poetry: the oxymoron, or intellectual paradox, a rhetorical figure that combines contradictory or incongruous words. Such a figure is consistent with the paradoxical notions this literary tradition propounds: the idea that loving is synonymous with solitary suffering and that woman is at her most desirable when she is distant and unattainable. This rhetorical link signals a deeper connection between futurist misogyny (in particular, the degeneration of desire into violence vividly illustrated in the passage above) and the literary idealization of woman that emerged in the twelfth and thirteen centuries with the lyric of courtly love and was later codified in Petrarch's *Rime sparse* (Scattered Rhymes). Marinetti's "sacred" dancer is a degraded, fin de siècle successor of the *donna angelicata*, or angel-like woman. The latter is disembodied as she is idealized and transformed into a goal whose pursuit elevates the poet to new spiritual and intellectual heights. Petrarch, in particular, aspires to the supreme summit of poetic glory and constructs a literary "monument" of himself as a poet divided between sacred and profane love (but, by virtue of this division, autonomous from his literary father Dante, the poet of divine love). He does so by capitalizing on the idealized body of Laura, which is reduced to a composite of chaste parts (notably hair, hand, foot, and eyes).[16] Through this synechdochic representation, the woman's precious "fragments" are "scattered" in Petrarch's verses, without ever constituting a portrait of a whole individual interacting as a subject in an interpersonal love experience. Marinetti's divine but promiscuous beauty, by contrast, is literally turned into shreds, food for the fish of Mafarka's aquarium, in order to eliminate (the object of) a desire or (the projected image of) a lack that fragments and dissolves the self.[17] As will become apparent, the "wholeness" reclaimed with this gesture is a figure for literary autonomy. Both the rhetorical scattering of woman in Petrarch and the fantasy of her literal destruction in Marinetti can be traced to a one-sided ideal of individuality and self-sufficiency that is traditionally celebrated in Western literature and that may have been strengthened rather than diminished by the modern crisis of authority.

Marinetti's recurrent association of the maternal image with the experience of overwhelming desire can be understood in light of Benjamin's critique of the "mentality of opposition which pits freedom against nurturance" and "confusion between total loss of self and dependency" that sustain Western notions of individuality (*BL*, 172–173). She argues that the radical repudiation of (identification with and dependency on) the mother, postulated by the oedipal model, is not a "royal" road to freedom, but a potentially troubled, painful journey after impossible ideals: "The vision of perfect oneness, whether of union or of self-sufficiency, is an *ideal*—a symbolic expression of our longing—that we project onto the past. This ideal becomes enlarged in reaction to the experience of helplessness—in the face of circumstance, powerlessness, death—but also by the distance from mother's help that repudiation of her enforces" (*BL*, 173; emphasis in original). A cultural environment that devalues nurturance and dependency, confining them to infancy and to domestic space, radicalizes the dualism between the ideal of powerful autonomy and the experience of helplessness. When nurturance must be given up in exchange for autonomy and "individuals lose access to internal and external forms of maternal identification, independence backfires: it stimulates a new kind of helplessness, one which has to be countered by a still greater idealization of control and self-sufficiency" (*BL*, 174). The repudiated mother, as a consequence, is an impossible goal, part of a utopian effort at escape from the adult world of ambitious self-reliance. Or else she is the dangerous and nearby threat, the dreaded magnet of a relapse into smothering dependency—Medusa and engulfing womb. This pattern occurs throughout Marinetti's works.

Invoking Georges Bataille's reflections on the erotics of death, Benjamin notes that "love of death takes the place of primal continuity with others" in male fantasy: "The consequence of repressing this sense of bodily continuity may be [. . .] that the desire for it becomes tied to eroticized images of death and murder" (*BL*, 286 n. 75). Mafarka's proclamation of his violent sexual politics (addressed to the virgins that the citizens present to him as a tribute on the night of his victory) displays this paradoxical dynamics of desire and offers further evidence of the ideological and psychological underpinnings of the "inevitable pleasure" of total, annihilating possession.

> I love you and I understand you with all the intelligent thirst of my flesh, with *deep, dry black wells* dug into it . . . But when it's over, you will be unhappy! Because what I savor most in you is the desire to kill you! What can you ask from a live dagger like myself? . . . Ah! to lose you before the first caress, after the first surrender of your eyes liquified with passion! . . . Ah! to lose you today, as you are, all locked up inside your shell of decency! But I dream, alas! of the ineluctable pleasure of soon ripping it slowly off, strip by strip, as if undressing a large tropical fruit . . .
>
> To stop at this: scorching ecstasy! That's the honey of my desire! But it is written that you will be ripped apart by the harshness of my strength, flayed and smashed like so many ruts, by the toothed, fiery wheel of my selfish, rapacious lust! (103; emphasis added)

This delirious speech postulates not only an irreconcilable dualism but also an intrinsic link between an ideal of absolute wholeness (the untainted fruit protected by its shell) and a desire for total possession through destruction. Violence is the underside of frustrated idealism: through total annihilation, Mafarka achieves absolute control of an other he cannot possess in a state of ideal integrity and perfection. The origin of this "thirst" for violence lurks in the depths of the "deep, dry black wells"—marks of insatiable lack—hollowed out in his own flesh. Mafarka's display of phallic violence as well as the inflation of phallic imagery that characterizes the text assume the semblance of an exasperated apotropaic reaction.

The drama of Mafarka's victimization by forces beyond his will resonates with a number of episodes that stage the scene of his engulfment by abject, horrifying sites. Similarities touch both on the thematic level—the loss of self-control—and on the figural ground—the rhetoric of liquidity and decomposition. The most obvious examples are Mafarka's two descents into the uterine "Hypogées"—the sacred caves of the dead where Mafarka meets his mother's ghost (161–162, 217–219)—and the mass rape of the slaves, during which Mafarka and Magamal are drawn into a "tenebrous hall" (36) by a woman's cry, seemingly gushing out of "a mortal wound [. . .] flowing with blood, inconsolable for having been ignored and left with no hope" (35).[18]

The topos of engulfment by a maternal "cave" is taken up and elaborated with a puzzling twist in the episode of Mafarka's access into the Whale's Womb or Belly ("le Ventre de la Baleine"), which signals the onset of the hero's confrontation with his paternal legacy. The Whale's Womb, a subterranean labyrinth under the bastions of Tell-el-Kibir, is an architectural monster projected by Mafarka's father, Ras-el-Kibir, "in order to meet with all his vassals and to offer them the spectacle of the agony of his enemies shredded by hungry fish" (107). It extends, underground, the city's maze of viscid, dark alleys, culminating in a fantastic crystal aquarium located under the sea. Such a monstrous construction provides a disquieting subtext for what appears to be a typical oedipal situation. A solid, upright, paternal symbolic order is represented by the formidable walls that "flout" the sea and by the sovereign will of the lighthouse that "lacerates" the darkness, "bearing witness to the genius of its creator" (106). But this dead, idealized paragon of power seems to deny identification: Mafarka quivers before "the earthly imprint" of his "demigod" father and wonders whether he will ever be able to match his genius (106–107). Furthermore, the towering paternal construction has an abject underside; the fortress with its illuminating (phallic) lighthouse rises above a womb—a "flaccid," fetid, dark, and disquieting site, saturated with signs of abjection.[19] The threat of a collapse of identity looms large in this womb. The entrance to the cave evokes the topos of the gaping mouth ("Mafarka and his horse felt themselves being sucked into the gluttonous mouth of a furnace," 107), along with the correlated images of the *vagina dentata* and the gate to the underworld. The Whale's entrails are the theater of unleashed libidinal drives, unmanning, and death. Here Mafarka faces rebellion against his authority, orders his enemies' execution by dismemberment, and is threatened by a surge of sensual pleasure (his own engulfing "entrails") capable of reducing him to "a drenched rag" (un linge mouillé).[20] Moreover, this is the place where Mafarka gives a retrospective account of the power struggle with his now-dethroned uncle Boubassa, declaring that he has been gestated in, and evacuated from, the fetid "ventre" of this inept, dropsical[21] leader.

> [. . .] it's he, Boubassa, who put the fatherland in jeopardy! I'll settle for banishing him.
> —In the bellies of your fish! Sabattan murmured, as his friends grabbed him by the waist.
> —Yes, in the bellies of my fish! Why not? Wasn't I exiled to Boubassa's belly during my entire youth? Fortunately, I survived it, like a swallowed beautiful diamond. I came out of it with the nocturnal excrements of his loose bowels . . . I must say that he is still a little sick because of it. Ah! Ah! (115)

The implications of such a preoedipal, "cloacal" fantasy of parturition can be pursued in more than one direction.

The most obvious interpretation is that of a confrontation with an abject authority figure: a grotesque surrogate father (the evil half of a split paternal imago) who embodies the recurrent theme of gender confusion. The two symbolic wombs—the labyrinth created by Mafarka's father and the pregnancy of his uncle—condense the image of all-embracing maternity and the idea of an authoritative, withholding, castrating paternal figure who thwarts the son's yearnings for identification and power. Like his vulnerability to destructive sensuality, Mafarka's frustrating confrontation with paternal authority suggests that the ideal of autonomous individuality has failed or is in a state of crisis. The splitting of the father into an absent, idealized figure and an immanent, oppressive one is symptomatic of such a crisis. Both bear the mark of feminine abjection; both conspire to bar Mafarka from power and keep him prisoner in the maternal reign of dependency—the former by setting up an unattainable ideal of perfection, the latter by excluding him from the legacy of his father's role. Interestingly, this configuration of the family romance presents an analogy with Benjamin's paradigm for fascist domination: the authoritarian, withholding father who thwarts identificatory love engenders submission to an idealized locus of absolute power and fear/desire of engulfment by the maternal (the underside of the ideal of total separation). In Marinetti's fantasy, as in the scenario envisioned by Benjamin (*BL*, 146), the good, "nurturing" authority figure is missing, and a bad one is introjected in the struggle for identity and autonomy. Mafarka's tall tale of the horse trader, the Devil, and the stuffed fish presents the introjection of a negative, destructive power in literal terms, as an actual ingestion. The hero, in the role of a horse trader, sells a fiery stallion to the Devil, who is disguised as a merchant. The stallion copulates with all the mares in sight and sets the world ablaze with its flaming tail and mane. It turns out to embody an unquenchable "fire" of lust and destructive fury that even the master of evil cannot control. Unable to ride or tame the animal, the Devil castrates it and, presenting it to him as a stuffed fish, tricks Mafarka into eating the penis. As a result, Mafarka acquires the stallion's violent prowess. With his now hyperbolically elongated member, he brutally "possesses" an unspecified number of maids. He subdues his antagonists, reducing them to powerless femininity, and takes possession of their properties—the Devil's palace and Boubassa's scepter.[22] Mafarka's storytelling abilities play an instrumental role in securing his final victory over Brafane-el-Kibir, supreme chief of the black hordes.[23] If Boubassa, the Devil, and the enemy leader are embodiments of a negative authority figure,[24] the "stuffed fish" that determines the outcome of the power struggle is a degraded phallic symbol. By ingesting this surrogate of the paternal phallus, Mafarka inherits a reign infected with abjection and ruled by violence.

Another possible interpretation of the cloacal fantasy unlocks even more convoluted realms. The choice of anal evacuation as a figure for the male power struggle makes sense within the context of the homoeroticism that saturates Mafarka's tale. The Devil castrates the stallion, feeding the transfigured penis to Mafarka; the latter threatens the Devil with rape and eventually seduces Boubassa—

a feat that leads to the king's overthrow. These fantasies recall the central theme of uncertain borders and affective valences: they play on the slippery boundary between male homosocial and homoerotic bonds, the not-so-obvious underlay of the all-too-obvious abhorrence of women.

The ambivalences that contaminate authority intimate a crisis in the old symbolic order. The corrupt, inept uncle seems to represent political passéism: Boubassa stands for decay, pathology, oppressiveness, and hypocrisy—a constellation of attributes that Marinetti typically associates with the political establishment he rejects. The crisis is manifested by the dissolution of family relationships, no longer held in place under the aegis of paternal symbolic construction. Scenes of a gruesome family romance are conjured up by the jester's riddles, which allude to sibling rivalry, adultery, and parricide.[25] Later, Mafarka's enemies, relatives of his uncle, are fed to the sharks and horribly dismembered. The execution of the two men is a displaced parricide: Ibrahïm-Gandakatale, with his "huge belly" (118), evokes the dropsical Boubassa, who is in turn a surrogate father; Aciaca (Ibrahïm-Gandakatale's son) recalls Magamal in his "feminine frailness" (116). The recurrent motif of the sun's demise also points to a state of crisis in the aged symbolic order. Often characterized as a father, sovereign, or god, the sun symbolizes a less than omnipotent male authority: his belligerent, muscular figure is inevitably defeated by night's languors. At twilight, while the sun "bleeds" to death and the boundaries of day and night are confused, the sky dons the colors of abjection ("the pale sky turned green, and wretchedly began to rot," 139). The monologue that Mafarka addresses to the entropic solar system (52) lends support to this interpretation.[26]

The development of the theme of contagious abjection reaches a climax in the episode that recounts Magamal's homicidal fury and death, the result of the bite of a rabid dog. The abyss of guilt, despair, and self-doubt that engulfs Mafarka as a result of his brother's death echoes his previous (literal) descent into the Whale's Womb. Once again, this crisis is described in terms of inundation, liquefaction, and putrescence as Mafarka receives the first intimation of Magamal's sickness.

> Mafarka [. . .] felt his heart harden like a knot and little by little *flood* his chest with tears.
>
> And the burning pain *liquified* his will, which irked him.
>
> —Have I then been *rotten* since birth, for a single piece of inconsequential news is enough to turn me into *a tear-drenched rag*? (125–126; emphasis added)

Kristeva's psychoanalytical observations provide a gloss to this leitmotiv, linking it to the modern crisis of identity: "fear of being rotten, drained, or blocked," she notes, is the symptom commonly displayed by "patients who have recently come to the couch (borderline cases, false selves, etc.)" (*PH*, 63). The "borderline" case is one in which "the object no longer has, or does not yet have a correlative function bonding the subject. On that location, to the contrary, the vacillating, fascinating, threatening, and dangerous object is silhouetted as non-being—as the abjection into which the speaking being is permanently engulfed" (*PH*, 67). The object, in other words, becomes abject as a consequence of the dissolution of the borders that shore up identity.

Indeed, the threatening abject looms up everywhere, haunting Mafarka as he rushes to Magamal's deathbed. The workings of the crisis are graphically suggested by the disease of rabies, which spreads voraciously throughout the city, particularly among women and children. The rabid dog that bit Magamal now seems to infect Mafarka's imagination, generating a proliferation of monstrous phantasms: the sea, stars, moon, and Mafarka's slave all reproduce the frightful image of the infectious agent (127–128). This technique of obsessive repetition, a trademark of the unconscious, culminates in the description of the room where Magamal's metamorphosis has taken place (134). His horrible transformation is prefigured by the mythological carvings of sphinxes and chimeras that decorate the bridal chamber, now turned into a deathbed. The sculptures provide a clue to the nature of the monstrosity that ravages this scene: both the Chimera and the Sphinx are images of a hybrid nature, a mixture and (con)fusion of differences, which Magamal himself will incarnate in successive paragraphs.[27]

A profusion of gory details illustrates the fragmentation of identity and confusion of codes—human and beast, eros and thanatos, fecundation and destruction—wrought by Magamal's disease, the most extreme manifestation of his horror-inspiring ambiguous nature.

> Mafarka slipped on a soft paste and didn't understand. But *a warm and sweet smell of human sap and putrefaction bit his nostrils*; and his eyes, having little by little adjusted to the semi-darkness, discerned the shreds of a feminine corpse, spread everywhere, all around him, in sinister scatterings, as after a whipping.
>
> [. . . .]
>
> The bed appeared all soiled with *scarlet mud,* and as though broken down by a diabolical struggle. From its hollow inundated with blood emerged an amalgam of hair, vertebrae, and bones which seemed to have been gnawed on by a tiger in heat.
>
> *And Mafarka, his heart floating in a daze, stared for a long time at this pitiful refuse which exuded a black smell of lust.* They were indeed the pitiful remains of the divine Ouarabelli Charchar! . . .
>
> An enormous brown stain attracted his horrified eyes. He got closer. Up there, under the ceiling, there was a strange crouched silhouette, stuck to the top of a column, a blackish monster which looked like both a giant snail and a colossal nocturnal bird. But its contortions were those of a gorilla hanging from a branch, its body crouched and its head buried in its shoulders.
>
> A white flow of slobber was running along the column and dripping onto the floor, punctuating the mourners' chant, which languished nostalgically, as if it had been swept away with fatigue. A distant red barking, in hot pursuit, interrupted it abruptly.
>
> Then, suddenly recognizing Magamal's contracted body on top of the column, Mafarka collapsed to the ground, wringing his hands in despair. (134–135; emphasis added)

This affect-laden description is reminiscent of Mafarka's earlier address to the sensual virgins. The sadistic urge to destroy seductive women announced in that impassioned speech, and later unleashed against the sacred dancers, here finds a climactic outlet via Magamal's madness, which turns a desirable body into bloody, putrid sludge. To paraphrase Marinetti, the text "exudes" a "black lust"—undoubtedly the predominant emotion in this scene, where the smell of· death is perceived as "warm and sweet" (*chaude et sucrée*). Horrified and fascinated, Mafarka does not avert his eyes; he stares, as if lost in a dream, at "this pitiful refuse"—until another shapeless mass, his dehumanized brother, "attracts" him. The scene corresponds strikingly to one that recurs obsessively in the texts analyzed by Theweleit: the transformation of an object (most often a woman's body) into the desired, transfixing perception of a "bloody mass." Theweleit finds the psychological source of this configuration in the soldier male's compulsion to achieve self-differentiation "by mashing others to the pulp he himself threatens to become" (2:274). The macabre lust that inspires such fantasies allows for a violent eruption and flow of emotions without breaching the ego's "integrity." In Mafarka's case, the mechanism fails as he confronts the heartbreaking spectacle of Magamal's death, which irreparably crushes the walls of his "dike," opening the way to a surge of despair, remorse, and melancholia. The implication is that Mafarka falls apart because he has not *entirely* converted his affective energy into aggressive impulses. Unlike his desire for women, successfully transformed into sadistic violence, his fraternal love becomes a self-destructive force. Furthermore, Mafarka's consuming remorse indicates that the two shapeless masses he confronts are produced by the same perverted drive. Just as Magamal, possessed by rabid rage, has chewed apart his loved one, Mafarka's ambitions drive him to sacrifice his brother, whom rabies has transformed into a "brown stain," a bestial "blackish monster." The infecting agents are designated as "dogs of the Sun"—further proof that the solar ideal of glory that "justifies" his sadism toward women is also responsible for the loss of his beloved brother. The designation may seem odd in view of Marinetti's tendency to celebrate virile solar energy and deprecate enfeebling lunar influence; but it is consistent with my argument that Mafarka ingests, or identifies with, a negative, destructive source of power (an abject father figure). Additional evidence in support of this reading can be found in Marinetti's prefuturist works, in which rabid rage is recurrently associated with pride, ambition, and remorse.[28]

Mafarka's feelings of guilt, his suicidal thoughts, and, in particular, his claim to be "the victim of the victim of the dogs of the Sun" (144) suggest that the lost object of love continues to haunt him. Having "destroyed" the other, he becomes contaminated by the other's nature. In the desperate psychological aftermath of Magamal's death, a turning point in the narrative, the ambiguity and self-division initially identified with Magamal are incorporated by Mafarka, who becomes the protagonist of a fatal confusion of roles and codes, leading to his final self-destruction. At play in this metamorphosis is the melancholic strategy of incorporation: the refusal of loss through "internalization" of the one who is lost.[29] The same notion, as we shall see, can be invoked to account for Mafarka's final identification with the maternal ghost.

Magamal might also be regarded as the hero's monstrous double; confronting him triggers the onset of a crisis in which Mafarka displays his own abjection. A turning point in the narrative, Magamal's death signals the protagonist's withdrawal from the human establishment and from political commitment, a total retreat from reality: "Everything was dead; everything was abolished. The city, the walls, the armies had been swept away, far away from him" (136). However, the radical crisis engenders a "religious" fantasy of regeneration: the conception of a new self, immune to the threats that the narrative, striving toward a polarized reconstruction of difference, ultimately conflates with the feminine. Mafarka decides to re-create himself by generating, without any contact with woman, an immortal son. Gazourmah, the pure and incorruptible product of willpower and technology, is free from weakness, disease, death, emotions, and gender confusion. In his founding of a new religion, Marinetti appropriates and revises the Christian dogma of the immaculate "vessel" of divine incarnation: Mafarka, impregnated by a nonperson and without female intervention, achieves a futurist version of the Immaculate Conception. The Church Fathers based their dogma on an association between sexuality and death: in the words of John Chrysostom, "where there is death there is also sexual copulation, and where there is no death there is no sexual copulation either."[30] Marinetti pushes this logic to an extreme of male paranoia. The omnipotent god/machine Mafarka creates in his "ovary" is the embodiment of a defense fantasy targeted against woman's baneful power, that of generating an imperfect life without eternity.

The scene of fecundation imaged as the product of dreamwork invokes a psychoanalytic reading that identifies the symptoms of the crisis even in the conception of its regenerative solution. Mafarka's (pro)creative experience is governed by unconscious mechanisms, as identification with the mother and homoeroticism are displaced in a sublime experience of intercourse with divine solar power. In his dream, the protagonist reaches a velvety, shimmering wheat field and is seized by a desire "to sprawl out in it, with his legs up in the air, like a donkey" (153). As he is lying on his back, the "heavenly body" sets rapidly on him and takes the shape of "a colossal, solid copper hen [*une poule colossale de cuivre massif*], spreading its wings of light over the horizon." The homoerotic configuration of the scene is displaced even further by the feminine gendering of the fertilizing agent—the metamorphosis of the sun into a hen—and by the representation of fecundation as anal evacuation: "When she was very close to him, she flapped her wings, crapped on his eyes, and crashed into his heart." This fantasy, which simultaneously allows for appropriation and denial of the feminine, seems to enact what Freud referred to as the oedipal boy's "wish to be the father of himself."[31] Keller calls attention to the preoedipal subtext in this "poetic" fantasy of the young boy's unconscious: "Through condensation and elision, it allows for the subterranean survival of wishes no longer deemed acceptable, wishes regarded as feminine. Thus, in identifying himself with the race of fathers who can give birth, the young boy can simultaneously assert his independence and safeguard the earlier and conflicting wish for identification with the mother; in presuming to father himself, he satisfies his wish for omnipotent self-sufficiency."[32]

Invoking this deep structure of anxiety and regressive, conflicting wishes helps unravel the puzzling turn of events at the end of the novel. The all-male creative act turns out to be "tainted" by femininity, even though Mafarka's project (expounded in his "futurist Speech") virulently excludes woman from (pro)creation and from the new program of life—"the religion of manifested Will and daily Heroism" (169). Even as Mafarka professes to repudiate his past and ostensibly situates himself beyond desire, his fragmented, self-contradicting speech is overwhelmed by desire.

> As for the distant past of my youth, gone, gone forever! . . . I too experienced nights of love when I liked to blindfold myself with the fresh arms of a virgin . . . And plunged my head into perfumed breasts, in order not to see the multifarious remorse rise like clouds on the horizon. Yes, love, women . . . they can hide the sky for a moment and fill up the empty pits of space . . . But I have erased them from my memory! And yet there were some soft shadows in my country, where the light was gracious and intimate at dusk . . . [. . . .] In the arms of women, I could feel the memory of my daytime weaknesses crawl over my feet, reach up to my heart, feeling their alley over my unknotted, feverish nerve endings, while my imagination had delectable, golden jerks, at the fugitive flight of each sensation . . . All of that is life's poison! . . . So I dreamed and suffered from everything: from living and desiring, from dreaming and listening to my pain in the dark! . . . Poetry! Poetry! Oh sublime decay of the soul! (171–172)

In this poetically and emotionally charged moment, Mafarka appears to remain under the sway of feminine sensuality. Moreover, the homoerotic and incestuous motifs that recur throughout the novel are heavily accented in the conclusion. Mafarka becomes increasingly feminized as he assumes a generative role: he loves his son, as he loved Magamal, in the way that his mother loved her son (158). In addition, the procreation of Gazourmah, initially presented as a male triangular transaction (between Mafarka, God/the Sun, and the son), takes place entirely under the maternal tutelage, and the three-person family ends up being carved out of the material of too many feminine figures.

First, Mafarka is "impregnated" by the virile sun, which then dissolves into the image of a gigantic hen hatching Mafarka's "ideal" egg. The condensation of maleness and femaleness in the sun mirrors Mafarka's own ambivalence, while the dream of hatching recalls the earlier fantasy of Boubassa's "cloacal" parturition. Seen in retrospect, that delivery entails the first stage of a symbolic liberation from the anus qua locus of physical baseness. In Ernest Becker's words, it is "the anal protest of culture," or "the reversal of things with a vengeance: using the locus of animal fallibility as the source of transcendence."[33]

Mafarka then turns to Langourama, his dead mother, as to a venerated, in-spiring goddess. He will bear her a new child—a perfect, immortal version of himself—to replace the lost one: "Yes, in order to comfort your heart and to dis-tract you from your solitude, I bring you a son, my mother, do you hear? . . . The son of your son, the son of my womb!"[34] (159). The aura of veneration that sur-rounds Mafarka's mother apparently sets her apart from the feminine abject. Having been mummified, she is preserved from decay; this fact places Lan-gourama on a metaphorical island of purity, confirmed by the actual location of the Hypogeums on a templelike island. At the same time, Mafarka's veneration of his mother is consistent with his dictum that women can be loved only when they are dead, or rather after they have been killed ("You will love them more when they are dead! . . . But alive, no! no! . . . They cannot live among us!" 122). Fur-thermore, idealization is a form of "devivification" that may harbor latent ag-gression toward the mother.[35] The distance between sacred maternity and abject femininity collapses as Mafarka confronts Coloubbi, Langourama's sexual and monstrous double, the object of desire that emerges from the depths of his past ("cleansed by the memory of a moonlight savored long ago in his childhood," 188). At first, the protagonist abandons himself to the allure of the woman's per-fume "like long ago in his mother's arms" (189). When she draws his mouth to her breasts, however, he responds violently ("Oh! don't make the gesture of my mother! . . . Your breasts are cursed and dried up! . . . Go away!" 193). As the lover conjures up the mother and the two feminine faces are phantasmatically su-perimposed, Coloubbi's breasts become the horror-inspiring image of abjection. Later on, this contamination of the maternal is dramatized as Coloubbi's pig-faced hyena lacerates the mummy's "sweet" face (218).

The theme of ambivalent maternity is played out in recurrent images of breasts and milk. On the one hand, they stand for archetypal pleasure ("the ideal sweetness of maternal milk," 101). On the other, they signify an archaic link to the mother's body (source of an already decay-tainted nourishment) that threatens to swamp the subject's identity.[36] As with the paternal imago, this split representa-tion of the maternal figure originates in the ideal of autonomous individuality. Benjamin offers a poignant account of the dynamics and consequences of such splitting: "On the social level, male rationality sabotages maternal recognition, while on the psychic level, the oedipal repudiation of the mother splits her into the debased and the idealized objects. The reparation for debasing her takes the form of sentimentalizing and idealizing the mother, a strategy that locks both men and women into an inner fantasy world and evades the real issue: recognition of each other" (*BL*, 214–215). The results are deleterious, not only for the mother, who suffers being symbolically idealized and tangibly undermined, but also for the "au-tonomous" subject. "The more the individual repudiates the mother," says Ben-jamin, "the more he is threatened by his own destructiveness and her all-powerful weakness and retaliation" (*BL*, 215). The more the self rejects his dependency, the more he becomes unconsciously dependent on and threatened by the rejected other. When pushed to extremes, the subject's pursuit of absolute independence at the expense of the other paradoxically dead-ends in self-destruction.

Benjamin's analysis of the catastrophic consequences of absolute independence offers a fitting interpretive key for the novel's conclusion, where Mafarka founders in the jumbled waters of the oceanic maternal. The last stage of the transformation that drives him to the ultimate abyss begins when Coloubbi, the dangerous siren who radiates an unrelenting threat to male self-control, returns to the scene of creation, claiming to be the mother and lover of Mafarka's newborn: "You know he is my son, for his first gaze was directed at me! . . . I melted with pleasure beneath the rough caress of his eyes! . . . He is also my lover, and I gave in to all of his whims, in that first gaze!" (215–216). The hero must face the surreptitious power of woman and the infiltrated enemy acting from within his heart (his own violent emotions of jealousy and horror, in Coloubbi's words: "a poison tainted with both terror and love," 217). Again, the call of the feminine draws him into a tenebrous, slimy landscape. As Coloubbi's piercing voice and the lugubrious howls of her hyenas resonate in the sacred cave, Mafarka follows, fearing the profanation of his mother's corpse. What ensues is an emotionally charged encounter with Langourama's mummy, signaling Mafarka's terminal plunge into the maternal.

> It was his mother who was plaintively whispering:
> —Rock me, my child, as I rocked you, long ago! . . .
> Upon hearing these words, Mafarka felt his knees giving away.
> —Yes, yes, my adored mother, I will endlessly rock you, in order to lull you, and for the second time I will close your eyes with extended kisses! Because the time has come! . . . Oh! my mother! kiss me on my forehead like you did long ago, when you used to sit between my brother's bed and mine! . . . And you held your breath so as not to wake us up! . . . I am so little, mother, and I am frightened like a child, when the desert wind suddenly blows open the door to death, on stormy nights! Be happy! Forget me!
> —Here, Mafarka, I offer my lips behind the wood of the sarcophagus . . . Yes! Yes! I feel the warmth of your lips! . . .
> —Mother! Mother! I adore you more than my youth! . . .
> —Mafarka, kiss also my son for me, on the lips! . . . Do not forget! (220–221)

Langourama's legacy is a kiss of death: it terminally infects the hero with "maternal" love for Gazourmah, precipitating his lapse into feminine abjection. As Mafarka fulfills his mother's wish, the lofty intention of transfusing his élan vital into Gazourmah's sculpted mouth through the mandated kiss gives place to a (presumably maternal) "murderous desire," an impulse to bite or devour that his "paternal will" resists (223). Torn by a morbid attachment to his creature, the protagonist ultimately transforms into a jealous, paranoid, enwrapping mother unwilling to abandon "his beloved work of art [. . .] to the bleak future" (223).[37] He clings to Gazourmah's neck "like a heavy necklace of tenderness" (223), thus becoming the ballast that the newborn hero must drop in order to ascend from the earth. The impatient Gazourmah flings his creator away "just as a furious bull frees himself from the yoke" flattening him, like a "drenched rag," against a rock (224). The image that seals Mafarka's death is the *terminus ad quem* of the motif previously associated with the hero's crisis of self-control: his unsettling doubt, his fear of being "rotten," is thus realized. Tracing this motif to the prehistory of futurism, we can view Mafarka's lot as the realization of the death wish announced by the poetic "I"—the frustrated idealist—at the beginning of *Destruction*. "Fatally inebriated with the Infinite," the poet's dream must be submerged in the gigantic "vat" of the sea, fermenting with "old frantic musts" (*SF*, 153–154).

Finally, Gazourmah crushes the mother/mistress Coloubbi. The whole earth is torn apart by volcanic forces erupting from its bowels, and the new hero rises to conquer the skies in a climax of apocalyptic delight (228–229). Gazourmah's parricide and matricide, followed by annihilation of the mother earth, put a drastic end to the spread of contagion. Fear, guilt, self-doubt, ambivalence, and impotence are finally expunged in the triumph of an all-male creation predicated on destruction and distancing—the ideal architecture of a totalizing thought with no ambivalent residues.

TOTAL ART

Mafarka's tragic story places the abject (which the manifestos tend to project onto the "other side") within the confines of the self. Desire opens breaches in the subject's bounded, autonomous self, allowing the abject to infiltrate and dissolve the barriers between male and female, interior and exterior, pure and impure. Finally, the advent of Gazourmah mends the fragmented identity, polarizing difference and reconstituting wholeness. Such a solution is mythical, in that it proceeds by means of exclusion, according to the logic of myths and rituals: in Girardian terms, the progressive erosion of all boundaries is reversed through an act of generative violence. Woman's contaminated matrix is liquidated, and the expenditure is capitalized on in order to construct a fiction of power that inflates the limits of (male) subjectivity beyond the human. The founding myth of the futurist "religion" differs in significant ways from those of ancient religions. As previously noted, the scapegoating mechanism does not successfully displace the effects of the crisis onto one "sacrificial victim." Rather, the whole earth is sacrificed: instead of the restoration of the community's order and sense of unity through the sacrifice of an individual, the novel dramatizes the destruction of the community for the sake of boundless individual creativity. Rejection of the natural/traditional/communal realm does not quite square with the generally shared assumption that fascist mythology typically valorizes the organic, the down to earth, and the unity of the people in the homeland.[38] Mafarka's new religion, however, does anticipate the regime's rhetoric of self-sacrificial heroism and its catastrophic results.

Readers familiar with the work of Theweleit may have noticed correspondences between the futurist fiction of power and the *Freikorps'* male fantasies.

Marinetti's mythopoeia pivots on some of the central axes around which, according to Theweleit, the novels of the soldier males perpetually revolve: "nonfemale creation," "rebirth," "the rise upward to hardness and tension [. . .] from a world that is rotten and sinking," in the "morass of femaleness" (2:360–361). The fundamental trait that links these fantasies and denotes their kinship with totalitarian ideologies is a desire to expand individual limits through identification with "absolute" totalities. However, the soldier male's extended boundaries coincide with rigidly hierarchical totality formations, such as the army, whereas the soaring Gazourmah is enveloped in the "total music" and "poetry" created by his own wings.

> Suddenly, a suave and strange melody charmed his ears, just as his flight was slowing its pace.
>
> He then realized that it was coming from his wings, more resonant and lively than two harps. Drunk with enthusiasm, he playfully modulated these harmonious rhythms, languishing over each vibration, pushing ever higher their exalted returns.
>
> That is how the world's great hope, *the great dream of total music*, finally came into being in Gazourmah's flight . . . The soaring of all of the earth's songs ended in the grand flapping of inspired wings! . . . *Sublime hope of Poetry! longing for fluidity!* Noble counsels of smoke and flames! (232–233; emphasis added)

As compared to military institutions, the "totality machine" of art allows for more "fluidity" (and less susceptibility to alienation) in individual desire. While the soldier male's "rise upward" is supported by discipline and antisexual organization of libidinal drives, Gazourmah's flight is sustained by sexual tension with the feminine breezes, making a timely display of his virile prowess. Great emphasis, however, is placed on the hero's contemptuous detachment from his lovers: "Like a swimmer's hand which *hits* the wave, his mistress, nonchalantly leaning on her and then *thrusting* his body forward . . . like a tired lover slipping out of the bed of a sleeping woman, that's how I will fly! [. . . .] It is *by force* that I will open up a pathway through your flaccid hips, and my weight will allow me to keep balance under your *brutal* caresses!" (227; emphasis added). The "force" that resounds in these words (amplified by repetitions and exclamations) ultimately bespeaks a connection with the antisexual violence that reverberates in the writings of the soldier males. Arguably, the noted differences between sexual and antisexual scenarios are related to cultural factors such as upbringing and the social structuring of gender roles, which produce varying degrees and modes of absorption of individual desire into external totality formations.

My examination of futurist erotica in chapter 4 will further verify and expound the sexual configuration of Marinetti's fantasies. For the moment, it is important to note that the conclusion of *Mafarka* is consistent with the "logic" underlying the gender-inflected rhetoric of the manifestos. According to this logic, the feminine other cannot be totally obliterated; if it were, all boundaries (including those that demarcate gender differences) would crumble and the subject would be lost in the resulting chaos. Therefore, when the "absolute" self triumphs at the cost of the world's destruction, the text immediately re-creates tension by filling the void with personified breezes that provide the necessary friction for Gazourmah's flight. Furthermore, the superman's defiant challenge to the Sun, "the scarlet Emperor" (232), and his imperial ambitions to conquer the infinite in a sort of science fiction star wars re-create the necessary antagonist for an externalized conflict— "the eternal enemy that we would have to invent if it did not exist" (*TIF*, 16).

The delirious tone of Marinetti's fantasy invites a comparison with psychotic delusions. Mafarka's story is the psychodrama of a self unable to cope with the horrors of life and death except by a solution much like the psychotic's: a split between the symbolic self and the body and an escape into an imaginary fabrication of megalomanic self-expansion, magical omnipotence, and immortality. Marinetti's fantasies provide a caricature of "normal" defensive mechanisms, exposing the link between creation and delusion; in Becker's words, a condition of uprooting from cultural programming into life.[39] For the futurists, as for other modern artists, such a condition coincides with the sense of a rupture, or lack of organic continuity, between the modern world and the cultural constructs that are supposed to make sense of it. Marinetti envisages his utopian solution in terms of rejection and transcendence of the natural order, through the death of the old "I" and the parthenogenesis of a new hero delivered from abject reality and free to ascend to a luminous reign of the future. Gazourmah's flight hyperbolically illustrates a relationship to the past that is characteristic of modernity. Paul de Man describes it as "a desire to wipe out whatever came earlier, in the hope of reaching at least a point that could be called a true present, a point of origin that marks a new departure."[40] The ideal egg that hatches Mafarka's "conception" is a grotesque metaphor for the creative labors of modernism. Indeed, it recalls the caricatural picture of the modern literary scene depicted by a disgruntled contemporary critic: "For the healthy-minded man of today it is a matter of complete indifference what alien cuckoo's eggs the more extreme specialists of the Modern hatch out in their little *fin-de-siècle* chapels and brothels, wagging their little 'isms' like tails behind them: symbolism, satanism, neo-idealism, hallucinism . . . Give things a few years, and no cocks will crow for any of this ultra-modern charlatanism practised by these comic turns of literature and art."[41]

The novel's mix of *superomismo*, hyperbolic tone, and exotic setting calls for comparison with the genre of the serialized novel, or feuilleton. As already mentioned, Rinaldi disparagingly classifies *Mafarka* in that genre and accuses Marinetti of plagiarizing Emilio Salgari's novels while passing himself off as an avant-garde artist. His reading, however, is not supported by the theoretical framework of a structural and ideological analysis of the genre, such as that provided by Umberto Eco in *Il superuomo di massa*. Marinetti's text differs from a typical popular novel in one crucial respect: Mafarka's existential brooding, manic-depressive swings, and tragic destiny define him as a problematic hero, unlike those of Salgari and, in general, the one-dimensional protagonists of the feuilleton, who are always destined to success. His dramatic vicissitudes narrate a crisis of values that leads to the creation of a new symbolic order. As Eco points out, the aim of the *romanzo popolare* (popular novel) is to gratify the reader's desire for entertainment and evasion: its ideological structure tends to confirm current systems of expectations and values. The most important question raised by such a comparison is not whether Marinetti was influenced by Salgari's novels or by other feuilletons, or whether *Mafarka* should be classified as a romanzo popolare. Rather, it is the question of locating the ideological roots of the superuomo myth, the origins of which seem to extend into the cultural terrain of the nineteenth century, traversing boundaries between high and low literature, between philosophy and the popular novel. Expanding on Antonio Gramsci's insights, Eco argues that the superuomo is created in the forge of the serial story and only later ascends to philosophy.[42] The most significant ideological trait of this pervasive myth—or, in Eco's words, the "original sin" of the superuomo—consists of its separating the exceptional individual from the people: even the positive hero of the "democratic" popular novel, the earliest phase in the history of the genre, is the "bearer of an authoritarian (paternalistic, self-warranted, and self-grounded) solution of society's contradictions, over the heads of its passive members."[43]

In his role as a leader, Mafarka bears the mark of this "original sin": his subjects are mere slaves that he can sacrifice to his ambitions. Later, the same master-slave dynamic is reproduced in his relationship with the masses of workers that he needs to realize "the great sublime creation" (184). The hybrid nature of Mafarka's prodigious child points to a link between the creative experience staged in the novel, which mythicizes the futurist project, and the productive process of modern industry, which stands as an icon of mass culture. Gazourmah flies like an airplane and is termed a "mechanical bird"; he is created by the quasi-divine genius of Mafarka, who sculpts him from the wood of a young oak and then concocts a mysterious formula to transform vegetable fibers into living flesh and solid muscles, but he is also the product of manual labor—the skilled "weavers of Lagahourso" and the brutal "blacksmiths of Milmillah." Significantly, these enslaved masses are presented in a negative light, even though their contribution to the project is indispensable: their material concerns and divisive greed threaten to compromise the "sublime" enterprise. Mafarka's contempt and his assumption that he must withdraw from the social establishment in order to realize his spiritual mission equally bear witness to a persistent elitist/romantic bias in Marinetti's avant-gardist assimilation of mass culture. Furthermore, Mafarka's rejection of the political realm and Gazourmah's final flight from reality prefigure the developments of the futurist movement in the years of fascism, during which Marinetti renounces politics and embraces a consolatory, escapist conception of art.

Gazourmah himself may be said to embody an ideal of escapist aestheticism. In his initial ascent, buoyed by sensual breezes, he is in control of the feminine element, which serves as an antithetical force capable of polarizing differences—a medium of aggressive self-affirmation, rather than exploration of difference. Once the New Man's maleness is unmistakably established, however, his libidinal energy is sublimated into pure aesthetic pleasure. Realizing the romantic "dream of total music," Gazourmah creates a new art that, detached from the feminine and human, soars high above them. The new symbolic order of "harmony" ultimately receives the designation of *Poetry*, "Sublime espoir de la Poésie!" The reader's attention thus culminates in issues of writing, authorial control, and literary genealogy. The final emphasis on aesthetic transcendence is only one of a number of clues that identify Mafarka's drama as a tension between a feminine-connoted, "putrid" poetry of the past (172), which still retains its hold on Mafarka's (and Marinetti's) "soul," and the virile, "metallic," voluntarist aesthetic of futurism, which requires a drastic uprooting from the decadent literary tradition. As we have seen, Mafarka's father is an author, a creative genius who embodies the oppressive weight of the past. Mafarka himself is cast into the role of artist at two different points in the narrative. In the episode entitled "The Stratagem of Mafarka-el-Bar," he becomes a "comedian" (50) and a "storyteller" (56), and the illusionistic power of his storytelling is enough to vanquish his enemies. The most substantial manifestation of his identity as artist, however, occurs when he relinquishes the scepter to re-create himself in a living sculpture.

Mafarka's conversion to his new vocation contains disguised elements of an ideologeme much exploited in decadent literature: sickness and convalescence as necessary conditions for the development of an aesthetics attuned to the new times. In her insightful study of the decadent and antidecadent rhetoric of sickness, Spackman analyzes the various steps of the artist's "regeneration" or "aesthetic conversion": the liquidation of the crowd and expulsion of woman from the scene of creation; the return to a childlike state of conscience as a condition of tabula rasa and renewed, sharpened perception; and the feminization of the artist, whereby "the mind's activity is described in terms of corporeal activity marked as feminine."[44] Spackman argues that convalescence and femininity function in this context as figures for "psychic alterity"—in other words, for a renewed relationship between body and thought, the desire for which implies a valorization of the corporeal, a coming to terms with the irrational roots of the mind. Referring in particular to Nietzsche (unquestionably one of Marinetti's intellectual fathers), she observes that the new philosopher in *The Gay Science* is figured as a convalescent and a "mother-type." On the one hand, the borderline condition of convalescence is valorized as a desirable state, in that it stands for perceptiveness to the urgings of the body and mobility of perspective (i.e., a perspective that avoids totalizing solutions). On the other hand, maternity represents "a supposed, peculiarly female, interanimation between mind and body" characteristic of the convalescent philosopher's creative ability. "We philosophers are not free to divide body from soul as the people do; we are even less free to divide soul from spirit. We are not thinking frogs, nor objectifying and registering mechanisms with their innards removed: constantly we have to give birth to our thoughts out of our pain and, like mothers [*mütterlich*], endow them with all we have of blood, heart, fire, pleasure, passion, agony, conscience, fate and catastrophe."[45]

Initially, the story of Marinetti's artist-hero appears to conform to the decadent topos of the aesthetic conversion. Strictly speaking, Mafarka suffers no illness, but the despair caused by his brother's death entails the psychical and physical symptoms of illness, as if he had himself been bitten by the rabid dog. As already noted, the stricken hero withdraws from the social establishment to find a new abode in a sacred island, where he then liquidates his crowd of sailors (164). During his "nocturnal voyage," he is healed and purified by the therapeutic power of music (145–146). It is at this moment that the idea of a son with melodious wings is conceived. The very same music, however, reveals an affinity with "putrid poetry" and a link with feminine abjection: "The music alternatively slowed and became impassioned, like a lusty caress swollen with love and murder" (146–147). Indeed, the caressing melody causes "a bloody brawl" in Mafarka's heart and entices him into an almost fatal sleep that leaves him exposed to a traitor's murderous plot. Later, as he moves through the oneiric scene of his "fecundation," the topos of the childlike artist is evoked: "Gliding over those ephemeral images, the king suddenly felt overwhelmed by the childish pride of a young naive artist. [. . . .] A new light penetrated his eyes in supple, bright spurts that cleansed his soul and, little by little, arranged his exhausted body in a bath of ineffably icy, bluish, pristine sleep" (153). Finally, the artist assumes a feminine role when his ideal egg is fertilized by the sun. As in the narratives analyzed by Spackman, woman is excluded from the creative process so that her creative function may be appropriated. For Mafarka, this is the first step into the lethal feminizing sway of the maternal, which will provoke his regenerative death—a prerequisite to the birth of a new artist whose music is "total" and whose scope of activity is infinite.

In the final creation scene, Marinetti radically departs from the topos of decadence: he abandons the notion of art grounded in pathology and in the feminine body, just as Gazourmah "liquidates" (both in the sense of disposing of and, literally, reducing to a liquid state) his feminized father and his earthly feminine matrix. Mafarka's violent family romance is paralleled by the parricidal avowals of manifestos such as "Noi rinneghiamo i nostri maestri simbolisti ultimi amanti della luna" in which Marinetti repudiates his symbolist origins. Written three years before "words in freedom" and still weighed down by the fetters of conventional syntax and by symbolist imagery, Marinetti's genealogical tale of parricide, self-regeneration, and destruction of origins narrates his determination to create a new aesthetic free of links with the past. The music produced by Gazourmah's mechanical wings prefigures the aesthetic of "geometric and mechanical splendor" elaborated in the manifesto of 1914. As we shall see in the following chapters, however, neither the old "putrid" poetry nor the feminine phantasms created by desire are ever totally excised from Marinetti's writing. His production following the 1912–1914 technical revolution confirms Coloubbi's prophecy: "If you kill me, I will be reborn, I will be born again and again in your son's heart, like a poison tainted with terror and love!" (217). The penalty for killing the mother is to be haunted by the return of the repressed.

FOUR

The Heart with Watertight Compartments and the Travel-Size Woman

Futurist Strategies in Love and War

We are convinced that love—sentimentalism and lust—is the least natural thing in the world. Only coitus, the purpose of which is the futurism of the species, is natural and important.[1]

While celebrating the advent of metallized, mechanized man, Marinetti's futurist manifestos posit a radical stance against love, both in its erotic and in its sentimental aspects.[2] Entirely consistent with this crusade is his political program for devaluating marriage and the family, first elaborated in the 1918 "Manifesto del partito futurista italiano" (Manifesto of the Italian Futurist Party). Its agenda included abolition of the marital license, easily obtainable divorce, and the advent of free love (*TIF*, 154).[3] Once the unnatural hypocrisy of love is exposed and eradicated, Marinetti observes, sexuality will be confined to its biological function— reproduction of the species.

On the whole, however, Marinetti's output belies this forceful credo. Eroticism saturates his work, particularly during and after World War I. Furthermore, the last years of Marinetti's career saw the production of several texts in which the affective dimension of love, along with other previously rejected values, is recuperated. Under close scrutiny, Marinetti's statements seem puzzlingly inconsistent. Little wonder, then, that critics lack in interpretive consensus. While Macciocchi, for instance, valorizes Marinetti's antibourgeois, revolutionary sexual policy, Spackman identifies its reactionary underpinnings. Such conflicting readings point to elements of ideological continuity and discontinuity between futurism and fascism. Marinetti's nationalistic rhetoric of virility and his insistent concern with the fecundity of the "race" foreshadow reactionary fascist rhetoric, in which sexuality becomes a matter of national import. However, his anticonventional pronouncements also resonate with earlier, socialist positions. The attack on bourgeois mores and the program of free love and divorce propounded by the Futurist party had had wide currency among the socialists in the debate on the "woman question," which had been raging in the forum of *Critica Sociale* since the early 1890s. By contrast, fascist propaganda celebrated familial values and the role of woman as mother and "angel of the house."[4]

79

As Piero Meldini remarks, fascist efforts at institutionally controlling female desire and behavior were provoked by capitalist society's radical disruption of the patriarchal family. Unable to react, or perhaps even to identify, the causes of socioeconomic crisis, fascist leaders concentrated on such symptoms of modernization as women's changing familial and social role and the decline in population statistics. Such antifeminism was neither an isolated nor a specifically fascist phenomenon. Its roots can be traced to earlier manifestations of nationalism, as well as Catholic reaction. Their common inspiration was the ideal of a static, hierarchical organization of family and society. Likewise, fascism's call for a reconfiguration of gender roles can be seen as a recycling and politicization of positivist anthropology's "scientific" justification of oppression against women. Alarm over and policies enacted to counter demographic decline were a broad European phenomenon, fostered by anxieties about the decline of the West in the face of perceived advances by nonwhite peoples. Antifeminism, like other manifestations of fascism, was ultimately rooted in the general desire for economic and social revanche among the masses, whose discontent constituted the basis for fascist consensus.

Sandra Puccini emphasizes that resistance to women's emancipation was common and deeply rooted at all social levels, from the working class to the intelligentsia (including leftist intellectuals).[5] Within the working class, she notes, male antagonism toward working women was exacerbated during the postwar crisis, when veterans reclaimed the jobs taken over by women during the war (39). Surveying the various, sometimes divergent, pronouncements by socialist intellectuals on the "woman question," Puccini detects reactionary concerns about the consequences of the dissolution of patriarchal authority. For instance, concerns voiced by the socialist Mario Pilo in *Critica Sociale* foreshadow the apocalyptic assessments of family degeneration in *Critica Fascista*. "Heaven help us," Pilo admonishes, "if everybody in the house had the power to command and nobody the duty to obey: there would be a lack of discipline in the family; ruin would inevitably follow" (60).

The status of women beyond Italy's borders confirms that the antifeminist obsession traversed chronological, ideological, and national boundaries in the prefascist and fascist periods. Focusing on French literature and culture, Michelle Perrot discusses the phenomenon of antifeminism in relation to the "masculinity crisis," which developed concomitantly with the new feminine identity and found a heroic outlet in World War I.[6] Other analyses of the impact of World War I and World War II on women in Great Britain and the United States indicate that military discourse on all sides was imbued with misogynistic feeling. In all the combatant nations, including the so-called liberal ones, policies directed at women aimed at reinforcing patriarchal organicist notions of gender relations: the social and professional subordination of women to men was endorsed, and motherhood was celebrated as a natural function of all women. In other words, the repressive encoding of gender roles was a widespread reaction to modern attempts to reshape gender roles—a reaction that was exacerbated during wartime and during periods of crisis, such as the economic crises coinciding with the first affirmation and successive consolidation of fascist power in 1922 and in the late 1920s.

Seen from a rigid ideological perspective, Marinetti's discourse on love appears hopelessly ensnared in contradiction and ambivalence. Seen against its historical backdrop and through a nuanced psychological prism, it is revealed as a shifting defense strategy against the decaying structure of gender domination—a complex reaction to the myriad changes in gender roles and power relations that threatened male identity in modern society.

GRIM PICTURES OF THE HOME FRONT

A large number of texts in a variety of genres (pamphlet, manifesto, newspaper editorial, short story, synthetic theater, social-erotic novel) attest that the increasingly active role played by women in modern society was a persistent source of concern for the futurists.[7] Marinetti addresses questions of sexual politics at different times and in different contexts. Particularly interesting are those in which he abrogates mythmaking and propaganda, focusing instead on gender relations in contemporary society: here we find grim pictures of life in the modern family. In the 1919 "Contro il matrimonio" (Against Marriage), for instance, he saw women's entry into the workforce (which World War I had greatly accelerated) as undermining traditional gender roles and power relations.

> The vast participation of women in the national work produced by the war has created a recurring grotesque of matrimony: The husband had money or was earning it, now he has lost it and is hardly able to make any more.
>
> His wife works and finds a way of earning good money at a time when life is essentially expensive.
>
> Because of her job, the wife has little need for a life of domesticity, whereas the nonworking husband's activities are all focused on an absurd preoccupation with domestic order.
>
> Complete overturning of a family in which the husband has become a useless woman with the overbearing ways of a man and the wife has doubled her human and social value.
>
> Inevitable clash between the two partners, conflict and defeat of the man. (*TIF*, 371)

In this economic view of the postwar home front, women's enhanced value erodes both male privilege in the public sphere and patriarchal authority in the family, resulting in man's devaluation and "grotesque" degen(d)eration. Although the discourse on woman's sexuality is formulated in terms of a struggle against hypocritical, repressive mores and institutions, and in spite of his professed concern for the liberation of woman from the slavery of "marriage as legal prostitution" (*TIF*, 371), Marinetti's attempted subversion of the family ultimately becomes a reactionary assault on woman. Her value is reappropriated as a national asset: "Woman does not belong to a man, but to the future and development of the race" (*TIF,* 370).[8]

Nevertheless, the general focus of Marinetti's argument is not on the future and enhancement of the race but on salvation of the male as individual, threatened by family life and by woman's "contagious" will to corrupt and corrode his identity. Here recurs a familiar strain of imagery. The dissolution of identity evokes the specter of castration and a retinue of images of abjection.

> The family, as it is presently constituted, by marriage without recourse to divorce, is absurd, harmful and prehistoric. Almost always a prison. Often a Bedouin tent full of a lurid mixture of old invalids, women, children, pigs, asses, camels, hens and dung.
>
> [. . . .]
>
> The most energetic and marked characters wear themselves out in this unceasing friction of elbows.
>
> There is an outbreak of infection and sometimes an actual epidemic of exaggerated stupidities, catastrophic manias, nervous *tics* that develops into the mechanistic regimentation of German troops or the ragtag confusion of emigrants packed in a ship's hold. (*TIF*, 368; emphasis in original)

> Little boys—according to us—must develop far away from little girls so that their first games can be distinctly masculine—lively, pugnacious, muscular, and violently dynamic—in other words, free from all emotional morbidity, all womanly delicacy. (*TIF*, 370)

The modern family is a confusion, contamination, and erosion of differences: between young and old, male and female, human and nonhuman, strong and weak, sane and insane, foreign and germane. Marinetti's phobic scenario testifies to the deep-seated fears mobilized by the collapse of social structures. Woman functions as a pole of merging anxieties: the rhetoric of abjection establishes the connection between woman in her social, historical reality (as partner in the modern family) and in her mythical form (as Magna Mater, eternal feminine). The remedy that Marinetti proposes—the "liberation" of woman from her maternal role through state-run child rearing ("il figlio di Stato" or child of the State)—results in a more crucial liberation of man from the threat of the engulfing feminine: "We will finally abolish the mixing of males and females, which—during the early years—produces a harmful effeminizing of males" (*TIF*, 370; fig. 3).[9]

Announcing his plan to destroy, along with marriage, the property of wives, Marinetti advocates a "new" kind of relationship between the sexes. Resorting to the topos of woman as field, to be "worked" by the plowman, he postulates, "We want to abolish not only the ownership of land, but also the ownership of women. Whoever cannot work his land must forfeit it. Whoever cannot give his woman joy and strength must never force his embrace and his company upon her" (*TIF*, 369). This metaphor evokes the idea of a different, primitive kind of property, based on the "natural" right of the strongest, most able *maschio*, rather than on the legal right of marriage. Concerns about male identity are conflated with those relating to the biological production of manpower (the destiny of the "race") and

Fig. 3. "Futurismo e maternità": Benedetta Cappa Marinetti with her daughters Vittoria and Ala. *Oggi e domani*, 27 November 1930, 2. Reprinted courtesy of the National Library of Florence.

the patriarchal power system (of moneymaking and decision making) in the family. The control of female sexuality and gender roles is bound up with efforts to reinforce the boundaries of identity and preserve socioeconomic privilege.[10]

Self-defense, then, is the primary impetus for Marinetti's unconventional tirade against marriage and the family. At stake is the complete destruction of institutions that, because they are in crisis, threaten the foundations of patriarchy and male identity. Marinetti's remedy: allow the disease to run its decadent course. Once the old, inefficient sociosymbolic structures have collapsed, new and revitalized ones may emerge to take their place.

A similar strategy is at work in "Contro l'amore e il parlamentarismo." Marinetti declares himself in favor of women's access to the political scene because, he prophesies, their emancipation will precipitate the last stage of decay in both the parliamentary system ("Let women hasten, with lightning speed, to give proof of the total animalization of politics," *TIF*, 295) and in the family ("feminism's victory and especially women's influence on politics will hasten the demise of the principle of the family," *TIF*, 296). Implicit in this argument, especially in the term "animalization," is the infamous "scorn for woman," glossed as contempt for the conventional (erotic, sentimental, idealistic) conception of woman/love: "We despise woman conceived as the sole ideal, the divine vessel of love, the poison woman, the tragic plaything, the fragile woman, obsessing and fatal" (*TIF*, 292).[11] The contempt is further qualified when Marinetti, referring to the contemporary debate on "the supposed inferiority of woman," considers the determinant role of sociohistorical factors: "we think that if [women's] bodies and spirits had been subjected, over many generations, to the same education of spirit and body as have been men, it would perhaps be possible to speak of equality between the sexes" (*TIF*, 293). This stance appears progressive in comparison with the biologistic arguments that still prevailed in intellectual and political circles.[12] As Spackman observes, however, such consideration "is equivocal at best, for equality is postponed until some future, and rather dubious ('sarebbe forse possibile') date."[13] Emphasis is placed on women's present condition: their "intellectual and erotic slavery," their "absolute inferiority in character and intelligence" (*TIF*, 293).

Within the discourse on inferiority and ineptitude emerges a sort of counterdiscourse—a stance that is not so haughtily and contemptuously self-assured. Evoking a different, powerful and threatening, picture of contemporary women, Marinetti predicts that their "aggressive entry" into the political arena will have the explosive effect of "dynamite" (*TIF*, 294); their "resentful claws" will kill the parliamentary system (*TIF*, 295); their emancipation will result both in "pacifism," synonymous with emasculation, and in a more dangerous kind of belligerence: "We will have [. . .] the war of the sexes, undoubtedly prepared by the great agglomerations of capital cities, love of nightlife, and the regularization of working women's salaries" (*TIF*, 296). Given the possibility of a future urban war, the end of the traditional family seems more a matter of necessity and endurance than a desired goal. "If the family, suffocator of vital energies, disappears," Marinetti concludes, "*we will try* to do without it" (*TIF*, 296–297; emphasis added). The choice of phrasing is telling; it suggests an attempt to deal with loss and adapt to historical developments that are beyond men's control.

SOUR GRAPES

Could a similar mechanism account for Marinetti's attack on love? "Contro l'amore e il parlamentarismo" presents some evidence to this effect. The scornful denunciation of love as "the least natural thing in the world" (see the quote at the beginning of this chapter) is followed by a passage that offers a different angle: "Love—romantic obsession and voluptuousness—is nothing but an invention of poets, who gave it to humanity . . . And poets will take it away from humanity as if withdrawing a manuscript from the hands of a publisher who has shown himself to be incapable of printing it decently" (*TIF*, 293). Poets, in other words, are to reclaim their original creation—uncorrupted love—and repudiate the "product," which has been perverted in its encounter with the marketplace. Since the original version (the "manuscript") fails as a blueprint for actual relationships, Marinetti welcomes any change that divests woman of her sentimental and sexual appeal and thus facilitates the attainment of the ultimate goal, which is nothing short of total liberation from the "tyranny" of love: "In our campaign for liberation, the suffragettes are our most useful collaborators, because the more rights and powers they win for woman, the more she will be deprived of love, and the more she will cease to be a furnace [*focolare*] of sentimental passion and lust" (*TIF*, 293). Politicization empowers woman in the social arena but impoverishes her in the arena of love, where she (eventually) ceases to be a "focolare" of passion or, one might say, a "focolaio" (hotbed) of the malady of love. Like the campaign against marriage and the family, the futurist "effort of liberation" seems to be a reaction to a breakdown of values and institutions that men (and poets in particular) have endured and not initiated. Marinetti's attitude toward love begins to sound like the Aesopean fox: the greener the grapes, the easier it is to scorn them.

Contrary to antipasséist rhetoric, in which femininity (associated with nature and tradition) is synonymous with resistance to change, the discourse on the shifting socioeconomic structuration of gender roles targets women as the primary agents of change, signified by a revolution in their sexual behavior. How can we reconcile these seemingly contradictory representations? Woman, for the futurists, is a two-faced icon. One face is traditional, with static, eternal features; it looks backward, toward nature and the past, and symbolizes their fetters. The other is artificial and modern; adulterated by contemporary materialism, it looks to the future, evoking undesirable change.

As early as 1913, in "Distruzione della sintassi—Immaginazione senza fili— Parole in libertà," the following excursus on the contemporary depreciation of love sounds a jarring note in the celebration of the modern phenomena that have become elements of the new futurist sensibility.

> 8. Depreciation of love (sentimentalism or lust), produced by the greater freedom and erotic ease of women and by the universal exaggeration of female luxury. Let me explain: Today women love luxury more than love. A visit to a famous dressmaker's shop, escorted by a banker friend, pot-bellied and gouty but willing to pay, easily replaces the most passionate meeting with an adored young man. The woman finds all the mysteries of love in the selection of an extraordinary ensemble, the latest fashion, which her friends still do not have. The man does not love the woman who lacks luxury. The lover no longer has any prestige, Love has lost its absolute value. A complex question: all I can do is to touch briefly upon it. (*TIF*, 67)

According to Marinetti's diagnosis, the depreciation of *Amore* is a consequence, not of the futurist campaign against inflated "absolute values," but, rather, of changes in women's behavior (values and desires): increased (sexual) freedom and the excessive desire for conspicuous consumption brought about by a modern, liberated, materialistic way of life. It is especially the passion for fashionable apparel, according to Marinetti, that destroys women's sensuality and sentimentality. In view of the declared futurist objectives, such a change should be welcomed. Yet there is a distinct lack of enthusiasm for this by-product of modernity, as well as a certain nostalgia for the times when Love had "absolute value" and the lover ("adored young man") retained "prestige." The conclusive remark couples lack of enthusiasm with a reluctance to confront deeper, more complex implications.

These truncated reflections are taken up in "Contro il lusso femminile" (Against Feminine Extravagance; 1920), where Marinetti again correlates increasing luxury and decreasing lust, decrying disdain for love, in stronger and more explicit terms than previously, as a pathological phenomenon to be resisted. Women's passion for luxurious toilettes is construed as disease ("toilettite") and promiscuity; by killing love, they undermine the male "monopoly" and social order.

> 2. More and more, this morbid mania forces women to a masked but unavoidable prostitution. It happens in all walks of life, this careless and vain offering of the female body embellished by the *toilette*. Changing three *toilettes* a day is tantamount to displaying one's body in the window to a market of male buyers. The offering decreases her worth by diminishing her rarity and mystery [*L'offerta ribassa il valore di preziosità e di mistero*]. The offering drives away the male, who scorns loose women, who wants to discover and fight for his pleasure.
> 3. The public offering, even if it is not followed by a sale, eliminates the potential for monopolization. In order to desire, the male must be able to believe in this potential. (*TIF*, 546–547; emphasis in original)

Because it suggests an inconsistent attitude toward capitalism, Marinetti's use of marketplace terminology is intriguing. If male desire hinges on the "potential for monopolization," it follows that the economic system in which the concept of monopoly occurs is also a prerequisite. Yet it is precisely the artificial values and exchange mechanisms of capitalist commodification that Marinetti holds responsible for corrupting woman's desire and natural appeal, as well as (through contagion) man's virility. The apparent contradiction may be explained by referring to a distinction or tension between an exchange-oriented economy and the monopolist fetishism of commodities—the constitutive contradiction at the ideological heart of capitalism itself. On closer scrutiny, however, Marinetti invokes a more primitive value system.

> Jewels and fabrics, sweet to the touch, destroy in the male *his ability to savor the touch of the female flesh* [*l'assaporamento tattile della carne femminile*]. Perfumes are equally detrimental to true desire, as they seldom cooperate with the scents of the skin, often unpleasantly combining with them, always distracting and diverting the male's olfactory imagination.
>
> The male gradually loses *the power to sense the female flesh* [*il senso potente della carne femminile*] and replaces it with a faltering, totally artificial sensibility, that responds only to silk, velvet, jewels and furs.
>
> It is becoming harder and harder to find males capable of taking and *tasting* a beautiful woman without worrying about the *side dish* [*contorno*] and the touch of fabrics, shimmerings and colors. The naked woman is no longer pleasing. The males turn into jewelers, perfumers, tailors, milliners, launderers, embroiderers and pederasts. [. . . .]
>
> 7. This morbid mania increases woman's vanity to ridiculous proportions, takes her away from the male, and drives her to the banker. (*TIF*, 547; emphasis added)

The monopoly envisaged by Marinetti resembles a private hunting ground, established by means of virile prowess, rather than through the "artificial" power of money. Undoubtedly, Marinetti attacks the commodification of love for its deleterious effects on the "natural" value of masculinity, not for its reifying effects on woman. The object of desire evoked in the above passage is merely an unsophisticated, wholesome piece of "meat" (the Italian *carne* means both "flesh" and "meat"), which energizes man rather than detracting from his power and confusing his senses. The unpalatable, adulterated "commodity woman," unlike the genuine, appetizing "game-woman," is driven by her own "morbid mania" to circulate freely in the (sexual) marketplace. She offers herself to the highest bidder (the banker, who embodies the connection between capitalism and woman's mania for luxury), rather than to the most virile maschio. Her desire cannot be contained or assimilated within the private, monopolistic economy of phallic narcissism; it challenges the "natural bedrock" of male identity—the "value" and "right" of masculinity—in ways that the dissolution of the family does not. Even the politicized woman seems to be less threatening than the narcissistic woman, who has "perverted" but not lost her sexual appeal.

In Spackman's view, Marinetti's attack on feminine luxury is a countertext to Baudelaire's "Eloge du maquillage" (In Praise of Makeup), a sort of "Decadent manifesto" in which cosmetics and the *mundus muliebris* are praised "as the model for the artist whose poetics were those of cosmesis rather than mimesis," and where "proximity to the *mundus muliebris* is quite explicitly the incubator of genius," a path to androgynous completeness. By contrast, Marinetti argues that the morbid mania of fashion results in "pederasty."[14] Pursuing this comparison further, we can explore the distance that separates the decadent and the futurist anticonventional stance. The blurring of gender roles that accompanies the decadent aesthete's defiant experimentation with "artificial," "unnatural" pleasures is a way of transgressing natural limits, as well as the social constraints of bourgeois respectability. The artificial, cosmetic woman, particularly in her most extreme, blatant embodiment as prostitute and actress, is appropriated to this end because her masquerade exposes and subverts the hypocrisy of bourgeois mores and ideals. As Felski notes, the crossing of gender boundaries in decadent literature is one aspect of a more general tendency to emphasize the artificiality of the real in order to respond "to the presentation of bourgeois values and beliefs as rooted in an organic and unchanging reality." Such a response is based on the recognition that conceptions of authenticity are destabilized "within a society whose cultural expressions are increasingly shaped by commodity aesthetics and the logic of technological reproduction" (1097). With respect to the traditional, rigid construction of gender roles, the effects of decadent anticonventionalism would seem to be liberating. Women, however, are associated with the vulgar reality that the aesthete seeks to transcend through art; hence they are excluded from emancipation. The transgression of gender roles serves a symbolically liberatory purpose, which accrues to the benefit of the aesthete's superior, detached stance toward reality, with no subversive repercussion in the realm of sexual politics. Thus the gap between decadent and futurist subversion is less substantial than superficial consideration might suggest. Nevertheless, Marinetti's attack on artificial women is ideologically at odds with decadent positions. In his iconoclastic rhetoric against past value systems and in his celebration of the artificial world created by technology, Marinetti never undermines the "natural" foundation of gender identity; on the contrary, he consistently seeks to reinforce and build on it with the artificial support of a technological myth structure. Hence his rejection of those aspects of change, such as excessive desire for artificial pleasure, that undermine virility.

"Contro il lusso femminile" climaxes in an anathema that extends the dire effects of the pernicious mania of luxury to the motherland's destiny: "In the name of the great fecund and ingenious future of Italy, we Futurists condemn the rampant female idiocy and the devoted foolishness of males, which collaborate in the development of feminine extravagance, prostitution, pederasty, and the sterility of the race" (*TIF*, 549). The defense of virility and fecundity of the race is consistent with the polemics and discursive strategies of all the manifestos. However, the concern that Marinetti expresses in this text (and, in a more restrained fashion, in the 1913 excursus) over the demise of "love," "monopoly," and "mystery" seems to contradict his campaign for the evolution of humanity toward an unsentimental and lust-free form of life (the metallized, mechanized man). With this goal in mind, he launches "artistic propaganda" against the celebration of Don Juan and the ridiculing of cuckolds.[15] By removing these figures from "life, art and the collective imagination," argues Marinetti, "the great morbid phenomenon of jealousy, which is nothing but a product of a Don Juan-like vanity," will be eradicated. In the best of scenarios, romantic love is finally reduced to the "conservation of the species"; sexual contact is "freed from all tantalizing mystery, all appetizing spice and all Don Giovannian vanity," becoming "a simple bodily function, like eating and drinking" (*TIF*, 301).

Marinetti's contradictory discourse on love can be understood in terms of varying, but ultimately convergent, strategies. On the one hand, he is interested in formulating a utopian blueprint for the future; on the other, he seems to address immediate concerns, such as the threat posed by woman's postwar independence.[16] The ultimate goal—total rejection of love—will be attained only when man completes his evolutionary metamorphosis into a superhuman type. However, the pragmatist in Marinetti realizes that contemporary man still needs a healthy, ego-boosting "diet" of seduced women to sustain his undermined masculine identity. Despite occasional residues of nostalgia for the lost "mystery" and "absolute value" of *amore*, the "presentist" solution reveals a fundamental homology with the utopian model, in which the man of the future will purge his "heart" of love and reduce it entirely to its proper physiological function. In "L'uomo moltiplicato e il Regno della macchina," Marinetti invokes an alimentary metaphor to describe this end result: "The heart must in some way become a kind of stomach for the brain, which will methodically fill up so that the spirit can act" (*TIF*, 300). The instant cure for the ills of the postwar sexual economy is a purely sensual (or "nutritional") experience, in which absolute value is no longer sought in the idealized love object (the romantic solution), but in the male self and in the vitality and virility that the love object arouses.

COOKING WITH WOMEN

While the utopian discourse is characteristic of the earlier writings, pragmatism dominates the texts of the war and postwar period. The futurist manual *Come si seducono le donne* and the autobiographical war novel *L'alcova d'acciaio: Romanzo vissuto* (The Steel Alcove: A Lived Novel; 1921) exemplify the pragmatic move against change in the realm of sexual behavior and offer further insight into the underlying anxieties. Perhaps not coincidentally, these books can be seen as a moderation of futurist avant-garde poetics. By recuperating conventional syntax and narrative structures and by moving into a popular thematic field, Marinetti tailored his cultural product to the demands of the market. He thus "seduced" the general public and scored a best-seller. *Come si seducono le donne*, in particular, was the first and most successful of a number of futurist texts in the genre of social-erotic literature, which acquired great popularity immediately after the war.[17]

The manual (purportedly based on Marinetti's autobiographical experiences) is introduced by Bruno Corra and Emilio Settimelli as a didactic, "hygienic" treatise, meant to educate the passionate Italian male in the art of devaluing women.[18] This proposition appears to be consistent with the utopian goal of reducing love to "a simple bodily function, like eating and drinking" (*TIF,* 301). The protagonist-narrator, however, resembles a traditional Don Giovanni more than he does the futurist, metallized man. Rather than content himself with the satisfaction of physiological needs, he indulges in "guzzling" and "reveling." Essentially, it is a futurist version of the very phenomena castigated by Marinetti as deleterious to the futurist cause: glorification of the philanderer and denigration of the cuckold. By basing his myth of "irresistible futurist charm" (69) on the display of arrogant self-assertiveness, Marinetti hopes to "inject" his readers (and himself) with a dose of optimism: "[Women] love and respond to the man who desires them with the most force and the most arrogant drive. They adore the strength of the bravest, the most heroic. Heroism: here is woman's supreme aphrodisiac! . . . [. . . .] That is the reason why, during our great hygienic war for the realization of all our national ambitions, all or almost all the Italian neutralists (Germanophile professors and philosophers, the official socialist scum [*sozzalisti ufficiali*], Giolittians) are cuckolds" (140–141). However, this triumphant scenario is contradicted by a "compendium of moral maxims" that bitterly denounces woman's lack of regard for virile strength and heroism. Woman, complains Marinetti, is dazzled by the brave volunteer but will settle for the first man who comes along, no matter how *"unripe, reformed, or old,"* because "she likes a living donkey better than a doomed racehorse" (66–67; emphasis in original). She is, in fact, an opportunistic, manipulative cheat who will, given the chance, gladly take revenge on her husband or lover for her own inferiority and frustrations.[19] So much for the narrator's proclamation that heroism is "woman's supreme aphrodisiac"! Another vignette dramatizes the situation denounced in "Contro il lusso femminile":

> [. . .] a very fragile blond doll (cream gold smiles of fine glass) said to a biblical bald banker, who was hooking women (sailing ships or rowboats) with his rusty nose:
> —Oh! I find that *money is a powerful aphrodisiac.* Money is the greatest proof of love that a man can give us. (127; emphasis added)

The substitution of money for heroism dilutes the injection of optimism the book is meant to administer. No matter how old and rusty, the "grappling hook banker" stands a better chance of picking up women than the brave young soldier. The qualifier "biblical" and the hooked nose encode the "artificial" seduction of money with the attribute of Jewishness. In the texts analyzed by Theweleit, the rich, lascivious Jew embodies a threat to the desexualized ego, or body armor, of the Freikorpsmen (2:7–14). In Nazi propaganda, this stereotype recurs as "the agent of subversive social pleasures" (2:378). Unlike the armored ego of the German soldier male, constructed by molding desire through discipline and military drills, the identity of Marinetti's "strong and courageous volunteer" must be built with the trophies of conquered women. For Marinetti, the banker is despicable not because he connotes sexual pleasure but because he represents a devious antagonist who uses crooked means in the struggle for sexual power. He is a pirate, invading the territorial waters of heroic virility.

Come si seducono le donne has been read as an ironic, sarcastic demystification of the literary seducer.[20] The deeper significance of the futurist hero's about-face is lost if we see it solely or primarily as satirical. Keeping in mind the correspondences between the situations dramatized in this text and the arguments advanced (without any trace of self-irony) in manifestos such as "Contro il lusso femminile," the manual of seduction should be viewed, first and foremost, as Marinetti's self-asserting, defensive response to the challenges confronting the male individual in modern society. The prestige of virility is undermined by the free circulation of women; in response, Marinetti offers the myth of the futurist seducer, well armed (or armored) to cope with the new times. The soldier, whom Marinetti designates as his privileged addressee, is faced with the ineluctable destiny of being betrayed by his woman. The defense that Marinetti prescribes against suffering and ridicule—the lot of the cuckold—is that of rejecting the role of victim by negating jealousy and by assuming the opposite and complementary role of seducer. This strategy protects the threatened male ego with a glamorous shining armor, and it produces the collateral effect of enhancing male solidarity by turning it against the devalued woman. In their introduction, Corra and Settimelli point to this desirable by-product: "If Marinetti's concept could spread in our country of violent and passionate men, our social life would be freed from a terrible enemy [obsessive jealousy] which hinders all ascension, all novelty, all heroism, and which is a source of disintegration and incurable conflicts among men who, for the good of the Italian community, should be most in agreement" (23–24). Adopting a "healthy" attitude toward women is a matter of national, not just individual, importance; it can prevent an unproductive, divisive expenditure of male passion and aggressiveness.

This comment is representative of the tone and drift of the writings on love, marriage, and the family that proliferated in futurist periodicals, particularly in the postwar years. The discussion was aimed not only at fostering detachment from and domination of women but also at modifying and displacing desire in general. Emphasis was placed on virility, patriotism, heroism, and homosocial camaraderie, at the expense of care and affection. There were, however, differences and even disagreements among individual positions, as exemplified by Volt's (Vincenzo Fani Ciotti) polemics against Corra's plan for a new type of "superfamily." The plan hinges on, and confirms a concern for, the "health" of male homosocial relationships. It assumes that the mechanisms of alliance built around marriage have been undermined by the unstable, polymorphous deployment of sexual relationships. To counter this development, Corra argues, an alternative structure of alliance should be created—a new, legalized social organism, in which lovers share with husbands the financial burden of supporting wives. Without completely supplanting marriage and the family, the new "superfamily" structure would make it possible for the system of alliance (transmission and circulation of names and possessions, fixation and development of kinship ties) to be imbued with a new economy of power.[21]

Corra's proposal was criticized by Volt in "Matrimonio, adulterio, divorzio, amore libero" (Marriage, Adultery, Divorce, Free Love), which addresses the economic causes and revolutionary consequences of the demise of the traditional family.[22] Volt attributes the crisis to the redistribution of wealth following the war and vehemently defends the rights of virility against the power of money: faced with the extravagant demands of "honest" women, "every respectable young man, whose testicular capacity is inversely proportional to that of his billfold," will have the right to prefer the brothel over the family. "Virility," he prophesies, "will reassert its rights with revolutionary violence. The establishment of the family will be overturned." Decrying the "industrialization" of adultery proposed by Corra, Volt argues that such an economic solution undermines man's value ("The lover is nothing more than the economic complement of the husband. His individuality as a male does not count"). Economics, he objects, will not prevail over erotic instinct, which is "one of those dark and formidable forces that do not let themselves be repressed for long without blowing up. Reduced to a mere business, the family will explode amidst the collapse of all passéist society." Both writers recognize that the economic base plays a fundamental role in the changes affecting the structuration of gender roles. By transforming the adulterous love triangle into an economic partnership, Corra proposes the total assimilation of love. Volt, by contrast, declares a rebellion of virility, an explosive revanche of erotic instinct, and the total destruction of the degenerated family.

In his futurist *ars amandi*, Marinetti, like Volt, defends virility by celebrating erotic power against competing economic forces. At the same time, however, he also deploys defensive mechanisms against this "dark and formidable" natural force, which is deemed capable of destroying male individuality. In the manifestos, as well as in *Mafarka*, the threat is exorcised by constructing the myth of an invulnerable metallic self, armor-plated against sentiments and lust. *Come si seducono le donne* presents a more realistic, "diluted," hence vulnerable version of the futurist hero. The compromise solution is best illustrated by the following representation of "the power of the futurist heart" as a safety device for containing the damage produced by affective warfare.

> [. . .] the futurist affective power can be compared only to the steadiness of a dreadnought, which owes its stability to its watertight compartments. A fire, a blast or the explosion of a torpedo in some part of the dreadnought creates an opening to the sea, but the invading water stops in the watertight compartments and penetrates only a part of the ship.
>
> Automatically, the doors shut against the invading water. The general balance ignores or acts as if ignoring the localized danger. Everything is compensated for under the general law that governs the ship. Laws of navigation and dominion of the sea.[23]

A heart with watertight compartments is a less radical defense than the replacement of the "drenched" hero (Mafarka) by an impenetrable, totally metallized superuomo. In general, Marinetti's imagery of metallic armor and invading liquids recalls Freud's earlier model of the ego's agency, which relies on hydraulic or electric analogies.[24] According to this model, the ego functions as the boundary or surface that binds and regulates the circulation of energy (excitation, fantasy, unconscious desire, affect) in the psychical apparatus. In Jean Laplanche's words, "Inside the system of the ego, communications are good, whereas on the contrary, at its periphery, there exist barriers restricting exchanges; thus the ego appears as a kind of reservoir within which functions the principle of intercommunicating pipes, allowing the energy to be distributed at an equal level, whereas, in relation to the outside, a difference of level is maintained" (62). Both Marinetti's watertight heart and Freud's ego perform an inhibiting and defensive function against any disruptive eruption of libidinal energy. The ego does so by introducing "into the circulation of fantasy a certain ballast, a process of *binding* which retains a certain energy and causes it to stagnate in the fantasmatic system, preventing it from circulating in an absolutely free and mad manner" (63; emphasis in original); in the battleship-heart, the flow of affect is shut off—and any damage contained—by a system of multiplied internal barriers. The two models are not identical: Marinetti does not limit his to the function of stabilizing affect; rather, he envisages a dreadnought engaged in all-out war against a destructive enemy. In other words, the battleship-heart is a metaphor for the "armed" ego's perennial battle against the oceanic feminine.

The metallized man and the armored heart are icons of an aggressively defensive way of situating the self in relation to the outside world. Perhaps the most revealing emblem of Marinetti's attitude toward reality, however, is the recurrence of alimentary imagery, echoed by Corra and Settimelli in their introductory essay.

> It might seem that this book, which demolishes "sacred" concepts such as uniqueness, Eternity and Fidelity in love, should be inevitably a desperate, essentially pessimistic book, one of the usual spiritual failures, which are especially tragic if they are embroidered with false, spasmodic irony and cheerfulness. None of the above: Marinetti is a staunch optimist; he is an observer, and a lighthearted psychologist, although he is aware of all the human suffering and loaded with experience void of rhetorical illusions. [. . . .] The formidable vortex of his health and vital exuberance drives him *to process and chew this bitter food of perishability* [*amare vivande di caducità*] *so as to convert it into an effective source of nourishment. A formidable stomach! He assimilates the inevitable, renewing and purifying ferocity of war, the semicurable incomprehension of the masses and finally the painful but liberating infidelity of woman.* (22; emphasis added)

Marinetti's preoccupation with chewing, digestion, and assimilation can be traced to his prefuturist beginnings. In the early poems, the poet "hungers" for the Absolute; in the digestion scene of *Le Roi Bombance,* the character l'Idiot is a doubly alienated outcast who suffers for the degradation of all ideals, disgusted by material reality but unable to find any source of sustenance in the spiritual realm. As I have noted, Marinetti expresses futurism's evolutionist agenda in alimentary terms: man's heart, traditionally the seat of affective life, is to develop into "a sort of stomach for the brain," with the function of converting emotional matter into spiritual energy. According to Corra and Settimelli, the author of *Come si seducono le donne* has already developed such a "formidable stomach," capable of assimilating the bitter food of reality, transforming it into vital energy, and, we might add, rejecting undigestible experiences. The poet has come a long way since his early, frustrated yearnings. Once hungry for the Absolute, he has since undergone the futurist therapeutic program. He has educated his taste as to the ferocity of war, the obtuseness of the masses, and woman's infidelity. He has chewed them into manageable size and digested them into optimistic, assimilable food for thought. Finally, he has spewed them out again, in the form of healthy artistic products for the consumption of his public. The metaphor of assimilation can be extended to cover many aspects of the futurist project, including Marinetti's attitude toward fascism. Certain elements of modern reality (such as the efficiency, energy, and progress afforded by technology) were incorporated into Marinetti's fiction of individual and national power; he also identified with, and claimed paternity over, some of fascism's characteristics (most notably, national pride and aggressive, optimistic patriotism).[25] At the same time, he tended to eschew unpalatable aspects of modernity and fascism—social tensions, the alienation resulting from mechanized production, and the repression of individual freedom under the reactionary aegis of the regime.[26]

The trope of ingestion and assimilation elaborated by Corra and Settimelli in praise of Marinetti's hygienic vitality is echoed by the metaphors of sex as appetite and woman as food that abound in Marinetti's ars amandi and, in general, in his erotic scenarios. The following examples are from *Come si seducono le donne*.

> Sagacious conductor + fast train + August night + absence of passengers in the compartment × seducer = beautiful eaten and drunk Bolognese woman [*belissima bolognese mangiata e bevuta*]. (76–77)

> You are so beautiful that I grab you, eat you, drink you, my beautiful Italian woman, to satiate my thirst before facing death again with the bursting and burst laughter of a bomb from Italian artillery! (156)

Since gustatory and alimentary metaphors are stock material in erotic literature, this basic facet of Marinetti's representation of women might be discounted or even ignored. In light of Marinetti's overall strategy of aggressive defense, however, such stock material acquires special, disturbing significance. This becomes prominent when we read "La carne congelata" (Frozen Flesh), a novella in which the topos of erotic ingestion and the rhetorical strategy of synecdochically representing woman are deployed in a literal, gruesome fashion.[27] The narrative is presented as a guide to life. Alternating between prophetic utterances in the future tense and peremptory imperatives, it addresses a soldier who is on the verge of joining the *arditi* (shock troops). Its avowed aim is to dispel the "sentimental cowardice" of the soldier (106), who is anguished at the thought of abandoning his woman to the "turbulent and chaotic" city (105). A solution is offered in the form of Guzzo, a shock trooper who has devised the perfect remedy: killing his lover, "lovingly" devouring her head, legs, and arms, and carrying the rest in his backpack (114). The cannibalistic fantasy of devouring parts of the lover (perhaps, in view of several recent news stories, not so fantastical) manifests an obsessive wish for absolute control and possession: it annihilates and, at the same time, preserves the other within the self. In psychological terms, it is a fantasy of "incorporation," intended as a metaphorical displacement of the physiological function (ingestion) onto sexual drive (incorporation).[28] The *ardito*'s solution recalls the incorporative strategy of melancholy previously identified in *Mafarka*. In Guzzo's case, what seems to be at stake is a melancholic attempt to deny the loss, or impossibility, of an absolutely faithful, ideal love. This intertextual link further demonstrates the homology between the strategies of identity formation examined in the first three chapters and the love strategies under discussion here.

Synecdochic reduction of the feminine body to a mere vehicle of desire, the other erotic topos that Marinetti revitalizes through literalization, is similarly an objectifying mechanism for control of the frustrating love object (explicitly motivated, in the novella, by the soldier's anxiety about betrayal). Man makes himself independent from the desire of another self-willed individual by attaching his love to fragments, rather than to a whole person. In Mafarka's utopian solution, the subject who strives for omnipotent unity destroys the object of desire: the sacred dancers are torn to shreds and turned into food for the fish. In Guzzo's less radical strategy, the unmanageable whole is substituted by (or, in psychoanalytical terms, split into) controllable parts. The parceled woman bears physical evidence of a violently displaced sense of lack: she is made to assume man's losses as her own, thus making it possible for the male subject to reclaim his mastery. The narrator offers a poetically charged, idyllic description of the "travel-size" woman, in which a sprinkling of exclamation points highlight the marvel and excitement: "He really has a piece of flesh in his hands. Human flesh. A piece of naked, decapitated woman without arms and legs! The graceful torso of a petite woman! It seems chiseled and studded with lustrous salt. The round, delicate small breasts tremble alive, perhaps they will speak, especially since the lost distant head no longer speaks! The meek, naive, shy, humble belly curves toward the delicate dreamy small garden between the sensual thighs that are cut off midway. The two stumps are covered by shrouds of adherent black silk. So is the neck" (110–111). Certain details contribute to the fetishistic miniaturization of the female body. Black silk caps hide the traces of mutilation, while rhetorical figures change the trunk of the dead woman into a precious living sculpture that displays the desirable character traits of humbleness, shyness, and docility. Naturally, immobility, blindness, and inability to think (hence, to desire) are also desirable.

—Guzzo, do you like women?
—Yes, but not live women.
—I know.
—I don't love woman's head, or her feet.
—I know, but tell me, why?
—Because a woman must neither think nor walk. You see, I want mine flattened
and immobile . . . I don't want her to think of anybody else, see anybody else, or
ever run away! (113–114)

For the ardito, the only good (i.e., controllable) woman is a piece of flesh, cut to
manageable size, deprived of the ability to move and the power to experience and
express desire. Marinetti's concern with silencing is explicitly voiced in his diary,
in which the erotic fantasy is "cheerfully" proposed in all its obscene, cynical
glory, without touching it up in "gentle" imagery.

> I cheerfully propose that *the vulva,* with a side dish of women's thighs, be removed
> and given to the soldier. To be carried in his backpack and to be slipped on the
> member during guard duty. Eroticism at will, without female chatter, without the
> more or less fake smile of woman.
>
> I believe that man would love with a great absolute love the woman so reduced
> to her minimum expression—transportable silent and backpackable. He would de-
> fend her. He would defend himself, he would never be a prisoner, deserter, fugitive,
> a nostalgic person.[29]

The celebration of the self-grounded, heroic subject and the nostalgia for "a great
absolute love," which underpin the hypothetical argument in the second para-
graph, point to idealism as the reverse side of derogation and objectification.

The fundamental ambivalence of the figures inspired by desire can be further
explored in Marinetti's short story. The process of fetishistic transfiguration of the
"parceled" woman culminates in the complementary images of a damning, engulfing demon and of a saving, beatifying divinity: "I tumbled down from the desperate, black, torn and rolling sky of my dead life, down down on you, in you, in
your burning moist sucking heat! My heaven-my hell-my god, mine, mine! I drink
up the infinite in you, little immense divine one, full of every hope and every
benediction!" (112). Both figures bear witness to the phantasmatic power paradoxically wielded by the objectified feminine other: the power to (re)absorb into
the infinite gulf of nothingness and to reflect back an idealized image of blissful
oneness.[30]

If idealization, in intrasubjective terms, is the reverse side of degrading objectification, submission (devotional servitude, masochism) complements domination (mastery, sadism) in the intersubjective relationship. Predicated on the failure
of reciprocity and mutual recognition, such an imbalanced relationship cannot be
rehabilitated. It can, however, be reversed, as Guzzo's destiny illustrates. Though
decapitated and mutilated, the "incorporated" woman continues to speak within

the male subject, tapping an unexpected outflow of maternal tenderness from the
fierce ardito.

> He cries and, with a feeble voice of a woman, recites aloud a passage from a letter:
> —Take me to war with you. Take my flesh with you and kiss me night and day,
> kiss me, eat up my face with kisses, devour me, I am yours! yours!
>   Then, changing voice, Guzzo begins again:
> —I did what you wanted! I ate up your face with kisses, I ate your eyes, your
> forehead, and your whole, dear head with its hair! [. . . .] And now you are me! In
> my veins, my blood cradles you, little one, with the tenderness that dead mothers
> have in Heaven. (112–113)

An unresolved conflict and a fundamental affective ambivalence speak through
the body of the "maternal" soldier, who loses mastery and identity to the object
he needs to sustain his fantasy of absolute love. Ultimately, he becomes the
woman he has ingested. Guzzo's strategy founders on the paradoxical dynamic of
the master-slave relationship described by Hegel: the master gradually loses subjectivity to the slave on whom he grows dependent. Benjamin elaborates on the
paradox, using the following terms: in order to obtain recognition and maintain
the boundaries of domination-submission (an alienated form of differentiation en-
forced through distance, idealization, and objectification), the master requires
some residual subjectivity on the part of the slave; when the latter's objectification
is total, the master "can no longer use her without becoming filled with her thing-
like nature" (*BL,* 57).

Loss of identity culminates with death, which imparts another twist to the reversal of roles dramatized in the story's conclusion. As Guzzo is killed in what
appears to be a suicidal leap in front of a "teasing" bullet (114), he loses his
monopoly over his lover's body, which takes possession of the other soldier
(Marinetti's addressee), continuing to desire and to inspire desire: "you will hear
someone crying near you, on you, in you! It will be the delicious body of
Guzzo's sweetheart, already adulterous, all trembling with love for you! And
then her tears will drip down your back in slow, slow, voluptuous drops" (115).[31]
One is reminded of the "wisdom" of les Bourdes in *Le Roi Bombance.* Abandoned
by their dissatisfied women, they console themselves by complaining that women
cannot be served "on a plate" and cannot be easily "digested," since their desire
is insatiable and uncontrollable. These images of oral aggression also recall the
feminine "ravenous mouths" that threaten and ultimately engulf the embattled
masculine self in *Mafarka.* Following the suggestions of that text, I have argued
that the topos of erotic ingestion is played out by male anxieties regarding identity and power. The same anxieties emerge in the short story, as the ambivalent
effects of desire, initially directed against woman in the form of incorporating
violence, return to affect the male protagonist—thus dissolving the boundaries
of identity.

Could the violence displayed in Marinetti's texts be related to the wartime situation? It has been noted, after all, that the vulnerability experienced by men at
war leads to an escalation of the battle of the sexes.[32] Indeed, the production of futurist erotic literature, tinged with sadomasochism, increases during the years immediately following the war.[33] The phenomenon, however, is not at all confined
to the war and postwar period. Violence, especially oral sadomasochism, is a staple in futurist erotica.

A textbook elaboration of the topos of ingestion occurs in "Un pranzo che
evitò un suicidio" (The Dinner that Stopped a Suicide), which might well be entitled "Come si cucinano le donne," "Cooking with Women." Significantly, this
story serves as an introduction to the 1932 collection of futurist recipes, *La cucina
futurista* (The Futurist Cookbook).[34] It features three futurists, Marinetti, Enrico
Prampolini, and Fillia, in the role of heroes who brilliantly prevent the suicide of
a friend. For a more realistic effect, the latter's identity is disguised with the pseudonym Giulio Onesti. Giulio's troubles are, of course, love-related: his lover has
killed herself and is now "calling" him to join her. Another woman, who looks
"too much" but not "enough" like the lost one, has announced her arrival.
Caught between the competing desires of the two women, Giulio contemplates
suicide in order not to betray "the dead one." Both lovers personify the limitations to which man's desire is subjected. The first one stands for loss, regret,
melancholia, and death; the new one, synecdochically announced as a perturbing
"imminent mouth" ("la bocca imminente," 14), is characterized by attributes of
unruly desire: her voice is "aggressive," she moves like a "sophisticated wild beast"
(17), and she is called a "sculptress of life" (19)—an epithet that contrasts her life-
giving (and death-giving) power with the artistic power of the futurist "sculptors."
Against the power of feminine desire, the artists (whose mouths are also highlighted in synecdochic fashion, as "mouths of charming anthropophagi," 14) deploy a more "civilized" version of the cannibalistic solution adopted by the ardito
in the war story. They create a series of twenty-two edible, sensual culinary sculptures. These will "cure any suicidal desire" (12) by imprisoning "the fleeting eternal feminine" in the stomach and by finally satisfying "the painful, superacute
tension of the most frenzied lusts" (19). The suicidal lover will be healed by the
"erotic" experience of devouring the most perturbing and appealing of the sculptures, the masterpiece of all sensual pleasures—a synthesis of feminine, maternal,
natural, and mechanical elements, entitled "The Curves of the World and Their
Secrets." The futurists succeed where the ardito had failed. By displacing his desire for absolute possession onto the thus re-created woman, Giulio achieves the
ultimate ideal of freedom, oneness, and completeness: "He was at once empty,
freed, void and full. Enjoying and enjoyed. Possessor and possessed. Unique and
complete [*Unico e totale*]" (20).

As already noted, violent erotic fantasies, such as the one thinly disguised in
this story of sublimated cannibalism, are indicative of a sense of crisis that exacerbates need for control and desire for domination. Taking up the alimentary

metaphor offered by Corra and Settimelli, we can conclude that the sadistic violence recurrent in futurist texts is symptomatic of nondigested "bitter food of perishability."

BELLICOSE SEX AND SEXY WAR

Corra and Settimelli, who cite war and woman as among the unpalatable foods that Marinetti has assimilated and transformed into nourishment, lend support to my interpretation of the futurist eroticization of war. Formlessness and chaos constitute the metaphorical common ground in the equation woman = war. Caducity (with its implied meanings of limitation and death) is a corollary in the theorem of the world's abjection that the futurist hero seeks to transcend. Like the bellicose strategies in futurist erotica, Marinetti's sexy representation of war evokes the subjugation of a "shapeless" (feminine) object by a powerfully "bound" (male) subject.

Marinetti's autobiographical novel on the Great War experience, *L'alcova d'acciaio,* foregrounds the interplay between the eroticized scenario of battle and the embattled scenario of love.[35] Battlefield actions are depicted with an explosion of sensual imagery, the heroic protagonist makes love with "brutal vehemence" (185), and romantic love undermines the soldiers' stamina. There are just as many casualties in the "sweet and poisonous war of love" as there are in the "war of iron and mud" (104). Apparently, the deserters executed on the Italian side are not vile traitors, but men betrayed by their women, who want to go back to the home front in order to take just revenge. Other disillusioned victims of love find "refuge" in the brothel, the "only paradise" (8), where women can be metonymically reduced to "beds devoured and vomited lightheartedly" (115). Even this "junk food," however, produces its victims. The most horrifying image of death in Marinetti's novel is the graphic description of an officer killed by syphilis: "We approach the cadaver. The stench is unbearable. His nose is oozing greenish matter and large bubbles that pop, emitting a smell of advanced decomposition" (81). The affect released in this hideous scene is a powerful fear of dissolution; the decomposing interior oozes out of the body's orifices and bursts its boundaries. Marinetti dwells on this "tragic" story, relating the doctor's comments on the terrible disease that defies scientific progress. The only available cure, mercury, often proves as fatal as the ailment: "The ancient Greeks, Persians, Indians and Chinese used to rub the syphilitic body with a mercurial ointment. We have made little progress. In general, young men don't resist the 606, their bones are too fragile, they crumble, you see" (82). Arguably, Marinetti indulges in this medical digression not out of scientific interest, but because he perceives a connection between syphilis and mercury. The properties of this unique metal are fluidity, inconstancy, instability, and corrosion. These attributes also typically recur in Marinetti's representations of lust/love. In this respect, the doctor's odd remark on the frailty of young men's bones is illuminating, especially since bones are actually stronger in youth. What might be "too frail" (not yet ossified) is the framework (or armor) of cultural, ideological, and psychic barriers against the free circulation of affect. The destruction wrought by syphilis on the young officer's body offers physical evidence of the psychological effects that Marinetti ascribes to love.

Unlike *Zang Tumb Tumb*, in which the poetic "I" is identified with the mimetic power of futurist poetics, Marinetti's "lived novel" foregrounds the narrator's reflections and conflicting emotions. In the war between Bulgaria and Turkey that inspired his free-word poem, Marinetti was not a participant but a reporter. Most important, he was the creator and celebrator of a new kind of poetry capable of recording the chaotic experience of modern technological war. *L'alcova d'acciaio*, by contrast, celebrates the rebirth of the patriotic futurist hero and his victorious homeland. Marinetti's myth of the World War I hero develops thematically, from wounding and mutilation to healing and wholeness—a progression comparable to that in *Mafarka*, where inner conflict gives way to transcendent unity. In the later novel, however, emphasis is shifted from the drama of abjection (the humiliating breakthrough at Caporetto, an "enormous" wound that still festers) to the heroics of regeneration, and the final triumph of the hero coincides with the resurgence (not the destruction) of the land. *L'alcova d'acciaio* only covers the last months of the war, from the containment of the last Austrian offensive to the Italian counteroffensive that brought the conflict to an end in November 1918. In effect, Marinetti jettisons all but those aspects of the war that resonate with his vision of a victorious, unified army.

Under the challenging circumstances of war, the hero discovers many "unknown" souls (up to one thousand!) in himself; however, they all seem to be united and driven by the same passion for victory. They "press against his ribs to rush ahead" (141). This multiplicity of souls is celebrated as "elasticity," marking the superiority of the resilient Italian race (individualistic but patriotic, sentimental but audaciously virile, vengeful against the aggressor but compassionate against the weak and defenseless) over the rigid, discipline-worshiping enemy. The narrator prides himself on being able to change souls, like clothes, to suit the occasion: "I tossed the soul that I had previously needed on the sofa and I pulled out another one from the depths of my nerves" (39).

Love, however, turns this chameleonlike strategy into an inner war between the aggressive, "metallic," virile soul and the sentimental, "drenched," feminine soul. Latent throughout the novel, the conflict explodes in "I veleni del golfo" (The Poisons of the Gulf). It is the story of the protagonist's love sickness for Bianca, a "difficult" lover who is tellingly compared to an ultrasophisticated machine gun: "As I got off the train in Naples, I realized that a struggle had erupted between my willful brain, full of ideas about war and the impending attack, and my trembling, defeated, *melted*, Neapolitan heart. Extremely irritated, upset, and choking down my tears, I wobbled in the wobbling carriage along the night alleys" (103; emphasis added). When his "melted" heart gets the upper hand, the hero is ready to sacrifice himself for "absolute love." The unsentimental Bianca, however, does not let herself be "transform[ed] into a wife" (110) and rejects his capitulation: "Bianca inexplicably refuses in a resolute tone. She seems to have become my own active conscience. Transfer of souls. Bianca is the futurist man [*il futurista*]. I am the sentimental passéist with lacerated nerves who clutches at and desires continuity, eternity, the absolute of the heart!" (109). The unexpected role reversal seems to confirm my interpretation of the futurist's contemptuous, disparaging attitude toward love as a case of sour grapes.

The emotional crisis conjures up the drenched "handkerchief-heart" that is associated with Mafarka's downfall, but without the final tragic twist: "I fell asleep. As I woke up in the Rome station, I saw and felt my heart like a cloth soaked with tears wrung by the brutal hands of a very muscular Sudanese laundress. A wrinkled, but washed, very clean, heart. Freshly laundered heart" (111). The vigorous muscles of the Sudanese laundress recall the invigorating breasts of the black wet nurse in the first manifesto; in both cases, Marinetti transforms a threatening incident into a regenerative experience. His heart is as good and clean as new, although a bit "wrung" by woman's "virility" (Bianca's independence and the laundress's force). The protagonist promptly counterattacks and returns to his carefree conquests, glorified as the "gift of victory" from the homeland to her hero.

> Graziella's body was soft, elegant, slender, and fiery. It throbbed gracefully under my caresses, releasing a profusion of scents of a land happy to be reconquered. It was truly the gift of Victory.
>
> I did not have love for Graziella, but an overwhelming, most tender frenzy of spirit and nerves.
>
> I threw myself into the most marvelous pleasures with utmost delicacy and, at the same time, *a strange brutal vehemence,* and also a dazzling artistic impulse made of stylistic preciosity and musical cadence.
>
> —*Cleanse me, cleanse me,* love!
>
> I was a crazed ironsmith and a maniacal chiseler. *I was beyond every social, human, divine law like a happy cock with the ideal hen of the henhouse.* (184–185; emphasis added)

Victorious on both fronts, Marinetti triumphantly proclaims himself a superman (or "supercock") beyond good and evil. With artistic inspiration, delicate (but maniacal) craftsmanship, and a mysterious (yet, to the reader, quite familiar) "brutal vehemence," he "cleanses" Italy of the taint left by enemy occupation.

Once again, the embattled heart is called on to resist the lyrical overflow of sentiment that accompanies the joy of victory: "My heart skips a beat and pulses in my throat with brutal joy. Come on, stop, my heart, if you are not the heart of a woman! My heart yields under the grip of my will but immediately starts crying silently, almost dying in a vast lake of tears" (167–168). At the same time, love for the country at war facilitates a union and transcendence capable of assimilating even "feminine" sentiments, such as anguish, pity, care, and affection. By elevating his homeland to divine status, the poet satisfies his hunger for "the ideal." Meanwhile, patriotic love awakens sexually charged fantasies that allow the hero's virility to expand to ideal proportions. In an impassioned apostrophe, the poet commands his heart to transform into an engine, with which he will conquer the "divine" body of Italy, synthesis of all women, as he drives through the re-conquered homeland.

> Go on, rush, my engine heart, along this beautiful road that runs through the most lush, elegant, variegated lands on earth! This is the flowing hair of Divine Italy! We conquer her breast, her beautiful shoulders, up up, toward her two shapely arms that have been chained for so long, and the left hand ringed by the sea: Trieste! . . . and her rougher and more muscular right hand: Trentino!
>   [. . . .] The most virile impetus of my engine which is simultaneously heart, sex, inspired genius and artistic will, drives into you, with coarse delight for you, for me, I feel it! I am the extremely powerful Futurist genius-sex of your race, your favorite male who returns your vibrating fecundity by penetrating you! (195)

In this fantasy, the collective "we" of brothers in arms (united by the spirit of sacrifice, camaraderie, and love for the homeland) is supplanted by the "I" of a jealous, undemocratic superhero. Marinetti's many souls become cemented by patriotism, as are his "fragmented" cultural background and the still-fragile identity of imperial Italy. The power of Italian forces is joined by that of the poet's African soul and supported by the recently annexed colonial possessions. Soul and territory are symbolized by the Simun, a powerful African wind that is "no servant, but a lover of Italy" (246). This wind of alliance blends exotic and inebriating perfumes with the homegrown aromas borne on the Italian winds. Together, they sweep away the Austrian "stench" and prepare a suitable alcove for the divine spouse.

Even romantic love is salvaged through displacement onto Italy, "which sums up all feminine sweetness" (249). Love for woman (as the futurist Bianca painfully confirms) has lost its absolute value and is no longer a suitable vehicle for the poet's heroic endeavors. Love for Italy, however, offers an absolute measure of value and power. Religious terms and imagery abound in the representation of patriotic love: the liberation, for instance, is compared to the miracles of transmutation performed by Jesus (169), and the poet claims the role of "beacon" of faith and courage.[36] If the homeland is the beyond to which the "I" can expand, the battlefield is the locus where the interplay of individual and national identity can best take place and where libidinal drives can be heroically bound and sublimated. Unlike the broken helmet and sword of the prefuturist poet, shining armor awaits the futurist, who dons it in defense of a higher cause. As victorious champion of a threatened nation (the synthesis of all women in distress) and agent of the Italian race's procreation, he will attain immortality.

The armored car, or alcove, in which the love scene takes place, is a sort of fetishistic, magical object, endowed with the power of transforming or transcending a threatening reality. As such, it is a fitting battleground for the seducer-hero, for it represents simply another variation on the recurrent theme of metallic protection: a "presentist" version of the utopian *uomo metallizzato*. It is depicted as a fragrant island that floats above a "fetid river" of Austrian prisoners (245), "a double current of lurid, black, foul, and sullen forces" (249–250).

The mythicized symbiosis between the triumphant hero and his machine of love and war combines all the ingredients of the fiction of power to produce an ideal ego: artistic genius in action, virility, technology, the patriotic, purifying war that provides an absolute object of love, and an external enemy against whom libidinal energy can be channeled. Hate seems to be the ultimate binding agent; paradoxically, the embattled self achieves unity through destruction. The violent dynamics and repercussions of this binding mechanism are vividly illustrated in Marinetti's "explosive novel," *8 Anime in una bomba*. As in a chemical experiment, Marinetti separates the various components ("anime") of his personality. The eight "souls" are numbered, rather than named, and their essence is presented in action. Disconnected war episodes dramatize the narrator's goliardic heroism, power of seduction, artistic creativity, aggressive and resilient patriotism, lust, sentimental nostalgia, revolutionary genius, and fascination with spiritual abstractions. The episodes (and the souls) are juxtaposed without narrative or dramatic interrelation. However, when the sixth soul (the sentimental one) enters the scene, ushered in by the maternal image, and accepts the maternal legacy—tenderness and love for a single woman—the fourth soul (the violent, belligerent one) initiates a vehement attack and threatens to slaughter it (*TIF*, 862). In this way, Marinetti foregrounds the fragmentation of identity and the unifying mechanism less patently at work in other texts: the belligerent soul unifies the divided self by projecting, on the external world, a potentially self-destructive inner dissention. Final unity is achieved by binding the explosive mixture ("**92 KG. BOMB MARINETTI®**," *TIF*, 907; emphasis in original) and casting it against the abject enemy: "the [. . .] big lurid Austro-German trench full of cholera bedbugs priests moralists spies professors and policemen" (*TIF*, 916–917). The resulting discharge of hate and violence is graphically represented in a free-word table, which combines pictographic signs and onomatopoeic words to convey the impression of a bomb blast (*TIF*, 918; fig. 4). Warfare, like sexual violence, allows for a "legitimate" eruption of emotions: a destruction of boundaries that is predicated on the affirmation of difference. The futurist rhetorical arsenal produces ideological unity through emotional and textual explosions, transforming and assimilating the bitter food of reality into optimistic myths.

A third novel, *Un ventre di donna* (1919), stages Marinetti's authorial persona in the role of a World War I hero and illustrates the binding strategies deployed in the futurist war. It was written by the futurist woman writer Enif Robert and co-signed by Marinetti. His dramatic letters from the front counterpoint the female protagonist's dreary experience of physical and spiritual sickness. Offering friendly encouragement and advice in his correspondence, Marinetti still manages to appropriate the woman's difference as an image of lack to bolster his triumphant fiction

Fig. 4. The front cover of *8 Anime in una bomba* reproducing Marinetti's free-word table. Reprinted by permission of the University of Iowa Libraries (Iowa City).

of power. However, rather than simply echo the futurist hero's fantasies, the female voice maintains the role of protagonist and articulates an experience of writing as inner conflict and laceration. *Un ventre di donna* thus calls for a new perspective on the politics/rhetoric of gender in futurism—one that foregrounds the less sensational battles of the women who joined Marinetti's movement.

FIVE

The Hero's War and the Heroine's Wounds

Un ventre di donna

The feminine that constitutes the imaginary in male-centered futurist discourse does not correspond to the actual standing of women in the movement. Although the futurists upheld the spirit of a "male club"[1] and adopted blatantly misogynist rhetoric, several women joined the movement's ranks and participated in all its fields of action. In so doing, they expressed their rebellion against traditional codes of behavior, both personal and artistic.

Valentine de Saint-Point, a Parisian painter, writer, and performance artist, was the first woman to be officially associated with futurism. In two widely publicized manifestos, "Manifesto della Donna futurista" (Manifesto of the Futurist Woman; 25 March 1912) and "Manifesto futurista della Lussuria" (Futurist Manifesto of Lust; 11 January 1913), de Saint-Point rejected the reactionary notion that nonprocreative sex degrades woman.[2] Railing against the hypocritical preconceptions of Christian morality and the mystifications of an antiquated, sterile sentimentality, she celebrated untrammeled lust as a force of transgression and progress. At the same time, however, she condemned the "cerebral" aberration of feminism and valorized the stereotypical notion of the instinctive, irrational "essence" of woman, recasting it as aggressive, futurist vitalism.[3] Woman was hailed as "the great galvanizing principle" in the drive toward progress (MFL, 38), a "sublimely unjust" force of nature,[4] playing a fundamental role in any revolution as well as in the process of natural selection. Furthermore, while reacting against Marinetti's association of woman with the constraints of family, pacifism, and sentimental love (obstacles to the heroic destiny of man), she nevertheless circumscribed women's ambitions within the complementary and mutually exclusive roles of selfless mother and inspiring lover. These two roles were well within the scope of action traditionally reserved for women and reproduced the clear-cut distinction between "mother" and "prostitute" that had been drawn by, among others, the misogynist philosopher Otto Weininger. "Woman," claims de Saint-

Point, "must be a mother or a lover. True mothers will always be mediocre lovers, and lovers will be inadequate mothers through excess [*per eccesso*]. Equal before life, these two women complete each other. The mother who *receives* [*riceve*] a child makes a future from the past. The lover *dispenses* [*dispensa*] the desire that drives toward the future" (MDF, 35; emphasis added). Although woman's agency is celebrated, it is cast in a conventionally limited, dualistic, subordinate, and passive mold. Creation and desire are dissociated from it via the semantically passive "riceve," the economic idiom "dispensa" (recalling the noun *dispensa*, or pantry, which designates woman's traditional domain of delegated management), and a significant lack of possessive modifiers indicating feminine ownership or agency. The mother receives a child who is not her own, part of a future seemingly unrelated to her desire. Even as a lover, woman dispenses, rather than experiences, desire.

These prescriptive statements undercut de Saint-Point's initial rejection of a rigidly dualistic notion of sexual difference: "The majority of women are neither superior nor inferior to the majority of men. [. . . .] IT IS ABSURD TO DIVIDE HUMANITY INTO WOMEN AND MEN; it is made up only of FEMININITY and MASCULINITY. [. . . .] An exclusively virile individual is nothing but a brute; an exclusively feminine individual is nothing but a female [*una femmina*]" (MDF, 31–32). According to this preliminary polemic against biological sexual identity, femininity and masculinity—associated with, respectively, intuition and force—are shared in various degrees by both men and women. In the ensuing argument for the transformation of women's role in contemporary society, however, the distinction between femininity and woman becomes increasingly blurred, as de Saint-Point reproposes a series of stereotypical assumptions about woman's voluble, intuitive, and excess-prone nature. Ultimately, all the political objectives of feminism are peremptorily rejected and biology identified as a bedrock for the polarized construction of gender roles. In short, this first provocative attack on restrictive mores also charts the boundaries of the subversive territory explored by futurist women.

Some of the women who later joined the movement displayed nonconformist attitudes and looked to the shortcut of imitating the futurist *superuomo* as a means of emancipation from conventional roles. Fulvia Giuliani, dressed like a captain of the arditi, participated in futurist demonstrations; the *aeropittrice*, or aviation painter, Barbara (pseudonym of Olga Biglieri-Scurto), unbeknown to her parents, frequented an aeronautic club and became a pilot. After the war, some futurist women even proposed forming groups of ardite.

Writers such as Rosa Rosà (Edyth von Haynau), Enif Robert, Eva Khun, Emma Malpillero, and Benedetta (Benedetta Cappa Marinetti) rebelled against artistic and literary institutions and engaged in paroliberismo, *teatro sintetico*, and aeropoesia. During the war, Maria Ginanni took charge of the paper *L'Italia futurista*. Other writers, especially Robert and Rosà, contributed regularly to futurist periodicals and participated in a debate occasioned by the publication of

Marinetti's *Come si seducono le donne.* While futurist men responded to the modern reconfiguration of gender roles by deploying traditional rhetorical strategies, women like Robert and Rosà spiritedly resisted such representations; in so doing, they set about defining a new female subjectivity. The second edition of *Come si seducono le donne* (1918) included, as a final appendix, a selection from this debate— six texts, signed by Robert, Rosà, Shara Marini, and Volt. In the selection, we can clearly identify the thrust and limitations of futurist women's polemics.

The appendix opens with "Come si seducono le donne," a letter that Robert addressed to Marinetti in response to his recently published book.[5] Robert sets out to demystify the "fairy tale" of the weak, fragile, passive "prey-woman" evoked by Marinetti's title, identifying this figure as a myth or fantasy designed to foster male illusions of control and superiority. These, in turn, can be traced to male instincts of aggression and conquest. Rejecting the fantasy, Robert affirms that woman has the right and ability to enact her sexuality in a self-conscious, willful, and "healthy" fashion. However, she does not address the ideological and political implications of the manual's "paradoxical philosophy." Passing over the book's content, she hastens to absolve Marinetti of the charge of maliciously misrepresenting women, citing his "occasional" acknowledgment and appreciation of female qualities. While other men, including (to Robert's "horror") some futurists, theorize about and propose remedies against female vices and essential inferiority, Marinetti cheerfully accepts woman "for what she is." In conclusion, Robert expresses her desire for recognition and acceptance into the male-dominated movement, an overriding concern that frames her argument, stifling any radical criticism. "For your scornful laughter that resounds loudly amidst the whining chorus of our censors," she writes, "you are absolved also of the small perfidies in which you indulge with pleasure. What does it matter? As long as you deem us worthy of being at the side of the assailants of tomorrow, full of gigantic promises."

"Una parola serena" (A Serene Word), the other piece signed by Robert, predicates woman's value on her ability to strike a balance between feminine sensuality and "virile" intelligence and strength. She proclaims: "There are women who when they give themselves in a 'room of fragrances and shadows' are rendered delightful by a very happy correspondence, a perfect joining of soul and senses; however, at the appropriate time, they can be also lively, courageous, strong, VIRILE, INTELLIGENT, at their man's side."[6] In arguing against stereotypical representations of femininity, Robert confirms woman's subordinate role and value. She continues to define female subjectivity according to male-centered parameters that posit masculinity as the paradigm of worth against which woman's relative lack is to be measured. To be worthy of any esteem, she implies, women must strive for their share of virility and must be affiliated with a man ("at their man's side").

In "Rivendicazione" (Revindication), an impassioned defense of Italian women's virtues and dignity, Marini also shunts her critique of futurist misogyny into an unquestioning celebration of the movement: "I will not insult. I admire futurism too much!"[7] While refuting the futurists' disparagement of women as obstacles to progress, she reaffirms women's traditional role as supporting, self-sacrificing, and ultimately subordinate companions: "Have you not yet realized that woman's soul no longer entraps, but, rather, spurs on, follows, watches and suffers in silence? You are blind, totally blind!" In Marini's scenario, futurist men maintain a prerogative of power and agency disguised as a moral duty to protect woman from the attacks of malicious detractors: "It is up to you, then, to lift her up again with your pure hands and mighty arms, and the wings that are still sleeping in your flesh will be able to spread in the highest flight of untainted love." The influence of the futurist mythopoeia of virile power is compounded by prejudices and myths assimilated through literary conventions, particularly through the romance genre, which has traditionally been a popular form among women writers. Marini's rhetoric evokes the conventional topos of a valiant knight in shining armor, champion of pure love and rescuer of distressed damsels.

The two articles signed by Rosà place the woman question in a less conventional perspective. Rosà raises the possibility of a new female subjectivity, placing it in the context of momentous changes in the sociopolitical realm and in the realm of the individual psyche. In "Le donne cambiano finalmente" (Women Are Finally Changing), she sarcastically echoes the disparaging, reductionist representations of woman that had appeared in recent issues of *L'Italia futurista*. According to such arguments, she notes, woman's identity options would seem to be extremely limited. The disheartening alternative to the traditional role of "object-woman"—a doll or "dish" whose worth consists of her use value—is apparently that of being a sexually perverted, unattractive, independent *nonwoman*.

> Fine. The object-woman. The negligible woman. The illogical, inconsistent, irresponsible woman. The stupidity woman—the doll woman, with a side dish of vice and the sauce of amorality. There follows the verification of her contemptible inferiority.
>
> Otherwise: the woman—independent, liberated, ugly, intelligent, bitter, unpleasant because she does not desire to be appealing. There follow accusations of hermaphroditism, perversion of instincts, sentimental incapacity, egoism, etc., etc.
>
> Well, then: can anyone tell me how we should be?[8]

Rosà concludes with a warning to her male colleagues. Women are finding their own answer to the question of what they are or should be. They are gaining a new, inalienable self-consciousness that cannot be conquered or seduced: "They are about to acquire the awareness of a free, immortal 'I' who does not surrender to anybody or anything." Meanwhile, she adds, men are still entertaining the ancient notion that woman has no soul.

However, Rosà's definition of an autonomous female subjectivity remains cast in vague terms. In her second piece, "Risposta a Jean-Jacques" (Response to Jean-Jacques), she calls for an end to the senseless practice of dividing humanity along gender lines: "Let's quit splitting humanity into men and women (a division that seems to me as absurd as the notion of dividing humankind into blonds or brunettes); let's begin, instead, to draw the line between superior, strong, intelligent, healthy, valid individuals versus the idiot the cretin the maimed and the weak."[9] To stress her point, she speaks of incipient "psychological, sexual and erotic metamorphoses" that will prove the absurdity of the current value system. Gender, she predicts, will cease to be a discriminating factor in judging an individual's worth. Seemingly concerned with containing the politically subversive implications of her stance, Rosà concludes by denying any affinity with feminist radicalism: "I am not a feminist," she declares, "I am an 'ist' for whom the first part of the word remains to be found." Despite this disclaimer, Rosà's "ist" argument shares an early assumption of the feminist movement, the objective of equality between the sexes, without, however, embracing the concomitant political goal of a neutral justice for all. From the vantage point of a shift of concerns from principles of equality to questions of difference in recent feminist theory and practice, we are now in a position to see a significant drawback in the program of the women writers and activists who attacked the male-dominated establishment primarily to gain full access to it. In the early drive toward equality, the difference or differences in women's experiences were circumvented and silenced. Like feminist egalitarianism, Rosà's vision of a genderless future sidesteps such various, conflict-laden realities. In the case of futurist women, in particular, a concern with difference raises questions that were alien to the futurist debate: How did futurism's myths and formal innovations affect the creative experiences of female artists? Did the futurist fiction of individual transcendence empower women; or did it foster self-contempt, submission, and hero worship on their part?

Two other essays written by Rosà on the issue of the New Woman, both entitled "Le donne del posdomani" (The Women of Posttomorrow), were not included among the tokens of feminine dissent appended to Marinetti's book. In the first one, she reminds men that women have been made stronger by the trials and tribulations of war. They have grown equal to the grand events of their time, filling the positions left vacant by the men called to arms and setting a model of moral fortitude for those who must confront the pressing job of postwar reconstruction.[10] The second essay poignantly assesses the shortcomings of the ideal/reality of selfless motherhood. After wearing herself out in the care of her children, the self-sacrificing mother finds herself unable to have any impact on their development as teenagers and young adults: "The most important things, the most abstract aspirations, are jealously kept secret from the mother, for 'any attempt to explain would be useless, *she would not understand.*'"[11] Rosà argues for a radical change, prospecting a "posttomorrow" in which women, by acquiring their own "free personality," will be less maternal but better equipped to understand their children. She predicts, however, that woman's conquest of independence and individuality will result in the demise of love and in her ultimate evolution into the "superior type," that is, into a man. Such a conclusion echoes traditional/futurist notions of gender difference and the attendant anxieties about the catastrophic effects of female emancipation.

By excluding Rosà's speculations on the women of posttomorrow, the appendix dodges the most troubling questions raised by the debate in *L'Italia futurista*. Furthermore, it is a man who gets the last word: the final selection is Volt's open letter to Maria Ginanni (the editor of *L'Italia futurista*). It should be noted that the sequential ordering of the pieces does not follow the chronological order in which they originally appeared. Volt's letter was published in the 29 July issue, while the first three pieces—Robert's letter to Marinetti, Rosà's "Le donne cambiano finalmente," and Robert's "Una parola serena"—were dated, respectively, 31 December, 26 August, and 7 October.

Volt's comments provide an apt finale to the handbook, for they reproduce and expose the defense mechanism that drives Marinetti's strategies of seduction. He sets out to "to wipe out a colossal mistake that weighs heavily on the entire discussion of the woman question opened by *L'Italia futurista*."[12] Most of the women participating in the debate, he protests, advance the "absurd pretense" of being loved for their own intelligence and spiritual qualities. Volt does not let his self-serving view of the weaker sex be altered by women's call for the recognition of their subjectivity. He neutralizes such a threatening discourse by reading it through the deforming lens of a cliché: the conventional characterization of woman as a cheat and a tease. Woman's pretense of spirituality, claims Volt, can only fool "the puny decadent scholar." The futurist man, "less gallant but more manly," sees right through it. Woman, he warns, exhibits her would-be spirituality merely to set a trap. Her basic instinct is, in fact, to subjugate man by playing on and frustrating his "legitimate" sexual needs. Naturally, the manly futurist will not play the game by somebody else's rules: "he rebels and, with a well-placed kick, sends cards and table into the air." Like Marinetti's heroes, Volt constructs a psychological and rhetorical barrier between himself and women by regarding them as objects of sexual consumption. In the letter's conclusion, a metaphor of retreat and retaliation displays the consequent breakdown of any intersubjective relationship: "But if a physically desirable woman comes within 50 cm of the perimeter of my chest in order to offer her friendship to me, I withdraw behind the armored volt of my suspicion and fire the machine guns of my Irony." When a desirable woman confronts him with the alterity of her own desire, the futurist man's response is to interrupt all communications, entrench himself within an armored shield of prejudice, and unleash a barrage of machine-gun fire.

Despite such misogynist outbursts and occasional polemical exchanges, the futurist ranks remained open to women throughout the various phases of the movement's evolution. Marinetti himself married the futurist artist Benedetta (fig. 5), who, among other artistic and literary endeavors, played a primary role in the realization of "tactile tables." He also launched and sponsored the careers of several other women.[13] However, the recent revival of interest enjoyed by futurism has only marginally illuminated the work of its women. Their role has been perceived as a mimetic, entirely subordinated reflection of the artistic experience of futurist men.[14] Against this lack, I argue that futurism is a significant episode in women's

Fig. 5. F. T. Marinetti and Benedetta Cappa Marinetti in
their apartment in Piazza Adriana, Rome, ca. 1932. Portraits
of Marinetti by Depero (left) and Rougena Zatkova (right)
hang on the walls. Reprinted by permission of the Beinecke
Rare Book and Manuscript Library, Yale University.

activity on the Italian cultural scene at the beginning of the twentieth century: it
is the sole instance of Italian women's conspicuous participation in the historical
avant-garde. Far from being entirely reducible to a mere imitation, the writing of
futurist women articulates a different and conflict-laden representation of the
feminine, one that both internalizes and contradicts the notions and fantasies discussed thus far.

Robert's autobiographical novel *Un ventre di donna*, in particular, raises charged
questions, for it narrates the story of the female protagonist's initiation into futurism and of her relationship to the movement's charismatic leader. This text was
co-signed by Marinetti, who figures as the author of certain letters incorporated
in the narrative. The interplay between masculine and feminine voices fore-

grounds the issue of gender difference as a difference in (self-)representation.[15] I will address this issue by focusing on two interrelated tasks: that of plotting the locus of the woman writer's cultural identity, mapping the forces that intersect within her cultural field; and that of examining the different varieties of subjectivity that the two voices construct as they articulate ostensibly parallel wartime experiences.

The title of the novel and its thematic emphasis on an essentially female disease point to woman's biological nature as the intrinsic origin of her voice. Furthermore, Robert's programmatic introduction, by calling for the untrammeled expression of somatic symptoms and libidinal drives, identifies the body as the liberated and liberating domain of *écriture féminine*. The female body, however, remains the quintessential object of male-centered signifying practices. The novel's protagonist remains imprisoned within this "master's house."[16] Even as she strives for a gender-subversive identity, Robert's break with the past is not clear-cut and thus opens divisions and contradictions within her self-representation.

The fundamental dissonance that discriminates feminine from masculine voice in *Un ventre di donna* must be traced, therefore, not to the body *tout court* but to a gender-inflected *body of experience*. By this I mean a complex of perceptions, affects, and (self-)representations that are crucially shaped by culture and, in particular, by the "lenses" of gender: pervasive assumptions, such as biological essentialism, male-centeredness, and gender polarization, that are deeply embedded in our cultural discourses, social institutions, and individual psyches.[17] Robert proposes to articulate her experience as a woman in a transgressive fashion, by narrating the vicissitudes of her body in direct and unsophisticated language. Both her experience and her language, however, bear the unmistakable marks of male-centered discourses that transform the novel's central symbol of transgression, the exposed "woman's womb," into a figure of self-division and self-loathing.

A PRESCRIPTION OF COURAGE AND TRUTH

Echoing both de Saint-Point's glorification of women's sexual freedom and Marinetti's attack on passéist literature, Robert clamors for woman's emancipation from the conventional cant and coyness of contemporary feminine literature and from the dictates of bourgeois moralism. In a manifesto-preface entitled "Courage + Truth," she defines her objectives in terms of adherence to immediate concerns and real-life experiences: "No! everything has been said already about aesthetic sentiments, about airy fluctuations in the blue space: everything remains to be said, instead, about everyday reality, about the sinuosities that life relentlessly twists, again and again, in our tormented souls. This is, then, what we must confront."[18] In the spirit of the avant-garde's insistence on reintegrating art into life, Robert emphasizes the relationship between these two realms and criticizes the hypocritical, romantic rhetoric of the feminine "letteratura fremito," or quivering literature: "For pity's sake, don't waste any more gems of style [*tesori di bello stile*] to tell us that the sun is a divine lover, or that an autumnal garden can make you dizzy with the most intense pleasure!" Reading these "magnificent idiocies" gives Robert an irresistible urge to shake up the "the fluttering woman writer" and bring her back to reality: "No, dear: you are making a ghastly substitution of thoughts and things. A handsome young man with manly features is your sun and your garden" (XII–XIII). Robert's blunt, unceremonious formulation echoes her call for a plain, down-to-earth discourse. Her direct, intimate style of address clashes not only with "fluttery" romanticism but also with the epic, didactic, and vituperative rhetoric of the futurist manifestos. The epithet "dear," however, is anything but affectionate: rather than evoke female friendship, it indicates Robert's sarcastic, disparaging attitude toward the literary "nonsense" produced by contemporary women writers.

Her venom also targets the mealy-mouthed ladies whom this kind of mystifying literature portrays and fosters.

> A beautiful lady who is a friend of mine had been sick for a long time. To me and everybody else she told of nervous ailments, of . . . *fevers of thought* [. . . .].
>
> The ridiculousness of her outrageous aesthetic efforts to veil her true illness killed my compassion.
>
> I find a formidable logical link between my languishing friend, affected by a rectal tumor, and the *azure* women writers [*le scrittrici azzurre*]. And I am convinced that one, and not the least important, reason for her pitiful plastic poses was to be found in the literary genre for which she had a predilection. Books, newspapers, magazines in which women of letters, "*with fingers of azure*" [*con dita d'azzurro*], touch lightly upon the most inconclusive rarity of sensations which want to appear most refiiiined and affectedly vibrant [*raffinatiiiissimo e sedicente vibrante*]; in which the search for spiritual snobberies is so intense that it sometimes becomes incredibly ridiculous. (XIV–XV; emphasis in original)

What kind of connection does Robert draw between her sick friend and "azure" women writers? She offers only a causal explanation: this literary genre must somehow have contributed to inspire her friend's languishing pose. There may be, however, an unarticulated metaphorical ground for such a "formidable logical link." The woman's rectal tumor, like the gynecological disease affecting the novel's protagonist, bodies forth the reality of visceral "torments" that Robert intends to uncover ("everything remains to be said [. . .] about the sinuosities that life relentlessly wrings, again and again, in our tormented souls").

This introductory text sets the novel in a demystifying framework, in which sentimental clichés and spiritual abstractions are denounced as a displacement of real, bodily urgings. The proposed alternative is an energetic, futurist treatment of courage and truth—a new, feminine discourse representing a new woman, freed from the taboos of bourgeois moralism and from the hypocrisy of displaced language. Robert makes the case for an honest, open sexuality in the following terms: "But tell us, then, with rough frankness, your human and carnal desire as your legitimate and conscious sensibility suggests it to you; talk about your fecund and sensual right, without mixing it up with analogies of rays and perfumes that have absolutely nothing to do with your nakedness that sings love" (XIII). Her exhortation, like de Saint-Point's celebration of lust, seems to establish the limits of the proposed revolution within the domain of sexuality. The assumption that women's desires and experiences are contained entirely by their erotic yearnings and sexual behavior is informed by the traditional vision of separate, preordained roles for men and women, one that allows little or no overlap between their respective spheres and one that constrains women to a "natural," subordinate position ("A handsome young man with manly features is your sun and your garden"). However, the experience and ambitions that the novel articulates are not, in fact, entirely contained within these limits. The subject constituted in the text—a female author/narrator/protagonist—is actually a complex one; she represents an idiosyncratic experience that does not precisely conform to the models proposed by male-centered culture and literature, including the male futurists' theoretical and creative writings.

THE SURGICAL NOVEL

Alternating narrative, dialogic, and epistolary modes, Robert recounts an autobiographical struggle against a relentless disease that affects the womb.[19] The designation of the novel as "surgical" may have a formal relevance, in addition to an obvious thematic justification. The prevailing narrative form—a recording of events and conversations in the first person and in diary format—is interrupted by letters, sent mainly by Marinetti from the front. This "montage" technique grafts the éclat of the patriotic war onto the dreariness of the protagonist's private battle, producing a polarized or bifocal structure.[20] As will become apparent, such a structural split interplays with, and underlines, the conflictual thematics of the novel.

The protagonist is an unconventional, strong-willed woman, who, as a young and beautiful widow, has refused to submit to social laws and familial expectations, which require her to remarry.[21] Having embarked on a romantic affair that is not sufficient to fulfill her desires and confused aspirations, she suffers on account of her boring, uneventful life.[22] In addition, she is plagued by the symptoms of a mysterious illness. Only the attention of another man—the daring, brilliant, and athletic futurist Biego Fortis—brings a wave of vitality into the sleepy rhythm of her life. Interestingly, Biego's impetuous courtship does not sweep her away; rather, she "endure[s]" it ("lo subii," 13) with a mixture of conflicting feelings. The woman's health continues to deteriorate until a gynecological dysfunction is finally diagnosed and surgery recommended as the only way to escape death. The representation of the ensuing events—surgery, the patient's convalescence in the hospital, and her struggle with painful complications that prevent recovery—hinges on the themes of courage's victory over fear, the protagonist's loss of faith in "sullen Science" (78), embodied by a surgeon whose nickname is Jack the Ripper ("ironic, cold, viscid, cruel," 83), and her growing faith in the therapeutic power of futurism, which matures through readings and especially through an epistolary relationship with Marinetti. The futurist leader, "strong and precious friend" (127), a "wonderful exciter and diviner of latent forces" (129), advises a "futurist treatment" (subsequently expounded in a "therapeutic manual of desire-imagination" that the patient is advised to memorize), which consists of increasing "ardent links with earthly life" (124) through intensified desires.

Putting Marinetti's theory into practice, the patient pursues an ambitious program of artistic creativity ("spiritual inebriations," 116), using the futurist free-word style to articulate her "surgical sensations." Her therapeutic writing begins as follows:

> white white white blinding glare of sky of sun from bright tall windows [*silence*] little nuns candidandsilent smiling of sweet sweet faces habituation to the daily agony of sick flesh. Shuddering of my body at the cold touch of the small glass table—*COLD*—shiver of my warm naked body and correspondence of the tortuous blow to my back to my heart fast vigilant suspicious pulsation. . . . Bustling about of the confident quick ugly practical small nurse [*silence*] in large print on the facing wall. Chilling rigid entrance of the sullen cold bald "Science" anxious jump of the heart. (134–135; emphasis in original)

One might be tempted to identify a parallel progression from femininity to masculinity in the heroine's experiences and in the formal vicissitudes of the text. As she decides to take charge of her body, Robert shifts from typically feminine modes of writing—diary and letter—to futurist (hence "unsentimental" and "virile") ones.[23] Neither the thematic nor the formal development of the text, however, is consistent with such a clear-cut model. The new literary weapons, designed by Marinetti to capture the "drama" of matter in the context of modern, technological warfare, are deployed as a means of recording the drama of the woman writer's body ("the daily agony of sick flesh"), as it is violated by science. In other words, the "surgical" words in freedom do not multiply the feminine "I" by affording it power to master the life of matter; rather, they divide it by casting it in a conventionally passive, masochistic role. Furthermore, Robert limits her experiment of paroliberismo to a brief parenthesis and returns to the epistolary and diary format immediately thereafter.

The episode that follows the "futurist cure" also seems to contradict the hypothesis of progressive masculinization. In addition to experimenting with the therapeutic power of Marinetti's techniques, Robert submits herself to a healing intercourse with the personified sun, which appears to embody the "wonderful brutality" and uncompromising virile force characteristically celebrated by the futurists: "Naked in my open robe, I lie down on a deck chair and offer my womb to the sun. The incandescent astral body immediately shows his wonderful barbaric brutality hurling himself at my wound with savage fury and no diplomacy" (145–146). In Robert's erotic scenario, as opposed to Marinetti's sadistic fantasies of dismemberment, cannibalism, and necrophilia, aggression is directed toward the self, confirming stereotypical assumptions about female passivity and masochism.

No final recovery is represented. Instead, responding to the patient's rebellious feelings against inaction and to her (self-destructive) desire to fight at the front ("I would like to get up, go to war, in the trenches, shoot, kill myself, put an end to it. I am *fed uuuup!* [*sono stuuuufa!*]," 192; emphasis in original), Marinetti's letters develop a comparison between the "war" in the wounded womb and the battles that rend the "womb" of Italy.

> You don't know [. . .] that what is happening to your womb is deeply symbolic. In fact, your womb resembles that of the earth, which has today an immense surgical wound of trenches. (113)

> I navigate, wallow, row in the mudslop [*fangobroda*] of the communication trenches, fat, lurid bowels of this gutted plain. All these corridors of mud lead to one single vast latrine: the Austro-Hungarian empire. (139)

> You are wrong to fear another attack of high fever. One must acclimatize to danger.
> After all I am in your same situation. You are confined to your bed; I am confined to my muddy trench, in danger of being fancied by a machine-gun bullet or by a shell of the San Marco.
> *But I* [*Io, però,*] go around my trench with my chest swelling with pride for I am keeping a tight rein on my nerves under the sliding flights of death, who is dancing upstairs, ripping her silk train on the trees. (171; emphasis added)

The analogy that ostensibly equates the hero's and the heroine's experiences, establishing a symmetrical relationship between the two protagonists, actually foregrounds the asymmetry of their gender assignments. The third quoted passage spells out the antithesis implicitly developed via the novel's bifocal structure between the woman's war, consisting of humiliation, suffering, and impotence, and the man's, in which pride, exhilaration, and success are the main ingredients. Whereas the former scars the protagonist both physically and mentally, the latter scars the womb of the earth. Significantly, the abjection that the hero projects beyond Italy's borders ("one single vast latrine") remains an inner enemy for the heroine ("How disgusting to be a uterus in pain, while all the men are fighting!" 25).

THE WOMBS OF OTHER WOMEN

The last two chapters ratify and universalize the polarization of gender arrangements by extending the potential and actual threat of disease to the wombs of other women. In "Lotta di ventri femminili" (The Struggle of Women's Wombs), the female protagonist mentally strips female passersby and elaborates a feminine typology in the form of a classification of wombs: the hysterical womb of the passéist intellectual, the tired womb of the matron, and the happy womb of the beautiful figurine.[24] "Il ventre di un'altra donna" (The Womb of Another Woman) stages the drama of a woman affected by "intestinal putrefaction." Her husband's jealous protectiveness and the passéist doctors' pedantic opinions oppose a progressive doctor's surgical strategy. As the rich but miserly husband (symbolically named Prince Eutanasio De Ruderis [Euthanasius of the Ruins], "a stingy and maniacal multimillionaire," 209) is watching a parade of victorious troops, the doctors circle around the patient's bed in consultation. Suddenly, the crowd's outcry is heard, announcing that a futurist shock trooper of the 74th assault unit has stabbed Prince De Ruderis. In an emblematic finale, the liberating gesture of the "avenging" shock trooper is associated with the liberated gesture of the patient, who proclaims her courageous choice of action.

> But naked, strong and resolute, the princess stepped out on the balcony and leaned over as she cried:
> —I am ready! Operaaate on me [*Operaaatemi*]!
> And the soldiers, forgetting the assassin and the assassinated, applauded frenetically, *showing no surprise*, at the yet so very strange appearance of that marvelous naked woman. (218; emphasis in original)

This final scene provides an exemplary instance of the fundamental ambivalence that characterizes the feminine heroic stance in Robert's text. Even in her defiance, the princess is still presented, or rather exposed, in a posture that is substantially compatible with the traditional reductive representation of woman as mere body—the quintessential locus of pathology and object of male gaze.

Similarly, the protagonist's story constitutes a transgression with respect to traditional representations of sexual roles and gender identity (or, in the case of woman, lack of identity): she expresses the ambition of entering the male spheres of war and art, defies society's expectations about marriage, and confronts the unaesthetic truth of the disease hidden in her womb. However, the text's potential subversiveness is blunted by the heroine's association of "deviance" (and implied superiority over other women) with virility of spirit and her refusal to identify with members of her own sex. Toward the friends, nurses, and nuns who assist her with comforting kindness and affection the ailing protagonist manifests deep gratitude. But only in terms of the body's sexuality and pathology does she feel an affinity with other women—a feeling that ultimately results in an attitude of contemptuous antagonism and voyeuristic aggressiveness, rather than solidarity.

ECHOES IN THE MASTER'S HOUSE

The following passage unveils the rift between masculine will/genius and feminine body.

> I certainly have genius. As I am looking out of this window that drinks up all the hot, dazzling and fragrant Neapolitan gulf, I think that I would have been a bit of a

painter and a bit of a poet, if I had been born a man. Love is not enough for me. In this moment, I truly feel I am not much of a woman.

I have nothing in common with those flaccid, enormous Neapolitan matrons in their bathing suits; they are black, slimy and diluted like seals on the sand, with their darting and boiling litters spread around them.

I remember however the deeply carnal joy that I felt eight days after giving birth. (4)

It is precisely this rift that qualifies the protagonist as an exceptional woman in her own eyes ("I have the nerves of an uncommon woman, nerves that think and desire," 7), as well as in the "scientific" view of her physician. His final diagnosis appears to echo Richard von Krafft-Ebing's famous construct of lesbians as being endowed with a male soul in a female body:[25] "although it is difficult to define her, I will say that, to me, she seems to be an excessively virile brain in an excessively feminine body" (97).

The same paradigms that shape Marinetti's (traditional) opposition of masculinity and femininity also inform references to gender identity in *Un ventre di donna:* specifically, the recurrent association of man with creativity, heroism, and aggressiveness and the identification of femininity with sexuality, weakness, and pathology.[26] The disease that attacks the protagonist's womb destroys the biological "essence" of femininity, the reproductive function. Her stricken womb becomes the emblem of woman's "constitutional" vulnerability and passivity: "How disgusting to be a uterus in pain, while all the men are fighting! I don't even have the courage to take injections!" (25).[27] Moreover, the female genitals are evoked as the image of woman's weakening, emasculating influence on men.

My God! How Awful! Here is a very handsome Alpine soldier obscenely emasculated! I have imagined that the Viennese women compete with the Ethiopian ones and devour the sex organs of the Italian prisoners. . . .

The following night, my imagination sat down at the table of an archduke, between the very elegant wombs of two duchesses, sheathed in Parisian *toilettes,* which suddenly exploded.

Dynamite power of Italian virility! (169–170; emphasis in original)

In this example of "desire-imagination," the heroine fantasizes a link between the enemy threat and the unmanning power of the Austrian and Ethiopian women. Similarly, the explosive counterattack of Italian virility is directed against elegantly "armor-plated" wombs. It is easy to recognize the kinship of these images with the old fiction of the castrating, abject woman, especially with its futurist version, in which Marinetti posits woman as a threat to progress, courage, and virile determination—in other words, as a weakening, contaminating agent that must be dispensed with in order to pursue a religion of "manifested Will" and "daily Heroism."

Robert's text also seems to echo, in more than one way, Paul Julius Möbius's *L'inferiorità mentale della donna: Sulla deficienza mentale fisiologica della donna* (The Mental Inferiority of Woman: On the Mental and Physiological Deficiency of Woman).[28]

A classic in the tradition of "scientific" misogynist literature, Möbius's volume enjoyed wide popularity at the time the novel was written. Citing anatomical observations, Möbius elaborates a theory of woman's congenital deficiency and concludes that "every progress is the work of man" and, furthermore, that "woman weighs down on him like a load of lead" (9). Since women, he argues, are inherently destined to love and bear children, they are devoid of intellectual talent; in the rare case that a woman does possess intellectual attributes, they must be credited to a "masculine talent" (57).[29] The woman who violates natural and social laws by aspiring to individual realization is an abnormal being ("woman's individualism is not possible except on a morbid basis," 52); such a transgression is deemed so terrible a sin as to warrant the following curse, which takes the guise of a scientific diagnosis: "if she fails in her duty to the species and insists on living her individual life for herself, she is struck as if by a curse" (18). Aside from the more obvious analogies—the assumption that any intellectual talent is masculine, that any woman endowed with it is abnormal, and that progress is synonymous with man—one can perceive an even more disquieting link between the two texts: the drama of the protagonist—the struggle of a nonconformist female individual against a mysteriously powerful ailment—seems to fulfill the diagnosis/curse of the misogynist author.

As the protagonist defiantly articulates the "truth" about the female body, rejecting sentimental mystifications, other fictions take over. Other voices speak through her body, transforming it into an icon of traditional, male-centered values and fantasies. Robert's narrative is premised on the claim that giving voice to the body's urgings (desires and symptoms) is liberating. It can be read, more critically, as inscribing the heroine's experience within the constraints set on female pathology by male discourse, in which sickness is taken as a mark of femininity and the feminine (hysterical) voice as the body's conversion into language.[30] Such a discourse resounds in Robert's construction of sexual identity and gender roles. Furthermore, it is voiced by a male subject who, like Robert, figures as author, narrator, and protagonist. On the title page, Marinetti's name precedes that of "Signora [Mrs.] ENIF ROBERT," placing the latter in a subordinate position. This hierarchical relationship between the two authors is confirmed by the fact that Marinetti's seal of approval follows Robert's signature at the end of her preface:

ENIF ROBERT
futurist

I approve unconditionally.

F. T. Marinetti
futurist

Mrs. Robert's authorship is thus "authorized" by the famous author. As a narrator, moreover, Marinetti reads her suffering as an image of great historical events from which she is otherwise excluded. While apparently illustrating an affinity between the addressee of his letter and himself, he equates the war-torn land with her disease-ravished womb. Shifting from analogy to antithesis, he sets up a contrast between the bedridden female protagonist and the heroically active male subject ("But I go around my trench with my chest swelling with pride for I am keeping a tight rein on my nerves under the sliding flights of death"). The hero gloats with pride because, unlike the heroine, he dominates his body, instead of being dominated by it.

The *Taccuini* allow us to view Robert's autobiographical story from a different angle and illuminate a rich subtext to Marinetti's reading of it. Referring to Robert's experience in his notebooks, he adopts a clinical, explanatory, and titillating narrative that can be interpreted as a sexist discourse of male superiority and appropriation. The novel's protagonist views the tension between her feminine body and masculine "genius" as evidence that she is an exceptional woman. Marinetti, by contrast, reduces her difference to restlessness ("Restless soul," 189), deceptiveness ("Extraordinary power of fantasy and histrionic lies," 191), and deviant sexual desire.[31] He reports Robert's lesbian fantasies in great detail, so much so that one wonders whether this account may be, at least in part, a projection of his own fantasy. Alluding to the clinical case recounted in the novel, he comments,

> Enif became deeply interested in her doctor.
> The latter claimed that, after eight years of treating female genitalia, he did not desire women any more.
> Leaving her husband Enif went to Turin with the unavowed hope of arousing tormenting perturbing her doctor. Seducing him exciting him upsetting him [*scompagnarlo*]. Out of boredom restlessness *morbid* curiosity she ended up asking to be operated on by Dr. Carabba whom she declared most unpleasant. She felt horror terror and *morbid* desire for surgical instruments. Strange *sadistic morbid* heroic deviation of a bored uterine sensibility [*Strana deviazione eroica morbosa sadica di sensibilità uterina annoiata*]. (191; emphasis added)

Robert's imaginative power is characterized as deceit, and her experience—erotic desires, fantasies, and masochistic drives—is insistently qualified as "morbid" and ultimately confined to the bodily realm (in particular, the genitals: "bored uterine sensibility"). The attribute "sadistic" is problematic. If the qualification refers to "horror terror and morbid desire for surgical instruments," the appropriate term would be "masochistic." The use of "sadistic" could be a slip (perhaps not a casual one) or a deliberate choice: in either case, the effect is to shift focus back onto Marinetti's characterization of Enif as a tormenting seductress ("arousing tormenting perturbing her doctor"). Ultimately, regardless of how the word is interpreted, it conveys sexual perversion, thus adding to the diagnosed morbidity and resonating with lesbian fantasies. Marinetti appropriates Robert's story and in doing so denies its affective value, converting suffering into titillation.

The fundamental ambivalence underlying the central theme of the heroine's exceptionality also informs the collateral themes of maternity, marriage, and sexual life. Maternity, in particular, seems to provoke a radical split in the female protagonist's self. While she displays repulsion and contempt for the animalized "matrons" and their litters, the protagonist expresses maternal feelings and concerns for her son, Carlino, as well as considerable distress about her lost fertility: "You don't even let me laugh, you hateful enemy hiding here where only a great fecund flower should throb?! You are biting my children, those who I would expect to form and live under the radiant flow of creation" (201). Analogously, in spite of her nonconformist stance in sexual matters, she remains engaged in a monogamous relationship with the man whose love is avowedly insufficient to satisfy her desire. In fact, the only instance of "betrayal" occurs in her daydream of solar intercourse.

> It is both an enclosing embrace and a laceration.
> Each pore on my womb is a mouth that opens, throbs, and would like to flee.
> [. . . .] The whole sun, more vast than the earth, is in my wound. Around it, there are expanding concentric circles of decreasing heat, crossed by a delightful itching, and a very delicate fringe of the lightest spasms circulates all around my hips.
> They are spasms of pleasure, veiled by shades of pain. But the solar heat dominates them, nourishes and consoles them like affection dominates, nourishes and consoles the brutality in love and in violent games.
> I feel myself sinking into the semiunconsciousness of a faint, under the massive power of the solar fire. (146)

The exposure of human bodies to the healing power of the sun is a characteristic trope of the fin de siècle rebellion against bourgeois respectability.[32] As she exposes her scarred womb, Robert defies codes of decency and violates the taboo against revealing the body's pathological failures. In this respect, she displays a self-assertive attitude, which may be read as an attempt at overcoming her avowed "lack" through ostentation and boldness. The rhetoric of this passage, however, raises the possibility of analogies with the images and language of displacement that Robert criticizes in her initial tirade against sentimental literature "based on eroticism masked with chiseling grace" (XII). The fetishistic sublimation in the daydream resembles the "foolish substitution of thoughts and things" (XIII) stigmatized in her preface ("For pity's sake, don't waste any more gems of style to tell us that the sun is a divine lover, or that an autumnal garden can make you dizzy with the most intense pleasure!" XII–XIII). In effect, Robert reinscribes the notion of feminine passive submission to a divinely powerful, masculine force and displaces erotic desires through a fantasized interaction with an anthropomorphic natural phenomenon. The process of displacement is stripped of the prudish restraints and "graceful" rhetoric with which it had previously been disguised; in a sense, Robert's assault against "quivering literature" is directed more at its manners than at its message.

The daydream passage is not an isolated instance. The sun is consistently personified as a divine lover endowed with features of futurism's omnipotent and hypervirile superuomo. In describing the return of the sun after a storm, Robert naturalizes the intercourse between overpowering masculinity and submissive femininity by projecting it onto the marine landscape: "Now the sun is back, absolute *Master*, stubborn, solemn, obstinate, caressing and holding tightly all the curves, penetrating all the mouths of the possessed lascivious seashore, which delights in absorbing him" (22; emphasis in original). Subsequently, as the womb apostrophizes the sun, it becomes evident that the heroine's sadomasochistic fantasy reproduces the asymmetry of power relations dramatized in the novel: "Forgive me; I am yours; do what you want with me. I am nearly freed from consciousness. [. . . .] Cut! Wound! Rip! Tear to pieces! Burst open! I will be yours in shreds. Yours! Pierce me! Or crush me! Char me! Like this! Again! Again!" (149). Sexuality functions as a highly charged signifier for differentials of power, constituting a major locus for the reproduction and conservation of male ascendancy. The masochistic pleasure conveyed by the womb's acceptance of the sun's all-powerful violence testifies to the complicitous role woman plays in her own victimization. One way to interpret such complicity is to regard it as a search for identity (recognition) through the intercession of a powerful other who can bestow it vicariously—a search, or need, that is a consequence of woman's internalization of the idea of femininity as lack.[33]

The polarized dynamic of submission-domination played out in the protagonist's eroticized intercourse with the sun also informs Robert's intellectually ambitious relationship to Marinetti—the great artist, leader, and hero. The passage above bears comparison to the following excerpt from Marinetti's letters: "A cannon strike is the equivalent of an ardent epistolary love: one does not see or feel the mouth kissed from very far away. A mortar strike, instead, is the equivalent of a vehement radiotelegraphic embrace, or, rather, of a telephonic kiss" (139–140). While she subjects herself to the futurist leader's aesthetic prescriptions and experiments, Robert also echoes his brash language, rhetoric of sexual violence, and sadomasochistic identifications of death with eros.

THE SCARRED WOMB

Robert's reinscription of male-centered values and her use of Marinettian rhetoric do not warrant the conclusion that the novel fails to differ from the texts examined in previous chapters. An obvious difference is located at the level of thematic and narrative structures, which are traversed by the *unhealing*, intimate rift experienced by the female protagonist. At this level, Robert's woman is not merely a mirror of man's desires and anxieties. She is the author, narrator, and protagonist of an experience that she perceives and presents as a break with conventional gender identity. Still, given the unresolved ambivalence associated with her exceptional status (hysterical behavior, diseased body, confused gender identity), the futurist heroine is not an extraordinary individual in the way that the futurist hero is. Marinetti's letters in *Un ventre di donna* construct the myth of a virile, self-assertive, and aggressive individual who overcomes limitations, both intimate and external. Problematization is tendentially eschewed by defining the new hero in antithesis to passéist values and femininity. Even in this co-authored book, where the female voice plays a protagonist role, Marinetti assimilates woman's experience into his male fiction of power by rhetorically appropriating it as a figure for the material abjection (life in the trenches, fear of death) that he can master and transcend. In Robert's narrative, on the contrary, the protagonist's identity is radically problematized as she is placed in an uneasy, unstable position between masculine and feminine poles. The boundary dividing the two polarized spaces cuts through her in a way that correlates, in my view, with the central image of an incurable wound in the womb—an image of splitting that marks the protagonist's body with the unsuturable laceration between the self and the abject.

A less patent, but not less significant, site of difference is that of the text's political investment. The futurist heroine is not proposed as a model of emancipation to other women as the futurist hero is to other men: if her behavior is potentially subversive of traditional parameters, it is so in a way that allows no solidarity with other women. In fact, her exceptionality results in feelings of supercilious detachment toward other members of her sex, and there is no sense of sisterhood comparable to the futurist brotherhood (as portrayed, for instance, in "Uccidiamo il Chiaro di Luna!"), or to the male camaraderie in war represented in Marinetti's letters.[34] As I have already suggested, the experiences and aspirations shared with the other female characters are limited to the affective, physical, and sexual sphere: nursing and comfort in sickness, gossip about romantic adventures, the competitive desire to attract men, and vulnerability to the disease potentially hidden in each woman's womb. While war cements the male brotherhood-in-arms, the heroine's disease (an inner war) fosters a jealous, competitive attitude toward other women's healthy wombs, thus exacerbating an emblem of her inability to embrace female solidarity: "And why are all the other women, the slender ones I see passing by in the glowing wake of male admiration, why *are they healthy*, while I am not?" (203; emphasis in original). Finally, in the spiritual sphere of ambitious, artistic aspirations, the protagonist relates only to the futurist writer Marinetti, who demiurgically shapes her entrance into the literary world, and to whom she displays a hero-worshiping attitude.[35]

In conclusion, the novel offers a story of *unresolved* inner conflicts and malaise that significantly differs from the conflictual experiences dramatized in the texts of male futurist writers: the experience of an individual overstepping the boundaries of her preordained role and entering the sphere of culture and self-affirmation. In the charged image of the scarred, unhealing "woman's womb" we can identify a poignant emblem of the split furrowing the woman's self as a result of this transgression. We have seen how the female voice challenges behavioral and rhetorical codes that constrain women's role while at the same time internalizing prejudices—obstacles to self-affirmation—that result in self-loathing and self-division. We have also seen that the transgression is channeled out of the social and political realm into the turbulent stream of avant-garde artistic experience. Ultimately, the "cure" proposed by this text (unleashed creative imagination, paroliberismo) allegorizes the limits of the strategy generally adopted by futurist women: to follow an avant-garde program prescribed by a male-centered movement that did not provide a progressive ideological foundation for the restructuring of the social organization of gender.

SIX

Transformations in the Futurist Mythopoeia

The experience of futurist women calls attention to futurism's multifacetedness. Even without considering non-Italian efforts, we can speak of several different phases and "faces" of the movement.[1] Milanese futurism, the original modernist core of the movement, centered around Marinetti and Umberto Boccioni. In 1913–1914, the driving force behind Florentine futurism was the journal *Lacerba*, which played a prominent role in the campaign against bourgeois conventions and in the interventionist propaganda against Austria. During the war years, the so-called Pattuglia azzurra (Azure Patrol)—a second Florentine futurism developed in association with *L'Italia futurista*—imparted a presurrealistic flair to the movement. After the war, futurism shifted its capital from Milan to Rome, which became the site of Marinetti's Edizioni futuriste di «Poesia» and the major journals of the period—*Roma futurista, Il Futurismo, Noi,* and *Futurismo* (later *Sant'Elia,* and then *Artecrazia*).[2] The vicissitudes of these publications reflect the history of the movement into the 1920s and 1930s: the brief trajectory of the Futurist party and the confinement of the movement's ambitions to the artistic sphere after the political delusions of 1919–1920;[3] then the relationship with the fascist regime, marked by tension and by a persistent effort to claim for the movement a leading role in the cultural scene; finally, the links with other avant-garde movements and the defense of modern art against the most reactionary tendencies within the regime.[4]

The map of Italian futurism becomes more complex as we trace the movement's expansion into factions and provincial diffusion. Throughout these transformations, Marinetti maintained his role as founder, leader, animator, financier, and propagandist. Futurism's agenda, however, underwent considerable flux. Narrowing the focus to questions of poetics, four major phases can be distinguished: "free verse" (1909–1912), "words in freedom" (1912–1931), "aeropoetry" (1931–1944), and "poetry of technicalities" (1938–1944). Moving beyond literature into the numerous areas colonized by the futurists (politics, theater, painting, sculpture, architecture, music, dance, radio, cinema, fashion, cooking, interior design, and photography) and considering differences between theory and praxis, the issue of futurism's transformations becomes a complicated one. Scholars have tended to simplify matters by drawing a boundary between a utopian, experimental first phase (the so-called first or heroic futurism) and a more pragmatic, less innovative second phase (the so-called second futurism). Some writers locate the turning point in 1915–1916, with the outbreak of war and the deaths of Boccioni and Antonio Sant'Elia. Others look to 1920, and the disappointing conclusion of futurist political experiments, followed by the defections of such veterans as Carli, Settimelli, and Corra and the arrival of new young recruits.[5]

Such a periodization may reflect an attempt to dissociate the futurist aesthetic revolution from the movement's political connection with fascism.[6] It undoubtedly delineates a noticeable disparity in critical attention. The second period is invariably less known and less carefully studied. Particularly in Marinetti's case, scholars tend to evaluate summarily and often dismissively later developments as an involution and return to tradition—a tired recycling of the stock materials of the futurist warehouse, often merely serving a propagandistic function and lacking the aesthetic and ideological interest of the earlier works.

In his introduction to the 1968 edition of *Teoria e invenzione futurista*, De Maria notes that Marinetti's post–1920 works still await critical attention (LXVI). This assessment stands in the 1983 revised edition (XCIII) and remains valid today. My project in this chapter is to examine how sentiment, nostalgic memory, nature, and Christian love were reassimilated into the futurist mythopoeia as Marinetti's strategies shifted in reaction to historical change. I shall pursue this inquiry on two different but not unrelated levels: the diachronic dimension of the developments in the configuration of Marinetti's fiction of power and the synchronic dimension of the psychological and rhetorical processes that convert "deep structures" of existential angst into the "surface structures" of the futurist mythical vision of the modern age. My approach is premised on the belief that the diachronic developments actually point to the second kind of transformations and that an analysis of the former can be instrumental in the exploration of this other overlooked dimension of the futurist experience: its psychological foundation.

RESORBING THE REJECTED

Because Marinetti programmatically identified his futurist enterprise with the empowering developments of new technology, he is generally considered a paradigmatic modernist. The deep sense of crisis scholars find in other modernist authors is seemingly alien to Marinetti's vehement and single-minded vision of radical change. His manifestos hail the destruction of the past and its decrepit myths, while predicating a new mythology on the optimistic representation of technological progress. The role played by gender in the resulting fiction of individual and national regeneration indicates tensions and anxieties that subtend the paean to modernity. In Marinetti's later works, such tensions rise more visibly to the surface in the wake of a recuperation or (to use Marinetti's digestive metaphor for assimilation) resorption of previously rejected themes: sentiment, nature, and nostalgic memory.

Although it continues to celebrate technological progress, Marinetti's postwar writing shows signs of a reemergence of the pessimistic, fatalistic Weltanschauung of his prefuturist output. At the same time, the focus shifts from glorifying the machine to elaborating on changes in man and nature. Futurism's founding myth, as we have seen, celebrates the symbiosis between the beautiful, all-powerful machine and a multiplied, metallized superman, invulnerable to love, nostalgia, and death. In futurist poetics, the machine replaces woman in her traditional role as privileged aesthetic object, and the "intuitive psychology of matter"—capturing the secret life of molecules and engines—supplants the "exhausted" psychology of man (*TIF*, 50–52). The human element, specifically the workers' experience, is either absent from the technological scenario depicted in the manifestos or reduced to a dehumanized material instrument and decorative accessory for the aestheticized technological creation. When the victims of progress are considered, as in the following passage from the 1915 "Nascita di un estetica futurista" (The Birth of a Futurist Aesthetic), it is as the inevitable waste generated in the productive process: "To a well-built house we prefer the framework of a house under construction with its danger-colored scaffolds—landing platforms for airplanes,—with its numberless arms that scratch and comb out stars and comets, with its aerial quarterdecks from which the eye embraces a vaster horizon. The framework, with its rhythm of pulleys, hammers and hearts, and from time to time—so be it [*sia pure*]—the piercing cry and heavy thud of a fallen construction worker, a great drop of blood on the pavement!" (*TIF*, 316). The dangerous framework of a building in construction is an apt metaphor for the interplay of constructive and destructive drives that shapes futurist aesthetics. In this exultant celebration of dynamism, the worker's suffering, on which progress is predicated, is conceded ("sia pure"), then promptly discounted—reduced to a spot on the pavement.

In only one of Marinetti's later works, *Gli Indomabili* (The Untamables; 1922), is this marginal theme developed, becoming a grimmer but more sympathetic vision of working-class alienation. Returning to the overt existential and sociopolitical pessimism of the prefuturist play *Le Roi Bombance*, this allegorical narrative represents the human experience as an inferno of unruly instinctual brutality (the Untamables) and inevitable social oppression (the mass of workers, or River People), ruled by a contradictory and esoteric ideological domain (the translucent Paper People, supported by the Light and Paper Workers and led by King Contradictor).[7] The apocalyptic description of working conditions in the entrails of the future city—realm of spiritual freedom, but only for the privileged intellectual elite—is an emotion-laden critique of industrial civilization.

Around each wheel swarmed the minute labor of a complicated clockwork of small wheels, everyone of which was as tall as a man and wore, suspended from its crank, a black convulsed rag.

[. . . .] Those rags seemed to be panting. They were living be-
ʈʈ
ings. Limp, as if boneless, dragged around by the wheel
ʈʈ
itself, while in reality, the rotating force originated from them. From time to time, one of those flaccid, contorted men slowed down his convulsive movement. You could hear him panting and groaning from fatigue, while the wheels around him, all in gear, slowed their revolutions, and the giant perpendicular wheel, as it too lost speed, revealed its edge of bright silver teeth. A hiss immediately drilled the hot air.

—Harder! To work! Speed! Speed! Whoever stops will be punished! Work or death! Speed or death! (*TIF*, 988; emphasis in original)

The human "gears," mutilated and partly paralyzed by their monotonous, alienating toil, demand "the poetry of the body in freedom" (*TIF*, 989): creative, personal, inspired work. They want to break the dam of enslaved labor and flow freely to the great peaceful lake of Poetry. Their discontent erupts in a riot, led by one of the Untamables, who are intuitively inspired by the "frightening, mysteriously beautiful thoughts" of the futurist Paper People (*TIF*, 997). These words in freedom, however, exist only at a "celestial" level. Luminous but unilluminating, blinding yet obscure, they remain undeciphered hieroglyphs projected onto the unreachable screen of the sky. The revolutionary attempt to lift the workers out of their crippling oppression results in a flood of blind destruction and an eventual return to the status quo. This allegorical tale reflects Marinetti's political disappointment of 1920. One of the Paper People, the contradictory and opportunistic Mah, seems in fact to be inspired by Mussolini.[8]

Marinetti leaves the reader with no hope for social progress: revolutionary ideas and language fail to foster constructive change, and the imaginary world of the text appears to maintain the rigid hierarchical divisions between brutal instincts, blind oppression, enslaved labor, and illuminated (but esoteric) spiritual power. In the end, however, one of the Untamables opens up a way to spiritual metamorphosis by recalling an earlier experience prior to their arrival to the city. As he narrates his vision, all the others listen intently and peacefully: "Thus," read the final lines, "stronger than the cacophonic harshness of Sun and Blood, the superhuman, coolwinged Distraction of Art finally brought about the metamorphosis of the Untamables" (*TIF*, 1012). In discovering a possible avenue for change, the vision draws inspiration, not from a future of action in the social realm of the city, but from the past of reverie, with its consoling images of a natural, poetic oasis. This is the feminine, maternal oasis ("a paradise of fantasies," *TIF*, 964; "Oasis of the Moon," *TIF*, 968) in which the ferocious instincts of the Untamables had been temporarily tamed and purified through the experience of art and love afforded by the lake of Poetry and Feeling.

The moonlit scenery of the oasis, with sensual vegetation surrounding the luminous, poetic, and musical water of the lake, recalls similar moments in previous works such as "Uccidiamo il Chiaro di Luna!" and *Mafarka*. Once again, the feminine is evoked and identified with the seducing landscape.

> Up above, the crest of the Oasis was occasionally sagging like a bed, under the weight of an invisible, immense naked woman. There wafted about the perfume-memory of a night of love that had lasted one hundred years. As they marched, the Untamables and the negro soldiers threw back their heads to enjoy, with their eyes, cheeks and mouths, *the fresh aerial sea of arching foliage.*
>
> Baaaack and foooorth, uuuup and dowwwn, the leaves were trying to perfect the grace of their undulating rhythm with a languid softness. The path turned into *the carnal tenderness of the jasmine and the acacia.* (*TIF*, 963; emphasis added)

> No one was swimming in that still water; but *its surface rippled now and then with fleeting apparitions. Soft profiles of evanescent women, curves of delicate nude bodies, vaporous hair, bejeweled hands.* (*TIF*, 969; emphasis added)

There are distinct linguistic echoes between this scene and, for instance, the "seduction" episode in "Uccidiamo il Chiaro di Luna!": in particular, the "carnal tenderness" of the acacia reminds us of the "intoxicating milk of acacias" that drenches the moon, "the ancient green queen of loves"; the sealike foliage recalls the fluctuating prairies that assume feminine shape in the spellbound nocturnal scenario; and the vaporous female hair on the rippled surface of the lake echoes the image of swimmers evoked by the undulating motion of vegetation (*TIF*, 21–22). But these similarities underscore a crucial difference: in the earlier text, the deadly seductive powers of the feminine-connoted nature are exorcised by the power of technology (the moonlight is killed by "three hundred electric moons," *TIF*, 22); here, on the contrary, immersion in the sweet, tender, soothing elements of the feminine oasis results in the miraculous, albeit temporary, transformation of untamable brutes into sensitive, gentle human beings. Enraptured by the sensual delights of nature, they take each other by the hand, joining into "a new human chain" (*TIF*, 974).

However, the triumph of Sentiment, Peace, and Beauty is confined to the Oasis of Poetry. In his commentary to the text, Marinetti explains that ferocious instincts cannot be harnessed by "goodness" because they are the vital forces on which progress is predicated: "Only the ferocity, the cruelty, the destruction mastered yesterday and today conscious and willful can lead to the future. But the forces mastered for an instant break loose anew, anarchic, individualistic, ferocious. Again they become unconscious, brutal, and criminal instincts that must be chained up. And everything would start again. But in Humanity there is the continuity of consciousness" (*TIF*, LXXXVII). Such a cyclical conception of history is seemingly underlined by the temporal frame—the inescapable alternation of day and night—in which the narrative is set. The sole possibility for redemption, in this deterministic perspective, is escape into the consoling realm of aesthetic catharsis: "the superhuman coolwinged Distraction of Art." The power of art is thus both celebrated and restricted to a function of distraction (rather than liberation). Memory, as a means of escape, also acquires a crucial, positive role, in implicit contrast to Marinetti's previous railings against nostalgic literature.

FROM POLITICAL ACTIVISM TO AESTHETIC ESCAPISM

According to the movement's antipasséist program, nostalgic memories, as well as all emotions that threaten the integrity of the self, should be drained off, or at least dammed up. Instead, as will become apparent, they flow freely in Marinetti's later texts. Why the reversal? It could be hypothesized that a surge of pessimism, breaching the optimistic futurist fiction, opens a space for the "inundation" of sentiment and what Marinetti might have more predictably described as "putrid poetry."[9] These former enemies of the self become assimilated into a positive role of consolation and distraction, made necessary by social, political, and economic realities.

The 1922 manifesto "Ad ogni uomo, ogni giorno un mestiere diverso! Inegualismo e Artecrazia" (To Every Man, Every Day a Different Job! Unequalism and Artocracy), whose title recalls the demands of the crippled workers in *Gli Indomabili,* lends credence to such a hypothesis. In offering a fervid celebration of individuality and originality, Marinetti pitches Art, Love, and Pleasure against the abjection of politics.

> Only Unequalism, by multiplying contrasts, chiaroscuro, volumes, inspiration, warmth, and color, can save Art, Love, Poetry, Plastic Art, Architecture, Music, and the indispensable Pleasure of Living.
>
> Destroy, wipe out politics, which dulls all bodies. It is a most tenacious leprosy-cholera-syphilis! (*TIF,* 553)

Politics in general and egalitarian communism in particular are associated with virulent, infectious pathology and evoke the specter of monstrous loss of identity. In keeping with the rhetorical strategies deployed in the earlier manifestos, politics is not simply denounced but vehemently abjected and rejected. As in the prefuturist poems, Marinetti turns to the sea (his "favorite adviser," *TIF,* 549) for advice about the intricate "tangle" of sociopolitical problems that trouble the world. Having taken from nature an evolutionist lesson in inequality, injustice, agonism, and antagonism, he prophetically declares the advent of *artecrazia,* the rule of art, and advocates an artistic solution to labor issues: the introduction of art, variety, and individuality in the workplace. A similar proposal had already been advanced, and outlined in greater detail, in *Al di là del Comunismo* (Beyond Communism; 1920). The earlier text does not explicitly reject and abominate politics per se; however, it does represent a move beyond politics and modernolatria. The alienating effects of modern capitalism ("the hard, dark, dreary and convulsive rhythm of daily life,"

TIF, 485) are explicitly denounced but ahistorically postulated in terms of "economic hell"—the eternal, immutable underside of the escapist utopia of "life as a work of art" or "life as a festival": "We will have no earthly paradise, but the economic inferno will be cheered up and pacified by innumerable festivals of art" (*TIF*, 488). Thus social issues are translated into metapolitical, aesthetic terms, and the artist's agency is narrowed to a consolatory function.

This shift in direction is especially conspicuous and significant since it follows a phase of increasingly intense and constructive political commitment, culminating in 1918–1919. As Emilio Gentile notes, "With regard to the period before the outbreak of the Great War, it is more correct to speak of an *attitude* on Marinetti's part than a political *commitment*."[10] His political attitude was most explicitly formulated in three brief manifestos, launched before the elections of 1909 and 1913 and at the onset of the Libyan war in 1911. It was characterized by militant patriotism, antisocialism, and anticlericalism, by an agonistic conception of progress, and by the ideal of art as the driving regenerative force in the evolution of the country. The program that these texts outline is limited to a generic formula of renewal (regeneration through violence, unfettered creativity, and economic expansion) and to such nationalistic slogans as the famous "The word ITALY must prevail over the word FREEDOM. All freedoms but cowardice, pacifism, anti-Italianism" (*TIF*, 339).

In early references to the social function of art, Marinetti displayed an elitist, contemptuous attitude toward the obtuse mass audience, although he proclaimed his faith in art's mysterious, miraculous power to "infiltrate," or "rub off onto," the public's taste and sensibility.[11] At the end of World War I, he expressed a more optimistic view of the masses, who, he believed, had been galvanized and regenerated by the experience of victory: "Wonderful spectacle of an entire army gone to war with hardly any awareness and returned politicized and worthy of governing" (*TIF*, 382). The movement's political activity, previously confined to interventionist propaganda, was expanded in an ambitious effort to set the agenda for the renewal of national life. A futurist political party was founded, and a program for extensive sociopolitical change was outlined. In *Manifesto del partito futurista italiano* (Manifesto of the Italian Futurist Party; 1918) and in *Democrazia futurista*, Marinetti and his colleagues proposed a synthesis of nationalism, revolutionism, and democracy as an alternative to the traditional antithesis between clerical, conservative nationalism and pacifist, democratic internationalism. Such a synthesis was designed to subvert old ideological commonplaces and revolutionize politics to conform "plastically" and "elastically" to the shifting, violent dynamics of modern life (*TIF*, 353–360).

Gentile underscores the idiosyncratic nature of the futurist democracy envisioned by Marinetti.

> The "futurist democracy" [. . .] was not a modern mass democracy; despite its pretensions to modernity, it resembled the ideal of a small anarchic community. By

abolishing the family through free love and the adoption of children by the State, such a community would guarantee for all an equal starting point, leaving then to each individual total freedom to realize and continually surpass himself. The *heroic citizens* of this anarchic and individualistic democracy would be trained, in futurist fashion, for the love of risk, for personal physical defense (hence the abolition of police and prisons), for individual and spontaneous creation in the various fields of human activity.[12]

The utopian quality of the program is an early indication of Marinetti's tendency toward a transcendence of reality—which later manifests itself more dramatically in his abrupt switch from intense political engagement to a disillusioned rejection of politics.

The aftermath of the war was a turbulent, eventful period. Italy's economic and sociopolitical problems became greatly exacerbated. Chaos in politics formed the backdrop for several fateful developments in Marinetti's career and the progress of futurism. Citing a shared agenda of struggle against "unpatriotic" socialism, abolishment of the monarchy, protection of veterans' rights, and defense of Italy's victory (tainted by "unredeemed lands"), the futurists formed an alliance with Mussolini's Fasci Italiani di Combattimento and with the Associazione degli Arditi d'Italia (Association of Italian Shock Troopers) led by Ferruccio Vecchi.[13] However, the fascist ticket was soundly defeated at the polls. At the ensuing second congress of Fasci (1920), Mussolini set a new political course, advocating the restoration of order through compromise with conservative forces. In response, Marinetti resigned his Executive Committee post and broke with the organization, accusing it of passéism and reaction.[14] When he approached fascism again in 1923–1924, significant changes had taken place within the futurist movement, as well as in his own life: several old companions had abandoned the futurist ranks, the ambitions of futurism had been circumscribed to the artistic sphere, and he had contravened his antimatrimonial policies by marrying Benedetta Cappa, an artist who had recently joined the movement.

Futurismo e Fascismo (1924), the text that sanctions the new alliance with fascism (Marinetti's dedication on the title page reads "To my dear and great friend Benito Mussolini"), defines a division of roles: politics was to be the domain of fascism, while art remained the province of futurism. Rewriting political history in a self-aggrandizing fashion, Marinetti claims paternity over fascism and proclaims its coming to power "the realization of the most basic futurist program [*programma minimo futurista*]" (*TIF*, 494). The basic program evidently consists of an ideological common ground, marked by "optimistic proud violent overbearing and combatant patriotism" (*TIF*, 496).[15]

Marinetti's rejection of politics and retreat into art may well have been a reaction to the political disappointments of the postwar period. *Al di là del Comunismo* was written shortly after the electoral defeat of 1919, and the manifesto "Ad ogni uomo, ogni giorno un mestiere diverso!" was launched in November 1922, after the crisis of the alliance between futurism and Fasci (May 1920), the failed revolutionary experience in Fiume (December 1920), and the fascist March on Rome (October 1922). Both texts lack the political optimism that characterizes *Democrazia futurista*, substituting an escapist, consolatory conception of art. It might be concluded that Marinetti, in keeping with his "digestive strategy," abominated and rejected what he was unable to assimilate. In fact, however, he did manage to swallow many changes in the ensuing years: the fascist compromise with the monarchy and the Vatican, the reactionary involution of the regime, and even his own nomination to the passéist role of official member of the Fascist Academy of the Arts (1929). As some have noted, Marinetti's renunciation of politics and claim to the role of precursor to fascism might have enabled him to protect futurism from the growing reactionary tendencies among fascist cultural authorities.[16] If this was the case, it is not hard to see why the revolutionary, libertarian edge of texts previously published in *Guerra sola igiene del mondo* or *Democrazia futurista* was, when reprinted in *Futurismo e Fascismo*, blunted by the elision of references to universal suffrage and freedom.[17]

TACTILISM AND TRANSFORMISM

The developments in Marinetti's aesthetics after the war bear evidence to a shift from palingenetic, superomistic goals to more mundane concerns and immediate sensual pleasures. "Il Tattilismo" (1921) contains the first signs of an obvious realignment of values as compared to the earlier manifestos. The main argument in celebration of art's therapeutic power does not seem to depart from previous positions: Marinetti proposes the new *arte tattile* as a remedy against the postwar syndrome—pessimism, indecision, neurosis, lack of will. But this familiar rhetorical strategy results in an unexpected move: the recuperation of the passéist values of Love and Friendship. Love, previously regarded as a threat to the subject's unity and the target of exorcism through violence, mechanized sex, or a futurist-style Don Juanism, now figures as a positive force binding individuals and communities. Addressing his contemporary "artists" and "thinkers," Marinetti intimates something resembling a new humanism: "Heal [. . .] the postwar ailments by giving *new nourishing joys* to humanity. Instead of destroying human agglomerations, we must perfect them. Intensify the communication and the fusion among human beings. Destroy the distances and the barriers that separate them in love and friendship. Give total realization and beauty to these two essential manifestations of life: *Love and Friendship*" (*TIF*, 161; emphasis added). Whereas the syntactic revolution celebrated in the earlier technical manifestos aims at a superman's victory over matter and death, the new art form is meant to perfect spiritual communication among human beings by means of an increased, diffuse (not necessarily genital) sensuality of "tactile harmonies" (*TIF*, 166).[18]

According to Marinetti, the idea of tattilismo germinated during the war, in the underground tunnel of a trench. Groping his way through the darkness, he became acutely aware of the material objects surrounding him—bayonets, mess tins, and heads of sleeping soldiers (*TIF*, 165, 175). This initial experience with tactility was amplified by a subsequent "immersion," this time among jutting rocks in a sea, with the red flags of a worker's strike as a backdrop.

> Last Summer, in Antignano, [. . .] I invented Tactilism. Red flags were flapping over the factories occupied by workers.
>
> I was naked in the silky water that was being torn by rocks, foaming scissors knives razors, among mattresses of algae soaked with iodine. I was naked in a sea of flexible steel that heaved with virility and fecundity. I was drinking from the chalice of the sea, full of genius to the brim. With its long searing flames, the sun was vulcanizing my body and bolting together the keel of my forehead rich in sails. (*TIF*, 159)

The presence of fluttering banners associates the treacherous waters in which the artist is swimming with the turbulent "Red Biennium": the waves of leftist-inspired strikes, land occupations, and food riots that swept Italy in 1919–1920.[19] As if in reaction to the surrounding threat, the artist drinks from the "cup" of the sea (his inspiring muse). It brims with genius. Having partaken, the artist is transformed into a powerful ship propelled by the volcanic force of the sun. Once again, the assimilative strategy of metaphorically incorporating a hostile object/ environment is the precondition for artistic creation.

In the 1924 version of this manifesto, references to the postwar neurosis are omitted, and so is a declaration of solidarity with mass insurrections ("As for us futurists, who bravely confront the agonizing postwar drama, we favor all revolutionary attacks that the majority will attempt," *TIF*, 160–161). Instead, Marinetti expounds his theory of the discovery and development of new senses, introducing it with the vision-hypothesis of an apocalyptic event that could have "spontaneously" engendered the new art he has created "with an act of futurist whim-faith-will" (*TIF*, 178). "Suppose," he tells his readers, "that the Sun leaves its orbit and forgets the Earth! Darkness. Men stumbling about. Terror. Then, the birth of a vague confidence, and settlement" (*TIF*, 178). People would gradually adapt to the perpetual night, and their bodies, following the evolution of "nyctalopic" (night-seeing) animals, would develop previously unknown sensory powers.

Comparing the narrative frame of the two manifestos on tactilism with the mythopoetic introduction to the first technical manifesto, a crucial shift in perspective becomes apparent. The program of syntactic revolution was "dictated" by the whirling propeller of an airplane that afforded to the poet a foreshortened, all-embracing, transcendent point of view (*TIF*, 46, 52). Tattilismo, by contrast, is generated by an immersion in the dark, threatening chaos of phenomena. In both cases, art's evolution is presented as a consequence of, or an adaptation to, the evolving, challenging circumstances of life. In the later vision, however, man's lot is not the aerial, totalizing perspective of an omnipotent superuomo, but the compensatory "supersensibility" of a night-seeing animal. The image of groping in the dark is a telling metaphor for Marinetti's bleak outlook on life at this time. Furthermore, his apocalyptic vision of humanity's evolution into night vision can be read as a dismal parable of his transformist (Lamarckian) conception of art and his compromise with the shifting politics of fascism.

ART AS SALUTARY DISTRACTION AND COSMETIC COMPENSATION

In the cultural climate that accompanied the rappel à l'ordre of the interwar period, the futurists offered "new nourishing joys" and salutary distractions to mass audiences preoccupied with socioeconomic problems. The most obvious result was a vast production of social-erotic fiction. In this popular genre are the short stories Marinetti collected in *Gli amori futuristi, Scatole d'amore in conserva,* and *Novelle con le labbra tinte.* Futurist experiments in the field of culinary art were also products of this escapist tendency. As we have seen, an erotic story constitutes a kind of manifesto-preface to the recipe book *La cucina futurista.* An introductory note celebrates the "futurist culinary revolution" as a creative, economic antidote of optimism against the "dangerous depressing panic" caused by the contemporary world economic crisis. The goal is to create "harmony" between man's palate and modern life by "fortifying, dynamizing, and spiritualizing" the Italian diet.

Marinetti's erotic tales use the recurrent motif of incorporation to transform woman into food. As I have argued, the same (frustrated) desire for control that breeds sexual violence in earlier Marinettian texts is evident here. But whereas *Mafarka* and the first manifestos reject woman and sex for the sake of heroic male ambitions, later texts valorize them in the service of pleasurable evasion. This is clearly the role envisaged for feminine sensual appeal in "Ritratto olfattivo di una donna."

Olfactory Portrait of a Woman

(olfactory lyric - words in freedom)

The gate to the city of iron electricity coal fire smoke speed drinks the infinite green of the spring morning like a mouth   I am the bitter tongue of the city in search of coolness wandering in the sweet air
With my eyes closed nostrils open unraveling with my marching body the very elastic very vibrant mass of perfumes smells
It's she   This sweet most agile ovoidal volume of fresh rosy milky perfumes with 3   6   nine spirals of vanilla fragrances above

NOT SEEING HER SMELLING HER

To the left	To the right
roses	violets
roses	violets

roses   violets

roses   violets

roses etc.   violets etc.

20 curved fragrances   1000 tongues

of rose   of fragrances of violets

On the smell of
wet soil
the fresh warm
sharp and velvety scent
of her breasts
of twenty-year-old
Italianness
advances

Quickening my pace
       running
following
       3 spirals
of cigarette odor
     Stop
Warmsweetsour odor

of panting breath

in her invisible left hand swings a bunch of carnations stings and alcoholic romantic flourishes caresses passion etc.	in her invisible right hand swing 3 bananas smell melted with sweetness terror of dissolving into the damp shadow of death etc.

smell of hair
compressed by the sun
kindred smell of the smell
of scorching stones

To the left   and   to   the right
and globally over the head shifting arches
of the freshest milky fragrance of acacia
mother infancy *uè! uè!* beginning again[20]

The initial image of an engulfing mouth recalls the by now familiar metaphor of violent erotic incorporation. However, it proceeds to dissolve into an experience of olfactory assimilation: the poet's closed eyes allow him freedom of fantastic re-creation. The woman, meanwhile, is deprived of autonomous individuality. She is reduced to a synesthesia of olfactory, tactile, and gustatory sensations—a supple, ovoid mass of inebriating smells. Furthermore, she is assimilated as an object of desire and catalyst of existential anxiety through metonymic identification with

Italianness and youth ("breasts of twenty-year-old Italianness"), death ("sweetness terror of dissolving into the damp shadow of death"), intoxicating passion ("alcoholic romantic flourishes caresses passion"), and regression to infancy ("mother infancy *uè! uè!* beginning again"). The subject portrays himself as the bitter "tongue" of the city—possibly, a trope for poetic experience in the industrialized world. The expressions "bitter" and "in search of coolness" suggest that the "tongue," saturated with the poisons of modern life, seeks refreshment, evasion, and regeneration in the polymorphous sensuality of woman/nature. Such an image appears to reverse futurism's original move away from the realm of the feminine (which usually overlaps with the domains of nature and sensuality) and toward the metallic, electric splendor of technological artifacts. Still at play is the transfiguring, assimilating, and ultimately defensive strategy that constitutes the founding and driving impetus of the futurist fiction of power. But the avant-garde myth of art as action (destruction of the past and construction of the future) gives way to the decadent notion of art as cosmetic compensation (pleasurable transfiguration of, or evasion from, the real).

This development is also signaled by a shift in perspective from the exciting, utopian future to the consolations of a remembered past. Clear evidence of such a shift can be found in later manifestos and theoretical writings, such as *Marinetti e il Futurismo* (1929) and "La tecnica della nuova poesia" (The Technique of New Poetry; 1937). These, for the most part, commemorate the movement's accomplishments, recycling and commenting on passages in the earlier texts. Marinetti now claims a position of leadership in the artistic life of the nation, emphasizing the role played by futurism as a precursor to fascism's "revolutionary" spirit. As with his earlier disclaimer of politics, the apologetic, self-glorifying rhetoric can be seen as a defensive response to the marginal position to which futurism had been relegated by the fascist cultural establishment.

RECYCLING THE PAST

As he grew older, reality became increasingly alien to Marinetti's fiction of power. He responded by investing his fantasies in the past. In *Spagna veloce e toro futurista* (Speedy Spain and a Futurist Bull; 1931), for instance, the poet expresses yearning for youth's freshness through the voice of a "futurist" bull ("the king of bulls, a horned antisocial machine of exploding savage power," *TIF*, 1048), who is fighting time and death in the arena: "I'm on fire! Oh my fresh distant youth . . . / Green spasm! / Softviscous" (*TIF*, 1044). Time and death, however, are not the only dangers: "I'm surrounded! A new insidious danger [*nuova insidia*] spreads around me with splendors riches honors jests and gaudy sumptuousness. I can smell the corrupt scents of senile power and glory" (*TIF*, 1043). The definition of "nuova insidia" is significant to an understanding of Marinetti's attitude toward "senile power and glory," particularly if we assume that the personification of the embattled animal is symptomatic of a mechanism of identification—a hypothesis that is corroborated by a sympathetic exclamation in Spanish ("Pobre toro!") and an impassioned confession: "Who has pronounced these words? Maybe they slipped from the mouth of some beggar fallen in exhaustion at the crossroads of my desert veins that love poor beasts" (*TIF,* 1041). The affect expressed by Marinetti's slippage into the persona of a bull condemned to death and surrounded by "corrupted scents of senile power and glory" may reflect the way he felt about his predicament in the arena of politics.

Other texts are entirely inspired by the experience of nostalgic remembrance. In *Il fascino dell'Egitto* (Egyptian Fascination; 1933), Marinetti adopts the elegant, polished stylistic modes of art prose to record his travel impressions after a return to his native Egypt.[21] Marinetti's fascination with exotic, sensuous African ambience, detectable in several other works (most notably, in *Mafarka*), is manifestly displayed, as the title leads the reader to expect. Africa, for Marinetti, is not merely the distant, exotic setting typical of much orientalist literature. Even though he was almost certainly influenced by that literary tradition (in particular, by Gustave Flaubert's exoticism), what he absorbed through his readings is fused with reminiscences of the fantastic times of his childhood.[22]

The primitive, feminine-connoted setting conjures up the nostalgic, sensual dimension of memory. The experience of remembering is illustrated in terms of heightened sensibility and laceration of the self.

> My sensitivity ruptured and I became a heavy wound opened to grasp the arch of the sea-horizon with my living shredded tentacles.
> [. . . .]
> There is reborn the fragrant and sonorous feast of the Sacred Heart. The altar all fleshed out with jasmine was nested in the foliage of a baobab whose trunk was sweating rose petals. In the hot May afternoon the flames of the candles, the sparkling tinkle of the censers and the swift vermilion tunics intoxicated the turtle doves roosting on the high palm trees so much that their cooing of voluptuous water stirred to a spasm our childish senses. (*TIF,* 1053–1054)

> Another strip of my flesh had the sour honeyed and spoiled smell of the cassias that poked out of the railings of the Antoniadis garden to provoke the chaste and blind water of the Mahmudieh canal. (*TIF,* 1054–1055)

As he opens to the surge of lush sensations and reaches for the horizon, the narrator's self is torn into shreds of "organic" memory.[23] His dissolution is the result of a tension that echoes the conflict, in Marinetti's earlier writings, between the empowering influence of the new "machine aesthetic" and the weakening ("extenuating") effect of rejected passéist poetry. However, the conflict is no longer projected outside the authorial persona: it is, in Marinetti's words, "the tragic struggle that took place in [his] veins between that lamenting past and the magnificent future that strangled it" (*TIF,* 1056). In other words, the text dramatizes an inner struggle between the reemergence of emotions based in the primitive (feminine) Egypt of Marinetti's past and his admiration for the modern (virile) world foreign influence has brought about. The modernization of Egypt can be seen as symbolizing the "colonization" or repression of Marinetti's own sensual, "primitive" self—his mother-bound desires and anxieties. While the active, productive colony "resuscitates" a vision of his father's "iron life" (*TIF*, 1057), memories of his melancholic mother are associated with the sensuality and languor of decaying Egypt and with death (*TIF*, 1078–1079).

Unlike earlier texts, no incendiary, iconoclastic rhetoric is fired against the ruins of the past. Instead, change and modernity are represented with deep ambivalence. Memories "break" in the author's hands like fragile old toys as he surveys the new reality that has taken over the emotion-charged sites of his youth (*TIF*, 1058). Although the destructive effects of colonialism seem to be accepted as an inevitable fate, the triumph of productive, geometric, militaristic modernity over the past is figured in gloomy tones that culminate in an emblematic image of mutilation.

> But the ardent and sensual cassias of my adolescence were gone! Instead my nostrils were penetrated by a strong smell of tar coming from the keel of a barge overloaded with cotton. That tar of willpower travels dangers trades and adventures invaded my brain and forced me to raise my head.
> Beyond the camerus of the enchanted garden, a very high order of palm trees geometrically pointed with their metallic tufts at the route of the Italian mail plane. With the lamenting but tenacious drone of a bellicose bee, the plane flies over me. A black flute of war, it musically cut into [*ferì*] the blue. Its wings were the very hands severed from its musician, abandoned on earth. (*TIF*, 1058–1059)

The spellbound, enchanting *hortus conclusus* of youth is ousted by the same aggressive sensations and images of modernity that are stock ammunition of the futurist arsenal: the smell of tar, the drone of engines, the warlike music of technology. As Marinetti's word choice ("invase," "costrinse," "gemente," "ferì," "mozzate," and "abbandonato") indicates, they are now associated with violation, pain, and alienation. The natural realm is rhetorically transfigured into a symbol of the transforming power of progress: palm trees form a metallic sign indicating the route of the Italian mail plane; organic life forces are distilled and denatured into the viscous "tar" of a utilitarian, enterprising sensibility; the musician's hands have turned into airplane wings.

Futurist mythology usually celebrates such things as the airplane, which it sees as a mechanical extension of multiplied man, an inspiring muse, and a symbol of the empowering relationship between man and technology. By contrast, the plane in *Il fascino dell'Egitto* leaves behind a mutilated artist (held back by the old world he has ostensibly rejected), thus evoking the problematic, anxiety-causing aspects of progress. Earlier futurist texts strive to negate anxiety through a defense mechanism: the subject's internalization of, and identification with, the threatening technological object. Now, however, the process of identification fails to produce the sense of omnipotent, sadistic control that gives futurism its characteristic maniacal impetus. As the mechanized, metallized superuomo stands maimed in futurism's twilight, a way is opened for the emergence of anxieties—but also for the recuperation of the comforting, feminine-connoted themes of memory, nature, and love.

PATHETIC FALLACY IN THE TECHNOLOGICAL MYTHOPOEIA

Marinetti's later texts foreground sentiment and nostalgic memories even when they address the futurist themes par excellence—technology and war. Sporting a new coat of aeropoetic paint, the latter continue to occupy the center of the futurist showroom. In the late 1930s, a manifesto on "technicalities" and "Corporative Arts" recycled the concept of dehumanized poetry and presented Marinetti as the poet of the regime's autarchic and corporative policies. Poetry and other arts are, he proclaimed, bound to "idealize" the universe by reshaping and putting into words its "thoughts forms colors sounds noises fragrances and tactilisms." However, "the Fascist Imperial Italy born of the Speedy War" calls for an additional duty: "that of organizing with a profitable distribution of intuitions and creative efforts the idealization of the various chemical mechanical manual administrative conceptual jobs" (*TIF*, 1143).[24] The major work inspired by these dictates, *Il Poema non umano dei tecnicismi,* was dedicated to the chemical company Snia Viscosa, in homage to its "dynamic autonomous creative Italian spirit," by the "futurist aeropoets devoted to the originality of Imperial Fascist Italy" (*TIF*, 1139). As has been noted, this development of futurist poetics testifies to the end of the movement's utopian, polemical phase and the onset of a new conformism— an art devoted to celebrating the new regime.[25] The *poema* itself, however, delivers something more or other than what the introductory statements suggest.

A close reading of the second section, entitled "Poesia simultanea dei canneti Arunda Donax," illustrates the discrepancy between promise and product. The theoretical framework set up by the introduction leads us to expect a description of chemical transformations of processed matter—free of human drama and nostalgia and ultimately serving a propagandistic function of celebrating the regime's policy of self-sufficiency. Instead, the text compels recognition of an emotion-laden thematics. Rather than celebrate the productivity of national industry, it presents the plight of humanized nature: the lament of "heroic reeds" condemned to destruction by the "Goddess Geometry." The recurrent use of apostrophe and personification confers human status on the reeds that are to be sacrificed. Sensuality and femininity predominate in this prosopopoeia: "But to continue they would continue endlessly continue continue your contests of greetings curtseys ceremonious coaxing and the womanly flighty flirtings were burning hot with modesty and with the smooth shamelessness of rose willows these sweet reeds of love undress" (*TIF*, 1151–1152). Along familiar rhetorical lines, the poem sets up an antithesis between the sensual, languid *canne*—creatures of the moon—and the hard, materialistic Dea Geometria—a solar divinity. On the symbolic level, the usual conflict between organic nature and technological progress is thus staged. In an unusual role reversal, however, nature becomes the hero (or heroine) that cruel, materialistic technology victimizes, having enlisted and corrupted nature's traditional allies, the farmers.

The reeds scream

—Damned word damn utility profit calculation of numbers

Oh give us back the delight of the Absurd of the Void of the Abstract going haphazardly somehow or other aimlessly from agony to agony restrained by the apparent death that does not die

All is decided nothing saved or would have ever saved the heroic reeds devoted to languor

Whipped at full force by the cutting solar rays they were burning and cooking

Then half-burnt or overcooked but alive they are handcuffed like revolutionary female students [*studentesse rivoluzionarie*]

(*TIF*, 1157–1158)

Unlike Geometry, the reeds are given a voice with which to utter their rage and agony. Their malediction echoes Marinetti's recurrent invectives against materialist concerns, or "rights of the stomach."[26] Furthermore, the lexia associated with Geometry have negative connotations: "overbearing," "implacable," "terrorizer," "torturer," "grinds her immense dentures" (*TIF*, 1155).[27] Nature, by contrast, is associated with positive valences such as sweetness, splendor, and, most important, heroism: "sweet reeds of love," "splendid waters of the sumptuous Moon," "heroic reeds devoted to languor" (*TIF*, 1152, 1156, 1158). Such valorizations seem to belie the futurist credo advocated in the early manifestos, which Marinetti restates in the initial address to his readers: "While all the poets of the earth more or less continue to polish and embellish nostalgias and despairs in the verses of Leopardi, Baudelaire or Mallarmé, for many years the Italian Futurist Movement has praised its poets' and its artists' hope for creating poetry and arts that are 'nonhuman,' that is, unrelated to humanity through a systematic extraction of new splendors and new music from the technicalities of the mechanical civilization" (*TIF*, 1142).

Marinetti's credo is even more patently contradicted when the drama of humanized vegetation becomes the backdrop for the human drama of the futurist aeropoet. The latter abandons the evasive dimension of sky, which excessive flying has "poisoned," and lands among the doomed reeds. Drowning in the sensual, pathetic appeal of a progress-threatened natural environment, the *aeropoeta* falls prey to "voluptuous myriad reeds each maddened by feeling insufficiently naked silky smooth" and eager to "console [him] and convince him and convert him and kill him with kisses wearing out if necessary his virile shoulders" (*TIF*, 1156). Seduced, consoled, and overwhelmed by nature's sensual appeal and bewildered by technology's incomprehensible cruelty, the aeropoeta sinks in dismay, and the poetic "I" comments on his tragic destiny.

The futurist aeropoet implored

What absurdity for me to abandon the sky and the cutting aerial speed

I don't understand Goddess Geometry the cruelty of your chemistry and the crimes of your mechanics

TRALALÀ TRALALÀ so many women on the heart and on the head on the eyes and on the lips it's tragic the destiny of the man who was shipwrecked in an authentic ocean of caresses

(*TIF*, 1156)

Given that the change of voice is not marked by any punctuation and given that the poetic "I" presents himself as "aeropoeta" in the introduction, the distinction between the two personae blurs, and the tragic destiny of the aeropoet ultimately appears as the poet's own predicament.

The drama is abruptly resolved by a brief, concluding vision of prosperity and national pride.

Workers' swimming pools workers' children soccer fields and bowling greens

Vittorio Veneto and Arnaldo Mussolini avenues

Theaters and refectories for thousands of workers

High shelter of plane trees and horse chestnut trees for a population of bicycles

High above traveling traveling endlessly the new constellation whose stars form the word AUTARCHY

(*TIF*, 1159–1160)

But the plight of the sensual vegetation and the grounded, dejected aeropoet is far more charged, stylistically and emotionally, than this picture of progress under the regime's aegis. On balance, the excuse of progress and national self-sufficiency does not outweigh the pathos of nature's destruction; the final, happy scene of prosperity makes sense only as a convenient diversion from an inescapable impasse, or perhaps as a token gesture of compliance with the requirements of the epideictic situation.[28]

Even when the poem appears to fulfill the promise of a dehumanized description of matter's chemical transformations, as in the sections "Poesia simultanea

della luce tessuta" (The Simultaneous Poetry of Woven Light) and "Poesia simultanea di un vestito di latte" (Simultaneous Poetry in the Clothing of Milk), it soon
becomes evident that the power at play is fundamentally "la potenza miracolosa
della poesia" (*TIF,* 1145) and that the process being idealized and celebrated is
none other than the fantastic transformation of reality's raw materials into the
aesthetic product of the poet's imagination. The following passage illustrates the
metaphorical alchemies created in this process: "Thus the angel of fluid crystal
and incessant plumed flight of woven Light jumps out of the infernal desulfura-
tion with pathetic pallors neighs ringing jingle bells and cracking whips amidst
cursing tangles of harnesses horses manes" (*TIF,* 1163). Paradoxically, the result of
such figurative surfeit and imaginative expansion is that of cutting down reality to
manageable size, biting off only what can be ingested and assimilated and thereby
tendentially rejecting the vexed social dimension of industrial production and the
spiritual dissonances of modern life. By transfiguring the productivity of national
industry into a source of aesthetic pleasure, Marinetti indeed provides artistic le-
gitimization for the regime's autarchic policies.

FASHIONING A FASCIST DISCOURSE

The function played by the joint sensual appeal of woman and consumer art in
"Poesia simultanea della moda italiana" (Simultaneous Poetry of Italian Fashion;
section 8 of *Il Poema non umano dei tecnicismi*) provides striking evidence of the political implications of escapist aestheticism. In this text, Marinetti invokes an alliance between fantasy and sensuality for the purpose of creating a perpetual feast
for the senses. The alliance is enacted in the realm of women's fashion: fantastic,
capricious styles display futurism's originality and patriotism. "No comfort no
reasonability no logic," dictates Marinetti, "but glory to the arbitrary whimsical
and fantastic that know how to idealize the neck breasts waist hips so that they
can strum a carnival tune on man's tense nerves" (*TIF,* 1187). Anything goes, provided it is "made in Italy" and is "favorable to woman's feline softness" (*TIF,*
1188). Nothing less than national/male identity, the mainstay of Marinetti's fiction of power, is at stake when it comes to feminine apparel: "No more short hair
viscid fashion of the Northern seas mortified by asexual fogs to confuse the sexes
and derail the male wheels from the track that knows how to sting the pale
chastity of the sky" (*TIF,* 1189). Fashion is seen as providing sexual stimulations
capable of defending men against gender confusion and foreign influence. The
two dangers are conflated; sexual perversion becomes identified with the
degen(d)erated foreign "look." Besides positing an explicit connection between
aesthetics, sexual politics, and national supremacy, the poem also illustrates how
an art of evasion, even at the level of spectacle or pleasure, can lend itself to political power. The following scene highlights the link between the futurist carnival-
esque feast of the senses and the spectacular "happenings" of mass consent staged
by the fascist regime.

To create a festive mood of cheering crowds beneath Palazzo Venezia a massive lineup of
helmets and shining black umbrellas under the rotating projection of a nickel rain
wrap the woman [*fasciate la donna*] in orange velvet coiling up to the headdress of a
single emerald feather
All eyes will be captured by the woman dressed in a living mood of sky triangulated
by air force squadrons

(*TIF*, 1187; emphasis added)

Feminine apparel and virile military display are combined to tailor mass consent
and enthusiasm in a dazzling, multimedia spectacle of modern life in a modern
nation.[29] It might be objected that the glamorous costume depicted above does
not conform to the rustic, "wholesome" styles of clothing displayed in fascist
iconography and in the popular festivities choreographed by the regime at the
time of the poem's publication (1940). According to the so-called return to traditions policy, regime-sponsored festivals aimed at revamping folk customs and
thereby defending sound rural values against the degenerating effects of modern
life. However, the Marinettian goals of diversion and patriotic display are essentially consonant with the cultural strategies with which fascism stabilized its rule.[30]

Interestingly, Marinetti did not object to the folkish choreographies staged by
the regime. The evidence suggests that he too jumped on the bandwagon during
the national festivities sponsored by the government in celebration of the marriage of the heir to the throne (in January 1930). The ceremony's program, which
lists, by region and province, the contingents participating in the costume pro-
cession, contains a prefatory text signed by Marinetti. This consists of an impassioned apostrophe to a personified nation, whose seductive apparel draws from
the geographic and folkloric characteristics of various provinces and regions. In
the first half of the apostrophe, Italy is presented as a beautiful woman emerging
from her bath ("the warmblue tub of the Mediterranean") and donning her
dance attire.[31] In the second part, the bathing and dancing beauty is transfigured
into a dynamic transatlantic liner, built with polychromatic and polymorphous
regional components: "Italy, sailing pier of Europe, immense Transatlantic
Liner, you were made of firs dripping with sky, dramatic trunks of olive trees,
bright wagons of Palermo and fierce cacti of Sardinia! Your hull, bolted with Si-
cilian pride, has the rippling slenderness of a Sienese hill. Your flag is made of
Alpine snow, Milanese meadows and Neapolitan corals! Your engines, tested in
a frenzy of wheels on the swift planes of Lombardy, ensure you an Italian victory
over Time and Space, your slaves." As usual, patriotic idealism is the binding
principle that transcends and reconciles contradictions. It unites the superim-
posed images of the folkloric woman and the powerful ship, ready to conquer
time and space. The one is a familiar icon of futurist mythopoeia; the other is
clearly inspired by the nuptial cortege of costumed provincials. Although direct
references to the royal wedding are conspicuously absent, Marinetti offers his
consent to the marriage of futurist and traditional iconography, during which
the former assimilates the latter.

Another preface, this time to a collection of "dialect songs" by various authors (including the futurist Paolo Buzzi) in praise of fascism and its duce, offers further insight into the terms of Marinetti's espousal of tradition.[32] The assimilatory or colonizing strategy that we have seen throughout Marinetti's writings is once again present: "As it perpetually and indispensably evolves and creates words for the mechanical civilization, the Italian language rules and must rule increasingly in Italy and in the world, *absorbing also the precious juice of dialects*" (IX; emphasis added). Dialects are synonymous with regional particularism and stale poetic modes. In the hands of a creative genius, however, they can contribute to the cultural vitality and supremacy of the Italian language, which "absorbs" them. No doubt is left as to the futurist brand of such revitalizing (and assimilating) creative genius "that invents everything breaking away from rancid sentimentalism and the dusty picturesque style detested by the Duce in order to become the voice of the glorious military chemical motorized civilization" (X). Vernacular poetry can be redeemed by new inspiration, to be provided by the likes of Mussolini, the founder of the empire: "not at all like Roman or Napoleonic emperors as the cloying promoters of plagiarism and imitation would have it" (and Marinetti here lashes out against the neoclassic nostalgia that informs much of fascism's rhetoric and iconography). Ultimately, however, the vitality of dialect as poetic material ("the dialect-lymph of our land") depends on the life-giving power of the futurist "spirit" (XI–XII). Thus both the vernacular languages and the imperial thematics are claimed as provinces of futurism.

REALIGNMENTS IN THE MYTHOPOEIA OF WAR

Nowhere is futurism's apology for, and involvement in, fascist politics more evident than in the literature of war. Marinetti, who participated in the Ethiopian campaign (1935–1936) and World War II (he left for the Russian front), remained the bard of heroic patriotism and modern warfare throughout his prolific career. *Il Poema africano della Divisione "28 Ottobre"* (The African Poem of the "October 28" Division; 1937) and *Canto eroi e macchine della guerra Mussoliniana* (I Sing the Heroes and Machines of Mussolini's War; 1942) are among the most salient examples. When we compare these texts with more popular works in the so-called fascist-heroic genre, it becomes apparent that Marinetti's war literature, even at its most apologetic, cannot be labeled mere propaganda. The fascist-heroic genre built on a preexisting production of nationalistic, militaristic, and patriotic inspiration spurred on by World War I. In time, it acquired a more specifically fascistic character, incorporating themes inspired by the regime's rhetoric: Mussolini's biography, enterprises and heroes of fascism, and the fight against communism or the plutocratic nations. The works that best performed the function of publicizing fascist accomplishments, ideals, and objectives were generally in novelistic form and were characterized, both stylistically and thematically, by simplicity, conventionality, and repetitiveness. These features produced an effect of familiarity and ensured easy assimilation of an unequivocal political content.[33]

Despite a (partial) recuperation of syntactic and narrative structures, Marinetti's war poems hardly conform to the parameters of this genre. One episode in the uneasy relationship between the futurist leader and the minister of popular culture, Alessandro Pavolini, bears witness to a gap between Marinetti's efforts at offering poetic "support" to Mussolini's war and the response of both the fascist leadership and the public at large. Such a gap does not blot out the author's political commitment and the texts' essentially fascist political content; it does, however, pose an obstacle to reductionist and dismissive critical gestures. In 1941, Marinetti broadcast a series of war poems, which elicited a shower of protests from the audience: his lyrics were qualified as "ridiculous," "incomprehensible," and "counterproductive." Raoul Chiodelli, director general of fascist broadcasting, seized the occasion and asked Pavolini to intervene and terminate the program. He supported his request with the text of a lyric entitled "L'Aeropoema dell'aviatore Corinto Bellotti" (Aeropoem of the Aviator Corinto Bellotti), underlining the parts that he considered most obscure. Marinetti counteracted with a letter to Pavolini questioning the patriotic record of his critics and defending his "obsessive" goal of elevating the "Italian spirit to an atmosphere of heroisms and offer to the Fatherland."[34]

It is significant that the displeased audience complained not only about the poems' obscurity but also about their counterproductive effect. As Lucio Villari reports, "People loudly requested that Marinetti be silenced to make room for more entertaining broadcasting" (8). Indeed, the text singled out by Chiodelli sounds some mournful notes: it unearths the subjective, psychological dimension of the poetic "I" and posits the heroic self-sacrifice of Corinto Bellotti (who, interestingly, does not die fighting, but in a rescue mission) against *"a coalition of Pessimisms," "minute corporeal anguishes,"* and the quicksands of pedantic irony and catastrophism (10; Chiodelli's emphasis). The following lines seem to anticipate the public's criticism: "They will say that I wear a hood of dark conspiracy [*un cappuccio da complotto buio*], but *it is lined with meadows sun picnic snack hams / impertinent little girls and marriageable young women eatlaugh [mangiaridono] in blouses of snow and strawberries"* (10; Chiodelli's emphasis). This kind of reflective and fantastical digression clashed with the sounds of fanfare and popular song expected by the authorities. Furthermore, the irruption of the subjective, psychological dimension, taking the form of dark anxieties and bright, consolatory evasions, signals a break with Marinetti's prior representations of war and parallels the transformations, discussed earlier, in his technological mythopoeia.

The justification for such a break can be found in "Estetica Futurista della guerra" (The Futurist Aesthetic of War), in which Marinetti adds the ingredient of sentiment to his recipe for interventionist propaganda. The distinctive aesthetic value of war is no longer identified solely with the depersonalized dynamics of battle and the destructive power of mechanical weapons. It now also entails the fecund union of "strength" and "goodness," as well as the constructive, humanitarian potential of industrial warfare, which speeds up (hence reduces) destruction, thereby promoting a new "solidarity and generosity."[35] Relating this idealistic scenario to a specific historical context, we can see that Marinetti's "humanitarian" recipe easily translates into a prescription for imperialist expansion (where the triumph of goodness, solidarity, and generosity stand for the success of the Italian colonialist effort).

The manifesto was subsequently incorporated into the first section of *Il Poema africano della Divisione "28 Ottobre,"* inspired by the "imperial" war against Ethiopia. Marinetti, who took part in the campaign (fig. 6), sets out to commemorate the heroic enterprises of his division, culminating in a strenuous and victorious resistance against outnumbering Abyssinian forces. Oratorical eloquence and an epic tone are used to extol the Italians' "divine" heroism, honesty, power, and pride— as well as the "wise goodness of the government" and the quasi-supernatural power of Mussolini ("sanctified by his miraculous Speedy War").[36] According to a rigid Manichaean logic, these virtues are pitted against foreign vices. Italy's evangelical honesty, heroic sacrifice, and divine goodness are contrasted with other nations' diabolic greed: "Today our Italy becomes our crèche lit up with heroism and honesty / This crèche is besieged by 52 envious nations representing diabolical Money" (116). Furthermore, the colonial war is portrayed as a civilizing enterprise that will redeem the savage Abyssinian population by unlocking the gate to progress. And the enemy, tellingly figured as "humanized darkness" (227), is consistently associated with negative, racial traits: treacherousness, obtuseness, cowardice, cruelty, and greed.

The epic, apologetic framework legitimating the regime's colonial ambitions is fleshed out with a plethora of description, which foregrounds the natural environment and the poetic imagination as the true protagonists of the poem. The primitive, African setting—scorched by a torrid sun, populated by scavengers, and swarming with "armies of Abyssinian flies" (287)—is presented as the quintessential symbol of cosmic chaos ("elemental cacophonic chaotic wilderness," 242) and as the theater of an existential struggle against elemental forces, in which the drama of the abject promiscuity of life and death is played out with obsessive recurrence. Storms of relentless flies symbolize the "fecundity of death" (185). They are a formidable adversary, as are the aggressive smells of putrefaction. The human enemy, meanwhile, is metaphorically dehumanized, blended with the hostile, primitive environment, and portrayed as the embodiment of abjection. Marinetti confers abject status on the Abyssinians by attributing their despicable characteristics to an unfortunate, "dirty" mixing of races (the very word "Abyssinian," he informs the reader, is etymologically linked to "abescia," which means "mixture" in ancient Arab).[37] The same motif appears in the guise of degenderation, or gender mixing: the Abyssinians, according to a savage custom, threaten their enemies with castration and are occasionally portrayed as effete or outrightly feminine. In one instance, the threat and the appearance of emasculation are combined in the figure of an effeminate dancer designated "the black castrator," who grazes the spectators' groins with a shining blade (270–271). Finally, abjection is projected onto the foreign other by means of the antithesis between civ-

Fig. 6. Marinetti and other officers in Ethiopia, 1935–1936. Reprinted by permission of the Beinecke Rare Book and Manuscript Library, Yale University.

ilized Italian colonizers and dirty, smelly, obtuse savages. The protagonist-poet's repeated attempts to fend off their offensive smell with showers of eau de cologne—a defensive strategy he also deploys against carrion—underscore the association of the natives with the ultimate abjection of death and decay.

> Males sticking to females colliding of various shapes of snouts lit up by a spiritualizing sun that finally sets about to perfect them
> But descending streaming around dances of drops surprise showers the deifying softness of perfume fluttering aerial gardens motorized by the wind directed by my gesture toward those ebony ivory eyes almost thought almost love and new fast roads opening up in the still brains of sand
> [. . . .]
> And thus through vast circles the eccentrically incessant blessing of Italian *colonia* makes the heavy dusty opaque materiality of Abbi Addì elegant and exalts it toward the noble the terse and the divine
>
> (292–293; emphasis added)[38]

The Abyssinians (in particular, the inhabitants of the conquered town Abbi Addì) stand for the dull opaqueness of materiality, while the poet's eau de cologne symbolizes the redeeming spirituality of Italian civilization. The symbolism is reinforced by the pun on "colonia," which means both "colony" and "cologne." However, the dual meaning of "colonia italiana" has the effect of reducing Italian colonization to a merely cosmetic sprinkling of token progress (such as Marinetti's "fast roads") over the primitive world. The latter irony is probably unintentional.

Cologne also provides an apt metaphor for Marinetti's poetic imagination, with its inclination to transfigure excrement "frying in a shining oil of flies" into a "pincushion of emeralds" ("[sterchi] friggenti nell'olio lucente di mosche mosconi puntaspilli di smeraldi," 187). Descriptions often invoke other representational codes, such as painting, sculpture, and performance, to "repaint and resculpt the landscape" (180), or turn the theater of war into a stage for a cast and an audience of stars: "The Uorcamba theater is perfumed with ballistite and black powder [. . . .] two stars of the first magnitude are dancing [. . . .] Exploding applause of all the stars boarding-school girls giddy with Sunday joy through giggles eyes small teeth smirks small bracelets convulsing little feet adorned with pearls" (158–159). Such imagery recalls the glamorous, anthropomorphic stars of *La Con-quête des Étoiles* and, more generally, the rhetorical surfeit I have previously identified as characteristic of Marinetti's prefuturist poems. The later works confirm that the poet's often contrived, excessive efforts to transfigure reality are a fundamental tactic in his struggle against the abjection of materiality.

Here, rhetorical transfiguration joins forces with sentimental, religious, and patriotic sublimation. Memories and feelings are ushered in by intense sensory stimulation. The insidious dust of the desert, for instance, is sweetened by the sugary taste of candy, which in turn evokes the poet's children ("dust that I suck [. . .] with the sugar of strawberry candy manipulated both far and near by Vittoria Ala Luce," 134) and recalls the delightful, rejuvenating smells of his own childhood: "And I turn young again back to my childhood by the Mahmudieh canal of Alexandria Egypt because by now the aristocratic charming instinct of acacias rules governs all the vibratile nostrils of the landscape" (134). In another episode, the night's shadows are accompanied by memories of love.

Bristling with the longest peevish thorns the sunset prematurely arrives like a monstrous fruit of the tropical day and after the rosy little girls[39] have faded away the shadows of the Night that exquisite friend enemy of every overstrained human perfection enter the small valley of spurges in coiling gushes in large slow serpents
—Sleep well Masnata

Alone in my small cubical tent I search for contact with Europe with the point of my heart turned into a ray
[. . . .]
Hearing your voice and departing in its company it comes from far away or takes me away through space
You are here everywhere and in me in my arms unless I free myself from the overly thick fragrant and voluptuous forest of your hair
What a beautiful sea of limpid feelings around us and what a profundity of affection deep down joining corals of sensuality and slow sea stars of good fortune

> Like the most harmonious fish of crystal moiré and platinum in the immense basin
> of transparent darkness no no you are rather a shining good thought in the infinite
> black pupil of the Night
>
> (101–102)

The woman invoked by the poet embodies the harmonious fusion of sensuality
and sentiment. The mixture, formerly represented as lethal, is now charged with
positive connotations: the sea of sentiments that surrounds the lovers is beautiful
and limpid, deep with affection, blessed by good fortune, and made precious by
sentimentality.[40] The woman is both an icon of overflowing, enveloping sensuality (signified by her voluptuous hair)[41] and an image of pure goodness. Eros is no
longer the heroic self's archenemy. Only a faint echo of the old war between sensuality and the will remains: the ambivalent qualification of the night as "exquisite friend enemy of every overstrained human perfection."

Earlier in the poem, the antithesis between the Abyssinians and the Italians is
used to celebrate the joining of power and sentiment, heroism and love: "Thus
with bolts of Catholicism and precious sentiments fastened under the black shirt
the mechanical geometric power of fascist futurist simultaneous dynamism de-
feats the contemplative fragility of prehistory" (53). Why does the fiction of power
now incorporate the "bolts" of religion and "precious" sentiments? Clearly, the
strategy conforms to the colonialist view of a struggle between civilized (Catholic,
well-meaning, progressive) and primitive (non-Catholic, hostile, brutal) forces.
Pursuing the hypothesis proposed earlier in the chapter, it could also be argued
that the original supporting elements of the fiction of power—youthful optimism,
vital energy—fail to sustain the crushing impact of a formidable (internal) enemy
and thus require additional, reinforcing structures. This argument is corroborated by the following passage, in which the exhilarating hubris of victory is overcome by an unexpected note of despair.

> Joy of no longer feeling the stealthy but leaden tread of old age because every ges-
> ture of mine dripping with glory is virgin and however frenzied it can lean sturdily
> on the thickness of pride while my thought is an immense burst of brand-new sun
>
> In a dream I wrap myself in beautiful saffron-colored Abyssinian silk and I wait mo-
> tionless for the sun to embroider it with gold
> *But a strange repeated ringing of profound desperation forces me to search for a scrap of happiness
> in the perfecting of some lyric notes* for the present future African poem
>
> (242; emphasis added)

The shining halo of glory and pride only temporarily shields the poet from the approach of old age and is soon shattered by the reverberating call of despair. This
is not the first time it has appeared in Marinetti's work. In *Spagna veloce e toro futurista*, for instance, the poetic persona—engaged in a race against time and space—
finds himself wondering: "To conquer, to conquer, the dismal Infinite Nothingness? How? With what weapons? My choice: a steady great rosy absolute Love

which fixes with its watchful edges! . . . But if Infinite Nothingness resists, what then? To burst it open with the immense bloody fist of creative pride! To create, to fill the frayed Dark Void with an astonishing New Construction!" (*TIF*, 1034). Once old ideals have failed, the violent force of "creative pride" is the poet's final weapon in the war against nothingness. Marinetti's imagination persistently forges shields with which to cover the abyss of "Infinite Nothingness." In *Il Poema africano*, however, art and creativity allow him to carve no more than a "scrap of happiness" out of emptiness, darkness, and despair; heroic feelings, meanwhile, are easily overcome by angst.

The transformation of futurism's mythopoeia of war culminates in *Canto eroi e macchine della guerra Mussoliniana*, the last major work to be published in Marinetti's lifetime—two years before his death in 1944. His choice of title echoes the incipit of ancient epic and presents Marinetti as *aedo* of the fascist war. In the preface, "sublime" themes of patriotism, heroism, and martyrdom are introduced, couched in emphatic diction and religious imagery. Heroism, for instance, is defined as the greatest of spontaneous efforts to reach the divine.[42] The soldiers who inspire *aeropoeti* and *aeropittori* are portrayed as "haloed with sublime heroism by the deadly violence of machines and explosives" (19).[43]

The conspicuous religious inflection of this apologetic rhetoric is taken up and further accentuated at various points in the poem, as illustrated by this exhortation to the pilots and infantrymen.

> Angels of speed and of flashing TNT you who turned flight into a baptism of holy air and the engine into a wandering cradle in search of Jesus can now with the Absolute lubricate the gears of nerves hearts fantasies while gliding under the firmamental flaming cupolas of nocturnal bombardments
>
> And you fragile Infantrymen martyrs with halos of shrapnel and wandering bullets recite for them litanies of machine-gunning steps
>
> (139)

A familiar topos of the technological mythopoeia—the religion of speed, with its paraphernalia of angel-like airplanes and enginelike hearts launched to conquer the Absolute—seems to be played out here. The "angels of speed," in particular, recall the first manifesto's prophetic announcement: "soon we will see the first Angels fly" (*TIF*, 8). The "flashing TNT" echoes Marinetti's "destructive gesture of the freedom fighters" (*TIF*, 11). However, the transfiguration of the engine into a "wandering cradle in search of Jesus," as well as the characterization of infantrymen as "martyrs," creates an elegiac tone that differs radically from the exalted bombast of the manifestos. By commemorating the heroic deeds of the "martyrs," the poet (along with his fellow aeropoeti and aeropittori) seeks to combat insidious defeatism on the home front and defends patriotic love as a necessity. For the soldiers, he provides examples of selfless patriotism designed to inspire them to victory in the "Multifront War" (17). By claiming, for the futurist aeropoets and aeropainters, the role of celebrants of the ongoing conflict, he continues to wage literary war against the pedantic enemies of futurism. Marinetti's most important goal, however, seems to be an existential one: to rescue from death the fallen heroes, who crave the nourishment of glory ("heroes are thirsty hungry thirsty hungry thirsty hungry for liquid fleshy glory," 41).

As usual, rhetoric is the primary weapon in Marinetti's own multifront war. Against the objections of his "pedantic enemies," he deploys the "overbearing" power of his "stunning images" ("prepotenti immagini sbalorditive," 84). His imagination engages in metaphorical hand-to-hand combat with abjection; pleasurable images wrestle against horrifying visions: "In fact my aeropictorial fantasy furiously fights in the most violent shooting brawl wrapped with waste carrion and bloody hand-to-hand combat in order *to extract from it at any cost an elegant image*" (112; emphasis added). The correlative to this rhetorical strategy of fantastic transfiguration is the theme of metamorphosis developed in the choral interludes at the conclusion of the various sections (each dedicated to a particular heroic episode). These interludes, featuring the pathetic fallacy of "cosmic voices" that welcome and celebrate the dead heroes, evoke idyllic scenarios in which a fecund, sensual, and maternal nature provides a receptacle for the regeneration of the victims. The feminine continues to be identified with the organic world and its interbreeding of life and death. In developing this theme, however, Marinetti does not conjure up the familiar figure of abject Mother Nature (first embodied by the abominable Saint Putrefaction in *Le Roi Bombance*). Nor does he stage the antagonistic relationship between sensual, natural femininity and aggressive, mechanical virility that recurs in earlier works. Instead, the final solacing union between war's heroic victims and nature is intended to assimilate the anxiety-causing otherness of death. At the end of the second section, for instance, a submerged forest offers a maternal reception to the victims of a sunk torpedo boat (ominously named Nullo [Null]): "From the sapling to the veteran plant we are all stretching out to receive When is he coming? How can we celebrate the dead metallic hero? [. . . .] Let's quickly prepare our small roots woven like a bed in the comings and goings of the most loving maternal breaths" (68). The dead hero is still "metallico"—armored by his symbiotic union with the machine. But the machine in question is a sinking boat. A vulnerable, permeable cocoon, it has failed to protect him from death and fluid (con)fusion with nature. The boat's fatal leak is pictured as an "immersed mouth of lugubrious uterus" (59). This dismal mouth clearly echoes the negative valorization of the feminine that marks earlier works. However, this time it is associated with a technological womb, not a natural one, while Mother Nature's role is that of nurturer, soothing fears of the cold grave. A sense of intimacy with nature is evoked by such phrases as "small roots woven like a bed" and "the comings and goings of the most loving maternal breaths."

Comforting imagery and infantile vocabulary recur in the later works, in which the regressive dimension of the futurist utopia becomes more prominent.

In another choral interlude, images of the cradle and a caring mother are summoned to fill the gaping gulf of nothingness.

on the soft graves [*molli tombe*] to the rhythms of cradle fuel and

nothing [*a ritmi di culla nafta e nulla*] $\mathrm{SINKING}$
Sinking
          sinking
sinking smelling abysses
abysses

         COSMIC VOICES
800 meters deep fanning and fanning itself the kilometric forest of
seaweeds scolds warns caresses and enwraps in its tentacles the torn
steal of the submarine

                        (128–129)

The macabre vision of the submarine sinking into bottomless abysses is mitigated by the association of the undulating "molli tombe" with the swinging movement of the cradle, reinforced by the assonance between "nulla" and "culla." Furthermore, the marine vegetation offers a providential, maternal embrace that gently contains the hero's fall into the void.

The vegetation, in addition to comforting the hero with words of solace, blames his mother for abandoning her son to the sun's predatory rays: "Poor bloody little face dear honeyed little lips Gioacchino you know that your mommy was wrong to abandon you under the nasty clawed sun that tortures trees and butterflies" (43). As we have seen, Marinetti typically associates the sun with values such as ambition, vital force, aggressiveness, and paternal authority. Indicting the hero's careless "mommy" for sacrificing her child's "little face" and "honeyed little lips" to the cruel forces of life sounds an odd note in a poem intended to celebrate a family's patriotic love and heroic sacrifice (the mother, for instance, is earlier represented as a victim of the war). Susan Gubar has traced the scapegoating of the maternal in literature that, unlike Marinetti's writings, presents an unglorified vision of technological warfare. She argues, for instance, that George Orwell's *1984* "underlines the implicit anger with which many male writers, encased in what they call 'the womb of war' or 'the steel cocoon,' describe the juxtaposition between the biological mother and the military, for the mother who has given her son over to the state has exchanged her birth-giving function for a death-dealing one."[44] Marinetti's prosopopoeia of a compassionate, protecting, regenerating Mother Earth unexpectedly voices similar feelings.

Besides sheltering the dead hero from the defilement of decay, the sensual and loving vegetation provides the elements that perform his miraculous reincarnation.

In order to reincarnate feet legs thighs of the half-burnt hero Corinto Belloti quick quick lentisks oleanders figs in a tangle with the bitterish sourness of the calm sirocco

We will use a mix of oregano and rosemary and the pond's crust formed by
lacquers waxes varnishes textured with insects
Systematic recovery of one hundred thousand drops in the microscopic plants of
dryness of heat of light in electromagnetic equilibrium between precipitated
currents
The singing rain carries dishes and channels the heavy concentrated electric
charges
The reincarnation is already beginning under scorching ionic floods

of life

Functional rain

Life
   Life

(104–105; emphasis in original)

The language of religion ("to reincarnate") as well as the jargon of science and
technology ("plants," "electromagnetic," "electric charges," and "ionic floods")
are mustered to exorcise or disavow the horror of death. The war heroes are absorbed into cosmic life, regenerated by this interfusion, and transformed into the
living fuel of heroic patriotism: "alive they are live coals of fossil heroism and a
proud mine of Italianness" (180).

The idea of a metamorphosis of the dead into heroic energy recurs in Marinetti's last composition, "Quarto d'ora di poesia della X Mas" (A Quarter of an
Hour of Poetry of the 10th E-Boat Squadron), written just a few hours before his
death. This brief poem might be said to constitute Marinetti's spiritual testament:
it is an impassioned profession of patriotic faith, pervaded with feelings of bitter-
ness and disillusionment. The poet calls his fellow aeropoeti to join him in a last
ride to the front line ("almost holy ground," *TIF*, 1202), where they can offer their
heroic sacrifice like a prayer to Jesus. During this imaginary ride, he addresses the
Italian people, from whom he feels alienated: young generations of "resisters to
the draft of the Ideal" (*TIF*, 1201) and all the calculating, rationalizing, cowardly
enemies of selfless heroism who have dragged Italy ("the fragile delightful Italy
wounded but undying") down to the bottom of their "ideological dungheap"
(*TIF*, 1202). Against them, he invokes the explosive rage of the dead heroes: "The
cemeteries of great Italians unfasten their small rural walls in the cowardice of the
sirocco and shoot off irascible sparks crackling with the impatience of a powder
keg without doubt the taloned dead will explode they are exploding so move on
trucks [. . . .] A cemetery of great Italians explodes and cries Stop stop Italian dri-
vers you need TNT we give it to you we give it to you we the best TNT extracted
from our skeletons' marrow" (*TIF*, 1201–1202). The explosive bodies recall the
"live coals of fossil heroism" in *Canto eroi e macchine*, as well as a famous passage
from "Nascita di un'estetica futurista," in which Marinetti describes "the clearest
and most violent of futurist symbols": Japanese merchants' "absolutely futurist"
traffic in human bones, which feeds the industrial production of the newest and

most lethal of explosive substances. He concludes his description of the desecrating, cynical exploitation of human corpses with an exclamation: "Glory to the indomitable ashes of man, which come to life in cannons!" (*TIF,* 317). Such an utterance squares with Marinetti's repeated declarations of victory over death, a leitmotiv of his futurist fiction of power. What seems to be at play in all three passages under discussion is a strategy of sublimation: the negative materiality of death becomes a living source of heroic, meaningful force, a powerful fiction or myth erected against the primal fear of nothingness. Indeed, a kinship is evident between the reincarnated or "recycled" war heroes and immortal Gazourmah, the metallized man with replaceable parts.

In this respect, it seems significant that the motif of abjection, which recurs in gory descriptions of decay throughout Marinetti's production, is played down in *Canto eroi e macchine,* even though the theme of death is more prominent here than in any other of his works. From the vantage point of the interpretive hypothesis I have been pursuing, it is not surprising that, as he approaches the end of his life, Marinetti transfigures death into a pleasurable or somehow positive experience: a return to the cradle, a regenerative union with Mother Nature, and a miraculous reincarnation of the Christlike hero sacrificed for the love of his country. This strategy enables him, once more, to ingest and digest the unavoidable "bitter food" of reality, turning them into "an effective source of nourishment."

THE ULTIMATE TRANSFORMATION: ART AS TRANSUBSTANTIATION

The religious undercurrent of Marinetti's war poetry testifies to a final elaboration of his futurist mythopoeia. The technological "religion of speed" is now steered in the direction of tradition through an infusion of Christian ideologemes. In the earlier writings, iconoclastic subversion and radical anticlericalism had coexisted with a mystical appeal to the sublime, just as the degraded role of the artist as marketer of aesthetic commodities was accompanied by an idealistic belief in art's prophetic and heroic mission. In the late 1920s and 1930s, European culture was pervaded by transcendentalist tendencies. The spiritual side of futurism became increasingly prominent (as in Prampolini's "cosmic idealism") and expanded to assimilate even traditional religion. The "Manifesto dell'arte sacra futurista" (Manifesto of Futurist Sacred Art; 1931), signed by Marinetti and Fillia, underscored this development, which involved primarily the visual arts. Noteworthy productions include the religious paintings of Gerardo Dottori, Fillia's representations of "religious moods," and Alberto Sartoris's projects for a modern ecclesiastical architecture that combines rationalist functionalism and futurist dynamism. The most significant literary example of this tendency is one of Marinetti's later works, *L'aeropoema di Gesù* (The Aeropoem of Jesus), in which aeropoesia seems to have become the vehicle for a new sublime goal. No longer confined to the hubristic conquest of the "Infinite," it now includes the Christian quest for divine Grace.[45]

The text develops as a sequence of apparently unrelated episodes, or visions. Each presents a different thematic and geographic locus of Marinetti's imaginary: eroticism on a Parisian summer night, war and death on an exotic Ethiopian night, the explosive, polychromatic creativity of futurist evenings in Milan, and, finally, the prosopopoeia of Judaean and Italian landscapes. The former is presented as a cradle sanctified by the birth of Jesus; the latter as runway for a new, airborne encounter with the divine. The religious motif predominates only in the last two sections, but it is more or less crucially present throughout the text. The poet's impetuous sensuality is bound by his "metallic soul" (12); a "sanctifying" dawn dispels the sinful darkness of the Parisian night (13). Physical death, for the Italian troops under siege in the Ethiopian desert, is warded off by the "holy" water of life, more consoling than maternal milk and sublimely sweet, like the eyes of the divine Mother of Jesus.[46] And the futurist artists, who seek to expand man's physical and spiritual possibilities toward "new pleasures," join a pilgrimage toward the "goal" or "supreme synthesis" of a fulfillment described through the figures of a maternal, consoling religion: "the ultimate synthesis that tender physical and at the same time celestial abstract synthesis brimming with the immaterial milk of the Madonna is your blessed name oh Jesus Ave Ave Ave Maria Ave Ave Ave Mariaa" (24).[47]

The development of a futurist sacred art has been seen as an involution, scarcely relevant to an understanding of the futurist experience. Similarly, the technological mythopoeia's final elaboration in *L'aeropoema di Gesù* could be seen as a radical deviation, provoked by the final, sad circumstances of the author's life. Indeed, Marinetti wrote the poem shortly before his death in 1944, aware that his own condition and that of the nation at war held little hope for recovery. The preface presents the work as a prayer to Jesus, invoking protection for his family and for the nation. However, the broader significance of the poem and its relationship with Marinetti's previous work become evident when viewed through the lens of the psychodrama I have identified—in other words, if we regard Marinetti's often contradictory ideas and attitudes as a synergistic strategy, a consistent effort to ward off the abyss of nothingness. After the creation myth of *Mafarka*, with its technological Eden and immortal, prelapsarian New Adam, and after the empowering aesthetic/religion of speed celebrated in the manifestos, Marinetti turns to the Catholic ideologemes of resurrection, salvation, and divine love as new avenues for pursuing fantasies of transcendence, omnipotence, and immortality.[48] The attempt to exorcise his fear of the void ultimately leads Marinetti to recuperate the values whose decay and loss are lamented in his prefuturist poetry and welcomed in the manifestos.[49]

Art, religion, and technology are celebrated as the means to salvation and transcendence: the poet's soul, metallized through his union with the machine, is free to rise above human miseries—the weakness of the senses (44–45) as well as the economic inferno (54–55). His "transcendent" art, like prayer, should allow him to communicate directly with God, his ideal reader or interlocutor (44–45).

But sensualism and aestheticism, the most conspicuous common denominators of the mythopoeia's various elaborations, are never abandoned; the turn to traditional religion takes the form of an eminently aesthetic and sensual experience. The time and place of the union with Jesus is that of "everlasting beauty" (33); a proliferation of lush imagery forms the path that leads the poet from depths of sensual pleasure and abjection (symbolized by the Dead Sea) to heights of mystical bliss ("la Casa Degna" [the Worthy Home of Jesus], the place of the sacred), bridging the gap between nothingness and the absolute. Again, the difficult path to the real (the pain of divided reality and partial truth, the acceptance of human finitude) is forsaken in favor of the shortcut between desire and fantasy, with childhood's lost happiness as destination. Indeed, the itinerary to "the Worthy Home" (an image that evokes religion's sheltering function) is marked by figurations of regressive fantasies and libidinal objects: infantile innocence, the consoling maternal gaze, and—most saliently—the maternal womb, breast, and milk. As in other texts in which the religious motif is foregrounded, Marinetti identifies religion, not with the Logos of the Father, but with the Love of the incarnated Son and, especially, with the carnal mystique of the Mother with Child—an image that symbolizes, in Western eroticism, that which is most reassuring and sheltering against death's finality.[50]

Occasionally, however, the sensual, human dimension engulfs the poet in an abyss of anguish. The most significant moment of despair occurs at the end of the poem, during a "close encounter" between poet and machine, in which the illusory nature of the futurist technological myth is finally acknowledged. With a familiar rhetorical move, a personified engine speaks to the poet: "I am made of steel nickel copper and I live on castor oil and gasoline but I resemble the crazy heart of that beautiful woman with her excessively lavish dark hair" (61). The poet admits that the analogy is appealing to him because it evokes a familiar (feminine, natural) sphere of experience: "I like this image because I know [. . .] the voluptuous hair of all the women in love that compete with the almost-fluvial leafy ramifications of woods waters and desires of carnal passion." With these images, "enveloping musical delights," he hopes to appease the "fury" of the engines and to create the illusion of an empowering union between man and machine: "to render seamless the wedding of flesh and steel and the illusion of feeling metallic when one is in reality mere weeping flesh" (61). The defense mechanisms underlying the mythicization of the machine are thus exposed. By "marrying" the machine, man can sustain the illusion that he has overcome the miseries of his "weeping flesh." At the same time, he can exorcise his anxieties about technology (the "fury" of the engines).[51]

Besides confronting the illusory nature of the technological myth, Marinetti looks down the treacherous, slippery peak of human ambition: "the boasted overhang or pedestal predisposed to the gesticulating eloquence of the ambitious man intent on taming billows or rumps or backs or sheep-fleece or forests of rebellious horns / Limestone overhang without rails in fact with slippery edges for the necessary fall of power" (51). Because they are predicated on the fluid, magmatic moods and desires of the animalistic masses, power and glory are inherently unstable. Even the proudest of leaders may fall from the pedestal, becoming a putrid wreck on death's shores: "the new living loudspeaker haughty with domineering will cannot keep standing up and already slides slid would fall headlong and has been rotten for a long time his crushed skull amidst the shifting seaweeds noble buriers of shipwrecked men" (52). This bleak view of reality constitutes an undeclared premise to the final development of the futurist mythopoeia: following the collapse of earthly myths of power and glory, the Catholic faith of his childhood offers to the poet a last h(e)aven of hope.

As we have seen, a fundamental pattern recurs persistently (one might say compulsively) throughout Marinetti's writing: an unremitting war between self and other, whereby the threatening other is liquidated or assimilated into empowering symbolic structures. *L'aeropoema di Gesù* constitutes the last enactment of this war, reproposing the familiar pattern, in a more explicitly and traditionally religious fashion, as a conflict between the demonic and divine, immanence and transcendence, Flesh and Spirit, annihilating sensual pleasure and infinite celestial ecstasy, death and immortality.

Marinetti's rhetorical strategies cast the conflict in victorious terms: the futurist "I" shores up his identity by subjugating (transfiguring or denying) difference both within and without himself. Otherness is rejected and projected onto the external world as an enemy to be overpowered (woman, the past, the foreign aggressor, death) or disavowed through a process of self-inflating assimilation, in which the subject creates and identifies with an idealized, sublimated other (the "divinity" of speed, the "omnipotence" of the machine). However, the upward reach for symbolic sublimation results in an obsessive concern with, and rage against, the repulsive and fascinating (relentlessly threatening) enemy. Narcissistic union with the divine and will to power over the other are equally permeated with abjection and violence. Does the final configuration of the futurist religion avoid the pitfalls of domination and idealization? Do Catholic faith and Christly Love throttle abjection and violence in *L'aeropoema di Gesù*? These questions can be best addressed within the theoretical and historical frame of reference offered by Kristeva's queries into religion.

Kristeva explores the relationship between what she calls "the persecutive apparatus" (*PH*, 116) and the religious economy of sublimation and perversion in Judaism and Christianity. She points to the violent entailments of this economy: an identity founded on the rejection of otherness feels threatened by it and feels compelled to take measures against it—a compulsion that results in intolerance, repression, and persecution. The Christian version of the perversion-sublimation structure, she suggests, may enable an alternative economy of subjectivity and difference, whereby difference is accepted through internalization of abjection as sin, especially through love of the other (the "love your neighbor as yourself" precept).[52] But, she warns, sin "holds the keys that open the doors to Morality and

Knowledge, and at the same time those of the Inquisition" (*PH,* 122). She also notes that the Christian elaboration of abjection, while reconciling the maternal principle of the flesh with that of the subject, fails to revalorize or rehabilitate woman, who thereafter becomes identified with "sinning flesh" (*PH,* 117). As David R. Crownfield argues, extending Kristeva's insights, "dysfunctional dimensions" and "distortions" of the Christian strategy have historically come into play: "the patriarchal structure of Christian communities tends to transform the imaginary father of the original myth into a phallic father who validates male identities while abjecting female ones. This destabilizes the triadic structure, reactivating the original terror and rage in the form of abjection of mother, for which the feminine in general becomes the symbolic and transferential representative and victim."[53] Along with the patriarchal structures of gender domination, the bloody bench of history offers abundant evidence of this "dysfunctionality"—most notably, the intolerance, repression, and colonizing proselytism enacted by the Church.

Borrowing Crownfield's expression, we might say that Marinetti's "Gospel" enacts a dysfunctional distortion of the Christly ideal. On the one hand, it seems to embrace the precept of loving acceptance of otherness within and outside the self that Jesus embodies. The poem is, in fact, addressed to the incarnated Son of God, the mediating, synthetic Third term that can pacify the conflict between spirit and flesh through love that absolves sin, through sensual mysticism that sublimates the flesh, and through evangelical charity that opens up to the other. In a letter of Christmas greetings addressed to Cangiullo from the Ethiopian front, Marinetti spells out the loving lesson to be derived from the divine Child: "In his will for life redemption calvary cross resurrection immortality the Baby Jesus already contains all the Divine on earth made breathing moaning flesh like us [. . . .] To obey the bending love [*curvo amore*] of his mother the Baby Jesus prepares for the holy gesture that forgives Magdalen for her many lusts because they are all sublimated by an intense passion."[54] There are, indeed, echoes of the Christly message of love in the poem: the poet's persistent effort to reach the "more or less inauspicious crowds of the foolish, mediocre, and superficial" in order to offer them the light of art is explained as an "instinct to offer inspiration" (10). Marinetti also quotes Christ's forgiving words addressed to the prostitute and his warning to the self-righteous stoners: "Let he who is without sin cast the first stone" (43). In keeping with this admonition, the poet at one point calls himself unworthy of access to the Worthy Home ("Ma non sono degno io della Casa," 42).

On the other hand, the text is pervaded by the polarizing, Manichaean dynamics characteristic of Marinetti's previous works. With obvious religious symbolism, the colonial war against Ethiopia is figured in terms of a conflict between light and darkness, a legitimizing strategy commonly deployed in the discourse of European expansionism. The Italian spirit and genius must impose their illuminating rule over the "dark" enemy ("the brute opaque forces," 15) in order to fulfill their civilizing mission. When the ethnic other receives positive connotations—as in the case of the askari soldiers who "evangelically" bring the water of life to the Italians under siege, or the image of the black wet nurse who is likewise associated with the water of life (19)—it is by virtue of having been "colonized" through assimilation or incorporation into the economy of the self.

Femininity still bears the mark of abjection. Identified with "brutish malice," "toothless satanic bile," and "cruel joy" (43), it is relegated to a miasmic morass of sin, bestiality, and nauseating slime: "Remorses struggling in the convulsing chest of the earth especially as there flashes and reeks a viscid heap of crocodiles water mud thighs of naked women intertwined with nauseating filigrees in a webbed aquatic filth" (41). As the virginal "vessel" of God's incarnation, however, woman becomes also the abode of the sublime or a vehicle to the divine. Thus the feminine other remains inscribed in the dyadic intrapsychic (rather than triadic intersubjective) economy, where it stands for the abominated abject—unless assimilated as maternal milk. In the first case, the implicit psychological mode (i.e., attitude toward the other and the real) is one of conflict and subjugation; in the latter, it is one of escape into aesthetic and sensual consolations, regressive fantasies of comfort and oblivion (the mother-child synthesis, the cradlelike nature).

In the letter cited above, Marinetti blatantly twists the evangelical message: "In the manger of Bethlehem the Baby Jesus teaches goodness but the growing life that animates his fragile limbs heralds force and here comes the duel between Force and Goodness Be strong against an enemy who ignores and forgets or pretends to ignore our Goodness." Love reigns in the cradle, but Force takes over in adult life: the enemy, after all, is alien to Goodness. (In reality, the "enemy" is the Ethiopian people, struggling to resist Italy's colonial ambitions.) *Caritas*, in other words, is ousted by the materialist rule of the strong, which justifies violence, domination, and exploitation. According to this degeneration of Goodness into Force, the life-bearing "instinct" ("istinto d'offerta animatore," 10), with which Marinetti identifies his artistic mission, turns into intolerant, aggressive proselytism, as evidenced by the futurists' prodigal offer of "fingers full of punches and slaps" to unreceptive audiences (22), or into violent incorporation of the "neighbor," as illustrated by the epic celebrations of the colonial war.

Similarly, the balance of reality and transfiguration that Marinetti ostensibly identifies as the power/function of art ("The Worthy Home will be brimming with reality and transfigurations," 40) is, in actuality, no balance at all. The scales weigh heavily on the side of transfiguration, frequently toppling into abstract transcendentalism and consolatory sensuality. Describing the futurist artistic ideal, Marinetti becomes mired in symbolism.

> From the inside cracks in league with the most patient sticky viscous creeping and grating ivy maliciously try to bite the foundations [of the high walls of innocence]
>   But the Smooth the Polished the Reflecting and the ascensional innocence cleanse all the structures that love God
>   [. . . .]

Oh rigid ascensional walls of marble or reinforced cement in reality you constitute the concrete rebellion of humanity against the deemed indispensable sins of
softness languor cowardice mumbling hypocrisy indecision

(58–59)

Verticality, rigidness, and smoothness afford resistance against the erosive, crum-
bling effects of time (the cracks) and nature (the "sticky" ivy). In their upward
movement toward divine transcendence, however, the "walls of innocence" must
bend to accommodate a sensual Umbrian vineyard, where the "Spectacle" of
Jesus' incarnation is taking place (59–60). This double movement in the figuration
of the futurist artistic ideal is paralleled by the Worthy Home (the place of the
Other): on the one hand, it is defined as a pure and impermeable "blue sapphire";
on the other, the imagery-laden description of the sublime abode compels the
reader to recognize that a cradle is being fleshed out with the softest and most
comforting sounds, textures, smells, and colors that Mother Nature can offer.

The scenic Umbrian vineyard evokes (and was probably inspired by) Dottori's
paintings of "spiritualized" landscapes of his native Umbria.[55] More significantly,
it reminds the reader of the "festivals of art" Marinetti proposes as solution to the
economic inferno in *Al di là del Comunismo* (*TIF*, 488). In the same context,
Marinetti celebrates the power of art as "intoxicating" intellectual alcohol: "Art
must be an alcohol, not a balm. Not an alcohol that creates oblivion, but an alcohol of exalting optimism that deifies youth, multiplies maturity a hundredfold and
revives old age. This intellectual alcohol-art must be profusely offered to everybody. Thus we will multiply the creator-artists" (*TIF*, 487). The images of the
vineyard, grapes, and wine in the aeropoem invoke the notion of art's miraculous,
intoxicating power. Wine, the poet declares, elevates thought and artistically
beatifies the landscape (53–54). The vineyard is indeed the locus where the divine
becomes materialized, where grape bunches are metamorphosed into breasts,
and where the poet's hypersensibility harvests a wealth of olfactory, visual, tactile,
and auditory sensations. As advocated in *Al di là del Comunismo*, this wealth is
offered by the poet to alleviate the economic inferno. Such charity is symbolized
by the hauling of the grape harvest to the poor in the city: while being excluded
from any direct experience of earthly paradise, they will be allowed to enjoy a
"distillate" of its artistic surrogate (54–55). Notwithstanding Marinetti's claim to
the contrary ("Non un alcool che dia l'oblio"), the effect of this "alcoholic" art is
ultimately escape and oblivion.

The ideological and political implications of Marinetti's consolatory aesthetics
can be amplified by comparing his trope of art as inebriation with the symbolic
function of wine in Elio Vittorini's *Conversazione in Sicilia* (Conversation in Sicily;
1941). In his search for answers to the question of human suffering, the protagonist refuses escapist solutions and rejects intoxication as a degrading, dehumaniz-
ing loss of awareness: "and I thought of the nights of my grandfather, the nights
of my father, and the nights of Noah, the nights of man, naked in wine and de-

fenseless, humiliated, less of a man than a child or a corpse."[56] When man falls prey to illusion, Vittorini warns, he lets himself be seduced by "phantasms" of reality, such as fascism's mystifying rhetoric—embodied by a monument to fallen soldiers (a bronze statue of a naked, sexy woman). Against such "brazen" rhetoric, the novel's conclusion orchestrates a choral expression of human solidarity that culminates in an emblematic question voiced by the protagonist's interlocutors: "And is there much suffering?—asked the Sicilians." For Vittorini, art was neither mimesis nor transfiguration and transcendence of reality, but an instrument of transformation to be constructed through a pluralistic, choral discourse or "call."[57] Like many other contemporary authors, he resisted and criticized the seductive solutions that Marinetti embraced, first in his heroic utopia of destruction and creation, later in his retreat into political compromise and escapist aestheticism.

Afterword

The Rhetoric of Violence and the Violence of Rhetoric

Marinetti's representation of art's miraculous power in terms of inebriating transubstantiation may well stand, at the conclusion of this study, as the quintessential metaphor for the rhetorical strategies I have investigated. It conflates the religious and the alimentary sphere, intimating both a desire for exalted transcendence and a thirst for totalizing assimilation of the real. An early, more explicit formulation of this trope appears in one of Marinetti's first manifestos, "Distruzione della sintassi—Immaginazione senza fili—Parole in libertà," where he writes, "Discarding all stupid definitions and confused verbalisms of professors, I now declare that *lyricism* is the extraordinary *faculty* of *intoxicating oneself with life*, of *filling life with the inebriation of oneself.* The faculty of changing to wine the muddy water of life that engulfs and runs through us" (*TIF,* 70; emphasis in original). The violence that the futurists celebrated and enacted, particularly in the "heroic" phase of the movement, bears witness to the most disquieting implications of the will to mastery conveyed by the above image. Rejecting the inescapable "muddiness" of the real in favor of impossible, totalizing aspirations may afford consolatory evasion, but it may also result in intoxication with violence. The artificially inflated sense of self and bursting of boundaries open the door to explosive aggression against the other.

Futurism's rhetoric of violence is the most obvious manifestation of the aggressive potential inherent in its vision. Marinetti brashly glorifies war, preaches destruction of the past, and revels in scenarios of conflict, from the theater of military operations to the battlefield of futurist performances. Futurist "actions," with conflict as their governing premise, sought to turn rhetoric into reality. On the page, meanwhile, "formal violence" is enacted by means of suppressive and expansive mechanisms. Marinetti's destruction of syntax produces a fragmented, chaotic text that conforms to, and claims mastery over, the fragmentation and chaos of the modern world. The obliteration of syntax and logical links allows expressive force to expand "without strings," through a frenzied semiosis of sensorial effects and imaginary associations. The resulting explosion of imaginative energy stretches the boundaries of the subject to encompass the whole universe (**"art, this prolongation of the forest of our veins,** [. . .] spreads, outside the body, over the infinity of space and time," *TIF*, 54; emphasis in original). At the same time, the transfiguring force of language annihilates or assimilates the limits of the real ("chang[es] to wine the muddy water of life").

Metaphorical transfiguration is an especially effective device for amplifying the territory of the self and occupying that of the other. The subject figuratively incorporates empowering objects (as in the mythical construct of metallized and mechanized man), erecting a rigid and impermeable boundary or armor that channels affective energy into a struggle against a feminine or feminized other. Thus violence is intrinsically woven into the gendered configuration of the self-world relationship in the futurist fiction of power. The domain of subjective experience (be it artistic representation or imperialist expansion) is recurrently encoded as female, while woman is figured dualistically as the quintessential, forever unattainable object of desire (to be rejected or assimilated) and as the archenemy of self-expansion (to be destroyed).

Rhetorical strategies of suppression, expansion, and transfiguration engender insidious forms of discursive violence. Far from being confined to the order of language, the "violence of rhetoric" insinuates itself into the matrix of history and social practice, particularly the "reality" of gender.[1] Semiotic theory teaches us that the construction of human subjectivity in language relies on and (re)produces an asymmetrical, polarized, antagonistic configuration of sexual difference, which shapes virtually all aspects of social meaning, experience, and reality. Violence in rhetoric may assert itself in less conspicuous forms than those at which the futurists excelled. It is, nonetheless, a palpable force in discourses of domination ranging from scientific rationality to philosophical idealism—spheres of understanding/intelligibility ostensibly unrelated to futurism's excesses of imagination. In calling attention to the subtler configurations of violence in futurist texts, my aim is to suggest that the semiotic forces driving the futurist fiction of power are embedded in the signifying practices of our cultural past and continue to affect our historical present. Unquestioned and unchallenged, they may serve to generate an exclusionary politics of the future.

NOTES

CHAPTER 1. THE OTHER MODERNISM: FUTURISM AND ITS CONTRADICTIONS

My thanks to Lucia Re for suggesting the designation "the other modernism" to pinpoint the marginalization of futurism in modernist studies. The appellative "other" is also appropriate in view of the critical tendency to demonize the movement by association with fascism.

1. See Luciano De Maria, introduction, *Teoria e invenzione futurista* (hereafter *TIF*), ed. Luciano De Maria (1968; Milan: Arnoldo Mondadori Editore, 1983), XLVII. Subsequent page references to *TIF* will be given parenthetically within the text.

2. Jo Anna Isaak, *The Ruin of Representation in Modernist Art and Texts* (Ann Arbor: University of Michigan Research Press, 1986), 55–56.

3. Alice Yaeger Kaplan, *Reproductions of Banality: Fascism, Literature, and French Intellectual Life* (Minneapolis: University of Minnesota Press, 1986), 76. See also Arcangelo Leone de Castris (*Il decadentismo italiano: Svevo, Pirandello, D'Annunzio* [Bari: De Donato, 1974], 71–73), who speaks of futurist "terrorism"; and Edoardo Sanguineti ("La guerra futurista," in *Ideologia e linguaggio* [Milan: Feltrinelli, 1975], 38–43), who identifies the aesthetic celebration of war and the aestheticization of politics as the core of Marinetti's program, emphasizing its links with fascist cultural politics.

4. Marianne W. Martin, *Futurist Art and Theory: 1909–1915* (Oxford: Clarendon Press, 1968), 41.

5. Marjorie Perloff, *The Futurist Moment: Avant-Garde, Avant Guerre, and the Language of Rupture* (Chicago: University of Chicago Press, 1986).

6. I am paraphrasing the title of a book by Rinaldo Rinaldi, *Miracoli della stupidità: Discorso su Marinetti* (Turin: Tirrenia Stampatori, 1986), which in turn refers to Pier Paolo Pasolini's contemptuous judgment of Marinetti: "He is an enigma simply because he lacks intelligence. The instruments that serve to analyze literary forms, which are by definition products of intelligence [. . .] turn out to be absolutely useless in Marinetti's case. [. . .] In other words, Marinetti forces us to consider—*indeed, we could not honestly avoid doing so*—the presence of a fool where everything else is the product of intelligence. [. . .] Miracles of stu-

pidity" (emphasis added). This quote, which features as an epigraph in Rinaldi's book, is taken from Pasolini, *Descrizioni di descrizioni*, ed. Graziella Chiarcossi (Turin: Einaudi, 1979), 186–188. If the difficulty that Pasolini (and Rinaldi) experiences in dealing intelligently with Marinetti's "enigma" is merely due to the latter's stupidity, why does the honest critic feel compelled to deal with such an enigma in the first place?

7. For a history of the term's usage and a survey of various arguments for and against its validity, see Stanley Sultan, *Eliot, Joyce and Company* (New York: Oxford University Press, 1987), 96–101.

8. In *Rhetoric and Death: The Language of Modernism and Postmodern Discourse Theory* (Urbana: University of Illinois Press, 1990), Ronald Schleifer poignantly defines this crisis as a sense of the unintelligible materiality of language, life, and death—that is, a perception of reality as meaningless chaos and fragmentation, a pervasive feeling of futurelessness, and an apocalyptic foreboding of the end of culture in the modern age.

9. The literature on these issues is vast. I will limit myself to mentioning the studies to which I am most indebted: George L. Mosse, *The Culture of Western Europe: The Nineteenth and Twentieth Centuries* (Chicago: Rand McNally, 1961); Malcolm Bradbury and James McFarlane, eds., *Modernism: 1890–1930* (1976; London: Penguin Books, 1987); Stephen Kern, *The Culture of Time and Space, 1880–1918* (Cambridge: Harvard University Press, 1983); and Schleifer's *Rhetoric and Death*.

10. Still, as Bradbury and McFarlane point out, rationalist and irrationalist tendencies continue to coexist within modernism in an "explosive fusion" of reason and unreason, intellect and emotion, subjective and objective: "Modernism was in most countries an extraordinary compound of the futuristic and the nihilistic, the revolutionary and the conservative, the naturalistic and the symbolistic, the romantic and the classical. It was a celebration of the technological age and a condemnation of it; an excited acceptance of the belief that the old régimes of culture were over, and a deep despairing in the face of that fear; a mixture of convictions that the new forms were escapes from historicism and the pressures of the time with convictions that they were precisely the living expressions of these things" (*Modernism*, 46).

11. Mosse, *The Culture of Western Europe*, 220–221.

12. Such are the characteristic features of the avant-garde according to Renato Poggioli, *Teoria dell'arte d'avanguardia* (Bologna: Il Mulino, 1962). See also Peter Bürger, *Theory of the Avant-Garde*, trans. Michael Shaw (Minneapolis: University of Minnesota Press, 1984). Both Poggioli and Bürger tend to split off futurism from the modernist canon. In Poggioli's case, this tendency may be seen as an attempt to extricate aesthetics from politics in the analysis of the avant-garde; in Bürger's case, it appears to coincide with the agenda of "binding" the theory of a leftist avant-garde. Andrew Hewitt, in "Fascist Modernism, Futurism, and 'Post-Modernity' " (*Fascism, Aesthetics, and Culture*, ed. Richard J. Golsan [Hanover: University Press of New England, 1992], 38–55), pinpoints the political agenda underlying this strategy of exclusion: "Whereas Poggioli sought to relegitimate a depoliticized formalistic canon of modernism, it is *against* precisely this canon that Bürger wishes to reestablish the claims of a politically oriented avant-garde exemplified by Brecht" (40; emphasis in original).

13. See Charles Tilly, Louise Tilly, and Richard Tilly, *The Rebellious Century: 1830–1930* (Cambridge: Harvard University Press, 1975), 87–190. On the endemic institutional problems of the Italian state from unification to fascism, see also Nicola Tranfaglia, *Dallo stato liberale al regime fascista: Problemi e ricerche* (Milan: Feltrinelli, 1973).

14. See Sandra Puccini, "Condizione della donna e questione femminile (1892–1922)," *Problemi del socialismo*, 4th ser., 17.4 (1976): 9–71; Franca Pieroni Bortolotti, *Alle origini del movimento femminile in Italia, 1848–1892* (Turin: Einaudi, 1963); Bortolotti, *Femminismo e partiti politici in Italia, 1919–1926* (Rome: Editori Riuniti, 1978); Camilla Ravera, *Breve storia del movimento femminile in Italia* (Rome: Editori Riuniti, 1978); and Lucia Chiavola Birnbaum, *Liberazione della donna: Feminism in Italy* (Middletown, Conn.: Wesleyan University Press, 1986).

15. On this positivist trend, see Alberto Asor Rosa, "Il futurismo nel dibattito intellettuale italiano dalle origini al 1920," in *Futurismo, cultura e politica*, ed. Renzo De Felice, (Turin: Edizioni della Fondazione Giovanni Agnelli, 1988), 57–58.

16. See Niccolò Zapponi, *I miti e le ideologie: Storia della cultura italiana, 1870–1960* (Naples: Edizioni Scientifiche Italiane, 1981), 7–205; and the introductory essays in *La cultura italiana del '900 attraverso le riviste* (hereafter *LCI*), 6 vols. (Turin: Einaudi, 1960–1963).

17. Maffio Maffii, "Senescit iuventus," *Hermes* (May–June 1904): 175–179; rpt. in *LCI*, 1:408–413.

18. Giuseppe Antonio Borgese, "Il Vascello Fantasma," *Hermes* (February 1904): 100–104; rpt. in *LCI*, 1:375–379.

19. Giovanni Amendola, "Né ideale né reale," *Leonardo*, 3d ser. (August 1906): 222–237; rpt. in *LCI*, 1:317–328.

20. Enrico Corradini, "Per coloro che risorgono," *Il Regno* (29 November 1903): 1–2; rpt. in *LCI*, 1:441–443.

21. See Giuliano il Sofista [Giuseppe Prezzolini], "Decadenza Borghese," *Leonardo* (22 February 1903): 7–8 (rpt. in *LCI*, 1:129–131); and Gian Falco [Giovanni Papini], "Campagna per il forzato Risveglio," *Leonardo*, 3d ser. (August 1906): 193–199 (rpt. in *LCI*, 1:312–316).

22. D'Annunzian aestheticism, in particular, informs Papini's definition of "the imperialist ideal": refusing Corradini's "vulgar" desire for military domination, he embraces an "aristocratic" ideal of spiritual and intellectual supremacy. See Gian Falco, "L'Ideale Imperialista," *Leonardo* (4 January 1903): 1–3; rpt. in *LCI*, 1:90–95.

23. Papini, "I consigli di Amleto," *Hermes* (July 1904): 225–230; rpt. in *LCI*, 1:427–432. On the topos of de*gender*ation in decadent and antidecadent literature, see Barbara Spackman, *Decadent Genealogies: The Rhetoric of Sickness from Baudelaire to D'Annunzio* (Ithaca: Cornell University Press, 1989).

24. Papini, "Il massacro delle donne," *Lacerba* (1 April 1914): 97–99.

25. A sign of this concern is the debate on the "issue of sexuality" in *La Voce*, which sponsored two conferences in Florence (October 1910 and April 1912) to address the current interest in and "uneasiness" about sexual problems. See Prezzolini, "Convegno per la questione sessuale," *La Voce* (9 June 1910): 335; and the special issue "La questione sessuale" (10 February 1910).

26. Marinetti's biographies tend to romanticize and often lack scholarly rigor. See Walter Vaccari, *Vita e tumulti di F. T. Marinetti* (Milan: Omnia Editrice, 1959); and Gino Agnese, *Marinetti: Una vita esplosiva* (Milan: Camunia, 1990).

27. For an international map of futurist influence, see Claudia Salaris, *Marinetti editore* (Bologna: Il Mulino, 1990), 9, 241–263. Among other contemporaries, Guillaume Apollinaire, Gabriel Arbouin, Ivan Goll, Roch Grey, Ezra Pound, Vasilij Kandinskij, and Piet Mondrian acknowledged the historical importance of Marinetti's movement.

28. Marinetti, *La Conquête des Étoiles* (Paris: «La Plume», 1902); rpt. in *Scritti francesi* (hereafter *SF*), ed. Pasquale A. Jannini (Milan: Mondadori, 1983). All quotes refer to this edition.

29. Marinetti, *Destruction* (Paris: Vanier, 1904); rpt. in *SF*. All quotes refer to this edition. In the Italian translation, *Distruzione: Poema futurista*, trans. Decio Cinti (Milan: Edizioni futuriste di «Poesia», 1911), the final call for destruction ("Distruggiam! Distruggiamo!") is followed by a postscript that announces the beginning of the epic poem "La conquista delle stelle."

30. Rita Felski, "The Counterdiscourse of the Feminine in Three Texts by Wilde, Huysmans, and Sacher-Masoch," *PMLA* 16.5 (1991): 1102–1103. Subsequent page references will be given parenthetically within the text.

31. Felski emphasizes that the aesthete's colonizing move is concomitant with the "denial and repression of woman": "The appeal to the feminine in late-nineteenth-century writing entails a fundamental ambiguity; underlying the apparent subversion of gender norms is a persistent identification of women with vulgarity, corporeality, and the tyranny of nature, allowing the male aesthete to define his own identity in explicit opposition to these attributes" (1104).

For a more extended investigation of these issues, see Spackman's *Decadent Genealogies*. Spackman examines the topoi of eviration and feminization as constitutive elements of the decadent rhetoric of sickness, arguing that the appropriation of alterity through the occupation of the woman's body is a metaphor for a new interpretation of the body's relation to thought.

32. J.-K. Huysmans, *Against Nature: A New Translation of À Rebours*, trans. Robert Baldick (London: Penguin Books, 1954), 219. Subsequent page references will be given parenthetically within the text.

33. Sigmund Freud uses the term "oceanic" to designate a feeling of infringement of the ego's boundaries, an overwhelming sensation of being one with the external world. See "Civilization and Its Discontents," in *The Standard Edition of the Complete Psychological Works* (hereafter *SE*), trans. and ed. James Strachey, 24 vols. (London: Hogarth Press, 1953–1974), 21:64.

34. Marinetti, *Le Roi Bombance* (Paris: «Mercure de France», 1905). Page references will be given parenthetically within the text.

35. Marinetti, *Re Baldoria* (Milan: Treves, 1910). In his review ("Re Tobol e Re Bombance," *Corriere della Sera* [11 December 1905]: 1–2), Ettore Janni reports Marinetti's comment that the play was inspired by an "oratorical duel" between Turati (resembling the reformist Bechamel) and Labriola (resembling the revolutionary Emptystomach). Labriola actually wrote a favorable review of Marinetti's satirical tragedy in *L'Avanti*. Antonio Gramsci's famous article "Marinetti rivoluzionario?" (*L'Ordine Nuovo* [5 January 1921]; rpt. in *2000 pagine di Gramsci*, ed. Giansiro Ferrata and Niccolò Gallo [Milan: Il Saggiatore, 1964], 1:552–554) and other documents examined by Salaris indicate that left-wing circles appreciated futurist works and that significant contacts occurred between anarchosyndicalist groups and Marinetti's movement (*Marinetti editore*, 88, 118–120).

36. See Paul Ricoeur, *Freud and Philosophy: An Essay on Interpretation*, trans. Denis Savage (New Haven: Yale University Press, 1970), 315–316.

37. Marinetti, *La Ville charnelle* (Paris: Sansot, 1908); rpt. in *SF*. All quotes refer to this edition. The phrase "voyageur mordu" can be literally translated as "bitten traveler" or "crazy for traveling." In the Italian version, *Lussuria Velocità* (Milan: Modernissima, 1921), "mordu" becomes "stregato" (bewitched), one of the accepted figurative meanings of the French expression. The literal meaning, however, is important for future intertextual references: the association of "biting" with insatiable, uncontrollable, and frustrated desire or ambition is a leitmotiv in Marinetti's writing.

38. In Schleifer's words, the ahistorical attitude of modernist epistemology is predicated on "lack of an assured awareness of the continuity and power of the past—a lack of a sense of history, of a future as well as of the past" (*Rhetoric and Death*, 62). Because the past appears no longer logically (causally) related to the present, the present cannot be rationally comprehended (explained on the basis of past experience); the future is reduced, therefore, "to an accident that cannot be predicted" (65).

39. T. S. Eliot, "*Ulysses,* Order and Myth," *Dial*, no. 75 (New York, 1923): 480–483. Quoted in Bradbury and McFarlane, *Modernism*, 83.

40. Philip P. Wiener, ed., *Dictionary of the History of Ideas: Studies of Selected Pivotal Ideas* (New York: Charles Scribner's Sons, 1973), 3:551.

41. See Papini, "Introduzione al Pragmatismo," *Leonardo*, 3d ser. (February 1907): 26–37; rpt. in *LCI*, 1:335–342 (page numbers refer to *LCI* and will appear in the text).

42. Norbert Elias, *The Civilizing Process*, trans. Edmund Jephcott, 2 vols. (New York: Urizen Books, 1978). Gilles Deleuze and Félix Guattari (*Anti-Oedipus: Capitalism and Schizophrenia*, trans. Robert Hurley, Mark Seem, and Helen R. Lane [Minneapolis: University of Minnesota Press, 1983]) have also investigated this double movement of progress, particularly in "the social axiomatic of modern societies," which "are torn in two directions: archaism and futurism" (260).

43. Bruno Romani (*Dal simbolismo al futurismo* [Florence: Sandron, 1969]) has gone to great (perhaps excessive) lengths to demonstrate Marinetti's lack of originality by "unearthing" the sources of his theories, themes, and stylistic procedures. In particular, he points out the links with French movements such as symbolism, decadentism, naturism, integralism, parossism, impulsionism, and unanimism (93) and discusses "derivations" from artists such as Rosny Ainé, Paul Adam, Mario Morasso, and D'Annunzio. By contrast, Sergio Turconi credits Marinetti with being the "catalyst" of a diffuse climate, i.e., of shaping scattered and inactive elements into forms and structures that have left important traces in European literature. See his "I manifesti del futurismo e la visione lirica della tecnica e della scienza," in *Letteratura e scienza nella storia della cultura italiana: Atti del IX congresso dell'Associazione Internazionale per gli studi di Lingua e Letteratura Italiana, 1976* (Palermo: Manfredi, 1978), 831–838.

44. See Kern, *The Culture of Time and Space*, 36–64.

45. See "Noi rinneghiamo i nostri maestri simbolisti ultimi amanti della luna" (We Abjure Our Symbolist Masters, the Last Lovers of the Moon), *TIF*, 302–306.

46. See Mario Morasso, *La nuova arma (la macchina)* (Turin: Bocca, 1905), 30; and *L'Imperialismo artistico* (Turin: Bocca, 1903), 205. On Morasso's imperialist aesthetics and other sources of the futurist myth of the machine, see Roberto Tessari, "Macchine e rari merletti: Alcune fonti del futurismo nell'ideologia e nella letteratura," in De Felice, *Futurismo, cultura e politica*, 79–101. On modernist nationalism as the breeding ground of the futurist program of national palyngenesis, see Emilio Gentile, "The Conquest of Modernity: From Modernist Nationalism to Fascism," trans. Lawrence Rainey, *Marinetti and the Italian Futurists*, special issue of *Modernism/Modernity* 1.3 (1994): 55–87.

47. Several studies have combated or problematized the notion of an equation between Marinetti's futurism and Mussolini's fascism. Even among critics who oppose any crude identification, however, attitudes vary widely. The overall case against the fascism = futurism equation has been forcibly (and apologetically) made by De Maria in his ideological profile of Marinetti's Weltanschauung (see his introduction to *TIF*). Renzo De Felice also takes a defensive stance by confining Marinetti's wholehearted political commitment

(hence moral responsibility) to the prefascist era and by underscoring the idealistic and circumstantial reasons for his continuing "concessions and tributes" to fascism. See his "L'avanguardia futurista," in Marinetti, *Taccuini: 1915/1921* (Notebooks: 1915/1921), ed. Alberto Bertoni (Bologna: Il Mulino, 1987), VII–XXXV; and *Mussolini il rivoluzionario: 1883–1920* (Turin: Einaudi, 1965), 419–598. On the opposite side of the spectrum, Jeffrey Schnapp argues against this kind of "critical rescue mission" and, more generally, against "the common practice of placing a *cordon sanitaire* around the movement's first nine to ten years [. . .] to mark off the movement's greatest innovations" from the futurist/fascist connection. Asserting that futurism first anticipated and later complemented fascist doctrine, Schnapp finds evidence of a "fascist sensibility" in the futurist construction of subjectivity and space. See his "Forwarding Address," *Fascism and Culture*, ed. Jeffrey Schnapp and Barbara Spackman, special issue of *Stanford Italian Review* 8.1–2 (1990): 53–80. Robert S. Dombroski (*L'Esistenza ubbidiente: Letterati italiani sotto il fascismo* [Naples: Guida, 1984], 28–50) also underscores the "homology" between futurism and fascism, which he locates essentially in mythical structures of self-definition and problem solving. Striving for a balanced position, Emilio Gentile examines the formation of a futurist politics within a muddled ideological context of "national radicalism" and "modernist nationalism," in which a symbiosis between left-wing and right-wing radical movements created an environment favorable to the development of fascism. See his "Il futurismo e la politica: Dal nazionalismo modernista al fascismo (1909–1920)," in De Felice, *Futurismo, cultura e politica*, 105–159; *Le origini dell'ideologia fascista* (Rome-Bari: Laterza, 1975); and "La politica di Marinetti," *Storia contemporanea* 7.3 (1976): 415–438, revised and expanded in *Il mito dello Stato nuovo dall'antigiolittismo al fascismo* (Rome-Bari: Laterza, 1982).

The literature on the relationship between futurism and fascism is vast. In addition to the studies discussed above, the following ones constitute only a selected bibliography: G. Battista Nazzaro, *Futurismo e politica* (Naples: JN Editore, 1968); Enrico Crispolti, *Il Mito della Macchina e altri temi del Futurismo* (Trapani: Celebes, 1969), 580–843; Crispolti, *Storia e critica del Futurismo* (Bari: Laterza, 1986), 183–224; Niccolò Zapponi, "Futurismo e fascismo," in De Felice, *Futurismo, cultura e politica*, 161–176; and Judy Davies, "The Futures Market: Marinetti and the Fascists of Milan," in *Visions and Blueprints: Avant-Garde Culture and Radical Politics in Early Twentieth-Century Europe*, ed. Edward Timms and Peter Collier (Manchester: Manchester University Press, 1988), 82–97.

48. Carol Diethe epitomizes this tendency in her "Sex and the Superman: An Analysis of the Pornographic Content of Marinetti's *Mafarka le futuriste*," in *Perspectives on Pornography: Sexuality in Film and Literature*, ed. Gary Day and Clive Bloom (London: Macmillan, 1988), 159–174. For a discussion of the main loci of Marinetti's misogynist rhetoric, see David Dollenmeyer, "Alfred Döblin, Futurism, and Women: A Relationship Reexamined," *Germanic Review* 61.4 (1986): 138–145.

49. See Marinetti, preface, *Mafarka il futurista*, *TIF*, 253–254: "When I told them: '*Scorn woman!*' they all hurled lewd insults at me, like so many pimps infuriated by a police raid. And yet I am not discussing woman's animal value, but rather the sentimental importance attributed to her. [. . . .] I want to conquer the tyranny of love, the obsession with the ideal woman [*l'ossessione della donna unica*], the grand romantic moonlight that bathes the Bordello's facade" (emphasis in original).

50. De Felice, "L'avanguardia futurista," in Marinetti, *Taccuini*, XVIII.

51. Ezio Raimondi, "Il testimone come attore," in Marinetti, *Taccuini*, XLIX–L.

52. Maria-Antonietta Macciocchi, "Les femmes et la traversée du fascisme," in *Éléments pour une analyse du fascisme* (Paris: Union Générale d'Édition, 1976), 1:148.

53. See, for instance, Anna Nozzoli, *Tabù e coscienza: La condizione femminile nella letteratura italiana del Novecento* (Florence: La Nuova Italia, 1978), 49.

54. Kaplan, *Reproductions of Banality*, 86. Subsequent page references will be given parenthetically within the text.

55. Kaplan points out that fascism's earlier, utopian, "gathering" phase is a movement attuned to the "oceanic," preoedipal register, addressing infantile, maternal longings. Authoritarianism, repression, discipline, and pragmatism prevail over the utopian elements in the successive stage of reactionary entrenchment, when fascism becomes consolidated as a regime (*Reproductions of Banality*, 13, 24).

56. Jessica Benjamin, *The Bonds of Love: Psychoanalysis, Feminism, and the Problem of Domination* (New York: Pantheon Books, 1988), 151; hereafter abbreviated *BL*. Further page references will appear in the text. Benjamin's approach emphasizes the goal of relatedness to others, rather than the ideal of, or need for, autonomous individuality posited by "classical" psychoanalytic theory. In her view, such an ideal harbors the germ of domination, since the basic pattern of domination is predicated on "the breakdown of the tension between self and other" (between self-assertion and mutual recognition), which begins with the denial of recognition to the mother (the original other who is reduced to object) and "proceeds through the alternate paths of identifying with or submitting to powerful others who personify the fantasy of omnipotence" (*BL*, 219).

57. Benjamin views the theories of the Frankfurt school, as well as other theories based on the Freudian paradigm of the father-son struggle, as tending to obscure the question of woman's subjugation and, in general, the problem of gender relations. She also points out that such theorists as Wilhelm Reich, N. O. Brown, and Herbert Marcuse, who argued against authority and for the lifting of repression, still formulated the question of domination in terms of the oedipal paradigm, underplaying the role of gender relations in the dynamics of domination and subjugation (*BL*, 6).

58. Referring to Freud's writing on narcissim, where the ego ideal is defined as "heir to our narcissism" and the superego as "heir to the Oedipus complex," Benjamin underscores the role of the ideal father of rapprochement in the development of early narcissism. In the language of object-relation theory, rapprochement is the phase in which the toddler comes to terms with the limits of his/her effectiveness in the face of the parents' greater power and confronts the paradox of needing to be recognized as independent by the very people he or she depends on. Reinterpreting Jacques Lacan's mirror phase as "the relationship of identification with the idealized father as mirror of desire, with all its grandiosity," she argues that early love for the idealized (omnipotent) father solves the paradox: "the child idealizes the father because the father is the magical mirror that reflects the self as it wants to be—the ideal in which the child wants to recognize himself." Identificatory love results in "a particular kind of oneness with the person who embodies the power one now feels lacking." If such an identificatory love is frustrated, however, "this idealization can become the basis for adult ideal love, the submission to a powerful other who seemingly embodies the agency and desire one lacks in oneself" (*BL*, 100–101, 148).

59. Kaplan, *Reproductions of Banality*, 10: "Fascist subjects are virile, phallic, their devotion to the language they learn is total, boundary-less, and the language itself is a maternal one. In order for the state to generate a whole new type of man [. . .], it has to be female.

Its subjects are men; fascism itself is a woman, a new mother. The maternal language obviously makes them phallic, but authority is still feminine, its subjects masculine. There are many potential substitutions going on here: if fascist authority is feminine, then the leader is a woman of sorts."

Klaus Theweleit draws different conclusions from his study of memoirs and novels by *Freikorps* officers (vanguard of Nazism) and other widely read conservative writers (such as Ernst Jünger, Joseph Paul Goebbels, and Martin Niemöller) in *Male Fantasies,* trans. Stephen Conway, Erica Carter, and Chris Turner, 2 vols. (Minneapolis: University of Minnesota Press, 1987–1989). He maintains that the dynamic of unification in the fascist ritual of oratory is entirely inflected in the masculine gender and does not produce an undifferentiated unity, but a hierarchical totality formation (2:125–129). Subsequent page references will be given parenthetically within the text.

60. Rosemarie Scullion makes this point in her review of Kaplan's book (*Substance* 58 [1989]: 100–102) and cites Popular Front rallies in interwar France as an example.

61. See Margaret Randolph Higonnet, Jane Jenson, Sonya Michel, and Margaret Collins Weitz, eds., *Behind the Lines: Gender and the Two World Wars* (New Haven: Yale University Press, 1987).

62. Michel Foucault, "Powers and Strategies," in *Power/Knowledge: Selected Interviews and Other Writings, 1972–1977,* ed. Colin Gordon (New York: Pantheon Books, 1980), 139.

63. Renzo De Felice, "Fascism and Culture in Italy: Outlines for Further Study," *Stanford Italian Review* 8.1–2 (1990): 10. See also Delio Cantimori's comparison of a superficially unitary vision of fascism to "a kind of whale that swallowed everything indiscriminately, or that satanically carried everyone to their destruction, like Moby Dick." Quoted in De Felice, *Interpretations of Fascism,* trans. Brenda Huff Everett (Cambridge: Harvard University Press, 1977), 170.

64. For a discussion of futurist Don Juanism, see chapter 4 of this study. Theweleit maintains that antieroticism—attraction to male bonding, recoiling from sensual women, and persecution of sexuality—is a unifying trait in the fascist mode of production of reality (or fascist desire), which he characterizes as a particular form of libido perversion: the transformation of the life-producing energy of the unconscious into a murderous, explosive force of destruction. Although he takes the fantasies of a group of men with a rather homogeneous background as the basis of his broader speculations on fascist desire, he does pinpoint the specific cultural origins of the Freikorps' brand of terror. These men's compulsion to turn any potentially pleasurable situation into violent scenarios of aggression and annihilation (both in fantasy and in action) is viewed as the consequence of their early failure to cathect libidinally their own bodily periphery and thus form a stable sense of self "from the inside out" (*Male Fantasies,* 2:164). Such a failure, in turn, is traced to the educational methods commonly deployed in Wilhelmine society or, as Theweleit puts it, to "the whole terroristic process of their own acquisition of 'manhood' " (2:296): beating as a pedagogical practice, extenuating drills in the military academy, and an early estrangement from nurturing, comforting experiences in the family. The ego that external agencies beat and whip into shape is "a functioning and controlling body armor, and a body capable of seamless fusion into larger formations with armorlike peripheries," such as the troop, the military machine, and the nation (2:164).

65. Barbara Spackman, "The Fascist Rhetoric of Virility," *Stanford Italian Review* 8.1–2 (1990): 90. Subsequent page references will appear in the text.

66. In *Fascist Modernism: Aesthetics, Politics, and the Avant-Garde* (Stanford: Stanford University Press, 1993), Hewitt takes a different approach to the analysis of Marinetti's aes-

theticopolitical project. He explores the nexus theoretically, ideologically, and tropologically, focusing on the machine as a "central organizing metaphor" that serves as the "legitimation" or model for both aesthetic and political systems. Imperialism is seen as the common ideological root of both Marinetti's political commitment and his aesthetic achievements—a paradigm for textual production (an avant-garde aesthetic that privileges performance over the finished art object), a political structure that is at once totalizing and transgressive, and a (re-)productive/efficient libidinal economy. Despite his impressive theoretical subtlety and intellectual breadth, Hewitt reaches some excessively schematic conclusions. Such shortcomings, in my opinion, result from his failure to ground the ideological discussion in close readings of the futurist rhetoric and politics of gender relations. Adopting the theoretical model of Deleuze and Guattari's *Anti-Oedipus*, where the machine (unfettered "machinic" production) is the figure for a political project oriented toward the liberation of the body (a flow/exchange of desire that results in ego loss), Hewitt overemphasizes the "postmodern" aspects of Marinetti's project and concludes that futurism abhors any fixation of value, "even that minimal fixation of value that is the human body" (157). To account for the fascist turn of the futurist political course, he must then argue that the machine assumes "two quite distinct forms" (146), functioning as a figure of transgressive production in Marinetti's earlier writings and as a figure of order and totalitarianism in the texts that mark his rapprochement to Mussolini. However, as we shall see in the following chapter, discipline and precision are already among the features of Marinetti's early model of the machine (i.e., in the 1914 "Lo splendore geometrico e meccanico e la sensibilità numerica" [Geometric and Mechanical Splendor and the Numerical Sensibility; *TIF*, 98–99]). Conversely, "infinite" productivity is among the values celebrated in the 1925 "Introduzione a *I nuovi poeti futuristi*" (Introduction to *The New Futurist Poets*; *TIF*, 191). Hewitt's model runs into further complications when he confronts the apparent discrepancy between the different aestheticopolitical and libidinal economies entailed by the two forms of the machine metaphor. The transgressive configuration in the political and aesthetic realm seems to coincide with a phallocentric, genital libidinal economy. Marinetti's putative move toward a more "liberated," degenitalized, and "tactile" sensuality is concomitant, instead, with his shift toward a more constraining, totalitarian figurative organization and political stance. Hewitt invokes the principles of procreation (or industrialized fecundity) and efficiency (or full utilization of the body) to reconcile, respectively, the progressive model with the phallic economy of the "heroic" phase and the totalitarian one with the more "liberated" sexuality in the productions of the fascist years (150–154).

67. For a broad overview of this critical tendency, which places the politics and aesthetics of gender at the heart of a comprehensive understanding of early twentieth-century literature, see Bonnie Kime Scott, ed., *The Gender of Modernism: A Critical Anthology* (Bloomington: Indiana University Press, 1990).

68. Jessica Benjamin, "A Desire of One's Own: Psychoanalytic Feminism and Intersubjective Space," in *Feminist Studies/Critical Studies*, ed. Teresa de Lauretis (Bloomington: Indiana University Press, 1986), 80. Benjamin's essay offers a brief survey and a bibliography of the most significant developments in the relationship between feminism and psychoanalysis. She summarizes the terms of the feminist critique of Freudian and Lacanian theories of desire, where the phallus immutably represents the principle of desire/individuation/power and the central organizer of gender. Benjamin's own position refers to and develops Nancy Chodorow's gender identity theory, which integrates object relations psychoanalysis with feminism to elaborate a post-Freudian notion of desire. Emphasizing the impor-

tance of preoedipal maternal identification and the existence of a primal capacity for connection and agency that "later meshes with symbolic structures, but [. . .] is not created by
them" (93), Benjamin argues for an "intersubjective" (rather than intrasubjective, or phallic) model of psychic organization, whereby the subject's relationship to other subjects and
to its own desire is found in "freedom to be both with and distinct from the other" (98). The
intersubjective mode of desire, she holds, has "something to do with female experience"
and can be represented as "inner space," to be understood "as part of a continuum that includes the space between the I and the you, as well as the space within me" (95).

69. Benjamin, "A Desire of One's Own," 80. In her later book *The Bonds of Love,* Benjamin situates her investigations within a context of complementarity and revision, rather
than opposition and exclusion, with respect to the intrasubjective psychoanalytical approach. The theoretical and political viability of an alternative developmental model, she
argues, is grounded on the modern crisis of authority and on the increasing fluidity of
gender roles in contemporary society: "[The decline of authority] has revealed the contradiction once hidden within [the idealization of autonomous] individuality: the inability to confront the independent reality of the other. Men's loss of absolute control over
women and children has exposed the vulnerable core of male individuality, the failure of
recognition which previously wore the cloak of power, responsibility, and family honor"
(*BL,* 181).

Benjamin's analysis shares many assumptions and conclusions with Theweleit's work.
The most fundamental divergence appears to stem from differing approaches to the question of the social limitations to human desire. While Benjamin focuses on interpersonal relations and advocates a developmental model whereby the subject's desire is bound by
recognition of the independent reality of other subjects, Theweleit emphasizes and celebrates the revolutionary potential of untrammeled, free-flowing individual desire. As Benjamin and Anson Rabinbach suggest in their foreword to the second volume of *Male Fantasies,* his radical antiauthoritarian stance can be related to the intellectual milieu of the
West German student Left of the late 1960s and early 1970s (2:x).

70. Evelyn Fox Keller, *Reflections on Gender and Science* (New Haven and London: Yale
University Press, 1985), 95, passim. Subsequent page references will be given parenthetically within the text.

71. I refer more extensively to Kristeva's inquiries, in particular to her notion of abjection, in chapter 2.

72. Contrary to non-Lacanian feminist psychoanalysis, Kristeva's queries are premised
on the assumption that the self is merely a screen over an essential emptiness and that the
subject is constituted through accession to the symbolic space of language and culture governed by the Law of the Father. Her earlier elaboration of this problematic implies the impossibility of transcending the dynamics of violent separation, emptiness, and abjection
that sustain the formation of the split subject. But her later work (especially *Tales of Love* and
In the Beginning Was Love: Psychoanalysis and Faith) explores more positive, constructive, imaginative, playful possibilities for an alternative psychic economy that emphasizes love, con-
nectedness and relatedness in ways that somewhat resonate with Benjamin's model of in-
tersubjectivity. Furthermore, in spite of her Lacanian emphasis on the lack of a sustaining
core at the center of the subject, Kristeva has posited the "semiotic" (prelinguistic, somatic)
chora (the heterogeneous "process" from which the subject emerges, the locus of inscription
of primal experiences such as birth, nourishment, absence, motility, pain, and relief) as the
irreducible (albeit fluid, polymorphous, polyrhythmic) core of psychic life. One might say

that this maternally connoted chora (much like Benjamin's intersubjective space) is the (theoretical) breeding space for "tales" of love and *jouissance*.

CHAPTER 2. THE RHETORIC OF GENDER IN THE MANIFESTOS

1. Perloff, *The Futurist Moment*, 85.

2. Marinetti—founder, leader, promoter, and manager of the movement—is also to be credited with the creation of the new genre. He either wrote or presided over the writing of most of the manifestos. His editorial interventions, such as in Antonio Sant'Elia's "L'architettura futurista" (Futurist Architecture), show a consistent effort to reinforce the shock effect of the text. See Salaris, *Marinetti editore*, 166, 174.

3. On the aesthetic of the manifesto as a collage of different verbal strategies, and on the theatrical quality of the manifesto, see Perloff, *The Futurist Moment*, chap. 3, in particular p. 111.

4. Michael Kirby (*Futurist Performance* [New York: Dutton, 1971], 12, 8–18) has pointed out that the novelty of the genre is paired by that of the context in which the manifestos were delivered: the famous *serate futuriste* (futurist evenings). These multimedia events combined the declamation of futurist manifestos and poetry, improvised speeches, insults, noises, music, the display of paintings, and the use of unconventional props such as "vegetable ammunitions" provided by jeering audiences, with the purpose of eliciting the public's immediate enthusiastic consensus or outraged reaction.

5. Luciano Caruso and Stelio M. Martini's "La 'fuga in avanti' del futurismo" (in *Tavole parolibere futuriste (1912–1944)*, ed. Caruso and Martini, 2 vols. [Naples: Liguori, 1974–1977], 1:1–7) exemplifies this mystifying approach: the futurist linguistic revolution (the "liberation" of language from the referential/communicative function) is valued as a step toward the "liberation of reality" (4).

6. Mario Carli, "Arte vile e arte virile," in *Manifesti, proclami, interventi e documenti teorici del futurismo*, ed. Luciano Caruso, 4 vols. (Florence: Coedizioni Spes-Salimbeni, 1980), 2:131.

7. Francesco Cangiullo, "La scoperta del sostantivo anatomico o del sesso in esso," in Caruso, *Manifesti*, 2:180; emphasis in original.

8. On the "continuum" of homosocial and homoerotic desire, see Eve Kosofsky Sedgwick, *Between Men: English Literature and Male Homosocial Desire* (New York: Columbia University Press, 1985).

9. In *Psicoanalisi della guerra* (Milan: Feltrinelli, 1988), Franco Fornari traces the "bellicose-destructive" mode of conflict to its origin in the process of absolutizing the danger posed by the other as opponent in a conflictual relationship: "the very existence of an other who limits our omnipotence is experienced as a radical threat to our survival; such a radical threat can only be countered by the destruction of the opponent we perceive as a destroyer" (97). Fornari also notes that mechanisms of Manichaean splitting of reality inform the idealization and dogmatization process on which group formation is based (202–205).

10. Referring to Otto Rank's seminal theories, Ernest Becker describes the modern neurosis as an existential crisis born of the eclipse of secure communal ideologies of redemption, in *The Denial of Death* (New York: Free Press, 1973), 190, passim.

11. Examples of this kind of imagery are numberless. In the graphic "Sintesi futurista della guerra" (Futurist Synthesis of the War), for instance, one of the enemy countries, Austria, is associated with "filth," "clotted blood," and "bedbugs" (*TIF*, 327). This pamphlet was issued by the Direction of the Futurist Movement after Marinetti and other futurists

were arrested for staging patriotic demonstrations in Milan (15–16 September 1914). According to a letter by Marinetti to Luciano Folgore (Omero Vecchi), more than twenty thousand copies of the leaflet were distributed (Salaris, *Marinetti editore*, 178).

12. Julia Kristeva, *Powers of Horror: An Essay on Abjection*, trans. Leon Roudiez (New York: Columbia University Press, 1982), 12–13; hereafter abbreviated *PH*. Subsequent page references will be given parenthetically within the text.

13. Corporeal waste includes bodily fluids such as "menstrual blood and excrement, or everything that is assimilated to them, from nail-parings to decay" (*PH*, 70). According to Kristeva, such substances "represent—like a metaphor that would have become incarnate—the objective frailty of the symbolic order" (*PH,* 70).

14. Walter Benjamin, in an often quoted passage, qualifies Marinetti's aestheticization of war as a paradigmatic example of an alienated/alienating aesthetic sensibility, instrumental to the economic structure of imperialistic capitalism. See his "The Work of Art in the Age of Mechanical Reproduction," in *Illuminations*, trans. Harry Zohn (New York: Schocken Books, 1969), 241–242. In his analysis of Ernst Jünger's dehumanized descriptions of war, Jeffrey Herf points to another possible interpretation that focuses on the emotional underpinnings of the writer's fantasies rather than on the utilitarian logic of economic politics. He suggests that this strategy of representation is a defense mechanism to "ward off potentially traumatic shocks of fear and horror by freezing them at the level of conscious perception before their full emotional impact is felt." See his *Reactionary Modernism: Technology, Culture, and Politics in Weimar and the Third Reich* (Cambridge: Cambridge University Press, 1984), 99.

15. Marinetti's eroticization of war has been emphasized, in particular, by Kaplan, who views it as an example of the affinities between futurist and fascist propaganda. See her "Futurism and Fascism: Reflexions on the 70th Anniversary of the Trial of *Mafarka the Futurist*," *Yale Italian Studies* 1.3 (1981): 48. De Maria points out the fundamental role played by war in futurist ideology and notes the interweaving of war and eros in Marinetti's writing. However, he does not explore the latter issue in depth, referring, instead, to Marinetti's own statement on the defensive function of fecundation and proliferation in wartime (*TIF*, XLVI–XLVII). Mario Isnenghi (*Il mito della grande guerra: Da Marinetti a Malaparte* [Bari: Laterza, 1970]) relates Marinetti's eroticization of war to a universal psychic condition: "the contiguity of aggressive instincts, hence the affinity between bellicose instinct and sexual instinct" (172). This argument is highly problematic: it naturalizes, just as Marinetti's writing does, the degeneration of sex into violence. In view of Freud's final theory of instincts (which posits the dualism sexual instinct–death instinct), we can perhaps speak of "fusion," rather than affinity, of the two classes of instincts (*The Ego and the Id, SE*, 19:40–41). But I am more persuaded by Theweleit's argument that the pleasurable investment of destruction is a particular form of libido perversion that cannot be contained within the analytical framework of Freud's death-drive hypothesis. In Theweleit's view, this hypothesis is Freud's defense against the dilemma that "the agents of massive processes of contemporary destruction" posed for psychoanalysis: "the psychoanalysts would have been required to explain why the destroyers—who, in analytical terms, would certainly have been considered 'psychotic'—were so rarely associated with the psychiatric clinic, the lunatic asylum, or with what would normally be termed criminal delinquency" (*Male Fantasies*, 2:383).

16. Marinetti, *Taccuini*, 242. Subsequent page references will be given parenthetically within the text.

17. See, for instance, the section "Bombardamento" (Bombardment) in *Zang Tumb Tumb* (*TIF*, 773–779). In these "words in freedom," the chaos of battle is figured as a cacophonic theatrical performance and the triumphal march of the futurist bombardment as a dominant leitmotiv.

18. According to Freud's account, the castration complex can be traced to its origins in (the boy's realization of) woman's anatomical difference. See "Some Psychical Consequences of the Anatomical Distinction between the Sexes," *SE*, 19:252. Expounding on Lacan's reformulation of this theory, Kaja Silverman suggests that Freud's "refusal to identify castration with any of the divisions which occur prior to the registration of sexual difference reveals [his] desire to place maximum distance between the male subject and the notion of lack." His theory, in other words, is an instance of externalizing the displacement onto the female body of the symbolic castration (sense of loss, inadequacy, or existential lack) that undermines the male subject's plenitude and coherence. In Silverman's revised paradigm, castration is conceptualized in terms of the splittings through which the subject is constituted in the symbolic order, or the "divisions and losses suffered by the male subject in the course of his cultural history" (*The Acoustic Mirror: The Female Voice in Psychoanalysis and Cinema* [Bloomington: Indiana University Press, 1988], 15, 22, passim). Feminist psychoanalytic writers like Chodorow and Benjamin have imparted another critical twist to the trajectory of the castration theory by arguing that the Lacanian version does not dispute the central position of the phallus as the immutable principle of desire, individuation, and power. From this perspective, the radical splittings that engender subjectivity in polarized and asymmetrical interpersonal relations appear to be the product of ideological operations that can be challenged and changed. In other words, the male subject's preoccupation with "lack" exists in a directly proportional relationship with the idealization of totality, mastery, and autonomy in a given sociocultural system.

19. I refer here to the mechanism of the "surrogate victim" described by René Girard in his *Violence and the Sacred*, trans. Patrick Gregory (Baltimore: Johns Hopkins University Press, 1977): the transforming of reciprocal, disruptive violence into unanimous beneficial violence through the sacrifice of a surrogate victim, which, according to Girard's theory, is at the core of primitive myths and rituals. The main thrust of Girard's study is to examine the affiliation between violence and desymbolization. He asserts that myths and rituals respectively formulate and rehearse the outbreak and cathartic resolution of a "sacrificial crisis" (an eruption of violence and a crisis of distinctions affecting the cultural order). The mythical formulation transfers the crisis disrupting the cultural order onto a single agent that can be safely scapegoated (e.g., Oedipus in the homonymous myth).

20. See Kaplan, *Reproductions of Banality*, 86.

21. For a discussion of the Lacanian concept of suture, its function in the development of a logic of the signifier and in cinematic discourse, see Stephen Heath, "Notes on Suture," *Screen* 18 (1977–1978): 48–76.

22. Luigi Peirone (*Lo strumento espressivo di Marinetti* [Genoa: Tilgher, 1976], 27–28) notes that this mathematical logic is more rigid than the syntactical one.

23. My argument is based on Stephen Spender's definition of "organic" and "intellectualized" poetry: "We have the sense [. . .] that modern circumstances have set up a screen between nature and man so that the harmonious relationship realized in organic poetry in which the soul sees itself reflected in the physical environment, is prevented. The only way of return to the being-creating fusion is through spiritual or physical violence, tearing down the screen and forcing the inner sensibility into contact with the external. What I

have called intellectualized poetry is that in which the critical attitudes which determine the attitude of what is said and the technique of the poem, are an inseparable part of the consciousness which the poem conveys" (*The Struggle of the Modern* [Berkeley, Los Angeles, and London: University of California Press, 1963], 44).

24. From the beginnings of the movement, the futurists were attracted to the arcane and were inspired by contemporary developments in esoteric research. Marinetti, for instance, supports his vision of the multiplied man by referring to telekinetic phenomena (*TIF*, 299–300). The relationship between futurism and occult science is examined in Germano Celant's "Futurismo esoterico," *Il Verri* 33–34 (1970): 108–117. Sandro Briosi compares Marinetti's technical efforts to magic in his "Le 'paradoxe' de la littérature et sa 'solution' dans l'avant-garde," in *Vitalité et contradictions de l'avant-garde: Italie-France 1909–1924*, ed. Sandro Briosi and Henk Hillenaar (Paris: Corti, 1988), 51–58. According to Briosi, Marinetti's rigorous programmation of the techniques of literary creation is aimed at overcoming the paradox of literature (the otherness of meanings produced by the text that escape the author's control); the higher stake of this victory, however, is domination of reality through total control over all possible meanings, as if emancipating the subject from the otherness of meaning coincided with overcoming the otherness of life as well. Such an effort, says Briosi, is particularly accentuated in the visual poetry of the paroliberist tables and can be compared to the magic practice of killing one's enemy by killing its image, a practice in which the real loved/feared objects are substituted with their signifiers (53).

25. See Peirone, *Lo strumento espressivo*, 22–25; and Jeffrey Schnapp, "Politics and Poetics in Marinetti's *Zang Tumb Tuuum*," *Stanford Italian Review* 5.1 (1985): 75–92.

26. To advertise the movement's international resonance, futurist periodicals quoted some of the responses thus solicited. The penultimate issue of *Poesia* (April-May-June-July 1909), for instance, contained a selection of some 9,500 letters and articles for and against the founding manifesto. Many foreign newspapers and journals reported the launch of futurism. Salaris lists publications in France, Germany, Spain, Greece, the United States, Latin America, Japan, and Russia (*Marinetti editore*, 84–85). France, in particular, was "flooded" with fliers of the first manifesto. The responses published in *Poesia* came from aristocratic and academic circles and from intellectuals linked to Marinetti's prefuturist experience (like Paul Adam and Henri Bataille).

27. See Salaris, *Marinetti editore*, 167. Marinetti created Edizioni futuriste di «Poesia» in order "to protect, encourage and materially help" young revolutionary artists, stifled by the myopic, lucrative practices prevailing in the editorial world (11). He ran his enterprise out of his own home and supervised every phase and detail of production, availing himself of a small group of collaborators and hiring printers such as Angelo Taveggia. The volume of production and methods of propaganda, however, were those of an industrial enterprise. Marinetti's practices contrast strikingly with those of cubist, dadaist, and surrealist artists. These published their works in small, fine press editions, enhanced with drawings and etchings and aimed at an audience of art lovers and bibliophiles. Similarly, the small series self-published by the Russian futurists was aimed at a circle of initiates, not the general public. Daniel-Henri Kahnweiler, in Paris, published only one hundred copies of Apollinaire's books; Vladimir Majakovskij's works reached three to six hundred copies. Marinetti, however, aimed at a broad audience, disparaged the "rare book," and flaunted the length of his press runs—often inflating the figures. His editions ran an average of one to two thousand copies, with peaks of more than twenty thousand, as in the case of the profitable collection *I poeti futuristi* (The Futurist Poets; 1912), which was in high demand by

bookstores (15–16, 253–254). Edizioni futuriste di «Poesia» was also unlike other militant presses, such as Libreria della Voce and Piero Gobetti's publishing house, in that Marinetti privileged propaganda over profit. Prezzolini sardonically described Marinetti as a "disorganizer" who caused the value of futurist books to collapse through his practice of flooding the market with complimentary copies ("Marinetti disorganizzatore," *La Voce* [30 March 1915]: 510–517). Aldo Palazzeschi recalls that the preface to his *L'Incendiario* (1910) consisted of seventy-five pages of propaganda totally unrelated to the content of the book, and he emphasizes Marinetti's shrewdness in understanding and exploiting the power of advertisement in a cultural context wherein the application of commercial strategies to spiritual problems was considered "such an outrage that no dictionary contained a derogatory word to qualify it properly" (*TIF*, XXI). Futurist propaganda, which gained Marinetti the reputation of a "rich snob" intent on buying fame with "Americanized" systems, was apparently effective in reaching vast audiences. In "Marinetti rivoluzionario?" Gramsci notes that many groups of workers showed sympathy for futurism before the war, defending the futurists against attacks by "professional" artists and scholars. In her *Bibliografia del futurismo* (Rome: Biblioteca del Vascello, 1988), Salaris lists numerous parodies of futurist books, evidence of the popularity and scandal surrounding futurist publications (see also Salaris, *Marinetti editore*, 81). Salaris's work on Marinetti's role as cultural entrepreneur has been condensed and translated in "Marketing Modernism: Marinetti as Publisher," trans. Lawrence Rainey, *Modernism/Modernity* 1.3 (1994): 109–127.

28. F. T. Marinetti, Bruno Corra (Bruno Ginanni-Corradini), Emilio Settimelli, Arnaldo Ginna (Arnaldo Ginanni-Corradini), Giacomo Balla, and Remo Chiti, "La cinematografia futurista" (Futurist Cinematography), in *TIF*, 144; emphasis in original.

29. This manifesto is reproduced in *Ricostruzione futurista dell'universo*, ed. Enrico Crispolti (Turin: Museo Civico di Torino, 1980), 27–29; emphasis in original.

30. The playful, farcical side to the futurist style of action is exemplified by the 1910 Venetian prank in which Marinetti, strategically positioned in the Clock Tower of Piazza San Marco, showered the Sunday crowd with fliers of his manifesto against passéist Venice, while declaiming it through a megaphone; the other side, by the 1912 fistfight at the Florentine café Giubbe Rosse, one of many brawls the futurists sparked in their aggressive, bristling proselytism. Pranks and scuffles were staple ingredients of the volcanic futurist evenings; see Francesco Cangiullo, *Le serate futuriste: Romanzo storico vissuto* (Naples: Tirrena, 1930).

31. Marshall Berman, *All That Is Solid Melts Into Air: The Experience of Modernity* (New York: Simon and Schuster, 1982), 102.

32. While texts such as "La guerra elettrica" warrant the association of futurism with imperialistic militarism, Marinetti's writing overall defies easy pigeonholing. See, for instance, *Taccuini*, 402: "Absurdity of the nationalists' imperialism which is founded on the glories of the ancient Romans and on an impossible industrial commercial and colonial supremacy. Strength of the futurist Italian pride founded upon the mass of Italian individuals." This brief note (dated 30 December 1918) is echoed by anti-imperialist declarations in *Democrazia futurista: Dinamismo politico* of 1919 (Futurist Democracy: Political Dynamism; *TIF*, 373, 379). Differences between *Guerra sola igiene del mondo* (War, the World's Only Hygiene; 1911–1915), in which "La guerra elettrica" appears, and *Democrazia futurista* can be related to the different function of the two texts and to the different circumstances of their composition: the former contains interventionist propaganda and a futuristic "vision-hypothesis" aimed at galvanizing the country in view of the impending world conflict; the

latter, more pragmatically, elaborates a political program for the postwar situation and posits, for the Italian democracy, the "realistic" goal of "artistic," "creative," "innovative" supremacy among the other world democracies.

33. See also Fornari, *Psicoanalisi della guerra*, 195: "Edmund Husserl demonstrated that Western science, which he traces back to Galileo, at its origins performed a sort of repression of the *lebenswelt*. Francis Bacon's axiom 'Cognoscere est dominari'—which had consecrated the triumph of the new scientific era on the forces of nature and which seemed to mark the end of the mythological era of man—makes us think today that it may very well indicate a particular type of human knowledge, characterized by idealization of the sadistic component of epistemophilic impulsions."

34. Peter Nicholls, "Futurism, Gender, and Theories of Postmodernity," *Textual Practice* 3.2 (1989): 207. Subsequent references will be given parenthetically within the text.

35. Marinetti, to use Schleifer's terms, participates in "synechdochic" or "imperial" modernism, which seeks to recuperate transcendental meanings (the synechdochic scaffolding of order and hierarchy) from what it perceives as the "metonymic" chaos resulting from the twentieth-century crisis of Western culture (*Rhetoric and Death*, 57).

36. Unlike Nietzsche's idea of the *Übermensch*, Marinetti's notion of the superuomo seems to be predicated on theories of evolutionary perfectibility, such as Spencer's survival of the fittest and Lamarck's transformism (evolution by adaptation and inheritance of acquired characteristics). The latter is invoked in "L'uomo moltiplicato e il Regno della macchina" (*Guerra sola igiene del mondo*, in *TIF*, 299).

37. In his "Manifesto tecnico della letteratura futurista" he declares peremptorily, "It is not a question of rendering the dramas of humanized matter" (*TIF*, 50).

38. I have found two exceptions: Giorgio Celli's essay "In margine al futurismo: Storia di una ambivalenza," *Il Verri* 33–34 (1970): 118–123; and Roberto Tessari's chapter on futurism in *Il mito della macchina: Letteratura e industria nel primo Novecento italiano* (Milan: Mursia, 1973), 209–275. Celli identifies a vein of frustration and anxiety in the futurist love for the modern city and interprets it as evidence that the futurists shared in a fundamental, widespread feeling of ambiguity and unease about the artist's condition in the modern world. Tessari develops this hypothesis with a Marxist emphasis on the socioeconomic implications of Marinetti's mythical or "religious" transfiguration of industry, which he sees as a strategy instrumental to the capitalist design of "establishing at all costs the reign of God-Industry on earth" (252).

39. Contrary to today's usage, the noun "automobile" is inflected in the masculine gender. According to the *Dizionario Italiano Ragionato*, both forms were originally used, although there was an initial predominance of the masculine. Marinetti seems to follow this general tendency: he opts for the masculine in "Fondazione e Manifesto del Futurismo" (*TIF*, 8–10) and *Zang Tumb Tumb* (*TIF*, 653), but he adopts consistently the feminine in later works. Nevertheless, in the case of the example quoted above one might speculate that his choice of the masculine is contextually motivated: this text, in fact, celebrates the union between man and machine, setting up a contrast between the traditional feminine paragon of beauty and the futurist virile ideal.

40. In "Thanatophobia and Immortality" (*American Journal of Psychology* 26 [1915]: 550–613), G. Stanley Hall has described cults of death and resurrection as an attempt to attain "an immunity bath" from death and the dread of it (quoted in Becker, *The Denial of Death*, 12). From ancient myths and rituals to Christianity, writes Becker, "the hero was the

man who could go into the spirit world, the world of the dead, and return alive," thus enacting a victory over death (12).

41. I take issue here with Kaplan's reading of the image under discussion as a " 'maternal ditch' from which the poet escapes in his metal automobile" ("Futurism and Fascism," 41–42). The qualifier "factory" (d'officina) displaces the image from the organic to the technological realm, and the poet does not simply escape from the ditch but takes a regenerating dive into it.

42. During the journey to Asia, one of the futurist poets, Enrico Cavacchioli, dreams out aloud: "I feel my twenty-year-old body growing young again! . . . I return to my cradle with a step that is more and more infantile . . . Soon I'll reenter my mother's womb! . . . To me, then, everything is licit! . . . I want precious knickknacks to smash . . . Cities to crush, human anthills to mess up! . . . I want to domesticate the winds and hold them on a leash . . . I want a pack of winds, supple greyhounds to chase the flaccid, bearded clouds" (*TIF,* 18).

43. See Agnese, *Marinetti,* 56: "All the occupations that do not allow for distraction—from shaving with a razor to controlling a speeding car—are not suitable to Marinetti: in fact, on October 15, 1908, he was the cause and the victim of a frightful automobile accident: an accident which he elevated to a literary event, but with which he concluded without second thoughts his career as a driver, to start a new career as passenger and owner of spectacular cars."

44. Fornari, *Psicoanalisi della guerra,* 97. See also R. E. Money-Kyrle, "The Development of War: A Psychological Approach," *British Journal of Medical Psychology* 16 (1937): 219–236. Fornari's reflections on the psychology of war draw on Melanie Klein's object relations theory, based on her work on the earliest phases of the mother-child relationship.

45. The following passage contradicts Hewitt's argument (*Fascist Modernism,* 146–147) that "L'uomo moltiplicato e il Regno della macchina" celebrates the machine as a model of transgressive productivity rather than discipline: "Hence we must prepare the imminent and inevitable identification of man with the motor, facilitating and perfecting an incessant interchange of intuition, rhythm, instinct, and metallic discipline, which is absolutely unknown to the majority, and which is guessed only by the most lucid spirits" (*TIF,* 299). As we have seen, creative expansion and metallic discipline are also essential features of the aesthetic of "geometric and mechanical splendor" as defined in the 1914 manifesto.

CHAPTER 3. THE SUPERMAN AND THE ABJECT:
MAFARKA LE FUTURISTE

1. Marinetti, *Mafarka le futuriste: Roman africain* (Paris: Sansot, 1910); hereafter *Mafarka.* All quotes are taken from the new edition (Paris: Christian Bourgois, 1984). Page references will appear parenthetically within the text.

2. Marinetti et al., "Il processo e l'assoluzione di *Mafarka il Futurista*" (The Trial and Acquittal of *Mafarka the Futurist*), in *Distruzione: Poema futurista* (Milan: Edizioni futuriste di «Poesia», 1911), 7. When the novel appeared in Decio Cinti's Italian translation as *Mafarka il futurista* (Milan: Edizioni futuriste di «Poesia», 1910), Marinetti was prosecuted for "oltraggio al pudore." He was tried and acquitted in October 1910. On appeal, the prosecutor obtained a sentence of two months imprisonment, which was commuted to a fine and banishment of the book from circulation. Marinetti exploited this episode to promote his book and futurism. He had taken the stand, as an expert for the defense, in a similar

trial against Umberto Notari's *Quelle signore* (the book became a best-seller with eighty thousand copies sold). Following Notari's example, Marinetti orchestrated a clamorous defense strategy, hiring famous lawyers and presenting Luigi Capuana as a literary expert. The vicissitudes of the case were highly publicized through fliers that quoted supportive statements by writers like Marguerite Rachilde and Gian Pietro Lucini. The outcry surrounding the trial aroused interest in the book, which was later translated into Russian and Spanish (Salaris, *Marinetti editore*, 106–111).

3. James Joll, *Three Intellectuals in Politics* (London: Weidenfeld and Nicolson, 1960), 142.

4. Rinaldi, *Miracoli della stupidità*, 26.

5. Kaplan, "Futurism and Fascism," 40.

6. Kaplan, *Reproductions of Banality*, 76, 78, 83.

7. Giusi Baldissone, *Filippo Tommaso Marinetti* (Milan: Mursia, 1986), 114–126.

8. Glauco Viazzi, "Ainsi parla Mafarka-el-Bar," *Es.* (January–April 1978): 104–116.

9. Baldissone, *Filippo Tommaso Marinetti*, 123. For a more cogent study of the homoerotic (and homophobic) economy of the text, see a recently published essay by Barbara Spackman, "Mafarka and Son: Marinetti's Homophobic Economics" (*Modernism/Modernity* 1.3 [1994]: 89–107). Spackman reads the novel as a sexual fantasy of male autarchy—a "homophobic homoerotics"—that is intricately entwined with an economic fantasy. She argues that Marinetti's fable of phallic economics shares an ideological structure (or "ideo-logic") with the fascist discourse of economic (and cultural) self-sufficiency and colonial expansion. While I find Spackman's analysis compelling, I do not share her assumption that "the problem at the heart of the novel" is to maintain the threatened border between virility and homosexuality ("How can one remain a heterosexual male once sexual relations with women have been eliminated?" 92). From this perspective, the "bankruptcy" of virility seems to be solely a dreaded consequence (and not a motivating factor) of the economics of male autarchy. In my view, the question of gender difference (and, more generally, the motif of uncertain borders and affective valences) can be traced to a broader and more central problem: an expansive and expanding crisis of the symbolic order thematized through a pervasive rhetoric of abjection. As we shall see, Mafarka's fantasy of male parthenogenesis is born of a desire to shore up the collapsing ideal of autonomous individuality.

10. The expression is Kaplan's ("Futurism and Fascism," 50).

11. Questions of oral aggression and incorporation are examined in greater detail in chapter 4. On the image of the gaping mouth, see Mikhail Bakhtin, *Rabelais and His World*, trans. Hélène Iswolsky (Cambridge: MIT Press, 1968), and Barbara Spackman, "*Inter musam et ursam moritur:* Folengo and the Gaping 'Other Mouth,'" in *Refiguring Woman: Perspectives on Gender and the Italian Renaissance*, ed. Marilyn Migiel and Juliana Schiesari (Ithaca: Cornell University Press, 1991), 19–34. Bakhtin considers the "gaping mouth" a topos of folk culture and the predominant image in François Rabelais's *Gargantua and Pantagruel*. He emphasizes the links between this topos and a series of correlated images belonging to the "material bodily lower stratum": swallowing ("this most ancient symbol of death and destruction," 325); the gaping jaws of the earth or hell; the mother's womb; and the anus. Such images are presented as symbols of the ambivalences of birth-giving death, interwoven with a grotesque concept of the body and with a new concrete historic awareness that subverts the medieval transcendental world picture. Discussing the subversive function of the topos of the hag's *bocca sdentata* in macaronic literature, Spackman focuses instead on the feminine connotations of the "gaping mouth" as the displacement upward of the feminine "other mouth."

12. In Freud's interpretation, the snake-haired Medusa's head is a figure on which anxiety about feminine sexuality is focused. Freud equates the terror aroused by the sight of the decapitated head of the Medusa to the feelings stirred by "castrated" female genitalia. The sight of this "absence" results in an ambivalent reaction of recognition and disavowal of castration, which, if not overcome, becomes fixated in the fetishist's *Verleugnung*. Like the phallic snaky locks of the Medusa, the fetishist's object choice functions as a reassuring penis substitute ("Medusa's Head," in *SE*, 18:273–274; and "Fetishism," in *SE*, 21:149–151). Post-Freudian revisions, which are more relevant to my discussion, argue that this interpretation suppresses the real source of anxiety: a projected (externally displaced) sense of lack or loss. As Silverman lucidly puts it, woman is the "original" fetish covering the male subject's existential lack (*The Acoustic Mirror*, 20). Defensive operations that are deployed against, while relying on, the denigrated/idealized image of woman concur to promote the imaginary coherence of the male subject.

Other psychoanalytic writers have adapted Freud's view to an existential perspective. Following Alfred Adler, Carl Jung, Otto Rank, Médard Boss, and Norman Brown, Becker argues that "the horror of castration is not the horror of punishment for incestuous sexuality, the threat of the Oedipus complex; it is rather the existential anxiety of life and death finding its focus on the animal body" (*The Denial of Death*, 223–224). Fetishism, from this vantage point, is the exercise of a sort of symbolic magic: "the person hypnotizes himself with the fetish and creates his own aura of fascination that completely transforms the threatening reality" (236). This view of fetishism squares with my observations on the machine as a fetishistic love object in chapter 2: "men use the fabrications of culture, in whatever form, as charms with which to transcend natural reality. [. . .] [A]ll cultural contrivances are self-hypnotic devices—from motorcars to moon rockets—ways that a sorely limited animal can drum up to fascinate himself with the powers of transcendence over natural reality" (236).

In times of political turmoil, Medusan moments may also be charged with the anxiety of social emasculation. For a sociopolitical perspective on the trope of the Medusa's head, see Neil Hertz, "Medusa's Head: Male Hysteria under Political Pressure," *Representations* 4 (1983): 27–54.

13. From the economic and political vantage point of Spackman's analysis in "Mafarka and Son," the fantastic appropriation of Africa as the locus of destruction and rebirth appears to be significant in light of the crucial role played by colonial ambitions in Italy's quest for international status and economic self-sufficiency.

14. This detail is mentioned only in the story told by Mafarka at the enemy camp. Like several other risqué moments of the novel, it is omitted in the second Italian edition (Milan: Sonzogno, 1920). As for the peculiar size of Mafarka's penis, it is well known that eleven was Marinetti's lucky number.

15. See, e.g., p. 50: "Oh! he sighed, how maternal this silence is! . . . I feel it on my legs, in my stomach, and on my mouth, like the soft sheet of my childhood bed! . . . Oh! it is you, Langourama, my beloved mother, it is really you, circling my bed and tucking me in with your delicate, caring hand!"

16. Nancy Vickers puts it succinctly: "If the speaker's 'self' (his text, his 'corpus') is to be unified, it would seem to require the repetition of her dismembered image" ("Diana Described: Scattered Woman and Scattered Rhyme," in *Writing and Sexual Difference*, ed. Elizabeth Abel [Chicago: University of Chicago Press, 1982], 102). See also John Freccero, "The Fig Tree and the Laurel: Petrarch's Poetics," in *Literary Theory/Renaissance*

Texts, ed. Patricia Parker and David Quint (Baltimore: Johns Hopkins University Press, 1986), 20–32.

17. Silverman's inquiry into a different medium, "classic" cinema, offers a theoretical framework and a contemporary term of comparison for Marinetti's strategies. She examines the fetishistic function of the synecdochic representation of woman in Hollywood films, where the female subject's gaze and voice are excluded from symbolic power—the capacity for looking, speaking, or listening authoritatively. In this phallic visual and acoustic regime, she argues, the "female subject is the site at which the viewer's discursive impotence is exhumed, exhibited, and contained. She is what might be called a synecdochic representation—the part for the whole—since she is obliged to absorb the male subject's lack as well as her own. The female subject's involuntary incorporation of the various losses which haunt cinema, from the foreclosed real to the invisible agency of enunciation, makes possible the male subject's identification with the symbolic father, and his imaginary alignment with creative vision, speech, and hearing. Indeed, not only is woman made to assume male lack as her own, but her obligatory receptivity to the male gaze is what establishes its superiority, just as her obedience to the male voice is what 'proves' its power" (*The Acoustic Mirror*, 31–32). Silverman underscores that fetishistic operations may involve both disparagement and idealization: "In her vocal, as in her corporeal, capacity, woman-as-fetish may be asked to represent the phenomenal plenitude which is lost to the male subject with his entry into language. However, the female voice, like the female body, is more frequently obliged to display than to conceal lack—to protect the male subject from knowledge of his own castration by absorbing his losses as well as those that structure female subjectivity" (38–39).

18. This simile establishes a figural link between the antre leading into a putrid "pond" of lust and Coloubbi's mouth, which also evokes the image of a wound uncovered in the search for consolation (189). See also pp. 217–218.

19. Emphasis is placed on the stench permeating the womb and on Mafarka's intolerant reaction to it (111, 112, 113). One is reminded of the biblical episode of Jonah and the whale, in which the womb of the fish is glossed as "the belly of hell" (Jon. 2:2). A more profane antecedent may be the use of dungeons as the setting of gory crimes, a topos of the Gothic genre that is also appropriated by the historical and popular novel. See Umberto Eco, *Il superuomo di massa: Retorica e ideologia nel romanzo popolare* (Milan: Bompiani, 1990), 71.

20. The full passage reads: "By Allah! Mafarka cried; take all the lamps away! . . . I do not want to be surrounded by faces convulsing with lust! A man's face must be covered with darkness when rut crumples and twists it like a drenched rag!" (119).

21. Dropsy, or edema, is an effusion of serous fluid into connective tissue or into body cavities. Rabies (hydrophobia), the other disease playing a significant role in the novel, is also characterized by an abnormal relation to water: an inability or aversion to swallow liquids. The death scenes in *Mafarka* generally take place in water, traditionally considered woman's natural element. These include the human sacrifices in the Whale's Womb; the scene in which Mafarka, under the influence of sirenlike sea waves, is tempted to drown himself; and the final holocaust. An antecedent of this motif can be seen in *Destruction*, where Marinetti associates dropsy with the sea in order to convey the scientific, materialistic view of the universe that threatens to destroy the poet's romantic dreams: "[Scholars] despise your [the sea's] sobs / and the engulfing sadness in your eyes! . . . / They said that you wrap the curves of the earth / like the perverse humors of our bodies, / —dropsy of a decrepit world!" (*SF*, 149).

22. These acts of subjugation are presented in explicitly sexual terms. Mafarka threatens to sodomize the Devil, who is thus scared into leaving his palace (62–63). Boubassa, by contrast, is seduced by the miraculous virtues of Mafarka's "zeb" (slang in Arabic for "penis"; 64).

23. According to Kaplan, the point of the story is the phallic power of storytelling. Spackman goes further and reads it as a fable of phallic economics within an overarching fantasy of male autarchy.

24. Brafane-el-Kibir can be seen as a father figure in light of the monologue in which Mafarka characterizes himself as a child driven by "a whim" to win over the gigantic and wise king of the desert (51).

25. According to Girard, sibling rivalry, incest, and parricide, along with plagues and the floods, are the mythical and ritual motifs that symbolize the crisis of the cultural order in primitive and ancient societies (*Violence and the Sacred*, 74–76, 80).

26. Kern writes that "the discovery of the law of entropy in the 1850s and of atomic disintegration in the 1890s has given the life-sustaining energy of our world a time limit" (*The Culture of Time and Space*, 105). As in the previously quoted passage from *Destruction*, Marinetti alludes to scientific advances in physics and astronomy that undermined the orderly view of the Newtonian universe. The sun, as a literary trope, traditionally stood for ontological identity, symbolizing the completion of the self and its integration into the natural and political order. See Albert Russell Ascoli, *Ariosto's Bitter Harmony: Crisis and Evasion in the Italian Renaissance* (Princeton: Princeton University Press, 1987), 227.

27. Girard notes that in the Oedipus myth the Sphinx "plays a role similar to that of the plague [symbol of the sacrificial crisis], terrorizing all Thebes and demanding a periodic tribute of victims" (*Violence and the Sacred*, 87).

28. See, in particular, *La Ville charnelle*, in *SF*, 277 (quoted in chap. 1). As already noted, the first section of this poem is entitled "Le Voyageur mordu," "The Mad (literally, bitten) Traveler."

29. See Judith Butler, *Gender Trouble: Feminism and the Subversion of Identity* (New York: Routledge, 1990), 61. Butler addresses the question of melancholic incorporation in the context of her discussion of gender identification as complex cultural construction. Building on Freud's observations in "Mourning and Melancholia" and Lacan's notion of "masquerade," she views gender incorporation as part of the incorporative strategy of melancholy, whereby the mask (of gender identity) has a double function of refusing and simultaneously preserving an impossible (or forbidden) object of love and identification. The earliest loss is the same-sex love object, forbidden by the heterosexual imperative. But the parent of the other sex is also rejected as an impossible object of identification.

30. Quoted in Julia Kristeva, *Tales of Love*, trans. Leon S. Roudiez (New York: Columbia University Press, 1987), 239; hereafter abbreviated *TL*.

31. Freud, "Contributions to the Psychology of Love: A Special Type of Object Choice Made by Men," in *Collected Papers*, trans. Joan Riviere, ed. Ernest Jones, 4 vols. (London: Hogarth Press and Institute of Psycho-Analysis, 1953), 4:201. Quoted in Keller, *Reflections on Gender and Science*, 41.

32. Keller, *Reflections on Gender and Science*, 41. See also Kristeva, *TL*, 235–236; and Becker, *The Denial of Death*, 118–119.

33. Becker, *The Denial of Death*, 238, 240.

34. The original reads "le fils de mes entrailles," which resounds with the Hail Mary in French: "le fruit de vos entrailles" (the fruit of thy womb).

35. See Theweleit's considerations on the topos of split femininity in the writings of the soldier males (*Male Fantasies,* 1:100–107).

36. See, e.g., p. 148: "Meanwhile, the moon was pouring milk that had the rancid, empty taste of a sepulchre between Mafarka's white teeth! Pouah!"

37. Regarding the "paranoid woman" as a fictional character (namely, as a Célinian character), Kristeva observes that she "is perhaps a projection of the danger of death prompted within the speaking being by his perception of that part of himself he fantasies as maternal and feminine" (*PH,* 161).

38. See Kaplan, *Reproductions of Banality,* 26, 31. See also Russell Berman's foreword, "The Wandering Z: Reflections on Kaplan's *Reproductions of Banality*": "Perhaps more than any other motif, the desire for a nature as guarantor of unchanging order—and as the alternative to the metropolis as the locus of individuality and democracy—marks the various fascist literary imaginations: the German literature of blood and soil, Pound's invocation of the natural order of ancient China, and above all the cult of nature in Hamsun" (xvii).

39. Becker sums up the relationship between psychosis and creativity from an existential perspective: "By pushing the problem of man to its limits, schizophrenia also reveals the nature of creativity. If you are physically unprogrammed in the cultural *causa-sui* project, then you have to invent your own: you don't vibrate to anyone else's tune. You see that the fabrications of those around you are a lie, a denial of truth—a truth that usually takes the form of showing the terror of the human condition more fully than most men experience it. The creative person becomes, then, in art, literature, and religion the mediator of natural terror and the indicator of a new way to triumph over it. He reveals the darkness and the dread of the human condition and fabricates a new symbolic transcendence over it. This has been the function of the creative deviant from the shamans through Shakespeare" (*The Denial of Death,* 220).

40. Paul de Man, "Literary History and Literary Modernism," in *Blindness and Insight* (New York: Oxford University Press, 1971), 148.

41. Michael Georg Conrad, "Moderne Bestrebungen" (1892), rpt. in Erich Ruprecht, ed., *Literarische Manifeste des Naturalismus, 1880–1892* (Stuttgart: J. B. Metzlersche, 1962), 254–256. Quoted in Bradbury and McFarlane, *Modernism,* 42.

42. Eco, *Il superuomo di massa,* 53. See also Antonio Gramsci, "Origine popolaresca del 'superuomo,'" in *Letteratura e vita nazionale* (Turin: Einaudi, 1954), 122–124.

43. Eco, *Il superuomo di massa,* 83.

44. Spackman, *Decadent Genealogies,* 71, 33–104.

45. Friedrich Nietzsche, *The Gay Science,* ed. and trans. Walter Kaufmann (New York: Vintage Books, 1974), 35–36. Quoted in Spackman, *Decadent Genealogies,* 93.

CHAPTER 4. THE HEART WITH WATERTIGHT COMPARTMENTS AND THE TRAVEL-SIZE WOMAN: FUTURIST STRATEGIES IN LOVE AND WAR

1. Marinetti, "Contro l'amore e il parlamentarismo" (Against Love and Parliamentarianism; 1910–1915), *Guerra sola igiene del mondo,* in *TIF,* 292–293.

2. See Marinetti, "L'uomo moltiplicato e il Regno della macchina," in *TIF,* 297–301.

3. See also Marinetti, *Democrazia futurista,* in *TIF,* 351.

4. On the experience of women under fascism, see Victoria de Grazia, *How Fascism Ruled Women: Italy, 1922–1945* (Berkeley, Los Angeles, and London: University of California

Press, 1992). On the antifeminist politics and ideology of fascism, see also Piero Meldini, *Sposa e madre esemplare: Ideologia e politica della donna e della famiglia durante il fascismo* (Rimini-Florence: Guaraldi, 1975); and Enzo Santarelli, "Il fascismo e le ideologie antifemministe," *Problemi del socialismo*, 4th ser., 17.4 (1976): 75–108. Both Meldini and Santarelli point to different, although ultimately convergent, tendencies within fascism with respect to the issues of woman and the family: a moderate, or "revisionist," wing that acknowledged the historical and economic necessity of the ongoing changes in the structure of the family and a traditionalist, or "apocalyptic," wing (inspired by Spenglerian notions of decadence first and by the Nazi ideal of the "Aryan family" later) that advocated the demographic objective of racial fecundity and health. In the propaganda and legislation of the late 1920s and 1930s, fascist ideologues are united in their concern over demographics, but somewhat at odds over whether to emphasize the pronatalist agenda (related to militarist, imperialist ambitions) or the "moral" goal of restoring traditional order and values. However, as Meldini notes, the program of refounding the precapitalistic family (with the concomitant campaign for the "domestic segregation" of women, the battle against urbanization, and the more or less veiled critique of industrialization) is a utopian one "not only because it is objectively antihistorical, but because it runs profoundly counter to the plans of economic power, of which fascism is the most faithful interpreter as it descends from the nebulous realm of ideology to the ground of practical politics" (56).

In the 1930s the anticonventional edge of the futurist polemics was blunted, and some of Marinetti's companions became spokesmen for the sexual policies of the regime. Carli and Settimelli, for instance, having distanced themselves from the movement, founded *L'Impero*, which became the unofficial voice of the regime. Some futurists, including Marinetti, contributed to the paper, but the latter's contributions are confined to the literary sphere. Carli and Settimelli, by contrast, engage in the debate of sociopolitical issues. Their realignment in accordance with fascist orthodoxy is attested to by their diatribes against divorce and free love. See, for instance, Settimelli's "Contro il divorzio" (Against Divorce), *L'Impero*, 17 August 1923, 1; and Carli's ". . . e figli maschi!" (. . . and May You Have Sons!), *L'Impero*, 1 January 1929, 1. In these texts, the idealization of woman as mother is the feminine counterpart to the masculine ideal of the patriotic, disciplined individual. To my knowledge, Marinetti did not actively advocate such positions. However, as we shall see in chapter 6, his writing and personal life in this period show signs of a rappel à l'ordre.

5. Puccini, "Condizione della donna," 51–64. Subsequent page references will be given parenthetically within the text.

6. Michelle Perrot, "The New Eve and the Old Adam: Changes in French Women's Condition at the Turn of the Century," in Higonnet et al., *Behind the Lines*, 51–60. In the same volume, Margaret R. Higonnet and Patrice L.-R. Higonnet ("The Double Helix") examine the impact of the two wars on women, pointing out that misogyny was "inherent in militaristic discourse on both sides" (42).

7. The following are just a few examples of this vast production: Emilio Settimelli, *Nuovo modo d'amare* (A New Way of Loving; Rocca San Casciano: Cappelli, 1918); Settimelli, *Inchiesta sulla vita italiana* (A Report on Italian Life; Bologna: Messaggerie Italiane, 1918); Mario Dessy, *Vostro marito non va . . . ? Cambiatelo!* (Your Husband Doesn't Run . . . ? Trade Him In; Milan: Edizioni futuriste di «Poesia», 1919); Bruno Corra, *Io ti amo: Il romanzo dell'amore moderno* (I Love You: The Novel of Modern Love; Milan: Studio Editoriale Lombardo, 1918); and Ruggiero Vasari, "Donna del tempo" (A Woman of Our Time; *La testa di ferro* [20 February 1921]: 3). Especially in the futurist periodicals, the subject of sexuality

and gender roles provoked a veritable discursive explosion. In some cases, a periodical became the forum for an animated debate on a specific issue. The most significant case is the famous *querelle des femmes* on *L'Italia futurista*, stirred by the publication of Marinetti's *Come si seducono le donne*. See, in particular, the issues from June to December 1917.

8. This preoccupation with race is not necessarily an index of fascism. As Santarelli notes, myths and directives such as the fecundity of the race, the domestic role of woman, moral restoration, and demographic development became government policy under fascism but were not new ideas ("Il fascismo," 86–87). Earlier socialist denunciations of the work conditions in factories expressed concern for the "degeneration of the race," rather than for the physical degradation to which working women were subjected (Puccini, "Condizione della donna," 17).

I have indicated elements of convergence or analogy between futurist and socialist positions (both progressive and reactionary), not to obfuscate the clear connections between futurism and fascism, but to cast some light onto the complex historical context in which they coexisted. Recent studies have made a compelling case for the need to move beyond rigid distinctions between Left and Right in mapping the fascist period. See, for instance, Zeev Sternhell, *Neither Right nor Left: Fascist Ideology in France,* trans. David Maisel (Berkeley, Los Angeles, and London: University of California Press, 1986). With regard to the question of woman as reproductive asset, Luce Irigaray's discourse on the exchange and commodification of women in patriarchal societies should also be considered. See her *This Sex Which Is Not One,* trans. Catherine Porter (Ithaca: Cornell University Press, 1985).

9. Such calls for the socialization of procreative behavior and child rearing can be seen as a futurist prelude to the pronatalist campaigns of the fascist regime. There is, however, a significant difference: Marinetti attacks the institution of the family and negates the maternal role in child rearing, while the fascist plan for moral regeneration hinges on the recuperation of woman's traditional role in the patriarchal family. Fascist propaganda pursued this goal by constantly reiterating maternity's joys and duties. A poignant example is Stefano Mario Cutelli's "La famiglia generatrice d'aristocrazia," *Critica Fascista* 22 (1929): 435–437. Cutelli attacks free love, divorce, and state-run child rearing, defining the "child of the State" as a "socialistic triumph" accomplished in "Asiatic Russia" (quoted in Meldini, *Sposa e madre esemplare,* 172).

As I have already indicated, Marinetti's own family life in the subsequent decades contradicts these statements. An icon of the Marinettis' conformism to familial values is provided by the picture of Benedetta and her two daughters entitled "Futurismo e maternità" (Futurism and Maternity), *Oggi e domani,* 27 November 1930, 2 (fig. 3). The caption reads: "This joyous smile tells you how a true Italian woman of the Fascist Era can ingeniously reconcile the concerns of art with those of maternity. For example, we are offered the writer and painter BENEDETTA, Wife of our illustrious and dear Marinetti; she is the author of the book *Le forze umane* and of these two masterpieces named Vittoria and Ala." Granted the woman artist can write a book, her real masterpieces are, of course, her children.

10. Spackman, "The Fascist Rhetoric of Virility," 95n. 31. Spackman poignantly describes the advantages accruing to the male from the tactics of rejection of the family: "Divorce, free love and destruction of the bourgeois family are all tactics that will enforce intermittent proximity of men to women, as if to draw new boundaries that would protect virility from the 'effemination' that results from cohabitation, and at the same time refuel virility through sporadic contact with women" (96).

11. Marinetti had earlier provided a similar explanation of his slogan in the preface to *Mafarka* (*TIF*, 253–254).

12. See Meldini, *Sposa e madre esemplare*, 26–35. Examining the development of the querelle on woman's inferiority from the second half of the nineteenth century to the fascist period, Meldini underlines the continuing preponderance of the biologistic argument. Positivist culture, he notes, played a leading role in formulating the " 'scientific' model of the physiological, sexual, psychic, and intellectual difference-inferiority of woman"—a model that became canonical and was invoked even by followers of idealistic and spiritualistic currents (33).

13. Spackman, "The Fascist Rhetoric of Virility," 95. Lucia Re reaches similar conclusions in "Futurism and Feminism" (*Women's Voices in Italian Literature*, special issue of *Annali d'Italianistica* 7 [1989]: 253–272). "Rather than a liberation of woman," she notes, "the futurist vision at this juncture invokes a reduction of woman to sexual object and instrument of procreation" (254). Unlike Spackman, however, she points out that futurist ideas on sexual politics acquire "unexpectedly feminist overtones" when compared to contemporary disquisitions on woman's natural inferiority to man and when viewed in light of the regressive situation of women in Italy: "Futurism from its inception had the merit of raising issues regarding the representation and regimentation of sexuality, the political roots and ramifications of sexual behavior, and the ideological overdetermination of gender divisions and gender roles in contemporary society" (256–257).

14. Spackman, "The Fascist Rhetoric of Virility," 93–94.

15. Marinetti, "L'uomo moltiplicato e il Regno della macchina," in *TIF*, 300–301.

16. World War I gave impetus to women's rights movements. Italy, however, lagged behind other European countries. Although some women were active in Catholic and socialist groups, a feminist movement per se did not develop in Italy until the 1960s. After the war, women obtained the vote in England, Germany, Austria, Sweden, Czechoslovakia, Hungary, Holland, and the United States. A bill for women's suffrage was approved by the Italian House of Representatives (30 July 1919) but did not pass in the Senate. Italian women first exercised the right to vote only after World War II. A divorce bill proposed by the socialists Lazzari and Marangoni also failed to pass in 1919. At the same time, D'Annunzio introduced divorce in his Charter of Carnaro "in order to provide a 'revolutionary' aspect to his march on Fiume" (Bortolotti, *Femminismo*, 56). In "Ideologie sfasciate dalla conflagrazione" (Ideologies Shattered by War; *Democrazia futurista*), Marinetti describes the revolutionary impact of the war on love, sexuality, and the family in positive terms, as a healthy shattering of traditions and habits (*TIF*, 355).

17. After the first edition (Florence: Vallecchi, 1917), there was a second edition (Rocca S. Casciano: Cappelli, 1918) and an expanded edition with the title *Come si seducono le donne e si tradiscono gli uomini* (How to Seduce Women and Betray Men; Milan: Sonzogno, 1920). Marinetti had the book reprinted twenty-five years later, but the fascist minister of popular culture, Alessandro Pavolini, ordered its confiscation (Agnese, *Marinetti*, 283). Nevertheless, by 1943 it had sold fifty thousand copies. See Michele Giocondi, *Lettori in camicia nera: Narrativa di successo nell'Italia fascista* (Messina: D'Anna, 1978), 21. Giocondi provides interesting data about the popularity of erotic literature, which reached a peak during the years 1918–1924, a second peak in 1929–1932, and a less dramatic one in the late 1930s (70). Significantly, these watermarks of popular success coincided with three periods of historical crisis. Erotica, after all, is the escapist genre par excellence.

18. See Bruno Corra and Emilio Settimelli, "Marinetti intimo," preface, *Come si seducono le donne*, by Marinetti (Rocca S. Casciano: Cappelli, 1918), 21–24. Page numbers refer to this edition and will appear in the text.

19. A similar scenario is described by Bruno Corra in *Signora, torna vostro marito: Lettera aperta a una signora onesta* (Madam, Your Husband Is Coming Home: An Open Letter to an Honest Lady; Milan: Facchi, 1919), a disquisition on uxorial unfaithfulness in the form of a letter addressed to a woman whose husband is at war. According to Corra, the epidemic of infidelity, due primarily to women (instinctive creatures who, like animals, are excited by social cataclysm), is symptomatic of society's failure to contain "the overflowing restlessness of modern eroticism and sentimentality" (14). Corra proposes a series of remedies: most saliently, the legalization of adultery and sponsoring of "public love" (organized prostitution, to take place in an institute for the protection of young men, 25–26) as an antidote to romantic sorrows.

20. See Baldissone, *Filippo Tommaso Marinetti*, 143–144; and Claudia Salaris, *Storia del futurismo* (Rome: Editori Riuniti, 1985), 98. Spackman offers a more perceptive reading, based on the correct assumption that national borders coincide, in futurist rhetoric, with those of virility and on the acute observation that wartime "rapid-fire seductions" create an intermittent kind of proximity to women, which, unlike cohabitation, preserves rather than harms virility. However, she focuses on the celebratory, boastful aspect of the manual and therefore disregards its crucial defensive value with respect to the internal war between the sexes: "Only during the war can proximity to women be celebrated, for fighting on the national front allows the male to ease up on virility's front" ("The Fascist Rhetoric of Virility," 98). One may object that Marinetti's production of erotic literature continues after the war, with *Gli amori futuristi* (Futurist Loves; 1922), *Scatole d'amore in conserva* (Canned Love; 1927), and *Novelle con le labbra tinte* (Stories with Painted Lips; 1930).

21. Corra's argument for the legalization of adulterous relationships (or, one might say, partnerships) is developed in *Signora, torna vostro marito*.

22. Volt's article was published in *Roma futurista* (20 July 1919): 3.

23. This passage appears in the chapter "Donne complementari e cuore a compartimenti stagni" (Complementary Women and a Heart with Watertight Compartments), added in the revised edition, *Come si seducono le donne e si tradiscono gli uomini* (Milan: Sonzogno, 1920), 158.

24. See Jean Laplanche, *Life and Death in Psychoanalysis*, trans. Jeffrey Mehlman (Baltimore: Johns Hopkins University Press, 1976), 62–63. Subsequent page references will be given parenthetically within the text. Laplanche traces the problematic of the ego through different phases of Freud's thought. I refer to his discussion of the neurological or "economic" model developed by Freud in the *Project for a Scientific Psychology* of 1885, where the ego is not quite yet a subject of wishing and desire but "an internal object cathected by the energy of the apparatus," which performs an inhibiting or binding function and a defensive function (66).

25. See, e.g., Marinetti, *Futurismo e Fascismo* (Futurism and Fascism; 1924), in *TIF*, 496.

26. Marinetti persisted in emphasizing the links of futurism with the revolutionary spirit of Mussolini and the early phase of fascism as a movement (or *fascismo sansepolcrista*). It should be noted, however, that the official portrait of the fascist leader as a "wonderful futurist temperament" in the 1929 *Marinetti e il futurismo* (Marinetti and Futurism; *TIF*, 577) contrasts with the negative characterization of Mussolini as a megalomaniacal, reactionary, opportunistic, not-so-smart "raving energumen" in the 1918–1919 entries of *Taccuini* (392,

405–406, 409). Marinetti's early impressions about Mussolini were not univocally negative; he also referred to some aspects of Mussolini's attitude that seemed to denote a futurist sensibility: his confidence and his emphasis on the need to educate the Italian people to optimism and efficiency.

27. Marinetti expounded the central idea of this tale in the 1918 war diary (*Taccuini*, 188). The short story, however, was first published in *Gli amori futuristi* (Piacenza: Ghelfi, 1922). A slightly revised version by the title "Come si nutriva l'Ardito" (How the Shock Trooper Nourished Himself) was successively published in *Novelle con le labbra tinte* (Milan: Mondadori, 1930). Quotes are taken from the first edition; page references will be given parenthetically within the text.

28. See Laplanche, *Life and Death in Psychoanalysis*, 20: "The sexual *aim* is [. . .] in a quite special position in relation to the aim of the feeding function; it is simultaneously the same and different. The aim of feeding was ingestion; in psychoanalysis, however, the term used is 'incorporation.' The terms may seem virtually identical, and yet there is a slight divergence between the two. With incorporation, the aim has become the scenario of a fantasy, a scenario borrowing from the function its register and its language, but adding to ingestion the various implications grouped under the term 'cannibalism,' with such meanings as: preserving within oneself, destroying, assimilating" (emphasis in original).

29. Marinetti, *Taccuini*, 188; emphasis in original. The desire to silence that inspires this fantasy of beheading brings to mind a peculiar episode in *Taccuini*, in which Marinetti confesses his "mysterious" attraction and inhibition before a beautiful prostitute who produces "turbulent," foul language (207–208).

30. Drawing on Lacan's account of the speaking "I" as a masculinized effect of repression, Butler underlines the paradoxical and conflicting consequences of grounding identity on the repression of the maternal "body": "The masculine subject only *appears* to originate meanings and thereby to signify. His seemingly self-grounded autonomy attempts to conceal the repression which is both its ground and the perpetual possibility of its own ungrounding. But that process of meaning-constitution requires that women reflect that masculine power and everywhere reassure that power of the reality of its illusory autonomy. This task is confounded, to say the least, when the demand that women reflect the autonomous power of masculine subject/signifier becomes essential to the construction of that autonomy and, thus, becomes the basis of a radical dependency that effectively undercuts the function it serves. But further, this dependency, although denied, is also *pursued* by the masculine subject, for the woman as reassuring sign *is* the displaced maternal body, the vain but persistent promise of the recovery of pre-individuated *jouissance*. The conflict of masculinity appears, then, to be precisely the demand for a full recognition of autonomy that will also and nevertheless promise a return to those full pleasures prior to repression and individuation" (*Gender Trouble*, 45; emphasis in original).

31. In the revised 1930 edition, irony is tamed as the explicit reference to the woman's adulterous desire ("già adultera, tutta tremante d'amore per te!") is elided.

32. See Susan Gubar, "'This Is My Rifle, This Is My Gun': World War II and the Blitz on Women," in *Behind the Lines*, 227–259.

33. The following titles give an indication of this phenomenon: Corra, *Perché ho ucciso mia moglie* (Why I Killed My Wife; Milan: Facchi, 1918); Carli, *Sii brutale amor mio!* (Be Brutal, My Love; Milan: Facchi, 1919); Paolo Buzzi, *Il bel cadavere* (The Beautiful Corpse; Milan: Facchi, 1919); Emilio Settimelli, *Strangolata dai suoi capelli* (Strangled by Her Own Hair; Milan: Facchi, 1920); Settimelli, *Donna allo spiedo* (Woman on a Spit; Milan: Moder-

nissima, 1921); Fillia [Luigi Colombo], *La morte della donna* (The Death of Woman; Turin: Sindacati Artistici, 1925).

34. Marinetti and Fillia, *La cucina futurista* (Milan: Sonzogno, 1932), 9–20.

35. Marinetti had first enlisted as a volunteer in the Lombard Volunteer Bicycle Battalion. After attending the artillery school he went to the front and was wounded. He later passed to a bomber unit and finally to a unit of armored cars. The novel was first published in 1921 (Milan: Vitagliano) and presumably written between 1918 and 1920. Marinetti's 1918 war diary contains references to the composition of a "romanzo di guerra vissuto" (*Taccuini*, 387). *Cronache d'Attualità* [July 1921]: 49–55) published a selection of reviews celebrating the popular and critical success of *L'alcova d'acciaio*. Giocondi lists it among the best-sellers with runs of 20,000 to 40,000 copies (*Lettori in camicia nera*, 73). All references are to the 1985 edition (Milan: Serra e Riva Editori) and will be given parenthetically within the text.

36. The full passage reads, "You will tell me that one more lieutenant at the front is not worth much. But this lieutenant has a luminous name, and is an eloquent speaker, becoming therefore an example, a beacon, a call, a living flag of courage and faith for all those who believe in him" (38). In Marinetti's writing, the sacred is persistently mixed with the profane. He concludes this high-flown address to the readers by affirming his right to be compensated for his "selfless" heroic sacrifice with (feminine) prizes "to be grabbed with rough hands and with little regard" (39).

CHAPTER 5. THE HERO'S WAR AND THE HEROINE'S WOUNDS: *UN VENTRE DI DONNA*

1. Caroline Tisdall and Angelo Bozzolla (*Futurism* [London: Thames and Hudson, 1977]) speak of "a male club, with a puerile and indeed sinister insistence on aggressive virility" (157).

2. De Saint-Point's "Manifesto della Donna futurista," which was presented to audiences of artists and intellectuals in Brussels and Paris, stirred up a scandal fueled by ridiculing or moralizing comments by the press. The futurist Italo Tavolato, author of *Contro la morale sessuale* (Against Sexual Morality; Florence: Gonnelli, 1913) and "Elogio della Prostituzione" (In Praise of Prostitution; *Lacerba* [1 May 1913]: 89–92), applauded de Saint-Point's courage and took her side against the "moralist whining" of her detractors in "Glossa sopra il manifesto futurista della lussuria" (A Gloss over the Futurist Manifesto of Lust; *Lacerba* [15 March 1913]: 58–59).

3. "Attributing duties to woman is tantamount to making her lose all her fecund power. The arguments and deductions of Feminism will not destroy her primordial fatality; they can only distort it and force it to manifest itself through perversions that lead to the worst mistakes." See Valentine de Saint-Point, "Manifesto della Donna futurista: Risposta a F. T. Marinetti" (hereafter MDF), in *Le futuriste: Donne e letteratura d'avanguardia in Italia (1909/1944)*, ed. Claudia Salaris (Milan: Edizioni delle donne, 1982), 34. Quotes from "Manifesto futurista della Lussuria" (hereafter MFL) also refer to this edition; page numbers will be given parenthetically within the text. De Saint-Point's manifestos were included in the 1914 volume *I manifesti del Futurismo* (Florence: Lacerba) and then in the 1919 collection *I manifesti del Futurismo* (Milan: Istituto Editoriale Italiano).

4. The full passage reads, "WOMEN, BECOME AGAIN SUBLIMELY UNJUST, LIKE ALL THE FORCES OF NATURE!" (MDF, 34).

5. Enif Robert, "Come si seducono le donne (Lettera aperta a F. T. Marinetti)," *L'Italia futurista* (31 December 1917): 2. Rpt. in Marinetti, *Come si seducono*, III–VI; and Salaris, *Le futuriste*, 110–113.

6. Enif Robert, "Una parola serena," *L'Italia futurista* (7 October 1917): 1. Rpt. in Marinetti, *Come si seducono*, VII–X; and Salaris, *Le futuriste*, 108–110.

7. Shara Marini, "Rivendicazione," *L'Italia futurista* (1 July 1917): 2. Rpt. in Marinetti, *Come si seducono*, XII–XIV; and Salaris, *Le futuriste*, 117–119.

8. Rosa Rosà, "Le donne cambiano finalmente," *L'Italia futurista* (26 August 1917): 2. Rpt. in Marinetti, *Come si seducono*, VI–VII; Salaris, *Le futuriste*, 114–116; and Rosà, *Una donna con tre anime*, ed. Claudia Salaris (Milan: Edizioni delle donne, 1981), 120–121.

9. Rosa Rosà, "Risposta a Jean-Jacques," *L'Italia futurista* (1 July 1917): 2. Rpt. in Marinetti, *Come si seducono*, X–XI; and Rosà, *Una donna*, 115–116.

10. Rosa Rosà, "Le donne del posdomani," *L'Italia futurista* (17 June 1917): 1. Rpt. in Rosà, *Una donna*, 113–114.

11. Rosa Rosà, "Le donne del posdomani," *L'Italia futurista* (7 October 1917): 1. Rpt. in Rosà, *Una donna*, 122–126. Emphasis in original.

12. Volt, "Lettera aperta a Maria Ginanni," *L'Italia futurista* (29 July 1917): 2. Rpt. in Marinetti, *Come si seducono*, XIV–XVI.

13. Only four of the ninety-two books published by Marinetti's Edizioni futuriste di «Poesia» were written by women: Dina Cucini's *Aeropoema futurista delle Torri di Siena* (Futurist Aeropoem of the Towers of Siena; Rome, 1942); Maria Goretti's *Poesia della macchina* (Poetry of the Machine; Rome, 1942); Franca Maria Corneli's *La lingua del futurismo* (The Language of Futurism; Rome, 1942) and *L'aeropoema futurista dell'Umbria* (The Futurist Aeropoem of Umbria; Rome, 1943). There is evidence, however, that other works by women were published elsewhere with Marinetti's help. In a letter to Salaris, for instance, Goretti recalls that Marinetti contributed to the publication of her *La donna e il futurismo* (Woman and Futurism; Verona: La Scaligera, 1941) through a subsidy he obtained from the Ministry of Culture (Salaris, *Marinetti editore*, 328).

14. Nozzoli, for instance, reduces the value of futurist women's works to the petty level of literary "curiosity" and finds no significant difference between Marinetti's positions and the various positions articulated by the women writers (*Tabù e coscienza*, 41–43). Rita Guerricchio takes a similar stance in "Il modello di donna futurista," *Donne e politica* (August–October 1976): 35–37. Ignoring the subversive implications of futurist nonconformism, Bortolotti argues that the futurist women were the cultural and political precursors of the right-wing Fascio nazionale femminile, a national organization of fascist women that espoused a nationalist, antisocialist, and antifeminist program (*Femminismo*, 79–80). Giovannella Desideri, by contrast, emphasizes the polemical, nonconformist efforts of the first group of futurist women, as compared to Marinetti's "codifications" of gender roles and the realignment of the second generation of *futuriste* along positions of conservatism and conformism. See her "Alcuni modelli femminili futuristi," *Es.* (January–April 1978): 58–62. Re also departs from the reductive tendency exemplified by Nozzoli, calling attention to the "agonistic dialogue" between female voices and the male leaders of the futurist movement ("Futurism and Feminism," 259). Drawing on the framework of contemporary theory, she identifies modern, feminist inflections in those voices.

15. For a lucid discussion of gender as the product and process both of representation and self-representation, see Teresa de Lauretis, "The Technology of Gender," *Technologies*

of Gender: Essays on Theory, Film, and Fiction (Bloomington: Indiana University Press, 1987), 1–30. De Lauretis pursues a theory of gender difference that can account for sociocultural change. In her understanding of gender as (self-)representation, she underlines its concrete and real implications for the material life of individuals. Pointing to the deterministic limits of discourse theory and to the conservative effects of feminist notions of gender as sexual difference, she proposes a theory and practice of gender as a construction in progress. Such a construction, she argues, "is also effected by its deconstruction; that is to say, by any discourse, feminist or otherwise, that would discard it as ideological misrepresentation. For gender, like the real, is not only the effect of representation but also its excess, what remains outside discourse as a potential trauma which can rupture or destabilize, if not contained, any representation" (3).

16. For this feminist version of Nietzsche's metaphor of the "prison-house of language," see Audre Lorde, "The Master's Tools Will Never Dismantle the Master's House" and "An Open Letter to Mary Daly," in *This Bridge Called My Back: Writings by Radical Women of Color,* ed. Cherríe Moraga and Gloria Anzaldúa (New York: Kitchen Table Press, 1983).

17. See Sandra Lipsitz Bem, *The Lenses of Gender: Transforming the Debate on Sexual Inequality* (New Haven: Yale University Press, 1993). Bem argues that biological essentialism is the rationalizing, legitimizing frame for the other lenses: androcentrism, which posits male experience as the standard against which female deviation or lack is measured, and gender polarization, which shapes human experience according to a rigidly binary definition of sexual difference.

18. Enif Robert and F. T. Marinetti, *Un ventre di donna: Romanzo chirurgico* (Milan: Facchi, 1919), XIII. Subsequent page references will be given parenthetically within the text.

19. In an interview released shortly before her death, Robert confirms that the story is based on her autobiographical experience. See Mario Verdone, "*Un ventre di donna:* Il romanzo chirurgico di Enif Robert" (*La Fiera Letteraria* [4 July 1976]: 4–5). Marinetti refers to his relationship with Robert in his *Taccuini* (in particular, pp. 172, 189–191, 245). A note by the editor provides the following biographical information: "[Enif Robert] is the 'pen name' (obtained by using her husband's family name) of Enif Angelini (1886–1974), an actress and writer who joined the futurist movement" (552n. 41).

20. In "*Un ventre di donna,*" Verdone notes that the experimental structure of the narrative tends to realize the interpenetration of different settings that Marinetti propounded in his manifestos on "synthetic theater" and realized in several futurist plays.

21. "I am not crazy. I have the nerves of an uncommon woman, nerves that think, want, cling and disentangle, climbing up the impossible; nerves that cannot be satisfied by love" (7).

22. "In reality, I adore him. But my dissatisfied, ironic spirit springs away, while he is kissing me with tenderness, and rushes off elsewhere, searching, rummaging, far away, nearby, in the past, in the future, deep down in myself, another reality, another joy, a whim without shape, another man, without a body and a voice, an abstract type . . . a madness, in a word" (4).

23. This point is made by Barbara Zecchi in "Il corpo femminile trampolino tra scrittura e volo. Enif Robert e Biancamaria Frabotta: Settant'anni verso il tempo delle donne," *Italica* 69.4 (1992): 512.

24. "I want to see their wombs! . . . I would like to strip that gray statuette who is passing by now. Nude hips. A joyful pulsation of plastic whiteness; a wealth of blond and curly reflections throbbing with health and pleasure . . . And perhaps she is also hiding, in her

complex organic mass, the hostile germ that eventually will jump out to block her way to love!" (203–204).

25. Richard von Krafft-Ebing, *Psychopathia Sexualis*, trans. Franklin S. Klaf (New York: Stein and Day, 1978), 264. See also George L. Mosse, *Nationalism and Sexuality: Respectability and Abnormal Sexuality in Modern Europe* (New York: Howard Fertig, 1985), 106.

26. The same opposition also underlies the 1941 commentary of a woman critic, who applauds Marinetti's "mastery" and "generosity of heart" while conceding that the heroine inspires sympathy in spite of her "difficult, fickle character." See Artemisia Zimei, *Marinetti narratore sintetico dinamico di guerre e amori* (Rome: Le stanze del libro, 1941), 83–84.

27. In an open letter to Marinetti, Maria Ginanni (who was director of *L'Italia futurista* at the time) expresses similar feelings of admiration for the recently wounded futurist leader (whose "firmness" she sets up against Austrian impotence: "The impotent, flaccid Austrian machine gun smashed against the firmness of his body of tempered nerves") and of hate for her own constrained role as a woman, which she projects onto her constraining feminine clothes: "Well done: Well done my friend! I am shouting it to you with all my well-known enthusiasm! I am shouting it to you with my unwavering courage, which makes me hate my women's clothes that forbid me to take my place!" (*L'Italia futurista* [27 May 1917]: 1).

As Lynne Layton notes in "Vera Brittain's Testament(s)" (Higonnet et al., *Behind the Lines*, 70–83), "Both men and women experienced the inability to participate in war [World War I] as impotence and equated it with being female" (72). Rose Macaulay's envious address to the soldiers at war gives paradigmatic expression to this attitude: "Oh, it's you that have the luck, out there in the blood and muck / . . . In a trench you are sitting, while I am knitting / A hopeless sock that never gets done." Quoted in Jane Marcus, "Corpus/ Corps/Corpse: Writing the Body in/at War," in *Arms and the Woman: War, Gender, and Literary Representation*, ed. Helen M. Cooper, Adrienne Auslander Munich, and Susan Merril Squier (Chapel Hill: University of North Carolina Press, 1989), 131.

28. Paul Julius Möbius, *L'inferiorità mentale della donna: Sulla deficienza mentale fisiologica della donna*, trans. Ugo Cerletti (Turin: Einaudi, 1978). Page references will be given parenthetically within the text. The pamphlet was first published in Germany in 1900 with the title *Über den physiologischen Schwachsinn des Weibes;* it was first translated into Italian in 1904.

29. Cesare Lombroso (*La donna delinquente, la prostituta e la donna normale* [Turin: Roux, 1893]) had expounded analogous theories about the woman of genius: "And when genius appears in a woman, it is always associated with great anomalies: the greatest one is likeness to males—virility" (261). Similar notions were articulated in the futurist periodicals at the time in which the novel was written. See, for instance, Antonio Bruno, "Tema di 'Donne' " (Theme of "Women"; *L'Italia futurista* [2 December 1917]: 3): "Women, learn how to love us, and most of all, leave us in peace: we have so many serious things to do. Worship your mirrors and do not neglect perfumes. After all, what would you be without beauty? [. . . .] If a woman brags about being equal to a man—even to a genius—and she really is equal to him, she is certainly a monster."

30. Foucault, among others, discusses how women's bodies have been constituted in scientific discourse as being intrinsically pathological (in particular, neurotic, hysterical, and neurasthenic). See his *The History of Sexuality*. Volume I: *An Introduction*, trans. Robert Hurley (New York: Random House, 1980), 104, passim.

31. Marinetti attributes the following words to Robert in an entry dated 28 January 1918: "For many years I have lived all my loves with Duse in my fantasies. It is as if I had

lived them in reality. I bear their signs in my flesh. I decided to tell you, swear to you that they were not true because I felt that you found the words I had attributed to Duse interesting, and I wanted to satisfy my creative and novelistic vanity!" (*Taccuini*, 191). Robert worked in the theater with Eleonora Duse, one of Italy's most famous and glamorous actresses. In the novel, Enif is greatly comforted by Duse's loving attentions and enchanted by her "unique charm" (86). The lesbian motif that may be veiled in this relationship— another sign of the heroine's exceptional temperament—emerges in Robert's allusion to "Sapphic reminiscences" stirred by an old school friend (36).

32. See Mosse, "The Rediscovery of the Human Body," chapter 3 of *Nationalism and Sexuality*. Mosse points out that in the German volkish Right, particularly in the so-called life-reform movement, nudism and the celebration of the sun were associated with the mystique of national and racial regeneration, so that the rediscovery of the human body was ultimately stripped of its menace to the establishment (nationalism, respectability). Arguably, the futurist attack against bourgeois mentality also lost its subversive edge as it was integrated into the ideology of national regeneration.

33. See Benjamin, *BL*, 56. Benjamin investigates domination and submission (also in their adult erotic and sadomasochistic form) as results of the breakdown of the tension between asserting the self and recognizing the other. Taking issue with Hegel's and Freud's assumption that such a breakdown is inevitable, she argues that "the mother's lack of subjectivity, as perceived by both male and female children, creates an internal propensity toward feminine masochism and male sadism" (81). With respect to sadomasochistic relationships, she observes that pleasure for both partners derives from the violator's mastery and that pain is a route to pleasure only when it involves submission to an idealized figure (61–64). Both the desire for domination and the desire for submission signify absence of connection and mutuality in differentiation—"a breakdown of differentiation in which self is assimilated to other or other is assimilated to self " (73)—resulting in emptiness and alienation. From this vantage point, sadistic violation is "the attempt to push the other outside the self, to attack the other's separate reality in order finally to discover it" (68), or "to get outside the self into a shared reality" (73). Masochistic submission, which reflects the inability to express one's own desire and agency, manifests a wish to find one's own inner reality in the company of, and through, an other. Woman's propensity to occupy this role in the complementarity relationship is grounded in the girl's identificatory relationship to the self-sacrificing mother: the sadist's attack can be enjoyed by the masochist woman because "his assertion of subjectivity and difference is like a breath of the inaccessible outdoors. He embodies activity and difference for her. The vicarious quality of her enjoyment recapitulates the vicarious pleasure of the self-sacrificing mother with whom she identifies. Thus, submission for women allows a reenactment of their early identificatory relationship to the mother; it is a replication of the maternal attitude itself" (79).

34. See, for instance, the chapter entitled "Musica chirurgica in trincea" (Surgical Music in the Trenches), in which the harmony among the Italian soldiers is represented through musical imagery (185–188).

35. The idea that friendships among women are not to be taken seriously is a longstanding one. As Mosse writes, in the eighteenth century "the new and popular science of phrenology reflected general opinion when it sought proof through the study of the brain that women made friends only among men and never with other women" (*Nationalism and Sexuality*, 68).

CHAPTER 6. TRANSFORMATIONS IN THE FUTURIST MYTHOPOEIA

1. For a history of Italian futurism, see Crispolti, *Storia;* Salaris, *Storia;* Salaris, *Artecrazia: L'avanguardia futurista negli anni del fascismo* (Florence: La Nuova Italia, 1992).

2. *Il Futurismo* (1922–1925) was originally published in Milan (from 1922 to 1924, no. 9). In 1925, Marinetti himself moved to Rome. The Roman phase of Marinetti's publishing enterprise was characterized by a change in ambitions and managerial style. The volume of production decreased, advertising campaigns were less intense, and the trademark Edizioni futuriste di «Poesia» was "sold" to any futurist author who contributed money. Even under this new system, significant experimental texts were produced, such as the two famous *litolatte* ("litho-tin" books, made of tin with full-color serigraphs) by Marinetti and Tullio D'Albissola—the most innovative of futurist efforts toward the realization of books as artistic objects. The two phases of Marinetti's editions roughly coincide with the vicissitudes of the editorial market in Italy, which saw an increase between 1905 and 1914, followed by a drop in the war and postwar years.

3. I refer to the defeat of the Fasci Italiani di Combattimento, or Italian Battle Fasces (a coalition of futurists, fascists, and war veterans) in the 1919 elections and to the severance of the futurist alliance with Mussolini's Fasci in 1920, when Marinetti resigned his post in the party executive, accusing it of monarchism and clericalism. The process of reconciliation with fascism took place in the mid-1920s. See Salaris, *Artecrazia,* 7–63.

4. *Roma futurista* was the futurist forum for political debate in 1918–1920. *Noi* (2d ser., 1923–1925), edited by Enrico Prampolini, represented the predominant tendency to fashion futurism as an exclusively artistic movement. In the pages of *Artecrazia* (edited by Mino Somenzi, a Jewish intellectual) the futurists moved a defensive crusade against the fascist attempt at implementing an Italian version of the Nazi campaign against "degenerate art" in 1938–1939.

5. Enrico Falqui ("La poesia futurista," *Novecento letterario,* ser. 9 [Florence: Vallecchi, 1968], 7–43) and Gianni Scalia (introduction, *"Lacerba," "La Voce" (1914–1916),* vol. 4 of *LCI,* 11–76), among others, have posited the watershed between the first, experimental phase and the less innovative "second futurism" in 1915. De Maria indicates 1920 as the crucial divide (*TIF,* XXXI). Crispolti also refers to the futurist experience of the 1920s and 1930s as "second futurism" but argues that the movement continues to assume an "irreducibly revolutionary position" throughout its various phases (*Storia,* 185).

6. For this argument, see Schnapp, "Forwarding Address," 54; and Spackman, "The Fascist Rhetoric of Virility," 90.

7. The sociopolitical components are displaced by existential categories in "the philosophic-symbolic" explication of the text that Marinetti offered in an open letter to the critic Silvio Benco. In summary, the Indomabili, symbol of "untamed ferocity," are kept prisoners in a pit in the torrid sands of a desert island, under the watch of black Jailers, who represent "guided, utilized ferocity." Both the prisoners and the guards are ruled by the Paper People, "symbols of ideas and therefore of the Book that binds but does not tame instincts." As the scorching sun gives way to the night, brutal instincts can be drowned in the maternal Oasis and the pacifying, equalizing Lake of Goodness. But this is only a transitory experience, because "the human truth is not stasis even if happy, nor unconsciousness even if divine." The Untamables leave behind Feeling and enter the spiritual reign of ideas: the city of the Paper People. But the spiritual freedom and luminous dynamic abstractions that

rule the city are supported by the work of the River People, "the uniform, opaque and sad mass of the workers." Rebelling against their infernal conditions of life, the River People flood the city and rouse the destructive instincts of the Untamables, who must be returned to their original, captive state. Marinetti's final comments suggest that the dynamics of progress are intrinsically paradoxical. All-embracing harmony or goodness (humanity's supreme goal) is the very negation of "human vitality"—the anarchic, brutal instincts that must be alternately released and restrained so that they drive mankind toward its future and not toward its total destruction. See Bruno G. Sanzin, *Marinetti e il Futurismo* (Trieste: Sanzin, 1924), 29–31; rpt. in *TIF*, LXXXVI–LXXXVII.

8. Salaris, *Marinetti editore*, 293. Other pessimistic parables of the existential condition can be found in Marinetti's symbolic plays of the 1920s. *Prigionieri* (The Prisoners; first performed in 1925) and *Vulcano* (The Volcano; first performed in 1926) are paradigmatic examples. Imprisonment and volcanic eruptions symbolize the destiny of death and the chaos of passions to which men are captive. As in *Gli Indomabili*, rebellions are sterile retchings of a utopian desire for freedom, which results only in destruction.

9. Sentiment, syntax, and narrative structure return together in Marinetti's late production, just as his earlier attack on sentiment coincides with the aesthetic goal of suppressing organic form and subjective (emotional, psychological) subject matter.

10. Gentile, "La politica di Marinetti," 415; emphasis in original.

11. Marinetti acknowledges that the mass audience plays a crucial role in modern society but represents it in disparaging terms: as a female body to be seduced ("I have sufficiently experienced the femininity of crowds and the weakness of their collective virginity in the imposing of futurist free verse," *TIF*, 123); as a herd of animals to be watered by "trickle-down" art ("We are convinced [. . .] that art and literature exercise a determining influence on all the social classes, even the most ignorant, who are fed with them [*ne sono abbeverate*] through mysterious ways," *TIF*, 300); and as a mob of urchins to be tricked into learning a salutary lesson ("The great block of new ideas we have formed rolls around in mud and stones, pushed and soiled by the hands of cheerful urchins. These urchins, mocking the strange external colors of that unexpected enormous toy, are subjected to its incandescent and magnetic content," *TIF*, 332).

12. Gentile, "La politica di Marinetti," 427; emphasis in original.

13. Davies ("The Futures Market") finds the reasons for this alliance, as well as for the intrinsic contradictions of fascism and futurism, in Italy's complicated ideological and political situation. Noting that futurism and fascism shared in the same "hybrid theoretical ancestry" (an ideological ground where hybrids like "proletarian nationalism" and "nationalist syndicalism" were possible), she argues that the common ground of their alliance is demarcated by points of convergence between Right and Left, nationalism and syndicalism (94–95). See her useful summary and translation of the futurist program, in which correspondences with the platform of Mussolini's Fasci are highlighted in italics (93).

14. See De Felice, *Mussolini il rivoluzionario*, 596–597.

15. Benedetto Croce ("Fatti politici e interpretazioni storiche," *La Critica* [March 1924]: 189–192) and Piero Gobetti ("Marinetti, il precursore," *Il lavoro* [31 January 1924]; rpt. in *Scritti politici* [Turin: Einaudi, 1960], 579–582) offered a critical assessment of futurism as a precursor of fascism. Marinetti quoted Croce's comments in a leaflet (Salaris, *Marinetti editore*, 304). Other contemporaries, by contrast, argued that futurist avant-gardism was incompatible with the disciplinarian and hierarchical ideology of the fascist regime. See, for instance, Giuseppe Prezzolini, "Fascismo e futurismo," *Il Secolo* (3 July

1923); rpt. in *Per conoscere Marinetti e il futurismo,* ed. Luciano De Maria (Milan: Mondadori, 1973), 286–291.

16. See Luciano De Maria, *La nascita dell'avanguardia: Saggi sul futurismo italiano* (Padua: Marsilio Editori, 1986), 17; Salaris, *Storia,* 126; and Davies, "The Futures Market," 96–97. Marinetti courted Mussolini by giving him gift copies of the new futurist publications in artistically designed packaging. Mussolini, in turn, supported the old comrade "of the first hour" on several occasions. It was by his disposition, for instance, that Marinetti received a monthly check for fifteen thousand lira between 1941 and 1943. The money was used to sponsor the publication of futurist works and other activities of the movement (Salaris, *Marinetti editore,* 326–327).

17. See, e.g., *TIF,* 330, 413.

18. Like all other futurist manifestos, "Il Tattilismo" was sent to artists, opinion makers, important businessmen, libraries, and other cultural institutions. Some of the responses elicited by this propagandistic strategy were quoted in "Polemiche sul Tattilismo" (*Cronache d'Attualità* [May 1921]: 56–59). Two critical notes stand out against a chorus of enthusiastic comments. Rougena Zatkova and Gianni Calderone object to Marinetti's use of "passéist" capitalization (as in *Arte* and *Amore*). Volt expresses concern for the possible enfeebling effects of the new art ("If your hands become too delicate, how can you throw punches?") but declares himself interested in experiencing Marinetti's tactile tables and in comparing them with D'Annunzio's forthcoming *Notturno,* a literary experiment in tactile sensations. The article also reprints a French chronicle of Marinetti's conference on tactilism in Paris (January 1921), offering a colorful picture of the cultural context in which the manifesto was launched. According to the columnist of *Carnet de la Semaine,* the Théâtre de l'Œuvre was packed with "all the fighting spirits of the Parisian artistic circles." The dadaists, in particular, "tried to fight" but were "knocked down" by Marinetti who "had gone much further" in his experimentations and continued to renew himself "instead of lagging behind like the dadaists" (56).

19. The summer evoked in the manifesto is that of 1920, a year that "brought out the largest number of industrial strikes in Italian history. [. . . .] The main component of this spectacular increase lay in a new tactic, the factory occupation or sit-down strike, and in the month-long occupation of factories in the fall of 1920" (Tilly, Tilly, and Tilly, *The Rebellious Century,* 172–173).

20. The poem appeared in *I nuovi poeti futuristi* (Rome: Edizioni futuriste di «Poesia», 1925), 281–282; emphasis in original. In addition to "tactile tables," tattilismo and the concomitantly developed theory of "supersensualism" ("the discovery of new senses") inspired a series of "tactile," "olfactory," and "thermometric" lyrics, in which sensory images are instrumental to what one might call "assimilatory descriptivism": a descriptive technique that aims to convey the poet's sensorial impressions with intensified immediacy and intuitive precision. The oxymoronic principle of intuitive precision, which accounts for Marinetti's use of numbers and mathematical signs in his poems, is first formulated in "Lo splendore geometrico e meccanico e la sensibilità numerica" (*TIF,* 106–107). The same principle is developed in the 1941 manifesto on "qualitative, imaginative" mathematics, "La matematica futurista immaginativa qualitativa" (*TIF,* 226–231).

21. To the memorialistic genre belong also two autobiographical texts published posthumously in *La grande Milano tradizionale e futurista e Una sensibilità italiana nata in Egitto* (Great Traditional and Futurist Milan and An Italian Sensibility Born in Egypt), ed. Luciano De Maria (Milan: Mondadori, 1969).

22. With regard to Flaubert's influence on Marinetti's literary re-creations of Africa, evidence is provided by references to *Sallambò* in the manuscript copy of *Mafarka* held at the Beinecke Rare Book and Manuscript Library, Yale University.

23. On the notion of organic memory, see Kern, *The Culture of Time and Space,* 40–41. Marinetti's diction brings to mind contemporary developments in the conception of time. As Kern notes, some psychologists and philosophers "thought memories were locked in living tissue as a cumulative residue of voluntary movements and bodily processes" (40). Bergson, among others, maintained that "the past collects in the fibers of the body as it does in the mind" (41).

24. There are several versions (with slight variations) of this manifesto, which was first published as "Poesia Arti Corporative" in *Gazzetta del Popolo* (10 April 1937). Under the title "La poesia dei Tecnicismi," the manifesto appeared as an introduction to *Il poema di Torre Viscosa* (The Poem of Torre Viscosa; Milan: Off. Grafiche Esperia, 1938). Both the manifesto and the poem (the first under the title "Estrazione sistematica di nuovi splendori e nuove musiche dai tecnicismi" [The Systematic Extraction of New Splendor and Music from Technicalities], the latter under the title "Poesia simultanea dei canneti Arunda Donax" [The Simultaneous Poetry of the Arunda Donax Cane Fields]) were published also in *Il Poema non umano dei tecnicismi* (The Nonhuman Poem of Technicalities; Milan: Mondadori, 1940), 19–26, 37–51; rpt. in *TIF*, 1143–1146, 1151–1160.

25. See Antonio Saccone, *Marinetti e il futurismo* (Naples: Liguori, 1984), 112.

26. See, for instance, *Guerra sola igiene del mondo*, in particular "Discorso ai triestini" (Address to the People of Trieste: *TIF*, 248–249). Even in "Poesia simultanea degli affari del porto di Genova" (The Simultaneous Poetry of Business in the Harbor of Genoa; section 1 of *Il Poema non umano dei tecnicismi*), there is evidence of a fundamental ambivalence toward the business world, notwithstanding Marinetti's declared intent to idealize "trading finance and agriculture" (*TIF*, 1144). He refers to business transactions as "lugubrious circulating greed" (*TIF*, 1149) and represents the harbor of Genoa as polluted, both literally and metaphorically: "the harbor is an immense flooded tar dump better still it is the urinal of transatlantic ships where they trade in aromatic excrement from the other side of the world" (*TIF*, 1149–1150).

27. This description conjures up the image of a monstrous ogress, which is consonant with contemporary representations of technology. Cinema, in particular, displayed a preoccupation with the power struggle between man and technology; a recurrent theme was the embodiment of technology in a monster that escaped man's control and became his master. Famous examples are the motion pictures *The Cabinet of Dr. Caligari* (1920) and *The Testament of Dr. Mabuse* (1932).

28. The first edition of *Il poema di Torre Viscosa* coincides with one of the most difficult moments in the relationship between futurism and the fascist regime. In 1938, the racial laws were declared and an antimodern campaign against "degenerate," "subversive" art was stirred up by reactionary publications such as Telesio Interlandi's *La Difesa della Razza* and Roberto Farinacci's *Il Regime Fascista*. Marinetti, at the forefront of opposition, argued for the Italian origin of the avant-garde. See Salaris, *Artecrazia*, 137ff., esp. pp. 198–201.

29. Berman underlines the captivating power of the dazzling pageantry of military life and fashion in "pastoral modernism": "There is an important body of modern writing, often by the most serious writers, that sounds a great deal like advertising copy. This writing sees the whole spiritual adventure of modernity incarnated in the latest fashion, the latest machine, or—and here it gets sinister—the latest model regiment. [. . .] Armies on pa-

rade, from Baudelaire's time to our own, play a central role in the pastoral vision of modernity: glittering hardware, gaudy colors, flowing lines, fast and graceful movements, modernity without tears" (*All That Is Solid Melts Into Air*, 137).

30. De Grazia offers a detailed study of the stabilizing function of fascist mass organizations and low culture in *The Culture of Consent: Mass Organization of Leisure in Fascist Italy* (Cambridge: Cambridge University Press, 1981). On the broader issue of fascist cultural policies, de Grazia remarks that the regime demonstrated itself willing and able to assimilate a wide spectrum of "cultures" in the process of forming a single dominant culture: from "the verities of elitist practitioners of the old high culture" to "the technological utopias of the Futurists" to "the stock of folk traditions of precapitalist Italy." Because of the cultural background of fascist officials, however, and because of the regime's eagerness to gain cultural legitimacy, fascist cultural institutions gradually rejected avant-gardism "in favor of positions that might receive the support of traditional academic culture." They espoused the class-defined divisions between "high" and "low" culture and "the traditional intellectual elite's disdain for the popularization of culture" (187). De Grazia argues that fascist low culture, in its essentially diversionary nature, failed to produce "full ideological assimilation of the popular classes into a new national consensus." By fostering "passivity, ignorance, individualism, traditionalism, evasion," it was successful as long as "the government's overriding concern was to ensure normality," but was unable "to sustain mobilization with a firmer identification with fascist principles." Nevertheless, it performed a fundamental legitimizing function (223–224).

Regarding the "return to traditions" policy, de Grazia notes that "it was first announced [. . .] in 1929, when the regime, in its concern to reassure the crisis-stricken agricultural sector that its interests were being safeguarded, began to denounce the perils of urbanism and to defend sound rural virtues" (202). By fostering regional ethnocentrism, the return to traditions belied the national orientation of the fascist regime; however, "parochial and chauvinistic as it was, [it] offered to the regime a partially acceptable surrogate for national allegiance, one infinitely preferable to class identification" (214). Furthermore, state-managed festivals combined local custom, Catholic ritual, and fascist ceremony "with the recognition that veneration for the traditional cult might be transferred to the new fascist order" (210). Quoting the words of a leading ethnographer, de Grazia highlights the diversionary function of folkish fashion: "The comely peasant women who adorned the covers of *Gente nostra*, together with the sturdy peasant men who were 'so mirthful, yet so indefatigable in their work and so sober and thrifty in their habits,' symbolized 'the People,' whose customs, in Corso's words, expressed that 'passion and aesthetic sense' that 'beautifies their existence even amid the daily misery and drudgery of their lives' "(207).

31. See the program of the festivities, published under the title *Adunata del costume nazionale* (The Gathering of National Costumes; Rome: Bottega Danesi, 1930).

32. Marinetti, preface, in Filippo Fichera, *Il Duce e il Fascismo nei canti dialettali d'Italia* (Milan: Edizione del "Convivio letterario," 1937), IX–XII; subsequent references will be cited parenthetically in the text.

33. On the "genere eroico fascista," see Giocondi, *Lettori in camicia nera*, 84–107.

34. For a more detailed account of this episode and for a reprint of the texts under discussion, see Lucio Villari, "Inediti di F. T. Marinetti: Una poesia di guerra e una lettera," *Nuovi argomenti* 22.33–34 (1973): 7–11; further page references will appear in the text. An extended version of the poem was included in *Canto eroi e macchine della guerra Mussoliniana*. Vil-

lari notes that the letter to Pavolini had the desired effect of allowing Marinetti to continue his readings (albeit in a reduced time slot of ten minutes per month), which he attributes not so much to Marinetti's affirmation of his patriotic aims as to the veiled threat of retaliation conveyed by the letter's conclusive remarks: "You who are well informed know that if one had to pay attention to irony and sarcasm many of those who are talking would have to hold their tongues" (9). On the relationship between Marinetti and Pavolini, see also Agnese, *Marinetti*, 283, 295, 297, 301, 307–308; and Salaris, *Artecrazia*, 109, 165–166.

35. Marinetti, "Estetica Futurista della guerra," *Stile futurista* (November 1935): 9. Marinetti expanded on this later version of the futurist aesthetic of war (often recycling the same text with only slight variations) in the prefaces of poems and collections inspired by the Ethiopian campaign and by World War II.

36. Marinetti, *Il Poema africano della Divisione "28 Ottobre"* (Milan: Mondadori, 1937), 116, 301, 308. Subsequent page references will be given parenthetically within the text.

37. Interestingly, Marinetti equates the Abyssinians with the Italian communists, also labeled "miscela sporca" (103).

38. See also pp. 129, 239, 258. The same motif recurs in an episode of *La grande Milano*, where Marinetti recounts his experience as a guest speaker at an assembly of anarchists and socialists. He deploys bottles of flowery perfume against a stifling "equator of youthful sweat" and uses his gesture to illustrate his "argument of inequality" against "materialist opaque greyness" (89).

39. In this section (entitled "Simultaneità di cinematografo interstellare" [Simultaneity of Interstellar Cinema]) the nocturnal scenario is preceded by a luminous "cinematic" sequence, in which "the rosy little girls" are the protagonists: the poet "sees" his daughters, playing in a garden, as if he were watching them in a motion picture (99–100). Through such an explicit reference to cinematography, this section highlights the analogy between Marinetti's narrative techniques and the montage techniques of motion picture photography.

40. Passages like the one quoted above undermine Theweleit's argument that the pleasurable flowing of desire *neatly* distinguishes nonfascist from fascist writing (*Male fantasies*, I: 382), as well as other critics' claim that Marinetti is a *typical* fascist writer.

41. Exuberant, forestlike hair recurs as a quintessential feature of femininity in Marinetti's writing. His phantasmatic image of woman usually foregrounds the traditional connotative value of hair as a signifier of woman's sexual power—her desire and her capacity to generate desire.

42. Marinetti, *Canto eroi e macchine della guerra Mussoliniana: Aeropoema simultaneo in parole in libertà futuriste* (Milan: Mondadori, 1942), 27; subsequent page references will be given parenthetically within the text.

43. A secularized rhetoric of the sacred is characteristic of D'Annunzio's political speeches at Fiume and is also a staple of the fascist discourse on war. See Barbara Spackman, "*Il verbo (e)sangue*: Gabriele D'Annunzio and the Ritualization of Violence," *Quaderni d'Italianistica* 4.2 (1983): 219–229; and Jeffrey Schnapp, "Epic Demonstrations: Fascist Modernity and the 1932 Exhibition of the Fascist Revolution," in Golsan, *Fascism, Aesthetics, and Culture*, 1–37.

44. Gubar, " 'This Is My Rifle,' " 247.

45. *L'aeropoema di Gesù*, which Marinetti composed during his stay in Venice (1943–1944), remained unpublished until 1991. I conducted my study on the original manuscript (handwritten by Marinetti's wife, Benedetta Cappa), which is held at the Beinecke Rare

Book and Manuscript Library, Yale University. Quotes, however, refer to the published version edited by Salaris (Montepulciano: Editori del Grifo, 1991). Page references will be given parenthetically within the text.

46. See p. 14: "This [water] is holy and now flows in all fantasies like an unreachable maternal blessing"; and p. 19: "Thus the finally arrived water-bearing mules and askaris are evangelically approaching and their water bags are fresh breasts of a black wet nurse and the water that is so superior to any milk in its comforting sweetness has the translucent divine golden-brown softness of your Holy Mother's gaze oh Jesus."

47. The fact that Marinetti apparently did not revise the manuscript handwritten by his wife adds to the interpretive difficulties often posed by his "creative" texts because of unconventional syntax and lack of punctuation marks. Such difficulties are well illustrated by the passage above, in which the editor, presuming an error by the transcriber, has added an accent ("è il tuo nome" instead of "e il tuo nome")—changing the meaning from "and your name" to "is your name."

48. According to Agnese (*Marinetti*, 107, 239, 282), Marinetti had always been a believer in spite of his avowed anticlericalism, but he reapproached the sacraments only in 1940, when his youngest daughter received first Communion. A letter to Cangiullo from the African front (Christmas 1935) and a few lines addressed to Dessy from the Russian front testify to Marinetti's Christian faith. See Agnese, *Marinetti*, 272, 291; and Cangiullo, *Lettere a Marinetti in Africa* (Naples: Pironti, 1940), 35–36. In *La grande Milano*, Marinetti makes reference to the great devotion to Jesus impressed on him by his mother (202).

49. This recuperation parallels a shift in the general development of modernism, which Spender describes as follows: "In the early work of Joyce, Lawrence, Eliot and Pound, there is a straightforward willingness to regard the modern scene as being made up of hard, brutal, ugly appearances, which the poet was nevertheless determined to melt down and transform into strange and beautiful images, music harshly mechanical, yet disturbing, in his poem-novel or his poem. In their later work, all these writers turned away from that external scene of the modern—the poetry of the city, of the machine—which had at first fascinated them with its challenge. They become interested in ideas, or in levels of consciousness where the outside world is but a menacing evil on the fringe of a universal dream, a transforming ecstasy of love, or a compelling and timeless orthodoxy" (*The Struggle of the Modern*, 224).

50. See Kristeva, *TL*, 60. Kristeva explains the connection between maternal love and divine love as follows: "Man overcomes the unthinkable of death by postulating maternal love in its place—in the place and stead of death and thought. This love, of which divine love is merely a not always convincing derivation, psychologically is perhaps a recall, on the near side of early identifications, of the primal shelter that insured the survival of the newborn. Such a love is in fact, logically speaking, a surge of anguish at the very moment when the identity of thought and living body collapses. The possibilities of communication having been swept away, only the subtle gamut of sound, touch, and visual traces, older than language and newly worked out, are preserved as an ultimate shield against death" (*TL*, 252–253).

51. Evidence of a futurist anxiety about technology can also be found in the writings of other poets, especially in the works of Ruggero Vasari, where it becomes a predominant theme beginning in the early 1920s. See, in particular, his plays *L'angoscia delle macchine* (Machine Anguish) and *Raun* in *Teatro italiano d'avanguardia: Drammi e sintesi futuriste*, ed. Mario Verdone (Rome: Officina Edizioni, 1970).

52. In Kristeva's terms, the triadic structure of Christian Love or Agape comprises the loving Other (God the Father), the passion of the Son, through which the "body-Self has access to the Name of the Other," and the love of one's neighbor, reaching out from self to other (*TL*, 139–147).

53. David R. Crownfield, "The Sublimation of Narcissism in Christian Love and Faith," *Body / Text in Julia Kristeva: Religion, Women, and Psychoanalysis,* ed. David Crownfield (Albany: State University of New York Press, 1992), 60.

54. Cangiullo, *Lettere,* 35–36.

55. See Dottori's "Manifesto futurista umbro dell'aeropittura" (Umbrian Futurist Manifesto of Aeropainting), in Crispolti, *Ricostruzione,* 502.

56. Elio Vittorini, *Conversazione in Sicilia* (Turin: Einaudi, 1974), 153.

57. Elio Vittorini, *Le due tensioni: Appunti per una ideologia della letteratura* (Milan: Il Saggiatore, 1967), 67: "That which interests the author is not a 'mimesis' of reality, [. . .] but a *utilization* of reality that immediately is able to render and build, for historical forces, a weapon, an instrument of transformation, or in short a call to transform" (emphasis in original).

AFTERWORD: THE RHETORIC OF VIOLENCE
AND THE VIOLENCE OF RHETORIC

1. I refer to de Lauretis's notion of the "violence of rhetoric" ("The Violence of Rhetoric: Considerations on Representation and Gender," *Technologies,* 31–50), which takes into account the social dimension of the semiotic by addressing the "fact" of gender, unlike Jacques Derrida's notion of the "violence of the letter" (*Of Grammatology,* trans. Gayatri Chakravorty Spivak [Baltimore: Johns Hopkins University Press, 1976], 101–140).

INDEX

Abjection, viii, xi, 8–9, 103, 130, 152, 155; Kristeva on, 28, 35–36, 37, 56, 66–67, 158–159, 174n71, 174n72, 176n12; rhetoric of, in *L'Aeropoema di Gesù*, 157, 158, 160; rhetoric of, in *Mafarka le futuriste*, x, 56–59, 66–67, 182n9; rhetoric of, in *Il Poema africano della Divisione "28 Ottobre,"* 147–149; rhetoric of, in *Un ventre di donna*, 116, 118, 123

Adam, Paul, 169n43, 178n26

Adler, Alfred, 183n12

Aeropoesia (aeropoetry), 38, 125, 140–142

Agnese, Gino, 167n26, 181n43, 203n48

Ainé, Rosny, 19, 169n43

Amendola, Giovanni, 5, 167n19

Antifeminism: in early twentieth century, 24; in fascism, 80–81, 186n4, 188n9; in Marinetti, 2, 20–21; in Valentine de Saint-Point, 105–106

Apollinaire, Guillaume, 167n27

Arbouin, Gabriel, 167n27

Arte-azione (art-in-action/art-as-action), ix, 32

Artecrazia (artocracy), 125, 130, 197n4

Asor Rosa, Alberto, 167n15

Ascoli, Albert Russell, 185n26

Associazione degli Arditi d'Italia (Association of Italian Shock Troopers), 132

Bacon, Francis, 27, 45, 180n33

Bakhtin, Mikhail, 182n11

Baldissone, Giusi, 56, 182n7, 182n9, 190n20

Balla, Giacomo, 41, 179n28

Barbara (Olga Biglieri-Scurto), 106

Bataille, Georges, 63

Bataille, Henri, 178n26

Baudelaire, Charles, 19; "Eloge du maquillage" (In Praise of Makeup), 87–88

Baudrillard, Jean, 47

Becker, Ernest, 70, 175n10, 180n40, 183n12, 185n33; relation of psychosis to creativity, 75, 186n39

Bem, Sandra Lipsitz, 194n17

Benco, Silvio, 197n7

Benedetta (Marinetti, Benedetta Cappa), 83, 106, 110, 111, 132, 188n9

Benjamin, Jessica, 27, 28, 97, 173n68; *The Bonds of Love: Psychoanalysis, Feminism, and the Problem of Domination*, 171n56, 171n57, 171n58, 174n69, 196n33; on castration complex, 177n18; critique of Chasseguet-Smirgel, 23–24; on repudiation of the mother, 62–63, 71–72

Benjamin, Walter, 176n14

Bergson, Henri, 59, 200n32

Berman, Marshall, 42, 179n31, 200n29

Berman, Russell, 186n38

Birnbaum, Lucia Chiavola, 167n14

Boccioni, Umberto, 125, 126

Boine, Giovanni, 19

Borgese, Giuseppe Antonio, 5, 167n18

Bortolotti, Franca Pieroni, 167n14, 193n14

Boss, Médard, 183n12

Bozzolla, Angelo, 192n1

Bradbury, Malcolm, 166n9, 166n10, 169n39

Briosi, Sandro, 178n24

Brown, Norman O., 171n57, 183n12

Bruno, Antonio, 195*n*29

Bürger, Peter, 166*n*12

Butler, Judith, 185*n*29, 191*n*30

Buzzi, Paolo, 145; violent erotica, 191*n*33

Calderone, Gianni: criticism of "Il Tattilismo," 199*n*18

Cangiullo, Francesco, 179*n*30, 203*n*48, 204*n*54; "La scoperta del sostantivo anatomico o del sesso in esso" (The Discovery of the Anatomical Noun or of the Sex within It), 33, 175*n*7

Cantimori, Delio, 172*n*63

Capuana, Luigi, 181*n*2

Carli, Mario, 126, 186*n*4; "Arte vile e arte virile" (Vile Art and Virile Art), 32–33, 175*n*6; violent erotica, 191*n*33

Caruso, Luciano, 175*n*5

Cavacchioli, Enrico, 181*n*42

Celant, Germano, 178*n*24

Celli, Giorgio, 180*n*38

Chasseguet-Smirgel, Janine, 23

Chiodelli, Raoul, 146

Chiti, Remo, 179*n*28

Chodorow, Nancy, 173*n*68; on castration complex, 177*n*18

Cinti, Decio, 181*n*2

Conrad, Michael Georg, 186*n*41

Corneli, Franca Maria, 193*n*13

Corra, Bruno (Bruno Ginanni-Corradini), 126, 179*n*28; preface to *Come si seducono le donne*, 90, 91, 93, 94, 99, 190*n*18; *Signora, torna vostro marito: Lettera aperta a una signora onesta* (Madam, Your Husband Is Coming Home: An Open Letter to an Honest Lady), 190*n*19, 190*n*21; on "superfamily," 91–92; violent erotica, 191*n*33

Corradini, Enrico, 6, 19, 167*n*20, 167*n*22

Crispolti, Enrico, 169*n*47, 179*n*29, 197*n*1; on second futurism, 197*n*5

Critica Fascista, 80, 188*n*9

Critica Sociale, 79, 80

Croce, Benedetto, 198*n*15

Crownfield, David R., 159, 204*n*53

Cutelli, Stefano Mario, 188*n*9

Dadaism, 19

D'Albissola, Tullio, 197*n*2

D'Annunzio, Gabriele, 5, 6, 19, 21, 26, 32, 167*n*22, 169*n*43, 189*n*16, 202*n*43; *Notturno*, 199*n*18

Dante (Dante Alighieri), 62

Davies, Judy, 169*n*47, 198*n*13, 199*n*16

Decadence, ix, 7–12, 32; crossing of gender boundaries, 88; metaphors of carnality and decay, 9, 16; rhetoric of aesthetic conversion, 77–78; rhetoric of sickness, 77–78

De Felice, Renzo, 21, 24, 169*n*47, 170*n*50, 172*n*63

De Grazia, Victoria, 186*n*4, 201*n*30

De Lauretis, Teresa: notion of violence of rhetoric, 204*n*1; theory of gender difference, 193*n*15

Deleuze, Gilles, 169*n*42, 172*n*66

De Man, Paul, 75, 186*n*40

De Maria, Luciano, 2, 55, 197*n*5, 199*n*16, 199*n*21; *Teoria e invenzione futurista*, 55, 126, 165*n*1, 169*n*47, 197*n*5; on war in futurist ideology, 176*n*15

Depero, Fortunato, 41

Derrida, Jacques, 204*n*1

De Saint-Point, Valentine: "Manifesto della Donna futurista (Manifesto of the Futurist Woman), 105–106, 112, 192*n*2, 192*n*3; "Manifesto futurista della Lussuria" (Futurist Manifesto of Lust), 105, 192*n*3

Desideri, Giovannella, 193*n*14

Dessy, Mario, 187*n*7

Diethe, Carol, 170*n*48

Dollenmeyer, David, 170*n*48

Dombroski, Robert S., 169*n*47

Dottori, Gerardo, 155, 161, 204*n*55

Duse, Eleonora, 195*n*31

Eco, Umberto, 75, 76, 184*n*19, 186*n*42, 186*n*43

Edizioni futuriste di «Poesia» (Edizioni di «Poesia»), 7, 40, 178*n*27, 193*n*13

Elias, Norbert, 18–19, 169*n*42

Eliot, T. S., 17, 169*n*39, 203*n*49

Expressionism, 19

Falco, Gian. *See* Papini, Giovanni

Falqui, Enrico, 197*n*5

Farinacci, Roberto, 200*n*28

Fasci Italiani di Combattimento (Italian Battle Fasces), 132, 197*n*3

Fascism: cultural policies, 201*n*30; and futurism, 1, 20–26, 79, 132–133, 140, 143–146, 188*n*8, 198*n*13, 198*n*15, 200*n*28; literary imaginations, 186*n*38; and race, 188*n*8; theories of, 21–26; women under, 79–81, 186*n*4, 188*n*9

Fascist-heroic genre, 145, 201*n*33

Felski, Rita, 9–10, 88, 168*n*30, 168*n*31

Feminism: psychoanalytic theories, 27–28

Ferri, Enrico, 13

Fetishism, 58, 183*n*12; of commodities, 87; of the machine, 33, 102; rhetorical excess as, 8; and synecdoche, 95–96, 184*n*17

Fillia (Luigi Colombo), 98, 155; violent erotica, 191*n*33

Flaubert, Gustave, 138, 200*n*22

Fornari, Franco, 52, 175*n*9, 180*n*33, 181*n*44

Foucault, Michel, 24, 172*n*62, 195*n*30

Frankfurt school, 23, 171*n*57

Freccero, John, 183*n*16

Freud, Sigmund, 93, 168*n*33, 185*n*31; on castration complex, 177*n*18, 183*n*12; on narcissism, 171*n*58; *Project for a Scientific Psychology*, 190*n*24; theory of instincts, 176*n*15

Futurism: aeropoetry phase, 125, 140–143; antipasséist program, ix, 19, 130; anxiety about technology, 51–52, 157, 203*n*51; and automobiles, 48–49, 51–52; contradictions, 1–2; culinary revolution, 135; eroticization of war, 99–104; and expressionism, 19; and fascism, 1, 20–26, 79, 132–133, 140, 143–146, 188*n*8, 198*n*13, 198*n*15, 200*n*28; fiction of power, vii, ix, 16–20, 163–164; free verse (verso libero), 125; "futurist toy," 41; homoerotic undercurrents, 33–34, 56, 182*n*9; literary origins, 7–16; *litolatte* (litho-tin books), 197*n*2; manifestos, 29–31; and misogyny, vii, viii, xi, 2, 34, 54, 105 (*see also* Antifeminism); multimedia creation, 41; and nationalism, 1–2, 18, 41, 131; and occult science, 40, 178*n*24; origins of, vii–ix, 6–7; phases of, 125–126, 197*n*5; philosophical sources of, 17–18, 19; poetics of "the marvelous," 48; poetry of technicalities, 125, 140–143; polyexpressivity (*poliespressività*), 40; and postmodern nihilism, 47–48; and pragmatism, 17–18; pranks and brawls, 179*n*30; propaganda, 40, 178*n*27; rhetorical strategies, 40, 46–48; rhetoric of gender, viii–xi, 26–28, 32–34, 81, 85; rhetoric of violence, 163–164; simultaneity (*simultaneità*), 40; social-erotic fiction, 89, 135; synoptic and synthetic tables (*tavole sinottiche e sintetiche*), 40; synthetic theater, viii; tactilism (*tattilismo*), 1, 40, 133–135; tendency to primitivism, 14, 49, 59; theory of analogy, 46; violent erotica, 94–99, 191*n*33; visual poetry, 1; women in movement, xi, 104, 105–112, 193*n*14; words in freedom (*paroliberismo*), vii, 37–40, 46, 125; writings on love and marriage, 91–92, 187*n*7, 188*n*9

Futurismo (Sant'Elia; Artecrazia), 125

Gentile, Emilio, 131, 169*n*46, 169*n*47, 198*n*12

Ginanni, Maria, 106, 110, 195*n*27

Ginanni-Corradini, Bruno. *See* Corra, Bruno

Ginna, Arnaldo (Arnaldo Ginanni-Corradini), 179*n*28

Giocondi, Michele, 189*n*17, 192*n*35, 201*n*33

Giolitti, Giovanni, 4

Girard, René, 177*n*19, 185*n*25, 185*n*27

Giuliani, Fulvia, 106

Gobetti, Piero, 178*n*27, 198*n*15

Goebbels, Joseph Paul, 171*n*59

Goll, Ivan, 167*n*27

Goretti, Maria, 193*n*13

Gramsci, Antonio, 76, 168*n*35, 178*n*27

Grey, Roch, 167*n*27

Guattari, Félix, 169*n*42, 172*n*66

Gubar, Susan, 153, 191*n*32, 202*n*44

Guerricchio, Rita, 193*n*14

Hall, G. Stanley, 180*n*40

Heath, Stephen, 177*n*21

Hegel, Georg Wilhelm Friedrich, 97

Herf, Jeffrey, 176*n*14

Hermes, 6

Hertz, Neil, 183*n*12

Hewitt, Andrew, 166*n*12, 172*n*66, 181*n*45

Higonnet, Margaret Randolph, 172*n*61, 187*n*6

Higonnet, Patrice L.-R., 187*n*6

Hillenaar, Henk, 178*n*24

Husserl, Edmund, 180*n*33

Huysmans, Joris-Karl, 9–12, 168*n*32

Ibsen, Henrik, 19

Il Futurismo, 125, 197*n*2

Il Regno, 6

Incorporation, 64–65, 72, 95–98, 135–137, 182*n*11, 191*n*28; and colonization, 160; and melancholia, 68–69, 185*n*29; of hostile object/environment, 52, 134, 152. *See also* Marinetti—Fiction of power: alimentary imagery; Marinetti—*Mafarka le futuriste:* theme of sexuality as oral aggression

Interlandi, Telesio, 200*n*28

Irigaray, Luce, 188*n*8

Isaak, Jo Anna, 2, 165*n*2

Isnenghi, Mario, 176*n*15

Italy: femininist movement in, 189*n*16; fin de siècle crisis in, 4–5; militant journals, 5–6

James, William, 6, 17, 18

Janni, Ettore, 168*n*35

Jannini, Pasquale A., 167*n*28

Jenson, Jane, 172*n*61
Joll, James, 55, 182*n*3
Joyce, James, 17, 19, 203*n*49
Jung, Carl, 183*n*12
Jünger, Ernst, 171*n*59

Kahn, Gustave, 19
Kahnweiler, Daniel Henri, 178*n*27
Kandinskij, Vasilij, 167*n*27
Kaplan, Alice Yaeger, 2, 165*n*3, 181*n*41; on fascist desire, 21–22, 24; on *Mafarka le futuriste*, 55–56, 182*n*10, 185*n*23; on Marinetti's eroticization of war, 176*n*15; on Marinetti's fascism, 21, 25; *Reproductions of Banality: Fascism, Literature, and French Intellectual Life*, 165*n*3, 171*n*54, 171*n*55, 171*n*59, 177*n*20, 186*n*38
Keller, Evelyn Fox, 27–28, 45, 69–70, 174*n*70, 185*n*32
Kern, Stephen, 166*n*9, 169*n*44, 185*n*26, 200*n*23
Khun, Eva, 106
Kirby, Michael, 175*n*4
Klein, Melanie, 181*n*44
Kristeva, Julia, 28, 45–46; 174*n*71, 174*n*72; *Powers of Horror: An Essay on Abjection*, 35, 66–67, 176*n*12, 176*n*13, 186*n*37; queries into religion, 158–159; *Tales of Love*, 174*n*72, 185*n*30, 203*n*50, 204*n*52

Labriola, Arturo, 13, 168*n*35
Lacan, Jacques, 137*n*68, 171*n*58, 174*n*72, 177*n*18, 177*n*21, 185*n*29, 191*n*30
Lacerba, 6, 125
"La cinematografia futurista" (Futurist Cinematography), 41, 179*n*28
Laclau, Ernesto, 22
Lamarck, Jean Baptiste de: transformism, viii, 180*n*36
Laplanche, Jean, 93, 190*n*24, 191*n*28
La Voce, 6, 167*n*25
Lawrence, D. H., 203*n*49
Layton, Lynne, 195*n*27
Le Figaro, 7
Leonardo, 6, 18
Leone de Castris, Arcangelo, 165*n*3
Le Papyrus, 7
Libreria della Voce, 178*n*27
L'Impero, 186*n*4
L'Italia futurista, 106, 108, 110, 125
Lombroso, Cesare, 195*n*29
Lorde, Audre, 194*n*16
Lucini, Gian Pietro, 181*n*2

Macciocchi, Maria-Antonietta, 21, 79, 171*n*52
Maffii, Maffio, 167*n*17
Majakovskij, Vladimir, 178*n*27
Mallarmé, Stéphane, 19, 46
Malpillero, Emma, 106
Marcus, Jane, 195*n*27
Marcuse, Herbert, 171*n*57
Marinetti, Benedetta Cappa. *See* Benedetta
Marinetti, F. T.: background, 7; Christian faith, 203*n*48; cosmopolitanism, 7; critical studies of, 2–3, 20–21; and emergence of futurism, vii–viii, 19–20, 169*n*43; in Ethiopia, 148; and fascism, 20–26, 79, 94, 132–133, 137, 140, 142–147, 165*n*3, 169*n*47, 200*n*28; and his automobile, 52, 53, 181*n*43; influence of Flaubert, 138, 200*n*22; on Mallarmé, 46; marriage to Benedetta Cappa, 132, 188*n*9; military service, 145, 192*n*35; *modernolatria* (worship of modernity), xi; on Mussolini, 190*n*26; political activism, 131–132; promotion of futurism, 40, 178*n*26, 181*n*2, 199*n*18; publishing activities, 7, 40, 178*n*27, 193*n*13, 197*n*2; rejection of D'Annunzio, 32; rejection of politics, 130–133; rejection of psychologism, 17; rejection of symbolism and decadence, 32; relationship to Pavolini, 201*n*34
—Fiction of power: *aeropoesia*, 38; alimentary imagery, 9, 12–16, 57–59, 89, 90, 93–99, 168*n*37, 185*n*28 (*see also* Incorporation); *arte-azione* (art-in-action/art-as-action), ix, 32; binary structuring of reality in, 31–36; machine in, 48–54, 157, 172*n*66, 183*n*12; manifestos, vii, viii, ix, x, 29–54, 175*n*2, 175*n*3, 175*n*4; mixture of sacred and profane, 192*n*36; *paroliberismo* (words in freedom), vii, 37–40, 46; phallocentrism, 2, 42–43; on poetics of wireless imagination, 46; pragmatism, 18; prefuturist works, ix, 7–16; relationship of narrative techniques to cinematography, 202*n*39; and religious function of art, 34–35, 155–161; rhetorical strategies, viii, 40, 46–48, 143, 149, 163–164; superuomo myth, x, 44–45, 48–54, 59–69, 73–78, 89, 93, 101, 106, 121–122, 127, 133–134, 140, 180*n*36; syntactic destruction, 37–40, 163–164; technology in, 43–44, 139–140; theory of analogy, 46; undercurrent of decadence, 32; violence in, 36–41, 45–46; war in, 36, 43–44, 52, 99–104, 163
—*Mafarka le futuriste* (Mafarka the futurist): association of maternal image with desire,

60–63, 71; cloacal fantasy, 64–66, 70; comparison with feuilleton (serialized novel), 75–76; comparison with psychotic delusions, 75; consistency with logic of manifestos, 74–75; critical reception of, 55–56; and decadent theme of aesthetic conversion, 78; elitist/romantic bias, 76; homoeroticism, 56, 60, 65–66, 69, 70, 182*n*9; manifesto-preface to, 45; phallic imagery, 59, 63, 64, 65, 183*n*12; rhetoric of abjection, 56–59, 66–67, 182*n*9; rhetoric of decomposition, 57, 60, 63–64, 67–68; solar motif, 66, 68, 69, 75, 185*n*26; split representation of maternal, 71–73; superuomo myth, x, 45, 59, 69, 73–78; theme of aesthetic transcendence, 76–77; theme of contagious abjection, 66–68; theme of crisis in symbolic order, 66, 182*n*9; theme of self-dissolution and self-regeneration, 60–77; theme of sexuality as oral aggression, 57–59, 63; use of oxymoron, 61–62; violent sexual politics, 63; water motif, 60, 64, 66, 73, 78, 184*n*21
—Post-1920 period, xi, 126; ambivalence toward business world, 200*n*26; art as cosmetic compensation, 137, 149; art as transubstantiation, 155–162, 163; erotic fiction, 135; fascist discourse, 143–145; love in, 133; nostalgic remembrance in, 130, 137–140; notion of organic memory, 138, 200*n*23; principle of intuitive precision, 199*n*20; regression imagery, 152–153; resorption of previously rejected themes, 126–130; syntax and narrative structure, 198*n*9; *tattlismo* (tactilism), 133–135, 199*n*20; transformations in technological mythopoeia, 140–143, 146; war literature, 145–155
—Rhetoric of gender: association of sex and violence, xi, 10–11, 14–16, 36–37, 45–46, 96–99; attack on feminine luxury, 86–88; discourse on love, 79, 81, 85–89; discourse on marriage and the family, 81–85, 188*n*9; in *Mafarka le futuriste*, x, 57–59, 62–63, 64, 70, 74; in manifestos, 31–36, 50–51, 54; manual of seduction (*Come si seducono le donne*), 89–94; misogynism, viii–ix, 2, 110; primacy of, viii, 26–28; split representation of woman, 9, 62–63, 71, 96, 184*n*17, 186*n*35; "travel-size" woman, 95–96; woman-machine association, 51–52, 157
—Works: "Ad ogni uomo, ogni giorno un mestiere diverso! Inequalismo e Artecrazia"

(To Every Man Every Day a Different Job! Unequalism and Artocracy), 130, 132–133; *Al di là del Comunismo* (Beyond Communism), 130, 132–133, 161; *8 Anime in una bomba: Romanzo esplosivo* (8 Souls within a Bomb: An Explosive Novel), 42–43, 103, 104; *Canto eroi e macchine della guerra Mussoliniana* (I Sing the Heroes and Machines of Mussolini's War), 145, 151–155, 202*n*42; *Come si seducono le donne* (How to Seduce Women), 25, 89–94, 107–110, 189*n*17, 190*n*18; "Contro il lusso femminile" (Against Feminine Extravagance), 86–89, 91; "Contro il matrimonio" (Against Marriage), 81–84; "Contro l'amore e il parlamentarismo" (Against Love and Parliamentarianism), 84–85, 186*n*1; *Democrazia futurista* (Futurist Democracy), 131, 133, 179*n*32, 186*n*3; *Destruction*, 8–9, 10–12, 14, 168*n*29, 184*n*21; "Distruzione della sintassi—Immaginazione senza fili—Parole in libertà" (Destruction of Syntax—Wireless Imagination—Words in Freedom), 46, 85–86, 163; *Enquête internationale sur le Vers libre* (International Inquest on Free Verse), 7; "Estetica Futurista della guerra" (The Futurist Aesthetic of War), 146–147, 202*n*35; "Fondazione e Manifesto del Futurismo" (The Founding and Manifesto of Futurism), 29, 34, 48–50, 180*n*39; *Futurismo e Fascismo* (Futurism and Fascism), 132, 133; *Gli amori futuristi* (Futurist Loves), 135, 190*n*20, 191*n*27; *Gli Indomabili* (The Untamables), 127–130, 197*n*7; *Guerra sola igiene del mondo* (War, the World's Only Hygiene), 133, 179*n*32, 200*n*26; *Il fascino dell'Egitto* (Egyptian Fascination), 138–140; *Il Poema africano della Divisione "28 Ottobre"* (The African Poem of the "October 28" Division), 145, 147–151, 202*n*36; *Il Poema non umano dei tecnicismi* (The Nonhuman Poem of Technicalities), 140–144, 200*n*24, 200*n*26; "Il Tattilismo (Tactilism)," 133–135, 199*n*18; "Il teatro di varieta" (The Variety Theater), 30; "Il teatro futurista sintetico" (The Futurist Synthetic Theater), 30; "La carne congelata" (Frozen Flesh), 94–97, 191*n*27; *La Conquête des Étoiles* (The Conquest of the Stars), 7–8, 149, 167*n*28; *La cucina futurista* (The Futurist Cookbook), 98, 135, 192*n*34; "L'Aeropoema dell'aviatore Corinto Bellotti" (Aeropoem of the Aviator Corinto Bellotti), 146; *L'aeropoema di Gesù* (The Aeropoem of Jesus), 155–161,

Marinetti, F. T.—Works: (*continued*)
202*n*45, 203*n*47; *La grande Milano tradizionale e futurista e Una sensibilità italiana nata in Egitto* (Great Traditional and Futurist Milan and An Italian Sensibility Born in Egypt), 199*n*21, 202*n*38, 203*n*48; "La guerra elettrica" (Electrical War), 43–44, 179*n*32; *L'alcova d'acciaio: Romanzo vissuto* (The Steel Alcove: A Lived Novel), 89, 99–104, 192*n*35; "La matematica futurista immaginativa qualitativa" (Qualitative, Imaginative Futurist Mathematics), 199*n*20; "La nuova religione-morale della velocità" (The New Religion-Morality of Speed), 34; "La tecnica della nuova poesia" (The Technique of New Poetry), 137; *La Ville charnelle* (The Carnal City; Lussuria Velocità), 14–16, 168*n*37, 185*n*28; *Le Roi Bombance* (King Revelry), 12–14, 17, 93–94, 97, 127, 168*n*34, 168*n*35; *Les mots en liberté futuristes* (Futurist Words in Freedom), 7; letters in Robert's *Un ventre di donna*, 103–104, 116, 119–120, 122–123; "Lo splendore geometrico e meccanico e la sensibilità numerica" (Geometric and Mechanical Splendor and the Numerical Sensibility), 51, 78, 173*n*66, 199*n*20; "L'uomo moltiplicato e il Regno della macchina" (Multiplied Man and the Reign of the Machine), 44–45, 52–54, 89, 181*n*45, 186*n*2; *Lussuria Velocità* (Lust Speed), 16, 168*n*37; "Manifesto dell'arte sacra futurista" (Manifesto of Futurist Sacred Art), 155; "Manifesto del partito futurista italiano" (Manifesto of the Italian Futurist Party), 79, 131; "Manifesto tecnico della letteratura futurista" (Technical Manifesto of Futurist Literature), 46, 180*n*37; *Marinetti e il Futurismo*, 137; "Nascita di un'estetica futurista" (The Birth of a Futurist Aesthetic), 127; *Novelle con le labbra tinte* (Stories with Painted Lips), 135, 190*n*20; *Prigionieri* (The Prisoners), 198*n*8; "Quarto d'ora di poesia della X Mas" (A Quarter of an Hour of Poetry of the 10th E-Boat Squadron), 154–155; "Ritratto olfattivo di una donna" (Olfactory Portrait of a Woman), 135–137, 190*n*20; *Scatole d'amore in conserva* (Canned Love), 135, 190*n*20; *Spagna veloce e toro futurista* (Speedy Spain and a Futurist Bull), 137–138, 150–151; *Taccuini* (Notebooks), 21, 36–37, 120, 169*n*47, 179*n*32, 191*n*29, 192*n*35; "Uccidiamo il Chiaro di Luna!" (Let's Murder the Moonshine), 29, 31, 36, 50–51, 123, 129; "Un

pranzo che evitò un suicidio" (The Dinner that Stopped a Suicide), 98; *Vulcano* (The Volcano), 198*n*8; *Zang Tumb Tumb*, 7, 38–39, 100, 177*n*17
Marini, Shara, 107–108, 193*n*7
Martin, Marianne W., 2, 165*n*4
Martini, Stelio M., 175*n*5
McFarlane, James, 166*n*9, 166*n*10, 169*n*39
Meldini, Piero, 80, 186*n*4, 189*n*12
Michel, Sonya, 172*n*61
Möbius, Paul Julius, 118–119, 195*n*28
Modernism: cultural crisis of, 3–4, 166*n*8; in Italy, 4–6; rationalist and irrationalist tendencies, 166*n*10; role of gender in, 27, 173*n*67; shift in development of, 203*n*49; tenets and attitudes, 4
Mondrian, Piet, 167*n*27
Money-Kyrle, R. E., 181*n*44
Morasso, Mario, 19, 169*n*43, 169*n*46
Mosse, George L., 4, 166*n*9, 195*n*25, 196*n*32, 196*n*35
Mussolini, Benito, 1, 25, 26, 128, 132, 145, 146, 147, 169*n*47, 172*n*66, 190*n*26, 193*n*3, 198*n*13, 199*n*16

Nazzaro, G. Battista, 169*n*47
Nicholls, Peter, 47, 180*n*34
Niemöller, Martin, 171*n*59
Nietzsche, Friedrich, 6, 16, 19, 59, 194*n*16; *The Gay Science*, 77, 186*n*45; *Übermensch*, viii, 180*n*36
Noi, 125
Notari, Umberto, 181*n*2
Nozzoli, Anna, 171*n*53, 193*n*14

Orwell, George, 153

Palazzeschi, Aldo, 178*n*27
Papini, Giovanni, 6, 19, 167*n*21, 167*n*22, 167*n*23, 167*n*24, 169*n*41; magical pragmatism, 18
Paroliberismo (words in freedom), vii, 37–40, 46, 125
Pasolini, Pier Paolo, 165*n*6
Passatismo (passéism), 19
Pattuglia azzurra (Azure Patrol), 125
Pavolini, Alessandro, 146, 189*n*17; relationship to Marinetti, 201*n*34
Peirone, Luigi, 177*n*22, 178*n*25
Perloff, Marjorie, 2, 29, 165*n*5, 175*n*1, 175*n*3
Perrot, Michelle, 80, 187*n*6
Petrarch: *Rime sparse* (Scattered Rhymes), 62
Pierce, Charles S., 17, 18
Pilo, Mario, 80

Pirandello, Luigi, 14
Poe, Edgar Allan, 19
Poesia, 7, 178n26
Poggioli, Renato, 166n12
Poliespressività (polyexpressivity), 40
Positivism: in fin de siècle Italy, 5, 167n15; and pragmatism, 18
Postmodernism: and futurism, 47–48
Pound, Ezra, 167n27, 203n49
Pragmatism: defined, 17; and futurism, 18
Prampolini, Enrico, 98, 197n4
Prezzolini, Giuseppe, 6, 19, 167n21, 167n25, 198n15
Proust, Marcel, 31
Puccini, Sandra, 80, 167n14, 187n5

Rabelais, François, 182n11
Rabinbach, Anson, 174n69
Rachilde, Marguerite, 181n2
Raimondi, Ezio, 21, 170n51
Rank, Otto, 175n10, 183n12
Ravera, Camilla, 167n14
Re, Lucia, 165, 189n13, 193n14
Reich, Wilhelm, 171n57; *Die Massenpsychologie des Faschismus* (The Mass Psychology of Fascism), 22
Ricoeur, Paul, 168n36
"Ricostruzione futurista dell'universo" (Futurist Reconstruction of the Universe) (Balla and Depero), 41
Rinaldi, Rinaldo, 55, 71, 165n6, 182n4
Risorgimento, 4
Robert, Enif, 103, 106, 195n31; appendix to *Come si seducono le donne*, 107, 110, 193n5, 193n6; *Un ventre di donna* (The Womb of a Woman), xi, 111–124, 194n18, 194n19
Roma futurista, 125, 197n4
Romani, Bruno, 169n43
Rosà, Rosa (Edyth von Haynau), 106, 107; appendix to *Come si seducono le donne*, 108–109, 193n8, 193n9; "Le donne del posdomani" (The Women of Posttomorrow), 109–110, 193n10, 193n11

Saccone, Antonio, 200n25
Salaris, Claudia, 168n35, 190n20, 197n1, 202n45; *Le futuriste: Donne e letteratura d'avanguardia in Italia*, 192n3; on Marinetti as cultural entrepreneur, 178n27; *Marinetti editore*, 167n27, 178n26, 178n27, 198n8
Salgari, Emilio, 75
Sanguineti, Edoardo, 165n3

Santarelli, Enzo, 186n4, 188n8
Sant'Elia, 125
Sant'Elia, Antonio, 126, 175n2
Sanzin, Bruno G., 197n7
Sartoris, Alberto, 155
Scalia, Gianni, 197n5
Schleifer, Ronald, 166n8, 169n38, 180n35
Schnapp, Jeffrey, 169n47, 197n6, 202n43
Schopenhauer, Arthur, 17, 59; *Die Welt als Wille und Vorstellung* (The World as Will and Representation), 4
Scott, Bonnie Kime, 173n67
Scullion, Rosemarie, 172n60
Sedgwick, Eve Kosofsky, 175n8
Settimelli, Emilio, 126, 179n28, 186n4, 187n7; preface to *Come si seducono le donne*, 90, 91, 93, 94, 99, 190n18; violent erotica, 191n33
Silverman, Kaja: on castration complex, 177n18, 183n12; on synecdochic representation of woman, 184n17
Simultaneità (simultaneity), 40
"Sintesi futurista della guerra" (Futurist Synthesis of the War), 175n11
Slataper, Scipio, 19
Sofista, Giuliano il. *See* Prezzolini, Giuseppe
Somenzi, Mino, 197n4
Sorel, Georges: revolutionary force of myth, viii, 16
Spackman, Barbara, 25–26, 77, 78, 79, 84, 87; *Decadent Genealogies: The Rhetoric of Sickness from Baudelaire to D'Annunzio*, 167n23, 168n31, 186n44; on *Mafarka le futuriste*, 182n9, 183n13, 185n23; "The Fascist Rhetoric of Virility," 172n65, 188n10, 189n13, 189n14, 190n20
Spencer, Herbert: survival of the fittest, viii, 6, 180n36
Spender, Stephen, 177n23, 203n49
Sternhell, Zeev, 188n8
Stirner, Max, 6
Sultan, Stanley, 166n7
Surrealism, 19

Tattilismo (tactilism), 1, 40, 133–135, 199n20
Taveggia, Angelo, 178n27
Tavolato, Italo, 192n2
Tavole sinottiche e sinitetiche (synoptic and synthetic tables), 40
Tessari, Roberto, 169n46, 180n38
Theweleit, Klaus, 68, 73–74, 174n69, 176n15; on antieroticism in fascism, 172n64; on fascist notions of masculine identity, 24–25; on fascist ritual of oratory, 171n59; on Jewish

Theweleit, Klaus (*continued*)
stereotype in fascist writings, 90; on nonfascist *vs.* fascist writing, 202*n*40; on role of male-female inequality in patriarchal capitalist society, 27; on theme of split femininity in fascist writings, 186*n*35
Tilly, Charles, 166*n*13, 199*n*19
Tilly, Louise, 166*n*13, 199*n*19
Tilly, Richard, 166*n*13, 199*n*19
Tisdall, Caroline, 192*n*1
Tranfaglia, Nicola, 166*n*13
Turati, Filippo, 13, 168*n*35
Turconi, Sergio, 169*n*43

Vaccari, Walter, 167*n*26
Vailati, Giovanni, 17, 18
Vasari, Ruggero, 187*n*7, 203*n*51
Vecchi, Ferruccio, 132
Verhaeren, Émile, 19
Verlaine, Paul, 19
Viazzi, Glauco, 182*n*8; "Ainsi parla Mafarka-el-Bar," 56
Vickers, Nancy, 183*n*16
Villari, Lucio, 146, 201*n*34
Vittorini, Elio, 204*n*57; *Conversazione in Sicilia* (Conversation in Sicily), 161–162, 204*n*56
Volt (Vincenzo Fani Ciotti), 91, 107, 190*n*22; appendix to *Come si seducono le donne*, 110,

193*n*12; "Matrimonio, adulterio, divorzio, amore libero" (Marriage, Adultery, Divorce, Free Love), 92; response to Marinetti's *Il Tattilismo*, 199*n*18
Von Haynau, Edyth. *See* Rosà, Rosa
Von Krafft-Ebing, Richard, 118, 195*n*25

War: eroticization of in futurism, xi, 99–104; impact on women, 80–81, 109; Marinetti and, 36, 43–44, 52, 99–104, 163; Marinetti's eroticization of, 99–104, 176*n*15; Marinetti's literature on, 145–155
Weininger, Otto, 6, 105
Weitz, Margaret Collins, 172*n*61
Whitman, Walt, 19
Wiener, Philip P., 17
Women: under fascism, 80–81, 186*n*4, 188*n*9; femininist movement in Italy, 189*n*16; in futurism, 20–22, 105–112, 193*n*14; impact of world wars on, 80–81

Zapponi, Niccolò, 167*n*16, 169*n*47
Zatkova, Rougena, criticism of "Il Tattilismo," 199*n*18
Zecchi, Barbara, 194*n*23
Zimei, Artemisia, 195*n*26
Zola, Émile, 19

Designer: UC Press Staff
Compositor: Impressions Book and Journal Services, Inc.
Text: 10/12 Baskerville
Display: Baskerville
Printer: Edwards Brothers, Inc.
Binder: Edwards Brothers, Inc.